Gender Differences in Prenatal Substance Exposure

Gender Differences in Prenatal Substance Exposure

EDITED BY

Michael Lewis and Lisa Kestler

DECADE
of BEHAVIOR

2000-2010

AMERICAN PSYCHOLOGICAL ASSOCIATION

WASHINGTON, DC

Published by
American Psychological Association
750 First Street, NE
Washington, DC 20002
www.apa.org

To order
APA Order Department
P.O. Box 92984
Washington, DC 20090-2984
Tel: (800) 374-2721;
Direct: (202) 336-5510
Fax: (202) 336-5502;
TDD/TTY: (202) 336-6123
Online: www.apa.org/pubs/books
E-mail: order@apa.org

In the U.K., Europe, Africa, and the Middle East, copies may be ordered from
American Psychological Association
3 Henrietta Street
Covent Garden, London
WC2E 8LU England

Typeset in New Century Schoolbook by Circle Graphics, Inc., Columbia, MD

Printer: Edwards Brothers, Inc., Ann Arbor, MI
Cover Designer: Berg Design, Albany, NY

The opinions and statements published are the responsibility of the authors, and such opinions and statements do not necessarily represent the policies of the American Psychological Association.

Library of Congress Cataloging-in-Publication Data
Gender differences in prenatal substance exposure / edited by Michael Lewis and Lisa Kestler. — 1st ed.
    p. ; cm.
  Includes bibliographical references and index.
  ISBN-13: 978-1-4338-1033-6
  ISBN-10: 1-4338-1033-6
  1. Fetus—Effect of drugs on—Sex differences. 2. Children of prenatal substance abuse—Sex differences. 3. Fetus—Development—Sex differences. I. Lewis, Michael, 1937 Jan. 10- II. Kestler, Lisa. III. American Psychological Association.
  [DNLM: 1. Fetus—drug effects. 2. Prenatal Exposure Delayed Effects. 3. Abnormalities, Drug-Induced. 4. Sex Factors. WQ 210]
  RG627.6.D79G46 2012
  618.3'2—dc23

                                                                                                2011029646

British Library Cataloguing-in-Publication Data
A CIP record is available from the British Library.

Printed in the United States of America
First Edition

DOI: 10.1037/13092-000

APA Science Volumes

Attribution and Social Interaction: The Legacy of Edward E. Jones

Best Methods for the Analysis of Change: Recent Advances, Unanswered Questions, Future Directions

Cardiovascular Reactivity to Psychological Stress and Disease

The Challenge in Mathematics and Science Education: Psychology's Response

Changing Employment Relations: Behavioral and Social Perspectives

Children Exposed to Marital Violence: Theory, Research, and Applied Issues

Cognition: Conceptual and Methodological Issues

Cognitive Bases of Musical Communication

Cognitive Dissonance: Progress on a Pivotal Theory in Social Psychology

Conceptualization and Measurement of Organism–Environment Interaction

Converging Operations in the Study of Visual Selective Attention

Creative Thought: An Investigation of Conceptual Structures and Processes

Developmental Psychoacoustics

Diversity in Work Teams: Research Paradigms for a Changing Workplace

Emotion and Culture: Empirical Studies of Mutual Influence

Emotion, Disclosure, and Health

Evolving Explanations of Development: Ecological Approaches to Organism–Environment Systems

Examining Lives in Context: Perspectives on the Ecology of Human Development

Global Prospects for Education: Development, Culture, and Schooling

Hostility, Coping, and Health

Measuring Patient Changes in Mood, Anxiety, and Personality Disorders: Toward a Core Battery

Occasion Setting: Associative Learning and Cognition in Animals

Organ Donation and Transplantation: Psychological and Behavioral Factors

Origins and Development of Schizophrenia: Advances in Experimental Psychopathology

The Perception of Structure

APA Decade of Behavior Volumes

Contents

Contributors

Joel Ager, PhD, Professor Emeritus, Department of Family Medicine and Public Health Sciences, Wayne State University School of Medicine, Detroit, MI

Ekemini Akan, MD, Volunteering Trainee, Children's Hospital of Michigan and Department of Pediatrics, Wayne State University School of Medicine, Detroit, MI

Stephanie A. Beaudin, PhD, Assistant Research Scientist, Department of Microbiology and Environmental Toxicology, University of California–Santa Cruz

David S. Bennett, PhD, Associate Professor, Division of Child and Adolescent Psychiatry, Drexel University College of Medicine, Philadelphia, PA; Institute for the Study of Child Development, Robert Wood Johnson Medical School, University of Medicine and Dentistry of New Jersey, New Brunswick

Dennis P. Carmody, PhD, Professor of Pediatrics, Institute for the Study of Child Development, Robert Wood Johnson Medical School, University of Medicine and Dentistry of New Jersey, New Brunswick

Lisa M. Chiodo, PhD, Assistant Professor, College of Nursing, Wayne State University, Detroit, MI

Claire D. Coles, PhD, Professor, Department of Psychiatry and Behavioral Sciences and Department of Pediatrics, Emory University School of Medicine, Atlanta, GA

Chandice Covington, PhD, RN, CPNP, Professor, Anita Thigpen Perry School of Nursing, Texas Tech University, Lubbock

Nancy L. Day, PhD, Professor, Departments of Psychiatry and Epidemiology, University of Pittsburgh School of Medicine, Pittsburgh, PA

Virginia Delancy-Black, MD, MPH, Professor of Pediatrics, Wayne State University School of Medicine; Charles H. Gershenson Distinguished Fellow, Wayne State University School and Children's Hospital of Michigan, Detroit, MI

Diana Dow-Edwards, PhD, Professor of Physiology and Pharmacology, State University of New York, Health Sciences Center, Brooklyn

Nancy L. Fiedler, PhD, Professor, Department of Environmental and Occupational Medicine, Environmental and Occupational Health Sciences Institute, Robert Wood Johnson Medical School, University of Medicine and Dentistry of New Jersey, Piscataway

Mathew H. Gendle, PhD, Associate Professor, Department of Psychology, Elon University, Elon, NC

Mark K. Greenwald, PhD, Professor, Department of Psychiatry and Behavioral Neurosciences, Wayne State University School of Medicine, Detroit, MI

John H. Hannigan, PhD, Deputy Director and Professor, Merrill Palmer Skillman Institute, Department of Obstetrics and Gynecology and Department of Psychology, Wayne State University, Detroit, MI

James Janisse, PhD, Assistant Professor, Department of Family Medicine and Public Health Sciences, Wayne State University School of Medicine, Detroit, MI

Julie A. Kable, PhD, Assistant Professor, Department of Pediatrics, Emory University School of Medicine, Atlanta, GA

Sandra J. Kelly, PhD, Carolina Trustee Professor of Psychology, Department of Psychology, University of South Carolina, Columbia

Lisa Kestler, PhD, Senior Clinician, MedAvante, Inc., Hamilton, NJ

Noriyuki Koibuchi, MD, PhD, Professor, Department of Integrative Physiology, Gunma University Graduate School of Medicine, Maebashi, Gunma, Japan

Linda Lewandowski, PhD, RN, Assistant Dean, Family, Community, Mental Health and Elizabeth Schotanus Associate Professor of Pediatric Nursing, College of Nursing, Wayne State University and Children's Hospital of Michigan, Detroit

Michael Lewis, PhD, University Distinguished Professor of Pediatrics and Psychiatry, Director, Institute for the Study of Child Development, Robert Wood Johnson Medical School and University of Medicine and Dentistry of New Jersey, New Brunswick

Mary Ellen Lynch, PhD, Assistant Professor, Department of Psychiatry and Behavioral Sciences, Emory University School of Medicine, Atlanta, GA

Steven J. Ondersma, PhD, Associate Professor, Merrill Palmer Skillman Institute and Department of Psychiatry and Behavioral Neurosciences, Wayne State University, Detroit, MI

Nicha K. H. Otero, PhD, Postdoctoral Fellow, Department of Psychology, University of South Carolina, Columbia

Ty Patridge, PhD, Associate Professor, Department of Psychology, Wayne State University, Detroit, MI

Grace Patterson, BA, Research Assistant, Children's Hospital of Michigan and Department of Pediatrics, Wayne State University School of Medicine, Detroit

Gale A. Richardson, PhD, Associate Professor, Departments of Psychiatry and Epidemiology, University of Pittsburgh School of Medicine, Pittsburgh, PA

Elizabeth M. Sajdel-Sulkowska, DSc, Assistant Professor of Biochemistry, Department of Psychiatry, Harvard Medical School and Department of Psychiatry, Brigham and Women's Hospital, Boston, MA

Robert J. Sokol, MD, The John M. Malone, Jr., MD, Endowed Chair and Director of the C. S. Mott Center for Human Growth and Development, Distinguished Professor of Obstetrics and Gynecology, Wayne State University School of Medicine, Detroit, MI

Ann P. Streissguth, PhD, Professor Emerita, Department of Psychiatry and Behavioral Sciences, Fetal Alcohol and Drug Unit, University of Washington School of Medicine, Seattle

Barbara J. Strupp, PhD, Professor, Division of Nutritional Sciences and Department of Psychology, Cornell University, Ithaca, NY

Annelyn Torres-Reveron, PhD, Assistant Professor, Department of Pharmaceutical Sciences, Nova Southeastern University, College of Pharmacy, Ponce, Puerto Rico

Erica L. T. van den Akker, MD, PhD, Associate Professor, Department of Pediatrics, Division of Endocrinology, Erasmus MC–Sophia Children's Hospital, Rotterdam, The Netherlands

Nynke Weisglas-Kuperus, MD, PhD, Associate Professor, Department of Pediatrics, Division of Neonatology, Erasmus MC–Sophia Children's Hospital, Rotterdam, The Netherlands

Jennifer A. Willford, PhD, Assistant Professor, Department of Psychiatry, University of Pittsburgh School of Medicine, Pittsburgh, PA

Foreword

In early 1988, the American Psychological Association (APA) Science Directorate began its sponsorship of what would become an exceptionally successful activity in support of psychological science—the APA Scientific Conferences program. This program has showcased some of the most important topics in psychological science and has provided a forum for collaboration among many leading figures in the field.

The program has inspired a series of books that have presented cutting-edge work in all areas of psychology. At the turn of the millennium, the series was renamed the Decade of Behavior Series to help advance the goals of this important initiative. The Decade of Behavior is a major interdisciplinary campaign designed to promote the contributions of the behavioral and social sciences to our most important societal challenges in the decade leading up to 2010. Although a key goal has been to inform the public about these scientific contributions, other activities have been designed to encourage and further collaboration among scientists. Hence, the series that was the "APA Science Series" has continued as the "Decade of Behavior Series." This represents one element in APA's efforts to promote the Decade of Behavior initiative as one of its endorsing organizations. For additional information about the Decade of Behavior, please visit http://www.decadeofbehavior.org.

Over the course of the past years, the Science Conference and Decade of Behavior Series has allowed psychological scientists to share and explore cutting-edge findings in psychology. The APA Science Directorate looks forward to continuing this successful program and to sponsoring other conferences and books in the years ahead. This series has been so successful that we have chosen to extend it to include books that, although they do not arise from conferences, report with the same high quality of scholarship on the latest research.

We are pleased that this important contribution to the literature was supported in part by the Decade of Behavior program. Congratulations to the editors and contributors of this volume on their sterling effort.

Steven J. Breckler, PhD
Executive Director for Science

Virginia E. Holt
Assistant Executive Director for Science

Preface

This book is about gender differences in the effects of prenatal drug exposure on development. There is little doubt that exposure to such toxins as cocaine, marijuana, tobacco, alcohol, and lead have negative effects on children and their development. Indeed there is a large, rich literature that supports this contention. This volume is not about that issue; rather, it is about the differential effect of prenatal exposure on male and female children.

The study of sex differences is often motivated by a multitude of factors, including differences in biology, socialization at the level of family and siblings, and the culture at large. The argument often is made that the study of sex differences is motivated by political and sexist issues. This is not the case; certainly it is not involved in our attempt to understand sex differences in terms of the consequences of fetal exposure. We seek to place sex differences in the consequences of fetal exposure in the context of biological factors that may be involved. It is well known that male and female fetuses are differentially vulnerable to traumatic events. For example, more male human fetuses are conceived than female, a 120:100 male:female ratio, yet at birth the ratio has fallen to 105:100 (Shettles, 1961).[1] Such data suggest that independent of culture, male fetuses are more vulnerable than females. This vulnerability continues, and so by the age of 10 in any cohort there are more females than males alive, and, in fact, between males and females in most cultures, females live longer than males.

Although many factors may account for these sex differences in vulnerability, a careful study of their cause has not really been undertaken. More often than not, the blame seems to be placed on cultural factors, male risk-taking for example, or aggressive factors in that males commit and receive more violence than females. Our interest in this sex differences phenomenon is motivated in part by our work and that of our colleagues in the past 15 years. As the data on a variety of teratogens have become available, especially from long-term longitudinal studies, we have been struck by the differential vulnerabilities of males. Such differences are important to consider for any number of reasons. The most obvious, of course, is that these differences may give us a clue as to underlying biological, cultural, and interactive effects on development. Thus, sex differences, like individual differences, can reveal processes and effects that are not apparent without observing them.

Moreover, by considering the sample as a whole as opposed to considering sex differences, there is the danger of masking drug exposure effects. For the sake of example, let us assume that there is a Sex × Exposure effect. By not considering this interaction we may commit a Type II error because combining both males and females in the sample may wipe out the effects of a teratogen

---

[1]Shettles, L. B. (1961). Conception and birth sex ratios. *Obstetrical & Gynecological Survey, 18,* 122–130.

on only one sex. Thus, in the case of our own work on cocaine exposure, the strong Sex × Exposure cocaine effects often would be masked if we considered the sample as a whole without a sex differentiation. The same is true in our work on the effects of marijuana and cigarettes as well as alcohol; male fetuses seem more vulnerable.

The effects of prenatal exposure to drugs of abuse have been long-standing concerns for many, both in the human and animal literature. Studies of human exposure as well as animal models of exposure have reported adverse sequelae ranging from gross physical deficits to later cognitive and behavioral difficulties. As developmental teratology has become more sophisticated and as researchers continue their studies, they are now beginning to go beyond simple main effects in their teratological models of the effects of drugs of abuse. There is accumulating evidence that indicates sexual dimorphisms in prenatal exposure to several substances. This has important implications in terms of our basic understanding of the development of the central nervous system. An increased vulnerability to prenatal drug effects or, conversely, an increased protection from prenatal drug effects in one sex versus the other is potentially important in terms of understanding the mechanisms of action of teratogenic drugs. These kinds of findings also have practical implication for targeting the most vulnerable groups for intervention efforts.

Emerging findings of sex-dependent effects have led to increased awareness among researchers who study the long-term effects of teratogens. In fact, the National Institute on Drug Abuse recently issued several requests for proposals that examine sex differences as we come to appreciate the sex effects of drug exposure. In response to this growing interest in sex-dependent effects, a conference, with support from the American Psychological Association to Michael Lewis and colleagues, was organized to discuss what has been found across different types of teratogens and to explore potential common mechanisms. This conference served as a springboard for this volume and included papers from a variety of experts in both human and animal research in the field of developmental teratology.

We acknowledge with gratitude our colleague, the late Margaret Bendersky, whose commitment to the study of developmental teratology for over 15 years has made this book possible. Our thanks also to Stacey Napoli, without whose effort this volume would not have happened.

Gender Differences in Prenatal Substance Exposure

Introduction

Michael Lewis and Lisa Kestler

The effects of prenatal exposure to drugs of abuse, including cigarettes, marijuana, and alcohol, have been of long-standing interest and concern. When cheap crack cocaine became available in the mid-1980s, its use by pregnant women in poor urban areas became relatively common. Cigarette smoking during pregnancy continues to be a problem despite a general decline in smoking in this country. The demographic groups that have actually shown increased rates of smoking are teenage and young adult women, a fact that is of particular significance for prenatal exposure. Studies of human substance exposure, as well as animal models of gestational exposure, have reported adverse sequelae ranging from growth deficits to later cognitive and behavioral difficulties. Similarly, research on prenatal exposure to environmental toxins such as lead and polychlorinated biphenyl (PCB) has identified harmful effects on neurodevelopment and behavior. As the field of developmental teratology has become more sophisticated, researchers are going beyond simple main effects and teratological models to test models incorporating moderating influences. Exciting evidence accumulating from both human and animal studies indicates that there is sexual dimorphism in prenatal substance and toxin exposure effects. This has great implications in terms of our basic understanding of the development of the central nervous system, as well as practical implications for targeting the most vulnerable groups for intervention efforts.

This book is the first to present a broad view of the empirical and theoretical considerations about sex differences in response to prenatal toxin exposure. This volume brings together a group of human and animal researchers to present a timely view of the increased sophistication and refinement of our understanding of this societal problem and of sex differences in the fetal response to teratogen exposure.

The focus of this book is an often neglected yet extremely important issue: whether perinatal exposure to drugs or other toxins has different effects for males and females. Interest in the idea of sex differences in sensitivity to drugs or other agents has recently increased, and yet this question is still often neglected, as evidenced by the reviews presented in some of the chapters. The chapters to follow present what is currently known in developmental teratology research and make the argument for more research on issues related to sex differences.

The consideration of sex differences in the effects of teratogen exposure is important for a number of reasons because it is well-known that sex differences in vulnerability exist in any number of areas of behavior. Most important is that these differences may provide clues to the underlying biological, cultural, and interactive effects on development in general and in children exposed as fetuses to toxins. Given the increase in toxins, the understanding of their effects would be incomplete without the study of sex differences. By not considering sex differences in the effects of prenatal exposure, we may miss these effects; by combining the data by sex, we may miss the effects because summing across males and females who show differences but in different ways may wipe out overall effects. Moreover, because early differences, as a function of exposure, may interact with cultural differences based on sex differences, these interactive effects also may be lost.

Animal models are important to consider; not only are they useful in and of themselves, but they may also help clarify some of the complications that arise when we study humans. In humans, fetal exposure to specific teratogens is unlikely to occur in the context of the use of only that particular teratogen targeted. This gives rise to the concerns that many investigators face when trying to look at the effects of teratogens on human development. By using animal models, we can single out the target teratogen. Animal models provide a rich source of confirmatory data because it is only by using a series of regression techniques that we can study human exposure effects to targeted specific drugs in the face of polydrug use.

It is also important to keep in mind that in human studies, pregnant mothers who use drugs are likely to represent a proportion of the population who, because of poverty, violence, lack of education, and other factors, place both themselves and their children in risky environments. Because we know that risky environments play a prominent role in determining human developmental outcomes, statistical techniques are often needed to single out and target a particular teratogen independent not only of other drugs but also of effects of the environment. Because environmental effects can be minimized when we use animal models, confirmatory findings using animal models serve an extremely important role in our understanding, both of the general effects of teratogens as well as the specific effects of sex differences.

Sex differences can be found in both animal and human studies of the teratogens we have targeted for this volume. Such findings confirm our sense of the importance of considering sex differences when looking at the developmental effects of teratogens. Our task, in light of these findings, is to try to discern, through state-of-the-art approaches to the study of the effects of prenatal exposure, why it is that gender provides protective or risk factors to the children. Future approaches should focus not only on biological factors but also on genes and on Gene × Environment interactions.

This volume consists of 11 chapters that address the growing interest in sex-dependent effects in the field of developmental teratology. Some drugs of abuse or toxins have received greater attention than others. In organizing the book, our goal was to provide an in-depth review on the sex-dependent effects of each drug or toxin, including coverage of both preclinical and clinical research. Although there may be a vast literature on the effects of prenatal exposure to each of these drugs or toxins, for some there has been little exploration of potential sex-dependent effects of the substance. Often prenatal exposure researchers ignore sex differences or do not examine them at all. In this book, some substances are represented more than others. Our aim was to invite researchers who are considered to be experts within their field, rather than asking for rudimentary reviews of topics just for the sake of covering all bases.

The intended audience for this volume is wide. Its chapters may prove interesting and useful for psychologists with research interests in child development, vulnerability and resiliency, multifactorial underpinnings of health risk behavior, and development of children who are prenatally exposed to substances of abuse; neuroscientists and toxicologists interested in mechanisms of effects of toxin exposure; public policy makers; substance abuse counselors; and clinical psychologists, social workers, and educators who provide services to families and children.

We hope that the information presented here benefits researchers in the field of developmental teratology, given that the authors have written the way they would for academic journals in which they would typically publish. However, the conclusions reached in each chapter should be easily accessible to a range of professionals. The discussions of the clinical implications of the findings in these reviews may be especially useful for pediatricians, psychologists, developmental specialists, neurologists, and pediatric psychiatrists. For example, it may be helpful for clinicians to understand that there may be subtle differences in the manifestations of a prenatal exposure depending on gender.

A book addressing this issue of sex differences is very much needed in the field. Of particular importance is the need to point out conclusions that can be drawn from current research as well as areas of possible future research. As with many areas of science, research tends to be very narrowly focused, with little attention paid to bringing together related areas that can tell us more than if examined separately. An additional goal of this book is to provide both interdisciplinary and intradisciplinary insight into common mechanisms underlying the differential effects of prenatal exposures depending upon sex—whether there are common developmental factors that make one sex more vulnerable than the other or whether there are specific genomic and nongenomic (activational) effects of gonadal hormones that interact with toxin exposure to influence development.

Some issues of terminology arise in this volume. First, the terms *sex* and *gender* are both used. Many chapters focus on animal (preclinical) research, whereas others cover human (clinical) research. It is commonly understood that sex is a biologically determined category and gender is a socially constructed term meant to reflect certain characteristics (one of which is biological sex) that distinguish males and females. *Sex* is typically used in animal research, whereas *gender* is often used in human research. However, given the biological nature of the clinical research, much of which focuses on brain development and the impact of biological sex rather than other gender characteristics, some clinical researchers have chosen to use the term *sex* in describing differences between males and females in their research. Thus, there may be some inconsistency in the context in which the two terms are used.

In addition, research on rats often examines the effects of postnatal exposure to toxins on development. This is actually equivalent to prenatal exposure in humans. Because the period in the rat that corresponds to all three trimesters in the human with respect to brain growth includes both the prenatal and early postnatal periods, rat models often include exposure during the prenatal period, postnatal period, or both (perinatal) periods. Given that the rat model is meant to reflect similar events in human development, the term *prenatal* may be used more generally to discuss the effects of toxin exposure during these developmental periods.

Leeway was given to authors in order to gain different perspectives and approaches to the problem. Some chapters represent a fairly broad overview, whereas others focus primarily on the author's own work. Broad reviews can give a good summary of a fairly diverse body of literature; focusing on one's own work can give readers a more detailed understanding of the subtleties found in the sex differences observed based on a systematic sequence of hypotheses developed by the authors over time.

The book contains chapters on cocaine, tobacco, and marijuana, as well as alcohol and environmental toxins such as lead and PCBs. For each of these areas we have attempted to present chapters on both human and animal models of their effects. For some teratogens, there are more chapters than for others; for example, there are four chapters on cocaine exposure but only one on tobacco and one on marijuana. This reflects, in part, the interest of the editors but also the fact that the effects of cocaine exposure are quite severe.

The chapters on cocaine exposure cover both human (Kestler, Bennett, Carmody, & Lewis and Delaney-Black et al.) and animal literature (Dow-Edwards & Torres-Reveron and Beaudin, Gendle, & Strupp). Kestler et al. and Delaney-Black et al. review evidence from clinical studies that males are often more affected by prenatal cocaine exposure than females, at least in certain developmental domains from the animal studies; Dow-Edwards and Torres-Reveron point out that brain metabolism, gene expression within specific brain regions, and behavioral effects show that females are also affected but in different ways. They propose a number of possible mechanisms to explain these sexually dimorphic effects. Studying animal models, Beaudin et al. provide a comprehensive history of the research on prenatal cocaine exposure and methodological advances in animal research. They report results from their own studies, which focus primarily on the behavioral effects of prenatal cocaine exposure in rats. They find different sex-dependent patterns of impairment in domains of attention and emotion regulation and the potential physiological and neurochemical mechanisms underlying these behavioral effects, including developmental alterations in the dopamine and norepinephrine neuronal systems and their projections to the prefrontal cortex. The authors conclude that the sexually dimorphic pattern of cognitive and affective impairments seen in rats may have counterparts in humans and that it is important to consider the role of gender when evaluating the effects of prenatal cocaine exposure on the developing brain, as well as on neuropsychological and behavioral functions.

Coles, Kable, and Lynch review the research on the effects of prenatal tobacco exposure in humans. Although there is some evidence that exposed males have a higher level of behavior problems and later criminal behavior than nonexposed males, the design of most studies of such behavior has not allowed an adequate examination of effects on females. Findings from studies of other child outcomes have either neglected to examine gender differences or have revealed few gender differences in the effects of prenatal tobacco exposure. Coles et al. conclude that the question of interaction of tobacco exposure and sex on child outcomes is as yet unanswered. In the animal literature, Slotkin has found that the effects of prenatal tobacco exposure may be the result of the impact of nicotine on the cortical cholinergic systems and that there may be sex differences in response. Readers interested in the preclinical research on fetal tobacco exposure are directed to consult Slotkin, Lappi, and Seidler (1993).

Willford, Richardson, and Day examine the effects of prenatal marijuana exposure. They review findings from both the human and animal literature, which demonstrate sexually dimorphic effects of marijuana on neurotransmitter systems, the hypothalamic–pituitary–adrenal axis, and behavioral outcomes. Whereas human and animal research appears to be consistent with regard to the domains of functioning affected by prenatal marijuana exposure, few human studies have explored sex differences in these effects; those that have show mixed evidence. In the animal research reviewed, sex differences are apparent; sex affects different functions as a consequence of exposure. They recommend, as do most of the other authors in this volume, that sex differences found in animal studies should be further examined in human studies.

In examining the effects of prenatal alcohol exposure, Otero and Kelly review animal models and report sex differences in the effects of exposure on brain morphology, hormonal and neurotransmitter systems, and behavior, similar to the effects of alcohol on males that Streissguth observes. Ann Streissguth, one of the original researchers in the study of fetal alcohol spectrum disorders (FASD), takes a very different approach than other chapters, with a more anecdotal and first-person description of her findings. According to Streissguth, differential developmental aspects of males and females with FASD are rarely addressed in the scientific literature. However, she has noticed what appear to be male/female differences in the behavior of patients with FASD as they enter puberty, in particular the feminizing effect of prenatal alcohol on males.

Lead exposure is reviewed by Nancy Fiedler, who presents an interesting overview of a relatively mixed literature on the sex-dependent effects of prenatal exposure. One difference between lead and some of the other agents and drugs discussed in this volume is the extent of the literature that focuses on postnatal exposure. Although a great deal of research has focused on the effects of postnatal exposure to lead and other environmental toxins, it is important to understand the prenatal effects given that women who were previously exposed to lead may continue to confer increased risk of lead exposure during pregnancy because of the mobilization of bone lead stores.

Elizabeth Sajdel-Sulkowska and Noriyuki Koibuchi present a thorough overview of PCBs in preclinical models and discuss various aspects ranging from behavioral, structural, and neurochemical effects to the possible mechanisms by which PCBs exert their effects. Erica van den Akker and Nynke Weisglas-Kuperus from the Netherlands focus on estrogen disrupters more broadly rather than on just PCBs and relate the work on animal models to humans.

A general conclusion that can be drawn from many of the chapters in this book is that there are a number of important sex differences in at least some of the dependent variables examined. However, in some cases the research results have been less clear. In a great deal of research that has been conducted, either sex was not included in the analyses of the studies reviewed or the power to detect differences was too low to make reliable conclusions about interactions of sex with the effects of prenatal exposure. This is sometimes because females were excluded, the sample size was small, or sex differences were not considered variables of importance. We hope that this book encourages future study on this topic. Clearly, further well-designed research on the effects of prenatal exposures to drugs or other neurotoxins is needed to better understand how these effects may be differentially expressed in males and females. This is important both for theory as well as for clinical treatments.

Reference

Slotkin, T. A., Lappi, S. E., & Seidler, F. J. (1993). Impact of fetal nicotine exposure on development of rat brain regions: Critical sensitive periods or effects of withdrawal? *Brain Research Bulletin, 31,* 319–328.

Part I

Cocaine

1

Gender-Dependent Effects of Prenatal Cocaine Exposure

Lisa Kestler, David S. Bennett,
Dennis P. Carmody, and Michael Lewis

In the early 1990s, a number of longitudinal studies were initiated to investigate the effects of prenatal cocaine exposure. The need to understand these effects on infant and child outcomes was triggered by the availability of inexpensive and highly addictive crack cocaine leading to increased cocaine use among pregnant women, primarily in low-income urban environments. Although initial results showed that prenatal cocaine use does not lead to catastrophic outcomes (Frank, Augustyn, Knight, Pell, & Zuckerman, 2001), results from our 15-year prospective study show that prenatal cocaine exposure is associated with deficits in inhibitory control, emotion regulation, and cognitive abilities (Bendersky, Gambini, Lastella, Bennett, & Lewis, 2003; Bendersky & Lewis, 1998a, 1998b; Bennett, Bendersky, & Lewis, 2002, 2008; Dennis, Bendersky, Ramsay, & Lewis, 2006). In addition, we have found that cocaine exposure in utero predicts aggressive behavior at 5 years and more high-risk behavior at 10½ years (Bendersky, Bennett, & Lewis, 2006; Bennett, Bendersky, & Lewis, 2007). Other studies also have revealed subtle yet important long-term effects, including deficits in attention, executive dysfunction, and behavior problems. (For a review, see Chapter 2, this volume.)

Early research in this area was characterized by methodological limitations, including the use of small samples and failure to control for potential confounds such as environmental risk, neonatal medical complications, and prenatal exposure to other substances, which limit the validity of prior findings. These related risk factors are often elevated for children with prenatal cocaine exposure. Table 1.1 shows that in our sample, prenatal cocaine exposure is associated with elevated prenatal exposure to cigarettes, alcohol, and marijuana; elevated neonatal medical risk scores; and elevated environmental risk. In examining whether prenatal exposure to cocaine impairs children's later functioning, these confounding factors must be controlled.

In our studies of this sample, we use a conceptual model that examines cocaine exposure, exposure to other substances, medical complications, and environmental risk as potential factors influencing children's development (Lewis & Bendersky, 1995). By controlling medical risk, environmental risk, and exposures to other substances, we have been able to show that prenatal cocaine exposure affects infants', young children's, and preadolescents' inhibitory control and

Table 1.1. Sample Characteristics of Currently Active Participants

Characteristic	Exposed males (n = 40)		Unexposed males (n = 67)		Exposed females (n = 47)		Unexposed females (n = 56)	
	M	SD	M	SD	M	SD	M	SD
Prenatal alcohol exposure[a] (average no. drinks/day)	.96	1.59	.03	.15	1.84	3.90	.02	.06
Prenatal cigarette exposure[a,b,c] (number of cigarettes/day)	7.83	7.57	1.35	4.76	11.70	12.21	1.47	3.66
Prenatal marijuana exposure[a,c] (number of joints/day)	.08	.19	.04	.25	.51	1.94	.01	.03
Neonatal medical risk (log-transformed)[a]	.18	.23	.12	.22	.23	.26	.10	.22
Early environmental risk (composite score)[a]	54.01	8.01	48.86	8.90	52.73	8.46	49.25	7.82

[a]Main effect of cocaine exposure, $p < .01$. [b]Main effect of gender, $p < .10$. [c]Cocaine Exposure × Gender, $p < .10$.

emotional regulation abilities from infancy through 10 years (Bendersky et al., 2006; Bendersky et al., 2003; Bendersky & Lewis, 1998a, 1998b; Carmody, Bennett, & Lewis, 2011; Dennis, Bendersky, Ramsay, & Lewis, 2006).

Children who are prenatally exposed to cocaine are much more likely than nonexposed children to grow up in unstable, unsupportive, and chaotic homes (Bendersky, Alessandri, Sullivan, & Lewis, 1995). Family and neighborhood characteristics that may be more common in the environments of cocaine-exposed children include poor parental monitoring and supervision, lack of parental involvement, and harsh discipline (Castillo Mezzich et al., 1997; Clark, Neighbors, Lesnick, & Donovan, 1998; Gershoff, 2002). These environmental risk variables are associated with increased substance use, aggression, and openness to peer influence (Sameroff, Seifer, Zax, & Barocas, 1987; Wachs, 1991).

It also has been demonstrated that neonatal medical complications have an impact on subsequent development (Bendersky & Lewis, 1994; Landry, Fletcher, Denson, & Chapieski, 1993; Sostek, Smith, Katz, & Grant, 1987; Wildin et al., 1997). Newborns exposed to cocaine have more medical complications (Bendersky & Lewis, 1999; Singer, Arendt, Song, Warshawsky, & Kliegman, 1994; Woods, Behnke, Eyler, Conlon, & Wobie, 1995). Our sampling, which excluded infants with significant perinatal complications or medical conditions, led us to select relatively healthy infants; even so, our cocaine-exposed newborns had significantly higher medical risk scores than the unexposed group, indicating that medical risk should be controlled in analyses.

Finally, exposure to other drugs, such as cigarettes, alcohol, and marijuana, has been implicated as causes of developmental problems (Day, Richardson, Goldschmidt, & Cornelius, 2000; Fried, Watkinson, & Gray, 1992; Jacobsen, Slotkin, Mencl, Frost, & Pugh, 2007; Thompson, Levitt, & Stanwood, 2009; see also Chapters 5 and 7, this volume), and women who use cocaine are likely to use some if not all of these other substances (Nordstrom Bailey et al., 2005; Woods et al., 1995). In our sample, cocaine exposure is associated with all of these exposures (Bendersky, Alessandri, Gilbert, & Lewis, 1996), and therefore we have statistically controlled for these effects by including the amount of exposure to other substances as covariates when trying to understand the impact of cocaine on development. Deficits in inhibitory control, emotion regulation, and cognition appear to exist at least through late childhood and into early adolescence. It is notable that these cocaine exposure effects appear to be significant above and beyond the effects of exposure to other substances, neonatal medical risk, and environmental risk, which have been carefully measured and controlled for.

Our research has also shown that gender plays an important role in understanding the effects of prenatal cocaine exposure. We have shown that males exposed to cocaine are more adversely affected than females in many developmental domains. Although much has been written about the effects of prenatal cocaine exposure, in this chapter we review what we know regarding the gender-dependent effects. We also speculate on potential neural mechanisms responsible for these gender differences.

Gender-Specific Effects of Cocaine Exposure on Child Development

Gender differences have been found across a number of domains in prenatal cocaine exposure research. In particular, males appear to be negatively impacted by prenatal cocaine exposure, whereas exposed females often do not appear to differ from unexposed females on several outcome measures. Our work and that of others has suggested that, compared with exposed females, exposed males appear to be at greater risk for attention and inhibitory control problems, emotion regulation difficulties, health risk behaviors, and antisocial behavior (Bendersky et al., 2006; Bendersky et al., 2003; Bennett et al., 2002, 2007; Delaney-Black et al., 2004; Dennis et al., 2006; Singer et al., 2004; see also Chapter 2, this volume). Similarly, in the cognitive domain we have found exposed males to have lower IQ scores and more difficulty with abstract/visual reasoning tasks, whereas prenatally exposed females perform as well as unexposed females and males (Bennett et al., 2008). In fact, among the four groups (exposed/unexposed, male/female), exposed males show the worst performance on cognitive tasks and the highest levels of antisocial and risky behavior. These findings converge with those from animal studies that have shown that cocaine-exposed male, but not female, rats perform worse on cognitive, attention, and motor development assessments (Garavan et al., 2000; Gendle et al., 2004; Markowski, Cox, & Weiss, 1998). These gender-specific cocaine effects on behavior may be due to underlying gender differences in the effect of cocaine exposure on central noradrenergic or dopaminergic function (Booze et al., 2006; Ferris et al., 2007; Garavan et al., 2000; Glatt, Trksak, Cohen, Simeone, & Jackson, 2004).

In addition, we are now finding that cocaine exposure may affect the timing of pubertal development and the hormonal changes associated with puberty and that the direction of these effects differs for males and females. Our work indicates that gender is a very important moderator and that males are particularly vulnerable to prenatal cocaine exposure from early childhood through adolescence. In this chapter, we describe findings from our study in greater detail.

Study Description

The Growth, Learning, and Development program began in 1992 and has continued to follow the development of children whose mothers used cocaine during pregnancy. Pregnant women were recruited from two hospitals in Trenton, New Jersey, and Philadelphia, Pennsylvania. Of the women who were approached, 384 agreed to participate in the study. Infants were excluded ($n = 63$) if they were born prior to 32 weeks of gestation, required special care or oxygen therapy for more than 24 hr, exhibited congenital anomalies, were exposed to opiates or PCP in utero, or if their mothers were HIV+. Two hundred and fifty-eight subjects were first seen at age 4 months and have had regular follow-up visits every 4 to 6 months. As of 2009, there were over 200 active participants who had agreed to continue in the study, ranging in age from 13 to 16 years old. Demographic information is reported in Table 1.1. The outcome constructs that have been assessed at various ages throughout the study are listed in Table 1.2. In the sections that follow, we describe findings from the study that illustrate the gender-specific effects of cocaine exposure on several outcome domains.

Executive Functions

In our studies of executive functions, including inhibitory control, attention, planning, and set shifting, we have shown that from early childhood into early adolescence cocaine exposure negatively affects these functions, particularly for males and for children from high-risk environments (Bendersky, Bennett, & Lewis, 2005; Bendersky et al., 2003; Bennett, Carmody, & Lewis, 2011; Carmody, Bendersky, Bennett, & Lewis, 2007; Carmody, Dettwiler, Sugaya, Lubin, & Lewis, 2008; Carmody et al., 2011). These findings are consistent with animal research showing more pronounced dysfunction among males on tasks involving attentional processes (see Chapter 4, this volume).

We examined the ability of 5-year-old children to remember a rule and inhibit a prepotent motor response using a Contrary Tapping task (Bendersky et al., 2003). In this task, immediately after the experimenter tapped once with a wooden dowel, the child was to tap twice with the dowel; when the experimenter tapped twice the child was to tap once. Results indicated that cocaine exposure, high environmental risk, male gender, and low child IQ each were related to poorer inhibitory control. Exposed children made an error sooner than unexposed children. In addition, males made their first error sooner than females. A trend

Table 1.2. Outcome Constructs Potentially Affected by Prenatal Cocaine Exposure

	Source				
Construct	Self	Parent	Teacher	Bio assay	Lab task
Cognitive Abilities			X		X
Executive Functions					
Inhibitory Control and Attention		X	X		X
Planning, Organizing, Set Shifting				X	
Emotion Regulation	X	X			X
Physiological Stress Reactivity and Regulation				X	
Pubertal Development	X	X		X	
Risky Behavior					
Substance Use	X			X	
Antisocial Behavior	X	X	X		X
Sexual Risk Taking	X				
Risky Decision Making	X				X
Peer Relations	X				
Psychological Adjustment (e.g., internalizing/ externalizing)	X	X	X		X

also was found for gender to moderate the effect of cocaine exposure on inhibitory control. Although males in general made errors sooner than females, cocaine-exposed males tended to perform the worst ($p = .09$).

Inhibitory control and attention have been examined using computerized tasks from ages 6 to 12 years (Carmody et al., 2007; Carmody et al., 2008). We have used the Yale Child Study Center Attention Task (Mayes, Grillon, Granger, & Schottenfeld, 1998) to assess inhibitory control and attention at ages 6, 9, and 11. This task comprises three conditions: (a) a continuous attention task in which subjects respond with a button press to consecutive presentations of the go stimuli (i.e. a target letter); (b) a distracter condition in which go stimuli are interspersed randomly with distracters (i.e., no-go stimuli consisting of other letters); and (c) the inhibitory no-go condition, in which the rules are reversed and subjects are to inhibit responding to the target letter and instead respond to all other letters. The richness of go trials in the first two conditions sets up a prepotent response for the inhibitory response condition. The trials were scored such that correct attention occurred when the response was made within 1,500 ms of the presentation, and attention errors occurred when participants did not respond when they should. The inhibitory trials were scored such that correct inhibition occurred when no response was made; inhibition errors occurred when participants responded although they should not.

The task completed by the children in this study examined the effects of prenatal cocaine exposure on their attention and inhibitory control abilities at ages 6, 9, and 11 (Carmody et al., 2011). In the analyses, we controlled for the variables of polydrug prenatal exposure, perinatal medical complications, and environmental risk and found effects of cocaine exposure on both attention and inhibition, depending on gender. Specifically, exposed males are less capable than unexposed males of completing the task, make more attention errors, and make more inhibitory errors. These effects on performance are not evident for females. Prenatal cocaine exposure is not associated in females with attention errors or with inhibition errors.

In addition, the effects of prenatal cocaine exposure on attention and inhibition are dose related. Heavily exposed males show the poorest performance relative to unexposed males and lightly exposed males. Only 79% of the heavily exposed males completed the task, compared with 93% of the lightly exposed males and 97% of the unexposed males and in marked contrast to 93% of the heavily exposed females. Our analyses showed that when the poorest performing subjects are excluded, the heavily exposed males make more attention errors than the lightly exposed males and unexposed males. In contrast, levels of cocaine exposure are not significantly associated with attention errors for females; there is little variation in errors between the unexposed, the lightly exposed, and the heavily exposed females.

At 8 years of age we administered the Dots Task (Davidson, Amso, Anderson, & Diamond, 2006), which also measures inhibitory control. Children were asked to make a keyboard response on the same side that a solid dot is presented (congruent trials) and to respond on the opposite side when a striped dot is presented (incongruent trials). On the congruent trials, exposed subjects were slower than unexposed subjects. On the incongruent trials, exposed males were slower than unexposed males; however, there were no exposure effects for females on incongruent trials.

We have also seen gender-specific effects of prenatal cocaine exposure in children's ability to plan and problem solve (Bendersky et al., 2005). At age 6½, children were given a seven-puzzle Tower of Hanoi task, which requires planning, hypothesis generation, working memory, and inhibitory control. It consists of three rods and a number of disks of different sizes that can slide onto any rod. The objective of the puzzle is to move a stack of disks from one rod to another rod, moving only one disk at a time and without placing a larger disk onto a smaller disk. Differences in the number of moves used across the seven increasingly difficult trials were analyzed, including child IQ and environmental risk as covariates. There was a significant Cocaine Exposure × Gender interaction: Males who were prenatally exposed to cocaine required more moves across the seven puzzles.

Attention problems as rated by parents and teachers have also been shown to be greater in prenatal cocaine exposed children than in nonexposed children and especially in exposed males (Carmody et al., 2011). We examined prenatal cocaine exposure, gender, and environmental risk as predictors of teacher (Grades 2–5) and mother (at ages 8 and 11) ratings of child attention-deficit/hyperactivity disorder (ADHD) symptoms. Given significant relations between and within teacher and mother ratings, a single mean ADHD score was computed. The highest percentages of children with elevated scores were cocaine-exposed males from high-risk environments. Hierarchical logistic regression analyses examining high and low ADHD ratings also indicated effects of prenatal cocaine exposure and gender after controlling for neonatal medical problems and prenatal exposure to alcohol, cigarettes, and marijuana. Prenatal cocaine exposure and male gender made significant independent contributions to the ADHD ratings. Compared with non-exposed children, cocaine-exposed children were more than twice as likely to be in the high ADHD range. These results are consistent with past research indicating a gender-specific cocaine exposure effect on ratings of ADHD behaviors (Delaney-Black et al., 2004).

Brain Development

In our longitudinal study of prenatal cocaine exposure, we have found that exposure is related to difficulties with inhibitory control, attention, and emotion regulation, particularly in males. To examine whether there are effects on brain function that are associated with these difficulties, we have completed neuroimaging studies of the cohort in preadolescence while they were engaged in tasks that required attention, inhibitory control, and emotion regulation (Carmody et al., 2008; Zhang, Carmody, Dettwiler, & Lewis, 2009). Brain activation images were obtained using a 3 Tesla Allegra scanner and measured using blood oxygen level-dependent contrast with the acquisition of T2*-weighted gradient echo planar images (EPI). Functional images were acquired using an EPI pulse sequence with 31 slices in the transverse plane, covering the neocortex.

In the first study (Carmody et al., 2008), 30 preadolescent 10- to 13-year-olds (14 males; 16 females) completed the Yale Attention Task (Mayes et al., 1998) while functional magnetic resonance (fMR) images were recorded. Fourteen participants (six males, eight females) were exposed prenatally to cocaine, and 16 were unexposed to cocaine. The Yale Attention Task included an inhibitory-response phase in which participants were required to inhibit responding to the original target but to respond to distracters. The first phase of the task set up a prepotent response for the inhibitory phase.

We measured brain functioning using fMR images collected during the inhibitory phase of the study. Separate analyses were conducted for the four groups of participants: exposed males, unexposed males, exposed females, and unexposed females. Figure 1.1 shows the areas of brain activity for the four groups for the inhibitory (no-go) trials. Two major findings are shown in the composite images. First, in both the exposed and unexposed groups, females had greater levels of activity located in central and posterior brain regions than did males. Second, the exposed groups, both females and males, had less activity than the unexposed group. Figure 1.2 shows the areas of brain activity for the attention (go) trials. Again, the females had greater brain activity than the males in central and posterior brain regions in both the exposed and unexposed groups. The unexposed control females had greater activity than the exposed females in the same brain regions.

In a second neuroimaging study (Zhang et al., 2009), 22 preadolescent children (ages 11–13, 11 females) were scanned while viewing alternate blocks of disgusting and neutral pictures from the International Affective Picture System.

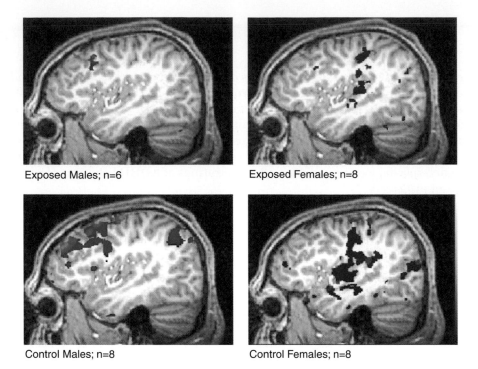

Exposed Males; n=6

Exposed Females; n=8

Control Males; n=8

Control Females; n=8

Figure 1.1. Brain activation showing gender and exposure differences in inhibition (no-go) trials. Red areas show increased activity, whereas blue areas show decreased activity. Note that females show greater volumes of increased activity than males; exposed males show the least activation for inhibition.

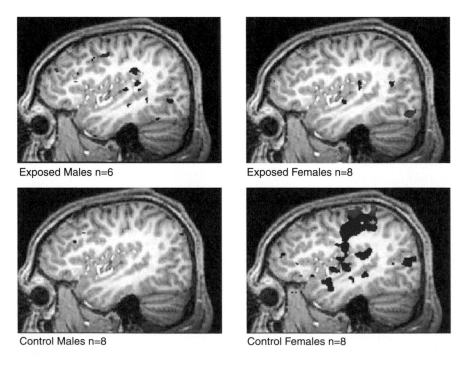

Exposed Males n=6

Exposed Females n=8

Control Males n=8

Control Females n=8

Figure 1.2. Brain activation showing gender and exposure differences in attention (go) trials. Red areas show increased activity, whereas blue areas show decreased activity. Note that females show greater volumes of increased activity than males.

The 10 exposed children and 12 unexposed children completed a rating scale of their emotional experience as well as the Level of Disgust Scale. We analyzed the ratings of emotions as well as the fMR images. Relative to the unexposed males, the exposed males had lower ratings of emotional reaction in general and disgust in particular to the disgusting pictures; relative to unexposed females, exposed females did not show this effect. The contrast of disgusting versus neutral pictures showed significant activation in several brain regions, including the bilateral occipital-parietal regions, bilateral cerebellum, bilateral middle frontal gyrus, insula, postcentral gyrus, precuneus, and parahippocampal gyrus. Cocaine-exposed males had greater activation than unexposed males in prefrontal cortex. This exposure effect in prefrontal brain activation was not evident in the comparison of exposed and unexposed females. Another brain region in males that was affected by exposure was the right hippocampal region in that exposed males had less activation than unexposed males. Again, this effect was not evident in the comparison of exposed and unexposed females. Thus, we found an interactive effect of prenatal cocaine exposure by gender on brain activation in an emotion-regulation task.

Emotion Regulation and Risky Behavior

Children prenatally exposed to cocaine may be at elevated risk for adjustment problems in early development because of reduced emotion regulation during challenging tasks. We examined reactivity to frustration and regulation of behavior during a problem-solving task (Dennis et al., 2006). Children age 4½ years were given the Impossible Pulley Task, a problem-solving task designed to elicit high levels of frustration. A toy or food is placed in a basket hanging from a pulley, just out of the child's reach. The child is encouraged to get the toy. If after 1 min the child has not discovered the knot at the end of the pulley, the experimenter points out that the basket is attached to the string, gesturing along the length of the string to the knotted end. The child is allowed 3 min to try to get it. Frustration reactivity was measured as latency to show frustration and number of disruptive behaviors, whereas regulation was measured as latency to approach and attempt the problem-solving task and number of problem-solving behaviors. Results indicated that cocaine-exposed children took longer than nonexposed children to attempt the problem-solving task, with cocaine-exposed males showing the most difficulties: They were quicker to express frustration and were more disruptive. This suggests that cocaine-exposed males showed greater emotional reactivity and less effective regulation. In contrast, cocaine-exposed females showed almost none of the decrements evidenced by cocaine-exposed males, and females overall responded to the challenging task with significantly more instrumental behaviors than did males.

The ability to regulate emotion also can be seen in children's externalizing behavior. We have examined aggression, risk taking, and antisocial behavior at several ages. We examined aggression in 5-year-old children in a multiple risk model that included cocaine exposure, environmental risk, and gender as predictors (Bendersky et al., 2006). We assessed aggression using multiple methods, including teacher report, parent report, the child's response to hypothetical provocations, and the child's observed behavior. Cocaine exposure, male gender, and a high-risk environment each predicted aggression at 5 years. Although the Exposure × Gender interaction was not significant, cocaine-exposed males had the highest scores on the composite measure of aggression that included the observation, mother report, and teacher report.

We also have examined health risk behavior, including self-reported use of substances, aggression, and disregard for safety (Bennett et al., 2007). The Youth Risk Behavior Survey (Centers for Disease Control and Prevention, 2005) was administered by computer to enhance anonymity of responses. At ages 10 to 11 years, cocaine-exposed males had the highest Total Risk Behavior Score (TRBS) and number of risks. Moreover, there was a significant Exposure × Gender interaction (see Figure 1.3). Cocaine-exposed males had higher TRBS than unexposed males, but the TRBS of exposed females was not higher than that of unexposed females. In addition, there was a significant Exposure × Gender × Environmental Risk interaction; exposed males with high environmental risk had the highest number of risks. Males who were prenatally exposed to cocaine, especially those from high-risk environments, had the most involvement in high-risk behaviors. Thus, there appears to be an Exposure × Gender interaction for high-risk behavior in early adolescence. Scores on the Youth Risk Behavior Survey indicated that at age 12, cocaine-exposed males were seven times more likely to have had sexual intercourse by age 12 (Kestler, Bendersky, Bennett, & Lewis, 2007).

Cognitive Ability

We examined children's cognitive ability at ages 4, 6, and 9 years using the Stanford–Binet Intelligence Scale (4th ed.; Bennett et al., 2008). Mixed models analyses controlling for neonatal medical problems, prenatal exposure to other drugs, environmental risk, and maternal verbal intelligence revealed a significant Cocaine Exposure × Gender interaction. Cocaine-exposed males had lower

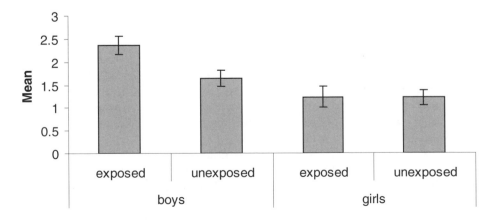

Figure 1.3.   Total Risk Behavior Score by gender and exposure to cocaine.

IQ scores (see Figure 1.4). Age did not moderate this relation, indicating that cocaine-exposed males had lower IQs across the 4- to 9-year age period. High environmental risk and low maternal verbal IQ also predicted lower child IQs. These findings indicate that cocaine-exposed males continue to be at risk for cognitive deficits across childhood.

Physical Development

The effects of gender and prenatal cocaine exposure on pubertal development, including salivary levels of dehydroepiandrosterone (DHEA), were examined in children between 11 and 12 years of age. DHEA is an adrenal androgen and a precursor to testosterone and estrogen that increases during childhood and adolescence. To assess the physical changes of puberty, the Pubertal Development Scale (PDS; Petersen, Crockett, Richards, & Boxer, 1988) was administered to 121 children at 11½, 12, and 12½ years. DHEA levels were assayed from two saliva samples at each visit. At age 12½ cocaine-exposed males had significantly lower PDS scores than unexposed males. There was no difference by cocaine exposure in the females at 12½ or in males or females at younger ages. Cocaine effects on DHEA also are gender dependent, with exposed females showing greater DHEA and exposed males showing less DHEA compared to unexposed children. Furthermore, the effect of cocaine exposure on female physical development shows up in early puberty (see Figure 1.5). Exposed females show significantly higher DHEA than unexposed females in pre- to mid-puberty (Tanner Stages I–III). In contrast, the effect of cocaine exposure on males is evident in late puberty. Exposed males show significantly lower DHEA than unexposed males in advanced puberty to postpuberty (Tanner Stages IV–V).

Our preliminary findings also indicate that although prenatal cocaine exposure is related to lower levels of puberty-related hormones in males, the cocaine-exposed males who are early developers are most at risk for engaging in risky

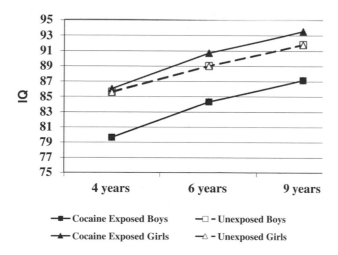

Figure 1.4. Change in IQ from 4 to 9 years.

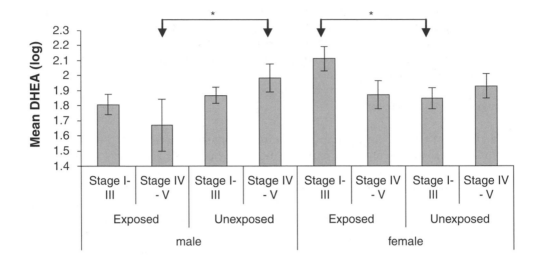

Figure 1.5. Cocaine exposure effects on DHEA as a function of pubertal development (Tanner stages). DHEA = dehydroepiandrosterone. *$p < .05$.

behavior. An analysis of covariance revealed main effects on risk behavior scores of cocaine exposure, gender, and pubertal status and an interaction between pubertal status and cocaine such that early developing males who were cocaine exposed were at greatest risk of engaging in risky behavior (Kestler et al., 2007).

Prenatal Mechanisms of Gender-Specific Cocaine Effects

The findings described in this chapter suggest that males appear to be more affected by prenatal cocaine exposure. This is consistent with research indicating that the male fetus is, in general, more susceptible to intrauterine factors affecting the central nervous system (research presented during the American Psychological Association, Science Directorate, Conference on Sex Differences to Fetal Exposure, October 7–8, 2006; Flannery & Liederman, 1994; Kraemer, 2000; Mathura, 1979; Moe & Slinning, 2002; Montagu, 1962; Pérez-Crespo et al., 2005; Spinillo et al., 2009; Tioseco, Aly, Essers, Patel, & El-Mohandes, 2006). These intrauterine factors to which male fetuses are more vulnerable and which are common sequelae of prenatal cocaine exposure, including hypoxia and vaso-constriction, may help to explain why prenatal cocaine exposure affects males and females differently.

Although the reasons for gender-specific effects are unclear, several possible mechanisms exist. Sex differences in a number of processes involved in placental transmission have been proposed to account for greater male vulnerability to teratogen exposure, including umbilical blood flow, the degree of drug ionization, maternal and fetal plasma protein binding, the anatomical structure of the placenta, and fetal metabolism and tissue uptake (van der Aa, Copius Peereboom-Stegeman, Noordhoek, Gribnau, & Russel, 1998). Males have been shown to be more susceptible to the effects of hypoxia and vasoconstriction (Hemmings,

Williams, & Davidge, 2005), which are common sequelae of prenatal cocaine exposure. Male fetuses have a greater velocity of intrauterine growth, placing them at greater risk for factors limiting fetal growth (Parker, Davies, Mayho, & Newton, 1984). High levels of gonadotropins and testosterone appear in the male fetus in the second trimester. The increased mortality and morbidity of the male infant might indicate sex differences in organ maturity at birth in which the different hormonal milieu may have been crucial. Because males grow at a faster rate but mature more slowly than females, males may be more dependent on a "perfect" placental environment (Zarén, Lindmark, & Bakketeig, 2000). Given that cocaine is associated with greater cerebral vasoconstriction among men than among women (Kaufman et al., 2001), cocaine exposure may cause greater vasoconstriction among male fetuses. Differences in oxidative stress may also be involved because prenatal cocaine exposure is linked to increased oxidative stress in the hippocampus (Bashkatova, Meunier, Maurice, & Vanin, 2005). Male rodents are more susceptible to oxidative damage in brain tissue (Katalinic, Modun, Music, & Boban, 2005; Pérez-Crespo et al., 2005). Iron deficient anemia also may be implicated, as males are at greater risk for this condition (Domellöf, Dewey, Lonnerdal, Cohen, & Hernell, 2002), and it has been found to be more prevalent among cocaine-exposed children (Nelson, Lerner, Needlman, Salvator, & Singer, 2004).

Evidence from animal research has suggested that particular mechanisms of effect of cocaine on the developing central nervous system may be more susceptible to damage in males (see Chapters 3 and 4, this volume; Booze et al., 2006; Brunzell, Coy, Ayres, & Meyer, 2002; Dow-Edwards, Freed-Malen, & Gerkin, 2001; Ferris et al., 2007; Garavan et al., 2000; Gendle et al., 2004; Glatt, Bolanos, Trksak, & Jackson, 2000; Markowski et al., 1998; Spear, 1995; Wood & Spear, 1998). Specifically, gender-dependent effects may be due to underlying differences in central noradrenergic or dopaminergic function (Booze et al., 2006; Ferris et al., 2007; Garavan et al., 2000; Glatt et al., 2004). Prenatal cocaine has been shown to reduce basal dopamine release from striata of juvenile male but not female rats (Booze et al., 2006). This was also shown in adulthood (Glatt et al., 2004), suggesting a selective and persistent vulnerability to exposure in male rats. Offspring following prenatal cocaine also show long lasting sex-specific alterations in D2, D3, and sigma receptor binding in accumbens and striatum (Booze et al., 2006) and D1 receptor, α2, and noradrenergic transporter binding alterations in prelimbic, hippocampus, and anterior cingulate regions (Ferris et al., 2007). These findings suggest that exposure differentially alters by sex the neurotransmitter systems and structures that underlie performance on tasks of attention and inhibition that are compromised by prenatal exposure in animals. All of the above indicate that male fetuses are more vulnerable than females to prenatal factors, especially to prenatal drug exposure.

Given that most prospective studies of prenatal cocaine exposure were started in the 1990s, few have yet to report findings from adolescence. Results from our study during childhood have shown that the cocaine exposure effects on inhibitory control, attention, and emotion regulation deficits are gender dependent. We also have shown evidence for a link between prenatal cocaine exposure and aggression–antisocial behavior, early sexual activity, and other risk behaviors from childhood through preadolescence and that these effects also are stronger in males than females. In addition, we are beginning to find evidence that cocaine exposure interacts with early pubertal development to further predict risky behavior.

Research has yet to examine whether gender interacts with prenatal cocaine exposure in adolescence, so we do not yet know whether the gender effects that we found at earlier ages continue. Gender differences play an important role in understanding the effects of drug exposure and may become even more pronounced at the onset of adolescence, when gender differences begin to emerge with the hormonal changes of puberty. For example, Spear and colleagues (Heyser, McKinzie, Athalie, Spear, & Spear, 1994; Heyser, Spear, & Spear, 1995) found more prevalent and consistent gender differences in adolescence and adulthood compared to testing during the preweanling period in prenatally exposed rats. Other animal findings show that cocaine-exposed males are at greater risk than exposed females for impairment into adolescence and beyond (Gendle et al., 2004; Markowski et al., 1998; Wood & Spear, 1998). In addition to neurobehavioral effects, prenatal cocaine exposure has been found to cause a sexspecific increase in heart susceptibility to ischemia and reperfusion injury in adult male rat offspring despite no evidence of fetal growth restriction or decreased contractility in the resting heart, suggesting that the vulnerability is not evident until stressed in later life (Bae, Gilbert, Ducsay, & Zhang, 2005). Furthermore, adolescence may be a critical period in which to assess gender moderation effects in exposed children, because males are more likely to engage in risky behaviors such as drug use and sexual activity during adolescence than are females (Byrnes, Miller, & Schafer, 1999). Given that exposed males are more likely to exhibit cocaine exposure effects at earlier ages, and the increased likelihood of males to engage in risky behavior during adolescence, the adolescent period is an important one in which to test the hypothesis that cocaine-exposed males are at increased risk for risky behaviors. As our sample progresses through adolescence, we will continue to explore these questions.

Summary

Well-controlled, prospective longitudinal investigations have yielded a growing knowledge about the impact of prenatal cocaine exposure on child development, from infancy through late childhood and now into adolescence. We now have a greater understanding of the subtle yet important deficits in emotion, behavior, and cognition that can result from prenatal cocaine exposure. We are beginning to understand how prenatal cocaine exposure also may impact physical development, first in fetal development and again in puberty. The effects of prenatal cocaine exposure are significant and long lasting, and they impact functioning across a number of domains. Whereas children exposed to cocaine in utero often are exposed to a number of other risks, including prenatal exposure to other drugs, perinatal medical complications, or environmental risk factors associated with drug use and poverty, analyses have been able to control for the effects of these other factors and find a unique contribution of prenatal cocaine exposure in predicting negative outcomes.

It is becoming apparent that the effects of cocaine on fetal development are gender specific, leading to different outcomes for males and females. Across several domains, exposed males appear to have the greatest deficits, whereas exposed females often do not differ from unexposed females. Brain imaging studies also have shown that prenatal cocaine exposure affects brain activation during inhibitory control tasks in males but not females. Rodent studies have illustrated gender-dependent effects in both brain and behavior and at different points in the life cycle. Gender differences in the susceptibility to the effects of neurotoxins in fetal development as well as greater male vulnerability to perinatal complications may underlie these gender differences in children prenatally exposed to cocaine. Gender differences in fetal growth velocity, organ maturity, cerebral vasoconstriction, oxidative stress, and sex hormone levels have all been implicated as possible prenatal mechanisms for gender-dependent effects of prenatal cocaine exposure.

The continuing effects of prenatal cocaine exposure on growth and development in adolescence are currently being studied. It is important to examine whether the effects vary by gender, given the number of gender-dependent effects that have been found across domains in early development. Further research must confirm and refine our understanding of these gender-dependent effects and their etiology and whether distinct approaches are needed to modify the detrimental consequences of cocaine exposure for males and females.

References

Bae, S., Gilbert, R. D., Ducsay, C. A., & Zhang, L. (2005). Prenatal cocaine exposure increases heart susceptibility to ischaemia–reperfusion injury in adult male but not female rats. *The Journal of Physiology, 565*(Pt 1), 149–158. doi:10.1113/jphysiol.2005.082701

Bashkatova, V., Meunier, J., Maurice, T., & Vanin, A. (2005). Memory impairments and oxidative stress in the hippocampus of in-utero cocaine-exposed rats. *NeuroReport: For Rapid Communication of Neuroscience Research, 16,* 1217–1221. doi:10.1097/00001756-200508010-00017

Bendersky, M., Alessandri, S., Gilbert, P., & Lewis, M. (1996). Characteristics of pregnant substance abusers in two cities in the Northeast. *The American Journal of Drug and Alcohol Abuse, 22,* 349–362. doi:10.3109/00952999609001664

Bendersky, M., Alessandri, S. A., Sullivan, M. W., & Lewis, M. (1995). Measuring the effects of prenatal cocaine exposure. In M. Lewis & M. Bendersky (Eds.), *Mothers, babies and cocaine: The role of toxins in development* (pp. 163–178). Hillsdale, NJ: Erlbaum.

Bendersky, M., Bennett, D., & Lewis, M. (2005, April). *Symposium: Is executive function compromised by prenatal exposure? Relation of prenatal cocaine exposure to executive function at 6½ years of age.* Paper presented at the Meetings of Society for Research in Child Development, Atlanta, GA.

Bendersky, M., Bennett, D. S., & Lewis, M. (2006). Aggression at age five as a function of prenatal exposure to cocaine, gender and environmental risk. *Journal of Pediatric Psychology, 31,* 1–14.

Bendersky, M., Gambini, G., Lastella, A., Bennett, D. S., & Lewis, M. (2003). Inhibitory motor control at five years as a function of prenatal cocaine exposure. *Journal of Developmental and Behavioral Pediatrics, 24,* 345–351. doi:10.1097/00004703-200310000-00005

Bendersky, M., & Lewis, M. (1994). Environmental risk, biological risk, and developmental outcome. *Developmental Psychology, 30,* 484–494. doi:10.1037/0012-1649.30.4.484

Bendersky, M., & Lewis, M. (1998a). Arousal modulation in cocaine-exposed infants. *Developmental Psychology, 34,* 555–564. doi:10.1037/0012-1649.34.3.555

Bendersky, M., & Lewis, M. (1998b). Prenatal cocaine exposure and impulse control at two years. *Annals of the New York Academy of Sciences, 846,* 365–367. doi:10.1111/j.1749-6632.1998.tb09756.x

Bendersky, M., & Lewis, M. (1999). Prenatal cocaine exposure and neonatal condition. *Infant Behavior & Development, 22,* 353–366. doi:10.1016/S0163-6383(99)00015-6

Bennett, D. S., Bendersky, M., & Lewis, M. (2002). Children's intellectual and emotional-behavioral adjustment at 4 years as a function of cocaine exposure, maternal characteristics, and environmental risk. *Developmental Psychology, 38,* 648–658. doi:10.1037/0012-1649.38.5.648

Bennett, D. S., Bendersky, M., & Lewis, M. (2007). Preadolescent health risk behavior as a function of prenatal cocaine exposure and gender. *Journal of Developmental and Behavioral Pediatrics, 28,* 467–472. doi:10.1097/DBP.0b013e31811320d8

Bennett, D. S., Bendersky, M., & Lewis, M. (2008). Children's cognitive ability from 4- to 9-years as a function of cocaine exposure, environmental risk, maternal verbal intelligence, and gender. *Developmental Psychology, 44,* 919–928. doi:10.1037/0012-1649.44.4.919

Booze, R. M., Wallace, D. R., Silvers, J. M., Strupp, B. J., Snow, D. M., & Mactutus, C. F. (2006). Prenatal cocaine exposure alters alpha2 receptor expression in adolescent rats. *BMC Neuroscience, 7,* 33. doi:10.1186/1471-2202-7-33

Brunzell, D. H., Coy, A., Ayres, J., & Meyer, J. (2002). Prenatal cocaine effects on fear conditioning: Exaggeration of sex-dependent context extinction. *Neurotoxicology and Teratology, 24,* 161–172. doi:10.1016/S0892-0362(01)00212-4

Byrnes, J., Miller, D., & Schafer, W. (1999). Gender differences in risk taking: A meta analysis. *Psychological Bulletin, 125,* 367–383. doi:10.1037/0033-2909.125.3.367

Carmody, D. P., Bendersky, M., Bennett, D. S., & Lewis, M. (2007, March–April). *Relations among prenatal cocaine exposure, gender and environmental risk in attention and inhibitory control tasks at age 9 and 11.* Paper presented at the Society for Research in Child Development, Boston, MA.

Carmody, D. P., Bennett, D. S., & Lewis, M. (2011). The effects of prenatal cocaine exposure and gender on inhibitory control and attention. *Neurotoxicology and Teratology, 33,* 61–68. doi:10.1016/j.ntt.2010.07.004

Carmody, D. P., Dettwiler, A., Sugaya, S., Lubin, M., & Lewis, M. (2008, March). *Gender differences in brain activity for attention and inhibitory processes in preadolescents prenatally exposed to cocaine.* Paper presented at the Society for Research in Adolescence, Chicago, IL.

Castillo Mezzich, A. C., Tarter, R. E., Giancola, P. R., Lu, S., Kirisci, L., & Parks, S. (1997). Substance use and risky sexual behavior in female adolescents. *Drug and Alcohol Dependence, 44,* 157–166. doi:10.1016/S0376-8716(96)01333-6

Centers for Disease Control and Prevention. (2005). *The Youth Risk Behavior Survey.* Atlanta, GA: Author.

Clark, D. B., Neighbors, B. D., Lesnick, L. A., & Donovan, J. E. (1998). Family functioning and adolescent alcohol use disorders. *Journal of Family Psychology, 12,* 81–92. doi:10.1037/0893-3200.12.1.81

Davidson, M. C., Amso, D., Anderson, L. C., & Diamond, A. (2006). Development of cognitive control and executive functions from 4 to 13 years: Evidence from manipulations of memory, inhibition, and task switching. *Neuropsychologia, 44,* 2037–2078. doi:10.1016/j.neuropsychologia.2006.02.006

Day, N. L., Richardson, G., Goldschmidt, L., & Cornelius, M. (2000). Effects of prenatal tobacco exposure on preschoolers' behavior. *Journal of Developmental and Behavioral Pediatrics, 21,* 180–188.

Delaney-Black, V., Covington, C., Nordstrom, B., Ager, J., Janisse, J., Hannigan, J. H., . . . Sokol, R. J. (2004). Prenatal cocaine: Quantity of exposure and gender moderation. *Journal of Developmental and Behavioral Pediatrics, 25,* 254–263. doi:10.1097/00004703-200408000-00005

Dennis, T., Bendersky, M., Ramsay, D., & Lewis, M. (2006). Reactivity and regulation in children prenatally exposed to cocaine. *Developmental Psychology, 42,* 688–697. doi:10.1037/0012-1649.42.4.688

Domellöf, M., Dewey, K. G., Lonnerdal, B., Cohen, R. J., & Hernell, O. (2002). The diagnostic criteria for iron deficiency in infants should be reevaluated. *The Journal of Nutrition, 132,* 3680–3686.

Dow-Edwards, D. L., Freed-Malen, L., & Gerkin, L. (2001). Sexual dimorphism in the brain metabolic response to prenatal cocaine exposure. *Developmental Brain Research, 129,* 73–79. doi:10.1016/S0165-3806(01)00184-5

Ferris, M. J., Mactutus, C. F., Silvers, J. M., Hasselrot, U., Beaudin, S. A., Strupp, B. J., & Booze, R. M. (2007). Sex mediates dopamine and adrenergic receptor expression in adult rats exposed prenatally to cocaine. *International Journal of Developmental Neuroscience, 25,* 445–454.

Flannery, K. A., & Liederman, J. (1994). A test of the immunoreactive theory for the origin of neurodevelopmental disorders in the offspring of women with immune disorder. *Cortex, 30,* 635–646.

Frank, D. A., Augustyn, M., Knight, W., Pell, T., & Zuckerman, B. (2001). Growth, development, and behavior in early childhood following prenatal cocaine exposure. *JAMA, 285,* 1613–1625. doi:10.1001/jama.285.12.1613

Fried, P. A., Watkinson, B., & Gray, R. (1992). A follow-up study of attentional behavior in 6-year-old children exposed prenatally to marijuana, cigarettes, and alcohol. *Neurotoxicology and Teratology, 14,* 299–311. doi:10.1016/0892-0362(92)90036-A

Garavan, H., Morgan, R. E., Mactutus, C. F., Levitsky, D. A., Booze, R. M., & Strupp, B. J. (2000). Prenatal cocaine exposure impairs selective attention: Evidence from serial reversal and extradimensional shift tasks. *Behavioral Neuroscience, 114,* 725–738. doi:10.1037/0735-7044.114.4.725

Gendle, M. H., White, T. L., Strawderman, M., Mactutus, C. F., Booze, R. M., Levitsky, D. A., & Strupp, B. J. (2004). Enduring effects of prenatal cocaine exposure on selective attention and reactivity to errors: Evidence from an animal model. *Behavioral Neuroscience, 118,* 290–297. doi:10.1037/0735-7044.118.2.290

Gershoff, E. T. (2002). Corporal punishment by parents and associated child behaviors and experiences: A meta-analytic and theoretical review. *Psychological Bulletin, 128,* 539–579. doi:10.1037/0033-2909.128.4.539

Glatt, S. J., Bolanos, C. A., Trksak, G. H., & Jackson, D. (2000). Effects of prenatal cocaine exposure on dopamine system development: A meta-analysis. *Neurotoxicology and Teratology, 22,* 617–629. doi:10.1016/S0892-0362(00)00088-X

Glatt, S. J., Trksak, G. H., Cohen, O. S., Simeone, B. P., & Jackson, D. (2004). Prenatal cocaine exposure decreases nigrostriatal dopamine release in vitro: Effects of age and sex. *Synapse, 53*(2), 74–89. doi:10.1002/syn.20036

Hemmings, D. G., Williams, S., & Davidge, S. (2005). Increased myogenic tone in 7-month-old adult male but not female offspring from rat dams exposed to hypoxia during pregnancy. *American Journal of Physiology. Heart and Circulatory Physiology, 289,* H674–H682. doi:10.1152/ajpheart.00191.2005

Heyser, C. J., McKinzie, D. L., Athalie, F., Spear, N. E., & Spear, L. P. (1994). Effects of prenatal exposure to cocaine on heart rate and nonassociative learning and retention in infant rats. *Teratology, 49,* 470–478. doi:10.1002/tera.1420490607

Heyser, C. J., Spear, N. E., & Spear, L. P. (1995). Effects of prenatal exposure to cocaine on Morris water maze performance in adult rats. *Behavioral Neuroscience, 109,* 734–743. doi:10.1037/0735-7044.109.4.734

Jacobsen, L. K., Slotkin, T. A., Mencl, W. E., Frost, S. J., & Pugh, K. R. (2007). Gender-specific effects of prenatal and adolescent exposure to tobacco smoke on auditory and visual attention. *Neuropsychopharmacology, 32,* 2453–2464. doi:10.1038/sj.npp.1301398

Katalinic, V., Modun, D., Music, I., & Boban, M. (2005). Gender differences in antioxidant capacity of rat tissues determined by 2,2′-azinobis (3-ethylbenzothiazoline 6-sulfonate; ABTS) and ferric reducing antioxidant power (FRAP) assays. *Comparative Biochemistry and Physiology Part C: Toxicology & Pharmacology, 140*(1), 47–52. doi:10.1016/j.cca.2005.01.005

Kaufman, M. J., Levin, J. M., Maas, L. C., Kukes, T. J., Villafuerte, R. A., Dostal, K., . . . , Renshaw, P. F. (2001). Cocaine-induced cerebral vasoconstriction differs as a function of sex and menstrual cycle phase. *Biological Psychiatry, 49,* 774–781. doi:10.1016/S0006-3223(00)01091-X

Kestler, L. P., Bendersky, M., Bennett, D., & Lewis, M. (2007, March–April). *Relations among pubertal maturation, DHEA and health risk behavior in adolescence: A sex by prenatal cocaine exposure analysis.* Paper presented at the Biennial Meeting of the Society for Research in Child Development, Boston, MA.

Kraemer, S. (2000). The fragile male. *BMJ, 321,* 1609–1612. doi:10.1136/bmj.321.7276.1609

Landry, S. H., Fletcher, J., Denson, S., & Chapieski, M. L. (1993). Longitudinal outcome for low birth weight infants: Effects of intraventricular hemorrhage and bronchopulmonary dysplasia. *Journal of Clinical and Experimental Neuropsychology, 15,* 205–218. doi:10.1080/01688639308402558

Lewis, M., & Bendersky, M. (1995). *Mothers, babies, and cocaine: The role of toxins in development.* Hillsdale, NJ: Erlbaum.

Markowski, V. P., Cox, C., & Weiss, B. (1998). Prenatal cocaine exposure produces gender-specific motor effects in aged rats. *Neurotoxicology and Teratology, 20,* 43–53. doi:10.1016/S0892-0362(97)00076-7

Mathura, C. B. (1979). The vulnerability of the male CNS to early trauma: Implications for clinical neuropsychology. *Clinical Neuropsychology, 1,* 34–35.

Mayes, L. C., Grillon, C., Granger, R., & Schottenfeld, R. (1998). Regulation of arousal and attention in preschool children exposed to cocaine prenatally. *Annals of the New York Academy of Sciences, 846,* 126–143. doi:10.1111/j.1749-6632.1998.tb09731.x

Moe, V., & Slinning, K. (2002). Prenatal drug exposure and the conceptualization of long-term effects. *Scandinavian Journal of Psychology, 43*(1), 41–47. doi:10.1111/1467-9450.00267

Montagu, M. (1962). *Prenatal influences.* Springfield, IL: Charles C Thomas.

Nelson, S., Lerner, E., Needlman, R., Salvator, A. N. N., & Singer, L. T. (2004). Cocaine, anemia, and neurodevelopmental outcomes in children: A longitudinal study. *Journal of Developmental and Behavioral Pediatrics, 25*(1), 1–9. doi:10.1097/00004703-200402000-00001

Nordstrom Bailey, B., Sood, B. G., Sokol, R. J., Ager, J., Janisse, J., Hannigan, J. H., . . . Delaney-Black, V. (2005). Gender and alcohol moderate prenatal cocaine effects on teacher-report of child behavior. *Neurotoxicology and Teratology, 27,* 181–189. doi:10.1016/j.ntt.2004.10.004

Parker, A. J., Davies, P., Mayho, A., & Newton, J. (1984). The ultrasound estimation of sex-related variations of intrauterine growth. *American Journal of Obstetrics and Gynecology, 149,* 665–669.

Pérez-Crespo, M., Ramírez, M. A., Fernández-González, R., Rizos, D., Lonergan, P., Pintado, B., & Gutiérrez-Adán, A. (2005). Differential sensitivity of male and female mouse embryos to oxidative induced heat-stress is mediated by glucose-6-phosphate dehydrogenase gene expression. *Molecular Reproduction and Development, 72,* 502–510. doi:10.1002/mrd.20366

Petersen, A. C., Crockett, L., Richards, M., & Boxer, A. (1988). A self-report measure of pubertal status: Reliability, validity, and initial norms. *Journal of Youth and Adolescence, 17,* 117–133. doi:10.1007/BF01537962

Sameroff, A., Seifer, R., Zax, M., & Barocas, R. (1987). Early indicators of developmental risk: Rochester Longitudinal Study. *Schizophrenia Bulletin, 13,* 383–394.

Singer, L. T., Arendt, R., Song, L., Warshawsky, E., & Kliegman, R. (1994). Direct and indirect interactions of cocaine with childbirth outcomes. *Archives of Pediatrics & Adolescent Medicine, 148,* 959–964.

Singer, L. T., Minnes, S., Short, E., Arendt, R., Farkas, K., Lewis, B., . . . Kirchner, H. L. (2004). Cognitive outcomes of preschool children with prenatal cocaine exposure. *JAMA, 291,* 2448–2456. doi:10.1001/jama.291.20.2448

Sostek, A. M., Smith, Y., Katz, K., & Grant, E. (1987). Developmental outcome of preterm infants with intraventricular hemorrhage at one and two years of age. *Child Development, 58,* 779–786. doi:10.2307/1130214

Spear, L. P. (1995). Alterations in cognitive function following prenatal cocaine exposure: Studies in an animal model. In M. Lewis & M. Bendersky (Eds.), *Mothers, babies, and cocaine: The role of toxins in development* (pp. 207–227). Hillsdale, NJ: Erlbaum.

Spinillo, A., Montanari, L., Gardella, B., Roccio, M., Stronati M., & Fazzi, E. (2009). Infant sex, obstetric risk factors, and 2-year neurodevelopmental outcome among preterm infants. *Developmental Medicine & Child Neurology, 51,* 518–525. doi:10.1111/j.1469-8749.2009.03273.x

Thompson, B. L., Levitt, P., & Stanwood, G. D. (2009). Prenatal exposure to drugs: Effects on brain development and implications for policy and education. *Nature Reviews Neuroscience, 10,* 303–312. doi:10.1038/nrn2598

Thorndike, R. L., Hagen, E. P., & Sattler, J. M. (1986). *Stanford–Binet Intelligence Scale* (4th ed.). Itasca, IL: Riverside.

Tioseco, J. A., Aly, H., Essers, J., Patel, K., & El-Mohandes, A. A. E. (2006). Male sex and intraventricular hemorrhage. *Pediatric Critical Care Medicine, 7*(1), 40–44. doi:10.1097/01.PCC.0000192341.67078.61

van der Aa, E. M., Copius Peereboom-Stegeman, J. H. J., Noordhoek, J., Gribnau, F. W. J., & Russel, F. G. M. (1998). Mechanisms of drug transfer across the human placenta. *Pharmacy World & Science, 20*(4), 139–148. doi:10.1023/A:1008656928861

Wachs, T. D. (1991). Environmental considerations in studies with non-extreme groups. In T. Wachs & R. Plomin (Eds.), *Conceptualization and measurement of organism-environment interaction* (pp. 44–67). Washington, DC: American Psychological Association. doi:10.1037/10100-003

Wildin, S. R., Smith, K., Anderson, A., Swank, P., Denson, S., & Landry, S. (1997). Prediction of developmental patterns through 40 months from 6- and 12-month neurological examinations in very low birth weight infants. *Journal of Developmental and Behavioral Pediatrics, 18,* 215–221. doi:10.1097/00004703-199708000-00001

Wood, R. D., & Spear, L. P. (1998). Prenatal cocaine alters social competition of infant, adolescent, and adult rats. *Behavioral Neuroscience, 112,* 419–431. doi:10.1037/0735-7044.112.2.419

Woods, N., Behnke, M., Eyler, F. D., Conlon, M., & Wobie, K. (1995). Cocaine use among pregnant women: Socioeconomic, obstetrical, and psychological issues. In M. Lewis & M. Bendersky (Eds.), *Mothers, babies, and cocaine: The role of toxins in development* (pp. 305–332). Hillsdale, NJ: Erlbaum.

Zarén, B., Lindmark, G., & Bakketeig, L. (2000). Maternal smoking affects fetal growth more in the male fetus. *Paediatric and Perinatal Epidemiology, 14,* 118–126. doi:10.1046/j.1365-3016.2000.00247.x

Zhang, Y., Carmody, D. P., Dettwiler, A., & Lewis, M. (2009). Decreased neural activation in prenatal cocaine-exposed children during emotional processing: An fMRI study. *NeuroImage, Abstract 394.*

2

Prenatal Cocaine Exposure and Age 7 Behavior: The Roles of Gender, Quantity, and Duration of Exposure

Virginia Delaney-Black, Chandice Covington,
Lisa M. Chiodo, John H. Hannigan,
Mark K. Greenwald, James Janisse, Grace Patterson,
Joel Ager, Ekemini Akan, Linda Lewandowski,
Steven J. Ondersma, Ty Partridge, and Robert J. Sokol

In this chapter, we review the literature on some key neurobehavioral effects of prenatal cocaine exposure in children. In addition, we present reevaluations of the relationships between new measures of the quantity and duration of maternal cocaine use during pregnancy on these outcomes. These analyses, made possible because of more detailed assessments of the original intake data and reexaminations of medical records, provide utilitarian cocaine modeling. The robust analyses we present expand on our original publications of data for behavior at age 7, which modeled pregnancy cocaine use initially with a dichotomous yes–no index and then with a measure of duration (persistent, across pregnancy) exposure and provided analyses stratified by gender.

In the 1980s, anonymous meconium testing at our urban university obstetrical center found that more than 30% of infants had been exposed to cocaine during pregnancy (Ostrea, Brady, Gause, Raymundo, & Stevens, 1992). Despite public health campaigns during the intervening years, cocaine use by adults has remained high (Mathias, 1995), particularly in urban settings like Detroit. The first National Institute on Drug Abuse (NIDA) National Pregnancy and Health Survey, a random sample of 4 million women delivering babies, revealed that 1.1% of pregnant women admitted to cocaine use during the index pregnancy

Funding and support for this research were provided by National Institute on Drug Abuse Grant DA08524 and the Children's Research Center of Michigan. We gratefully acknowledge the support of our program directors at the National Institute on Drug Abuse, Drs. Vincent Smeriglio and Nicolette Borek, and the vital role of the participating families and SCHOO-BE staff members who made this research possible. Our special thanks to the gentle urging of Dr. Margaret Bendersky, who sought our participation at the 2006 conference. We greatly miss her. Finally, our thanks to Dr. Michael Lewis and his team, who made this publication possible.

(Mathias, 1995), annually exposing at least 44,000 fetuses to cocaine. Maternal admission of pregnancy use, which likely greatly underreports true pregnancy exposure (Ostrea et al., 1992; Schulman, Morel, Karmen, & Chazotte, 1993), combined with the earlier epidemic use in the 1980s, translates into potentially millions of affected children, teens, and young adults. The potential long-term consequences from prenatal exposure to cocaine are still being investigated.

The predicted pandemic of prenatal cocaine effects on young children did not materialize. However, the earlier media and educational stigmatization of prenatal cocaine-exposed children as permanently damaged (Elliott & Coker, 1991) brought fierce reaction from pediatric researchers who correctly feared that these characterizations might become self-fulfilling prophesies as educators and others projected their expectations of cocaine exposure effects onto children (Rose-Jacobs, Cabral, Posner, Epstein, & Frank, 2002; Woods, Eyler, Conlon, Behnke, & Wobie, 1998). Reacting appropriately to these concerns, investigators suggested that problems attributed to prenatal cocaine exposure especially in early, often undercontrolled, convenience samples might be related to covariates, including poverty and prenatal exposures other than cocaine (Frank et al., 2001; Richardson & Day, 1994). As Richardson and Day (1994) noted in their article posing concerns regarding the "illusion or reality" of prenatal cocaine exposure, additional studies were needed. In controlled studies, their group reported brain abnormalities at 1 year of age related to prenatal cocaine exposure (Scher, Richardson, & Day, 2000) and attention problems at age 6 (Leech, Richardson, Goldschmidt, & Day, 1999). Today, researchers are charting a more appropriate approach to all prenatal exposures by avoiding stigmatizing labels and all assumptions, following the lead of Dr. David Lewis by urging the elimination of characterizations such as "ice" or "meth" or "crack" babies, even as they heed the warning of Zuckerman and Frank (1994) that "potential developmental deficits in areas such as social competence, complex language, and sustained attention may not be evident in infancy but may become measurable and functionally important during the school years" (p. 733).

In fact, as we elaborate in this chapter, animal studies of pregnancy exposure to cocaine have demonstrated significant behavior problems in young (Foltz, Snow, Strupp, Booze, & Mactutus, 2004; Lidow, 2003), adolescent (Morrow, Elsworth, & Roth, 2002), and adult (Crozatier et al., 2003) animals, with late development of some of these problems (Goodwin et al., 1992; Johns et al., 1994; Kosofsky & Hyman, 2001; Kosofsky & Wilkins, 1998), consistent with a pattern of increasing deficits found in the human prenatal alcohol literature (Whaley, O'Connor, & Gunderson, 2001). Several groups conducting clinical studies of preschool and school-age children now report prenatal cocaine exposure-associated cognitive deficits (Arendt et al., 2004; Bennett, Bendersky, & Lewis, 2002; Singer et al., 2004), executive dysfunction (Mayes, Molfese, Key Alexandra, & Hunter, 2005; Noland et al., 2003; Schroder, Snyder, Sielski, & Mayes, 2004), attention deficits (Bandstra, Marrow, Anthony, Accornero, & Fried, 2001; Delaney-Black et al., 2004; Leech et al., 1999; Noland et al., 2005; Savage, Brodsky, Malmud, Giannetta, & Hurt, 2005; Singer, Arendt, Minnes, Farkas, & Salvator, 2000; Singer et al., 2002; Singer et al., 2005), and behavior problems (Bada et al., 2007; Bendersky, Bennett, & Lewis, 2005; Delaney-Black et al., 2004; Delaney-Black et al., 1998; Linares et al., 2005; Nordstrom Bailey et al., 2005; Sood et al., 2005). Only some of these studies, however, evaluated for moderation by gender (Accornero, Anthony, Morrow, Xue, & Bandstra, 2006; Bada et al., 2007; Bandstra et al., 2001; Bendersky et al., 2005; Bennett et al., 2002; Brown, Bakeman, Coles, Platzman, & Lynch, 2004; Delaney-Black et al., 2004; Delaney-Black et al., 2000; Dennis, Bendersky, Ramsay, & Lewis, 2006; Hurt, Brodsky, Roth, Malmud, & Giannetta, 2005; Leech et al., 1999; Nordstrom Bailey et al., 2005; Phillips, Sharma, Premachandra, Vaughn, & Reyes-Lee, 1996; Singer et al., 2004; Sood et al., 2005). These behavioral findings are consistent with animal studies demonstrating deficits in attention (Kosofsky & Wilkins, 1998) and aggression (Estelles, Rodriguez-Arias, Maldonado, Aguilar, & Minarro, 2005; Johns et al., 1998; Spear, Campbell, Snyder, Silveri, & Katovic, 1998). Consistent with animal studies, preliminary data from our research group also suggest that these problems persist into early adolescence and are related to the quantity and timing of cocaine exposure and like many of the preclinical studies, are moderated by gender (Brunzell, Coy, Ayres, & Meyer, 2002; Dow-Edwards, Freed-Malen, & Gerkin, 2001; Foltz et al., 2004; Garavan et al., 2000; Johns, Lubin, Lieberman, & Lauder, 2002; Taylor, Freeman, Holt, & Gabriel, 1999; Torres-Reveron & Dow-Edwards, 2006; Wood, Bannoura, & Johanson, 1994). Most important, these variables are also powerful antecedents of high-risk behaviors in late adolescence. When gender effects are identified in the references below, this information has been provided.

Externalizing, Oppositional Defiant Disorder, and Conduct Disorder

Bendersky et al. (2005; New Jersey and Pennsylvania), Linares et al. (2005; Ohio) and a multicenter study (Bada et al., 2007) confirmed our prior findings in Detroit that prenatal cocaine is associated with increased externalizing behaviors in school-age children (Delaney-Black et al., 2004; Delaney-Black et al., 1998; Delaney-Black et al., 2000; Nordstrom Bailey et al., 2005; Sood et al., 2005) but did not identify differing gender effects. Using two measures of aggression, among 5-year-olds, Bendersky et al. (2005) reported positive relationships between aggression scores and prenatal cocaine exposure, male gender, and high environmental risk. In another report from the same group, boys exposed to cocaine prenatally demonstrated more frustration and were more disruptive in completing a difficult task than nonexposed boys or either group of girls (Dennis et al., 2006). Linares et al. (2005), using criteria based on the *Diagnostic and Statistical Manual of Mental Disorders* (4th ed.; *DSM–IV*; American Psychiatric Association, 1994), found that prenatal cocaine-exposed 6-year-olds were more likely to self-report oppositional defiant disorder and attention-deficit/hyperactivity disorder (ADHD) symptoms; however, caregiver Child Behavior Checklist (CBCL; Achenbach, 1991a) scores did not confirm these findings.

When child behavior was evaluated in the home environment, prenatal cocaine-exposed children in foster or adoptive homes were at greater risk for higher aggression and externalizing behaviors than nonexposed controls or cocaine-exposed children in kinship care or the care of their biologic mother. Cocaine-exposed children in foster or adoptive homes were also more likely to be rated as having more problems on the CBCL measure of Total Problems and Externalizing Behaviors & Aggression. Although investigators provide plausible explanations for divergent findings, clearly not all studies are consistent. Messinger et al. (2004) reported no differences between exposed (opiate or cocaine) and nonexposed toddlers on the Behavioral Record Score from the Bayley Scales of Infant Development. However, Brown et al. (2004), using three measures of toddler behavior, found a univariate relation with a dichotomous (yes–no) measure of prenatal cocaine assessed at delivery. Richardson, Conroy, and Day (1996) observed no behavioral effects on the Achenbach (1991b) Teacher Report Form in a small sample (N = 28) of 6-year-old children with "light" prenatal cocaine exposure (only one woman used cocaine throughout pregnancy), suggesting that lower doses may have smaller or fewer effects.

Accornero et al. (2006) found that caregiver depression, but not prenatal cocaine exposure status, predicted the parent's assessment of his or her child's behavior. Consistent with animal studies (described below) that demonstrate attenuation of the behavioral effects of prenatal cocaine exposure by enriched environment, Bennett et al. (2002) found that prenatal cocaine had a direct, negative effect on cognition for boys, whereas externalizing behaviors were indirectly related to cocaine (i.e., mediated by harsh maternal discipline and increased environmental risk). Accornero et al. (2002) did not evaluate gender effects, but they reported that environment, not cocaine exposure, affected children's behavior.

Moderation of Relations: Environmental Risk and Gender

Cocaine use during pregnancy is associated with various environmental factors known to alter child outcomes, including poverty (Evans & English, 2002), harsh parenting style (Pine et al., 1997), and continued family substance abuse (Habeych et al., 2005). Some investigators have suggested that the effects of prenatal cocaine may be related to these factors rather than the exposure itself (Hurt et al., 2005); indeed, enrichment services (Frank, Augustyn, Knight, Pell, & Zuckerman, 2002; Frank et al., 2005) and intervention (Schuler, Nair, & Kettinger, 2003) have improved outcomes for prenatal cocaine-exposed children. In rats, environmental enrichment attenuates both the prenatal cocaine-related behavior and changes in dopamine function in prefrontal cortex (Neugebauer et al., 2004). Similar effects were seen with early postnatal cocaine exposure (Magalhães, Summavielle, Tavares, & de Sousa, 2004). Thus, it may be that failure to recognize or control for a moderating effect of environment may explain important inconsistencies across human cohorts. Gender also is a recognized moderator of the behavioral effects of prenatal cocaine in four of our publications (Delaney-Black et al., 2004; Delaney-Black et al., 2000; Nordstrom Bailey et al., 2005; Sood et al., 2005). Bendersky et al. (2005) reported that both gender and environmental risk were risk factors for aggression in preschool boys. Animal studies have also recognized sex-specific effects of prenatal cocaine exposure for over a decade (Battaglia & Cabrera, 1994).

Potential Mechanisms for Gender Moderation

Evaluation of preclinical studies is essential to understanding how prenatal cocaine exposure may have gender-specific effects. Independent of prenatal cocaine exposure, sex differences have been observed in dopamine reuptake capacity (Reisert, Engele, & Pilgrim, 1989). In addition, sex-specific maturational differences have been observed in striatal dopaminergic and tyrosine hydroxylase immunoreactive fibers in rats (Beyer, Pilgrim, & Reisert, 1991). These observed sex differences in the timing of brain development mean that the same dose and timing of fetal cocaine exposure in an experimental model in fact occurs at different developmental stages for male as compared with female fetuses. Battaglia and Cabrera (1994) reported that male rats prenatally exposed to cocaine had potentiated $5\text{-HT}_{1\alpha}$ receptor-mediated functional responses to a $5\text{-HT}_{1\alpha}$ agonist. No sex difference was seen in basal hormonal levels or overall receptor number, suggesting that the effect was due to postsynaptic receptor variations. Although the overall receptor number was not altered, changes in receptor number in specific hypothalamic nuclei could not be excluded. Johns et al. (2002) identified a reduction in $5\text{HT}_{1\alpha}$ receptors in female rats prenatally exposed to cocaine on postnatal day 30. An in vitro model found a sex differential in striatal dopamine release after prenatal cocaine exposure with males but not females having lower dopamine release. Torres-Reveron and Dow-Edwards (2006) suggested that prenatal cocaine exposure has selective effects on different central neuronal circuits with prenatally exposed adolescent male rats having alterations in stereotypy and female rats having alterations in locomotion after a methylphenidate challenge. These findings are also suggestive of dose–response shifts and/or striatal dopamine effects, as the induction of stereotyped behavior is dependent on D1 activation (Chartoff, Marck, Matsumoto, Dorsa, & Palmiter, 2001). However, other brain areas also show sex-specific effects of prenatal cocaine exposure, including the hippocampus (Brunzell et al., 2002), anterior cingulate (Taylor et al., 1999), and limbic system areas (Dow-Edwards et al., 2001). In the latter study, glucose metabolism was reduced in cocaine-exposed male but not female rat pups in ventromedial and lateral hypothalamic nuclei, whereas the dorsomedial hypothalamus had fetal cocaine-associated reductions in glucose metabolism in both genders. In summary, brain development is sex specific, and prenatal cocaine exposure has unique sex-specific effects on the structure and function even of different nuclei in the same brain region; thus, it should not be surprising that human studies also demonstrate gender-specific findings in neurobehavioral function.

Impulsivity and Attention

Cocaine-related impulsivity, defined as sudden, often unreasoned activity, frequently without regard for rules or consequences and often leading to negative consequences (Stedman, 2000), can be assessed directly by measuring delayed gratification. Using the "forbidden cookie" paradigm, Bendersky and Lewis (1998) evaluated 2-year-olds ($N = 77$; 51 cocaine-exposed). After controlling for confounders, cocaine exposure shortened the latency to reach for, take, and eat the cookie (i.e., increased impulsivity). To date, this is the only clinical evaluation of delayed gratification. More research linking prenatal cocaine and impulsivity focuses on Continuous Performance Test (CPT; Conners, 1995) errors of omission (inattention) and errors of commission (impulsivity). Two groups reported an association between prenatal cocaine and CPT-measured inattention at early school age (Bandstra et al., 2001; Leech et al., 1999). In the Pittsburgh cohort, increased errors of omission in the age 6 group were related to any first trimester cocaine exposure; a gender effect was not evaluated (Leech et al., 1999). Bandstra et al. (2001) found no gender differences. Bandstra et al. (2001) identified a relationship between amount of prenatal cocaine and sustained attention in 7-year-olds. Similar to earlier studies, attention deficits in prenatally exposed children may be stress related. In a simple visual attention task, only under conditions of stress did performance of cocaine-exposed children deteriorate compared with controls (Heffelfinger, Craft, White, & Shyken, 2002). Savage et al. (2005) found that only when high arousal required sustained attention did prenatal cocaine-exposed 10 year olds show higher impulsivity. The relation between prenatal cocaine and impulsivity may be even more complicated. Similar to moderation seen in animals (Sobrian, Ali, Slikker, & Holson, 1995), prenatal exposure to nicotine reduced the detrimental effects of cocaine exposure as measured by CPT errors of commission (Noland et al., 2005). Although reevaluation of other data sets is needed to confirm the findings, impulsivity and attention problems are significant predictors of conduct disorder (Vitacco & Rogers, 2001). Furthermore, these clinical studies are consistent with results in mice, rats, and rabbits (Romano & Harvey, 1998; Wilkins, Genova, Posten, & Kosofsky, 1998). Attention deficits were identified following prenatal cocaine in preweanling (Mactutus, 1999), young adult (Thompson, Levitt, & Stanwood, 2005), and adult rats (Garavan et al., 2000). In the Garavan et al. (2000) study, both male and female cocaine-exposed rats displayed difficulties, with the males appearing to be more involved. To date, we are not aware of any published peer-reviewed data addressing relations between prenatal cocaine and delayed gratification in adolescence. Although there are no studies of prenatal cocaine-related changes in attention, impulsivity, and externalizing behaviors in young adults, studies of youth with ADHD confirm the significance of these symptoms in predicting young adult outcomes (Barkley, Fischer, Smallish, & Fletcher, 2006). Young adults with ADHD reported more social problems, high-risk behaviors, and indicators of risky sexual behaviors, including earlier age at first intercourse, more sexual partners, less protected sex, more sexually transmitted diseases and HIV tests for both boys and girls, and more pregnancies for girls. Educational and employment outcomes were similarly affected. One implication is that prenatal cocaine-exposed adolescents who show increased attention problems, impulsivity, and externalizing behaviors are also more likely to evidence more high-risk behaviors.

Social and Emotional Responding

Wood, Molina, Wagner, and Spear (1995) found that periadolescent rats exposed to cocaine (40 mg/kg/day; gestational days 8–20) elicited fewer and delayed play responses and altered responses to a novel foot shock stressor. These data show not only altered stress responsivity in cocaine-exposed rats but also altered use of social cues. Although no differences were seen in play between these periadolescent groups, in a prior study in adolescence with different housing regimes, cocaine-exposed rats were less playful (Wood, Bannoura, & Johanson, 1994). Similar human studies are limited by sample size, blinding, and lack of control, but prenatal cocaine has been associated with neonatal behavior problems, such as arousal and emotional state regulation (Black, Schuler, & Nair, 1993; Chasnoff, Burns, & Burns, 1987; Coles, Platzman, Smith, James, & Falek, 1992; Delaney-Black et al., 1996; Eyler, Behnke, Conlon, Woods, & Wobie, 1998; Phillips et al., 1996; Richardson, Hamel, Goldschmidt, & Day, 1996; Scafidi et al., 1996; Tronick, Frank, Cabral, Mirochnick, & Zuckerman, 1996) and dose-dependent autonomic stability (Chasnoff et al., 1987; Delaney-Black et al., 1996; Richardson, Hamel, Goldschmidt, & Day, 1996). Older cocaine-exposed infants showed higher irritability (Roberts, 1996) and lower frustration levels (Alessandri, Sullivan, Imaizumi, & Lewis, 1993) compared with nonexposed infants.

Aggression

At a neural level, reactive aggression is associated with impaired orbitofrontal cortex function (e.g., Blair, Peters, & Granger, 2004). Orbitofrontal modulation of amygdala function is also implicated in emotional arousal (Smith, Henson, Dolan, & Rugg, 2004). Increased reactive aggression is related to heart rate changes in response to challenges (Waschbusch et al., 2002; Williams, Lochman, Phillips, & Barry, 2003), consistent with responses by hyperaroused youth (Kagan, Snidman, & Reznick, 1989). Behaviorally, there is also a link among many cognitive–affective behaviors (sensation- and risk-seeking, attention, impulsivity) and autonomic and neuroendocrine measures and increased reactive aggression. Shields and Cicchetti (1998) linked early child maltreatment to increased levels of reactive aggression, mediated through poor emotional regulation, reduced attention, and socially inappropriate emotional expressions. Waschbusch et al. (2002) found that young teenage boys with various affective–cognitive deficits, including poor attention, impulsivity, and low response to consequences (oppositional defiant disorder), had increased levels of reactive aggression and more intense hostility following low-level peer provocation. Similarly, these transactional responses are also associated with increased attributions of hostile intent on the part of the provocateur (Williams et al., 2003). These findings are consistent with a social-cognitive model wherein reactive aggression results from attributions of hostile intent with little, if any, thought of consequences (Crick & Dodge 1996). Both of these models are relevant to interpretations of behavior among prenatally cocaine-exposed children and, given the previously noted associations between prenatal cocaine exposure and externalizing behavior, evaluation of aggression following prenatal exposure is warranted.

Behavioral Outcomes After Prenatal Cocaine Exposure

To reevaluate the behavioral effects of prenatal cocaine exposure at early school age, we assessed a prospectively identified cohort followed at Wayne State University. All procedures had prior approval of the Wayne State University

Institutional Review Board, and all caregivers gave appropriate informed consent and parental permission to participate.

Study Eligibility and Enrollment Procedures

Child participants were identified originally through a larger prospective pregnancy study that recruited women receiving prenatal care at our university maternity hospital. Because African American women constituted more than 90% of our prenatal clinic population, study participation was limited to this group. To reduce collinearity between alcohol and drug use, a block sampling design was used, with oversampling of the heavily and moderately exposed pregnancies. This technique helped to identify sufficient numbers of women with varying levels of cocaine and alcohol use. An unselected sample would likely have inadequately identified women using cocaine but not alcohol. Exclusions in the pregnancy study were limited to known maternal HIV and women with no prenatal care. This need for the latter exclusion was unfortunate because heavy drug and alcohol using and abusing women may be more likely to avoid prenatal care. However, this study design decision reduced the potential for misclassification of prenatal exposure that might be associated with retrospective data collection.

Mothers were screened extensively at each prenatal visit for use of tobacco, alcohol, and illicit drugs using a structured interview. Additional inclusion criteria for the longitudinal child study were singleton birth between September 1989 and August 1991 and continued residence in the Detroit area during the age 7-year assessments. Exclusion criteria for the longitudinal child study included multiple gestation (e.g., twins, triplets), known maternal HIV infection, and children with multiple malformation syndromes. Offspring from repeat pregnancies to the same participating mother were also excluded. Because prenatal cocaine exposure is associated with early delivery, prematurity was not an exclusion criterion. At the age 7 follow-up visit, six children were deceased and four others were recognized to have congenital malformations and were thus excluded. Families were geographically stable in that they remained in the area but moved frequently within Detroit. Of 656 eligible children at 7 years of age, 94% agreed to participate, and 85% completed lab testing ($N = 556$; 49.1% female). Participating children did not differ significantly from the 109 who did not participate on any newborn characteristic. Nonparticipating mothers did not differ from those taking part on any prenatal drug or alcohol variable, but mothers of participants were older and had more children.

Prenatal Drug and Alcohol Exposure

As detailed by Nordstrom Bailey et al. (2005), mothers were screened extensively at each prenatal visit to estimate pattern, quantity, and frequency of current and periconceptional drug and alcohol consumption using a semi-structured interview developed originally to assess alcohol use during pregnancy (Sokol, Martier, & Ernhart, 1985). All research interviews were conducted by trained researchers. A 2-week recall by drug and beverage type was obtained with questions linked to specific drug use and drinking habits, including details such as use at particular times of the day and days of the week and episodes of binging. At each prenatal visit, the use of cocaine, heroin, marijuana, and nonmedical opiates was ascertained by maternal self-report, and women's use of cocaine was classified as nonuser, user, or heavy user (i.e., two or more times per week). When clinically indicated, maternal urine samples were also assessed for drug use. From the drinking data, alcohol exposure variables were calculated as ounces of absolute alcohol per day and ounces of absolute alcohol per drinking day. In addition, at the first prenatal visit, the 25-item Michigan Alcoholism Screening Test (Selzer, 1971) was administered. Adverse fetal effects of drug use and alcohol consumption during pregnancy were explained, and women were advised to stop or at least to reduce their use.

Prenatal Cocaine Exposure: Refining the Predictor

Evidence of prenatal cocaine exposure was initially obtained prospectively from laboratory and historical sources for pregnant women participating in our longitudinal pregnancy study. These sources included (a) the previously described prospective structured interviews conducted throughout pregnancy; (b) the prenatal clinic record; (c) hospital records, including mother's admitted in-pregnancy drug and alcohol use obtained at delivery by obstetrical and nursery staff; and (d) retrospective report at the age 7 follow-up. Lab evidence of cocaine exposure consisted of positive maternal urine collected at the prenatal visits or at delivery and positive neonatal urine or meconium. Urine assays were available because hospital policy during the recruitment period mandated maternal and neonatal urine drug screens at delivery if there was a history of maternal drug or alcohol use, or known or suspected drug or alcohol exposure during the index pregnancy, or no prenatal care. This hospital policy resulted in screening more than 90% of our cocaine-exposed sample at the end of pregnancy or during the neonatal period. Meconium assays were initiated at the end of recruitment and hence were available for less than 10% of the sample. Sensitivity for cocaine and benzoylecgonine was < 35 ng/mL (the lowest reliable detected concentration > 0). Urine samples were collected by clinical staff and sent directly to the toxicology laboratory for analysis. All positive samples were retested with a second electromagnetic impedance translation assay. Although a continuous measure of cocaine "dose" was not available, in prior publications (Delaney-Black et al., 2004; Delaney-Black et al., 2000, 2004; Nordstrom Bailey et al., 2005; Sood et al., 2005) both a dichotomous ("None," "Any Exposure") and three ordinal levels of prenatal cocaine exposure based on duration of pregnancy exposure ("None," "Some," "Persistent") were modeled. We defined *persistent prenatal exposure* as continued cocaine use throughout pregnancy, evidenced by either a positive maternal urine sample at or within a week of delivery, and/or positive neonatal urine. Virtually all pregnancies defined as having persistent cocaine exposure (93%) also had earlier pregnancy samples and/or history that confirmed cocaine use across pregnancy. Among women in the persistent group who denied cocaine use, biologic measures confirming earlier pregnancy exposure were available for all but two women who did not initiate prenatal care until the third trimester.

We recently expanded our quantification of prenatal cocaine exposure to also include a measure of the frequency of exposure across pregnancy. In addition to

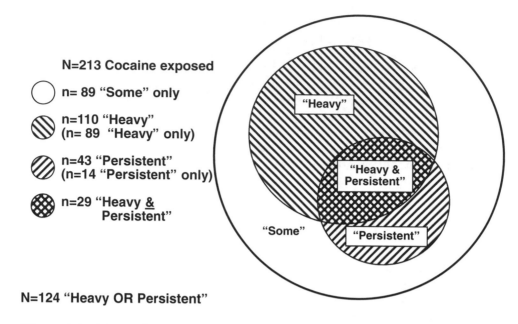

Figure 2.1.   Prenatal cocaine status of exposed children (N = 213).

our previous identification of persistent cocaine use, similar to other investigators (Jacobson, Jacobson, Sokol, Martier, & Chiodo, 1996), we also now report outcomes related to quantity of cocaine use, defining *heavy* use as two or more times per week during pregnancy. Children were described as having *some* cocaine exposure if there was any evidence of pregnancy use of cocaine but the fetus could not be characterized as having either persistent or heavy exposure. Because fetal cocaine exposure could be characterized as both heavy and persistent, as noted in Figure 2.1, we now characterize more extensive prenatal exposure as heavy or persistent (denoted "Heavy/Persistent"). The addition of frequency information ("Heavy") to the duration indicator ("Persistent") in our predictor (Heavy/Persistent) improved the sensitivity of our analyses. The assessment of the magnitude or level of prenatal cocaine exposure in the new modeling of cocaine exposure improves explained variance in our analyses.

Follow-Up Assessment at 7 Years of Age

Families were intensively sought by telephone, mail, or home visit to the last known address. Client files of all of the Detroit Medical Center hospitals and university-based practices were searched for updated contact information. Telephone directories were also searched. In addition, children were sought through private and public schools. After informed consent and parental permission, the child and caregiver (usually the biologic mother) were tested in our research laboratories. Caregivers completed the Achenbach (1991a) CBCL. Child testing was performed by research assistants blinded to prenatal exposure status. Testing included the children's self-report of violence exposure (Things I Have Seen and Heard; Richters & Martinez, 1993), whole blood lead level, and a measure of IQ, the Wechsler Preschool and Primary Scale of Intelligence–Revised (WPPSI-R; Wechsler, 1989). Additional testing included maternal psychopathology as measured by the Symptom Checklist (SCL-90; Derogatis, Lipman, & Covi, 1973), socioeconomic status (Hollingshead, 1975), social support (Norbeck, Lindsay, & Carrieri, 1981), and a modified lab assessment of the Home Observation for Measurement of the Environment (HOME; Caldwell & Bradley, 1984). Teacher-reported behavior problems were elicited with both a standardized measure, the Achenbach (1991b) Teacher Report Form and an investigator-developed measure, the PROBS-14 (Covington, Delaney-Black, Sokol, Ager, & Knoll, 2001; Covington et al., 2001). All teachers were sent a written request to return completed child assessments. Reminders and teacher appointments were successful in obtaining school data for 89% of the sample. Teachers were correctly told that the investigators were developing a new behavior measure and wished to compare the new measure with standard assessments. No other information was provided to teachers so that they would not be influenced by other potential reasons for the child's study participation. At age 7, the relation between heavy or persistent (noted Heavy/Persistent) prenatal cocaine exposure and behavior were assessed using two teacher-reported indictors: the Achenbach Teacher Report Form and the PROBS-14 (our previously validated and published measure; Covington, Delaney-Black, et al., 2001; Convington et al., 2001). Caregiver-reported behavior problems were assessed with the Achenbach (1991a) CBCL.

Data Analyses

Women who use cocaine may differ from nonusers in many ways (Delaney-Black et al., 2004; Delaney-Black et al., 2000). Indeed, as noted in Table 2.1, cocaine use during pregnancy in this cohort was associated with a variety of important maternal and child differences. Thus, in statistical analyses it is critical to evaluate the unique variance attributable to prenatal cocaine exposure. In addition to other prenatal drug exposures, we assessed important postnatal factors including whole blood lead levels, maternal IQ, caregiver psychopathology, custody changes, kinship care, enrollment in early intervention (e.g., enrichment) programs, postnatal drug use in the home and community, and community violence exposure assessed at age 7. Family and community violence exposure is particularly relevant because of its impact on child behavior and learning problems (Buka, Stichick, Birdthistle, & Earls, 2001; Lynch, 2003; Margolin & Gordis, 2000; Pratt & Greydanus, 2003; Stein, Jaycox, Kataoka, Rhodes, & Vestal, 2003).

Prior to analyses, checks were performed for missing and out-of-range data and for non- normal distribution of data. Because a control variable cannot be a confounder unless it is related to both exposure and outcome, association with either exposure or outcome can be used as a criterion for statistical adjustment (Schlesselman, 1982). In this study, control variables were selected for inclusion in the regression analyses based on their relations to outcome measures (Kleinbaum, Kupper, & Muller, 1988). All control variables that were even modestly related to each outcome ($p < .10$) were adjusted statistically by regressing the outcome on prenatal exposure level and the control variables related to that outcome. Pearson's r correlations were used to examine the relations of each control variable to each outcome. The covariates used included child's age and

Table 2.1. Comparison of Pregnancy, Child, and Family Characteristics by Prenatal Cocaine Exposure Status ($N = 556$)

Characteristic	None ($N = 343$)	Some ($N = 89$)	Heavy or persistent ($N = 124$)	
			S	F/χ^2
Pregnancy				
Age at delivery (years)[a]				36.6***
M	24.0	28.0	28.8	
SD	6.64	5.0	4.69	
Education at delivery (years)				0.5
M	11.4	11.6	11.6	
SD	1.6	1.6	1.7	
Married at delivery (%)	8.8	4.5	12.1	3.7
No. of cigarettes/day[a]				27.1***
M	6.1	12.5	11.7	
SD	8.9	9.7	10.1	
Alcohol (oz. absolute ETOH/day)[a]				10.2***
M	0.1	0.3	0.2	
SD	0.3	0.4	0.6	
Heroin use (%)	1.7	11.2	22.6	55.8***
Marijuana use (%)	25.1	57.3	49.2	44.9***
Child				
Birth weight (grams)[b]				12.1***
M	3096.9	2912.9	2793.2	
SD	604.8	615.9	644.6	
Gestational age (weeks)[c]				5.8**
M	38.9	38.6	38.0	
SD	2.4	2.6	3.3	
Apgar 1				2.3
Mdn	7.6	7.4	7.2	
SD	1.7	1.7	2.3	
Apgar 5				1.7
Mdn	8.7	8.71	8.4	
SD	1.2	1.4	1.7	
Gender (% male)	52.5	52.8	44.4	2.6
Age 7 whole blood lead (μg/dl)				2.3
M	4.9	5.2	5.0	
SD	2.8	3.1	3.4	
Age at visit (years)				2.0
M	6.9	6.9	6.9	
SD	0.3	0.3	0.2	
Family at Age 7 evaluation				
Biological mother is caregiver (%)	88.9	74.2	66.9	33.4***
Caregiver married (%)	27.3	21.3	30.9	2.4

Table 2.1. Comparison of Pregnancy, Child, and Family Characteristics by Prenatal Cocaine Exposure Status (N = 556) (*Continued*)

Characteristic	None (N = 343)	Some (N = 89)	Heavy or persistent (N = 124)	
			S	F/χ^2
Family SES-Hollingshead				0.7
M	29.6	28.6	28.5	
SD	10.1	10.4	10.1	
Caregiver years of education				0.2
M	11.9	11.9	11.8	
SD	1.9	2.5	2.4	
HOME				0.1
M	31.8	32.0	31.9	
SD	6.0	5.9	6.0	

Note.   SES = socioeconomic status; HOME = Home Observation for Measurement of the Environment (Caldwell & Bradley, 1984). [a]None is significantly different from some and heavy/persistent groups. [b]Some is significantly different from heavy/persistent group. [c]Heavy/persistent group is significantly different from none and some groups. **p < .01. ***p < .001.

sex, caregiver education and marital status, socioeconomic status, the HOME total score, mother's age at initial prenatal screen, caregiver performance IQ, maternal custody, and other prenatal exposures including alcohol (absolute ounces alcohol/day across pregnancy), smoking (cigarettes/day), marijuana (yes–no), and heroin (yes–no). Stepwise linear regression analyses were used entering all covariates in the first step (p < .05 to enter, p < .10 to remove) with the prenatal cocaine exposure variable in the second and final step. The impact of prenatal cocaine exposure on child behavior was initially analyzed on the total sample and then stratified first by gender and then by prenatal alcohol exposure status (Table 2.2). To avoid a potential confound between behavior problems and profound cognitive deficits when assessing behavioral outcomes, 14 boys and 15 girls with performance IQs ≤ 65 (15 cocaine-exposed, 14 non-exposed) were eliminated.

Sample Characteristics

At age 7, 94% of the 656 contacted families agreed to participate; 85% completed laboratory testing (N = 556; 213 = cocaine exposed, 49.1% female). The distribution of the prenatal cocaine exposure measure is provided in Figure 2.1. As previously noted, we have reevaluated the modeling of prenatal cocaine exposure and identified four clinically relevant levels of exposure: None, Some, Heavy (use two or more times per week at any time during pregnancy), and Persistent (use up to delivery). Women's pregnancy use of cocaine could also be characterized as both heavy and persistent. We evaluated 213 cocaine-exposed

Table 2.2.   Comparison of Regression Analyses Examining Teacher-Reported and Parent-Reported Behavior Problems at Age 7 by Prenatal Cocaine Exposure Status (None/Some vs. Heavy/Persistent)

Problem	All β	Boys β	Girls β
Teacher-reported problems (PROBS-14[a])			
Conduct-Hyperactivity	.09[†]	.15*	.01
High Distractibility	.08	.15*	.03
Inappropriate Social Skills	.07	.18**	.05
Unpredictable/Inconsistent Behavior	.07	.15*	.00
Hyperactivity	.08	.14*	.02
Difficulty internalizing personal code of behavior	.08[†]	.15*	.01
Demands attention inappropriately	.05	.10	.02
Problems with transitions	.09[†]	.14*	.02
Inability to handle Sensory Overload	.08	.16*	.03
Central Processing	.08	.10	.07
Problematic Academic Retention	.05	.03	.06
Extreme Disorganization	.09[†]	.15*	.06
Abstract thought problems	.09[†]	.12[†]	.07
Passive to animate/inanimate environment	.01	.02	.01
Delayed speech/language	.02	.03	.09
Motor Skill problems	.09[†]	.04	.13[†]
Total	.07	.13[†]	.04
Teacher-reported problems (Teacher Report Form[b])			
Attention Problems	.03	.08	.02
Externalizing Behavior Problems	.07	.15*	.02
Aggressive Problems	.06	.14*	.01
Delinquent Behavior Problems	.13*	.14*	.15*
Internalizing Behavior Problems	.02	.02	.03
Anxious/Depressed	.02	.03	.01
Withdrawn Behavior Problems	−.03	−.05	.02
Total Behavior Problems	.04	.11	.01
Attention Problems	.03	.08	.02
Externalizing Behavior Problems	.07	.15*	.02
Parent-reported problems (Child Behavior Checklist)			
Attention Problems	.09[†]	.10	.10
Externalizing Behavior Problems	.07	.18**	−.02
Aggressive Problems	.06	.17*	−.04
Delinquent Behavior Problems	.04	.15*	−.05
Internalizing Behavior Problems	.01	.01	.01
Anxious/Depressed	.01	.02	.00
Withdrawn Behavior Problems	−.04	.08	.02
Total Behavior Problems	.04	.11[†]	.00
Attention Problems	.09[†]	.10	.10

[a]Covington, Delaney-Black, Sokol, Ager, & Knoll, 2001; Covington et al., 2001. [b]Achenbach (1991b). [†]$p < .10$. *$p < .05$. **$p < .01$.

7-year-old children (Figure 2.1) and 343 nonexposed comparison children (the "Non" group; not shown in Figure 2.1). Eighty-nine children with documented pregnancy cocaine use (by history or lab measure), but who did not meet criteria for persistent or heavy cocaine exposure, made up the Some exposure group. Thus, a total of 124 (i.e., 213– 89) met criteria for either heavy or persistent exposure. Of the 124 heavy/persistent exposures, 81 were classified only as heavy, 14 as only persistent, and 29 were classified with both heavy and persistent exposure. Few differences were found in family–environment variables between nonexposed control and prenatal cocaine-exposed subjects with the exception of other prenatal exposures, maternal age at the first prenatal visit, and custody status (Table 2.1). Cocaine-using mothers were older than noncocaine-using mothers. In addition, at age 7, the biologic mother was less often the caregiver in the two cocaine groups than in the noncocaine group (see below). More similarity on environment and family measures between exposure groups allows us to examine the impact of cocaine exposure independent of these potentially confounding effects.

As previously noted, children in the no exposure group were more likely to be in the custody of the biologic mother at the age 7 assessment. In this group, 11% of children were not in their mother's custody. In comparison, the number of children not in the custody of the biologic mother more than doubled in the Some cocaine exposure group (26%) and tripled in the Heavy/Persistent exposure group (33%; χ^2 = 33.4, p < .001). Seventy-six percent of the children who were not living with the biological mother were in kinship care. Others have suggested that kinship care, unlike foster or adoptive homes, may not significantly change the home environment or consistently remove the child from the biologic mother's care (Frank et al., 2005). Children in adoptive homes may also have improved outcome because, at least in our study, these children were more likely to get early services (40%) compared with those in kinship care (8%) or those with their biological mother (7%; p = .001). Overall, few children (8%) received early intervention in our Detroit cohort, but the likelihood differed across exposure groups. A larger proportion of children in both the Some (12%) and Heavy/Persistent (13%) cocaine groups received early intervention services compared with children with no exposure (5.4%; χ^2 = 9.0, p < .01). As previously noted, many family characteristics did not vary across exposure groups. About 65% of caregivers had a high school diploma, and 73% were unmarried. Most families had low socioeconomic status based on income and employment. A dichotomous environmental status measure (positive vs. negative environment) based on median split was computed from both the HOME and socioeconomic status. In analysis by exposure group, negative environment was similar in all exposure groups (χ^2 = .85, p = .65). As at birth, caregivers were older in the prenatally exposed groups (F = 9.8, df = 2, p < .001).

Evidence of significant behavior problems was already evident by age 7. Based on teacher report (Achenbach, 1991a), 18% of children had clinical/borderline levels of total behavior problems. Cognitive and achievement data were well below national norms, and average full-scale IQ (WPPSI) was only 81; 19% had an IQ < 70. Standardized school achievement test scores were greater than 0.5 standard deviations below national norms; only 32% had a B or better grade point average (GPA). Average GPA was 2.47 (~ C). Child-reported community violence exposure was high: 80% reported witnessing someone being beaten up, 29% witnessed a shooting, and 23% a stabbing; 41% had been beaten up at least once; and about 11% reported someone had threatened to shoot or stab them. Drug deals had been witnessed by half of the children, and 15% had seen drugs in their home. Mean whole blood lead level was 5.0 μg/dl (25 children had values > 10 and two >15 μg/dl). There was a small relation ($r = .09$, $p < .05$) between violence victimization and blood lead level ($r = .11$, $p < .05$) but not with witnessing violence or prenatal cocaine exposure. Children with prenatal cocaine exposure had more violence victimization ($r = .09$, $p < .05$). There were no other significant covariate differences by prenatal cocaine status at follow-up.

Prenatal Cocaine and Behavior

All analyses reported are controlled for covariates. In each regression, heavy/persistent prenatal cocaine exposure accounted for 2% to 4% of the problem behavior variance, depending upon the behavior assessed. Table 2.2 provides the data for the Achenbach measures of child behavior. Compared with boys with no or some prenatal cocaine exposure, both parent (CBCL) and teacher (Teacher Report Form) reported measures indicated that boys with heavy/persistent prenatal cocaine exposure had significantly more externalizing behavior problems (delinquent and aggressive) than boys with some or no exposure. Teachers but not parents also identified that, compared with those with some or no exposure, girls with heavy/persistent prenatal cocaine exposure had more delinquent but not more aggressive behavior. In addition to the standardized Achenbach measures of child behavior, we also examined the relation between prenatal cocaine exposure and behavior using our specific and sensitive measure of cocaine-related behavior, the PROBS-14. In these analyses, even after controlling for covariates, boys with heavy/persistent exposure had a variety of conduct-activity related problems (i.e. distractions, inappropriate social skills, unpredictable behavior, hyperactivity, identifying a personal code of behavior, transitions, sensory problems, total hyperactive problems, and total behavior problems) compared with boys with some or no exposure. A trend was also evident for disorganized behavior, abstractions, and central processing problems. None of these behavior problems were seen in girls (Table 2.2). Heavy/persistent prenatal cocaine exposure accounted for 4% of the variance in PROBS total behavior problems.

Conclusion

Our review emphasizes that particular neurobehavioral effects of prenatal cocaine exposure may appear in children of one sex but not the other, so that generalizations about these teratogenic effects ought to be qualified by the sex of those exposed. Our previously published analyses used either a dichotomous (parent report: None vs. Any; Sood et al., 2005) or ordinal (teacher report: None vs. Some/Persistent; Nordstrom Bailey et al., 2005) cocaine exposure models. In Table 2.2, significant findings are now provided for our new modeling of prenatal cocaine exposure (None/Some vs. Heavy/Persistent). Biological and/or self-reported cocaine use late in pregnancy combined with self-reported heavy use is a more powerful predictor of behavioral teratogenic effects than previous dichotomous or ordinal measures of prenatal cocaine exposure use by us and others. In our new modeling, teachers and caregivers rated boys who had heavy/persistent prenatal cocaine as having significantly more delinquent, aggressive, and total externalizing behavior problems. In the absence of a continuous exposure variable, continued improvement in cocaine exposure modeling is essential to understanding the impact of pregnancy use of cocaine. Detection of prenatal cocaine exposure-related deficits, dysfunctions, and behavior problems is improved by a more precise description of the levels of prenatal exposure. Future directions for our research team include the assessment of the behavioral effects of prenatal cocaine exposure during early and late adolescence, including gender moderation, for this high-risk urban cohort.

References

Accornero, V. H., Anthony, J. C., Morrow, C. E., Xue, L., & Bandstra, E. S. (2006). Prenatal cocaine exposure: An examination of childhood externalizing and internalizing behavior problems at age 7 years. *Epidemiologia e Psichiatria Sociale, 15*(1), 20–29.

Accornero, V. H., Morrow, C. E., Bandstra, E. S., Johnson, A. L., & Anthony, J. C. (2002). Behavioral outcomes of preschoolers exposed prenatally to cocaine: Role of maternal behavioral health. *Journal of Pediatric Psychology, 27,* 259–269. doi:10.1093/jpepsy/27.3.259

Achenbach, T. M. (1991a). *Manual for the Child Behavior Checklist 4-18 and 1991 Profile.* Burlington: University of Vermont, Department of Psychiatry.

Achenbach, T. M. (1991b). *Manual of the Teacher's Report Form and 1991 profile.* Burlington: University of Vermont, Department of Psychiatry.

Alessandri, S. M., Sullivan, M. W., Imaizumi, S., & Lewis, M. (1993). Learning and emotional responsivity in cocaine-exposed infants. *Developmental Psychology, 29,* 989–997. doi:10.1037/0012-1649.29.6.989

American Psychiatric Association. (1994). *Diagnostic and statistical manual of mental disorders* (4th ed.). Washington, DC: Author.

Arendt, R. E., Short, E. J., Singer, L. T., Minnes, S., Hewitt, J., Flynn, S., . . . Flannery, D. (2004). Children prenatally exposed to cocaine: Developmental outcomes and environmental risks at seven years of age. *Journal of Developmental and Behavioral Pediatrics, 25*(2), 83–90. doi:10.1097/00004703-200404000-00002

Bada, H. S., Das, A., Bauer, C. R., Shankaran, S., Lester, B., LaGasse, L., . . . Higgins, R. (2007). Impact of prenatal cocaine exposure on child behavior problems through school age. *Pediatrics, 119,* e348–e359. doi:10.1542/peds.2006-1404

Bandstra, E. S., Marrow, C., Anthony, J., Accornero, V., & Fried, P. (2001). Longitudinal investigation of task persistence and sustained attention in children with prenatal cocaine exposure. *Neurotoxicology and Teratology, 23,* 545–559. doi:10.1016/S0892-0362(01)00181-7

Barkley, R. A., Fischer, M., Smallish, L., & Fletcher, K. (2006). Young adult outcome of hyperactive children: Adaptive functioning in major life activities. *Journal of the American Academy of Child & Adolescent Psychiatry, 45,* 192–202. doi:10.1097/01.chi.0000189134.97436.e2

Battaglia, G., & Cabrera, T. M. (1994). Potentiation of 5-HT1A receptor-mediated neuroendocrine responses in male but not female rat progeny after prenatal cocaine: Evidence for gender differences. *The Journal of Pharmacology and Experimental Therapeutics, 271,* 1453–1461.

Bendersky, M., Bennett, D. S., & Lewis, M. (2005). Aggression at age 5 as a function of prenatal exposure to cocaine, gender, and environmental risk. *Journal of Pediatric Psychology, 31*(1), 71–84. doi:10.1093/jpepsy/jsj025

Bendersky, M., & Lewis, M. (1998). Prenatal cocaine exposure and impulse control at two years. *Annals of the New York Academy of Sciences, 846,* 365–367. doi:10.1111/j.1749-6632.1998.tb09756.x

Bennett, D. S., Bendersky, M., & Lewis, M. (2002). Children's intellectual and emotional-behavioral adjustment at 4 years as a function of cocaine exposure, maternal characteristics and environmental risk. *Developmental Psychology, 38,* 648–658. doi:10.1037/0012-1649.38.5.648

Beyer, C., Pilgrim, C., & Reisert, I. (1991). Dopamine content and metabolism in mesencephalic and diencephalic cell cultures: Sex differences and effects of sex steroids. *The Journal of Neuroscience, 11,* 1325–1333.

Black, M., Schuler, M., & Nair, P. (1993). Prenatal drug exposure: Neurodevelopmental outcome and parenting environment. *Journal of Pediatric Psychology, 18,* 605–620. doi:10.1093/jpepsy/18.5.605

Blair, C., Peters, R., & Granger, D. (2004). Physiological and neuropsychological correlates of approach/withdrawal tendencies in preschool: Further examination of the behavioral inhibition system/behavioral activation system scales for young children. *Developmental Psychobiology, 45,* 113–124. doi:10.1002/dev.20022

Brown, J. V., Bakeman, R., Coles, C. D., Platzman, K., & Lynch, M. (2004). Prenatal cocaine exposure: A comparison of 2-year-old children in parental and nonparental care. *Child Development, 75,* 1282–1295. doi:10.1111/j.1467-8624.2004.00739.x

Brunzell, D. H., Coy, A. E., Ayres, J. J., & Meyer, J. S. (2002). Prenatal cocaine effects on fear conditioning: Exaggeration of sex-dependent context extinction. *Neurotoxicology and Teratology, 24,* 161–172. doi:10.1016/S0892-0362(01)00212-4

Buka, S. L., Stichick, T. L., Birdthistle, I., & Earls, F. J. (2001). Youth exposure to violence: Prevalence, risks, and consequences. *American Journal of Orthopsychiatry, 71,* 298–310. doi:10.1037/0002-9432.71.3.298

Caldwell, B. M., & Bradley, R. H. (1984). *Administration manual: Home observation for measurement of the environment* (Rev. ed.). Little Rock: University of Arkansas at Little Rock.

Chartoff, E. H., Marck, B. T., Matsumoto, A. M., Dorsa, D. M., & Palmiter, R. D. (2001). Induction of stereotypy in dopamine-deficient mice requires striatal D1 receptor activation. *Proceedings of the National Academy of Sciences of the United States of America, 98,* 10451–10456. doi:10.1073/pnas.181356498

Chasnoff, I. J., Burns, K. A., & Burns, W. J. (1987). Cocaine use in pregnancy: Perinatal morbidity and mortality. *Neurotoxicology and Teratology, 9,* 291–293. doi:10.1016/0892-0362(87)90017-1

Coles, C. D., Platzman, K. A., Smith, I., James, M. E., & Falek, A. (1992). Effects of cocaine and alcohol use in pregnancy on neonatal growth and neurobehavioral status. *Neurotoxicology and Teratology, 14,* 23–33. doi:10.1016/0892-0362(92)90025-6

Conners, C. K. (1995). *Conners' Continuous Performance Test.* Toronto, Ontario, Canada: Multi-Health Systems.

Covington, C., Delaney-Black, V., Sokol, R., Ager, T., & Knoll, J. (2001). Development of an instrument to assess problem behavior in first-grade students prenatally exposed to cocaine: Part I. *Substance Abuse, 17,* 87–99. doi:10.1080/08897079609444733

Covington, C., Nordstrom-Klee, B., Delaney-Black, V., Templin, T., Ager, J., & Sokol, R. J. (2001). Development of an instrument to assess problem behavior in first grade students prenatally exposed to cocaine. Part II: Validation. *Substance Abuse, 22,* 217–233. doi:10.1080/08897070109511464

Crick, N. R., & Dodge, K. A. (1996). Social information-processing mechanisms in reactive and proactive aggression. *Child Development, 67,* 993–1002. doi:10.2307/1131875

Crozatier, C., Guerriero, R. M., Mathieu, F., Giros, B., Nosten-Bertrand, M., & Kosofsky, B. E. (2003). Altered cocaine-induced behavioral sensitization in adult mice exposed to cocaine in utero. *Developmental Brain Research, 147*(1-2), 97–105. doi:10.1016/j.devbrainres.2003.10.006

Delaney-Black, V., Covington, C., Nordstrom, B., Ager, J., Janisse, J., Hannigan, J. H., . . . Sokol, R. J. (2004). Prenatal cocaine: Quantity of exposure and gender moderation. *Journal of Developmental and Behavioral Pediatrics, 25,* 254–263. doi:10.1097/00004703-200408000-00005

Delaney-Black, V., Covington, C., Ostrea, E., Romero, A., Baker, D., Tagle, M. T., . . . Long, J. (1996). Prenatal cocaine and neonatal outcome: Evaluation of a dose-response relationship. *Pediatrics, 98,* 735–740.

Delaney-Black, V., Covington, C., Templin, T., Ager, J., Martier, S., & Sokol, R. (1998). Prenatal cocaine exposure and child behavior. *Pediatrics, 102,* 945–950. doi:10.1542/peds.102.4.945

Delaney-Black, V., Covington, C., Templin, T., Ager, J., Nordstrom-Klee, B., Martier, S., . . . Sokol, R. J. (2000). Teacher-assessed behavior of children prenatally exposed to cocaine. *Pediatrics, 106,* 782–791. doi:10.1542/peds.106.4.782

Dennis, T., Bendersky, M., Ramsay, D., & Lewis, M. (2006). Reactivity and regulation in children prenatally exposed to cocaine. *Developmental Psychology, 42,* 688–697. doi:10.1037/0012-1649.42.4.688

Derogatis, L. R., Lipman, R. S., & Covi, L. (1973). SCL-90: An outpatient psychiatric rating scale: Preliminary report. *Psychopharmacology Bulletin, 9*(1), 13–28.

Dow-Edwards, D. L., Freed-Malen, L. A., & Gerkin, L. M. (2001). Sexual dimorphism in the brain metabolic response to prenatal cocaine exposure. *Developmental Brain Research, 129*(1), 73–79.

Elliott, K., & Coker, D. (1991). Crack babies: Here they come, ready or not. *Journal of Instructional Psychology, 18,* 60–64.

Estelles, J., Rodriguez-Arias, M., Maldonado, C., Aguilar, M. A., & Minarro, J. (2005). Prenatal cocaine exposure alters spontaneous and cocaine-induced motor and social behaviors. *Neurotoxicology and Teratology, 27,* 449–457. doi:10.1016/j.ntt.2005.01.002

Evans, G. W., & English, K. (2002). The environment of poverty: Multiple stressor exposure, psychophysiological stress, and socioemotional adjustment. [Erratum in: Child Dev 2002] [73]5:1. *Child Development, 73,* 1238–1248. doi:10.1111/1467-8624.00469

Eyler, F. D., Behnke, M., Conlon, M., Woods, N. S., & Wobie, K. (1998). Birth outcome from a prospective, matched study of prenatal crack/cocaine use: II. Interactive and dose effects on health and growth. *Pediatrics, 101,* 237–241. doi:10.1542/peds.101.2.237

Foltz, T. L., Snow, D. M., Strupp, B. J., Booze, R. M., & Mactutus, C. F. (2004). Prenatal intravenous cocaine and the heart rate-orienting response: A dose-response study. *International Journal of Developmental Neuroscience, 22,* 285–296. doi:10.1016/j.ijdevneu.2004.05.010

Frank, D. A., Augustyn, M., Knight, W. G., Pell, T., & Zuckerman, B. (2001). Growth, development, and behavior in early childhood following prenatal cocaine exposure: A systematic review. *JAMA, 285,* 1613–1625. doi:10.1001/jama.285.12.1613

Frank, D. A., Rose-Jacobs, R., Beeghly, M., Augustyn, M., Bellinger, D., Cabral, H., & Heeren, T. (2002). Level of prenatal cocaine exposure and scores on the Bayley Scales of Infant Development: Modifying effects of caregiver, early intervention, and birth weight. *Pediatrics, 110,* 1143–1152. doi:10.1542/peds.110.6.1143

Frank, D. A., Rose-Jacobs, R., Beeghly, M., Wilbur, M., Bellinger, D., & Cabral, H. (2005). Level of prenatal cocaine exposure and 48-month IQ: Importance of preschool enrichment. *Neurotoxicology and Teratology, 27,* 15–28. doi:10.1016/j.ntt.2004.09.003

Garavan, H., Morgan, R. E., Mactutus, C. F., Levitsky, D. A., Booze, R. M., & Strupp, B. J. (2000). Prenatal cocaine exposure impairs selective attention: Evidence from serial reversal and extradimensional shift tasks. *Behavioral Neuroscience, 114,* 725–738. doi:10.1037/0735-7044.114.4.725

Goodwin, G. A., Heyser, C. J., Moody, C. A., Rajachandran, L., Molina, V. A., Arnold, H. M., . . . Spear, L. P. (1992). A fostering study of the effects of prenatal cocaine exposure: II. Offspring behavioral measures. *Neurotoxicology and Teratology, 14,* 423–432. doi:10.1016/0892-0362(92)90053-D

Habeych, M. E., Sclabassi, R. J., Charles, P. J., Kirisci, L., & Tarter, R. E. (2005). Association among parental substance use disorder, p300 amplitude, and neurobehavioral disinhibition in preteen boys at high risk for substance use disorder. *Psychology of Addictive Behaviors, 19,* 123–130. doi:10.1037/0893-164X.19.2.123

Heffelfinger, A. K., Craft, S., White, D. A., & Shyken, J. (2002). Visual attention in preschool children prenatally exposed to cocaine: Implications for behavioral regulation. *Journal of the International Neuropsychological Society, 8*(1), 12–21. doi:10.1017/S135561770281102X

Hollingshead, A. B. (1975). *Four factor index of social status.* Unpublished manuscript, Yale University, New Haven, CT.

Hurt, H., Brodsky, N. L., Roth, H., Malmud, E., & Giannetta, J. M. (2005). School performance of children with gestational cocaine exposure. *Neurotoxicology and Teratology, 27,* 203–211. doi:10.1016/j.ntt.2004.10.006

Jacobson, S. W., Jacobson, J. L., Sokol, R. J., Martier, S. S., & Chiodo, L. M. (1996). New evidence for neurobehavioral effects of in utero cocaine exposure. *The Journal of Pediatrics, 129,* 581–590. doi:10.1016/S0022-3476(96)70124-5

Johns, J. M., Lubin, D. A., Lieberman, J. A., & Lauder, J. M. (2002). Developmental effects of prenatal cocaine exposure on 5-HT1A receptors in male and female rat offspring. *Developmental Neuroscience, 24,* 522–530. doi:10.1159/000069363

Johns, J. M., Means, M. J., Bass, E. W., Means, L. W., Zimmerman, L. I., & McMillen, B. A. (1994). Prenatal exposure to cocaine: Effects on aggression in Sprague-Dawley rats. *Developmental Psychobiology, 27,* 227–239. doi:10.1002/dev.420270405

Johns, J. M., Noonan, L. R., Zimmerman, L. I., McMillen, B. A., Means, L. W., Walker, C. H., . . . Lauder, J. M. (1998). Chronic cocaine treatment alters social/aggressive behavior in Sprague-Dawley rat dams and in their prenatally exposed offspring. *Annals of the New York Academy of Sciences, 846,* 399–404. doi:10.1111/j.1749-6632.1998.tb09765.x

Kagan, J., Snidman, N., & Reznick, J. S. (1989). Temperamental inhibition and childhood fears. In P. R. Zelazo & R. G. Barr (Eds.), *Challenges to developmental paradigms: Implications for theory, assessment, and treatment* (pp. 191–202). Hillsdale, NJ: Erlbaum.

Kleinbaum, D. G., Kupper, L. L., & Muller, K. E. (1988). *Applied regression analysis and other multivariable methods* (2nd ed.). Boston, MA: PWS-Kent.

Kosofsky, B. E., & Hyman, S. E. (2001). No time for complacency: The fetal brain on drugs. *The Journal of Comparative Neurology, 435,* 259–262. doi:10.1002/cne.1027

Kosofsky, B. E., & Wilkins, A. S. (1998). A mouse model of transplacental cocaine exposure. Clinical implications for exposed infants and children. *Annals of the New York Academy of Sciences, 846,* 248–261. doi:10.1111/j.1749-6632.1998.tb09742.x

Leech, S. L., Richardson, G. A., Goldschmidt, L., & Day, N. L. (1999). Prenatal substance exposure: Effects on attention and impulsivity of 6-year-olds. *Neurotoxicology and Teratology, 21,* 109–118. doi:10.1016/S0892-0362(98)00042-7

Lidow, M. S. (2003). Consequences of prenatal cocaine exposure in nonhuman primates. *Developmental Brain Research, 147*(1-2), 23–36. doi:10.1016/j.devbrainres.2003.09.001

Linares, T. J., Singer, L. T., Kirchner, H. L., Short, E. J., Min, M. O., Hussey, P., & Minnes, S. (2005). Mental health outcomes of cocaine-exposed children at 6 years of age. *Journal of Pediatric Psychology, 31,* 85–97. doi:10.1093/jpepsy/jsj020

Lynch, M. (2003). Consequences of children's exposure to community violence. *Clinical Child and Family Psychology Review, 6,* 265–274. doi:10.1023/B:CCFP.0000006293.77143.e1

Mactutus, C. F. (1999). Prenatal intravenous cocaine adversely affects attentional processing in preweanling rats. *Neurotoxicology and Teratology, 21,* 539–550. doi:10.1016/S0892-0362(99)00024-0

Magalhães, A., Summavielle, T., Tavares, M. A., & de Sousa, L. (2004). Effects of postnatal cocaine exposure and environmental enrichment on rat behavior in a forced swim test. *Annals of the New York Academy of Sciences, 1025,* 619–629. doi:10.1196/annals.1316.077

Margolin, G., & Gordis, E. B. (2000). The effects of family and community violence on children. *Annual Review of Psychology, 51,* 445–479. doi:10.1146/annurev.psych.51.1.445

Mathias, R. (1995, January/February). NIDA survey provides first national data on drug use during pregnancy. *NIDA Notes, 10*(1). Retrieved from http://archives.drugabuse.gov/NIDA_Notes/NNVol10N1/NIDASurvey.html

Mayes, L. C., Molfese, D. L., Key Alexandra, P. F., & Hunter, N. C. (2005). Event-related potentials in cocaine-exposed children during a Stroop task. *Neurotoxicology and Teratology, 27,* 797–813. doi:10.1016/j.ntt.2005.05.011

Messinger, D. S., Bauer, C. R., Das, A., Seifer, R., Lester, B. M., Lagasse, L. L., . . . Poole, W. K. (2004). The maternal lifestyle study: Cognitive, motor, and behavioral outcomes of cocaine-exposed and opiate-exposed infants through three years of age. *Pediatrics, 113,* 1677–1685. doi:10.1542/peds.113.6.1677

Morrow, B. A., Elsworth, J. D., & Roth, R. H. (2002). Prenatal cocaine exposure disrupts nonspatial, short-term memory in adolescent and adult male rats. *Behavioural Brain Research, 129*(1-2), 217–223. doi:10.1016/S0166-4328(01)00338-2

Neugebauer, N. M., Cunningham, S. T., Zhu, J., Bryant, R. I., Middleton, L. S., & Dwoskin, L. P. (2004). Effects of environmental enrichment on behavior and dopamine transporter function in medial prefrontal cortex in adult rats prenatally treated with cocaine. *Developmental Brain Research, 153,* 213–223. doi:10.1016/j.devbrainres.2004.09.001

Noland, J. S., Singer, L. T., Arendt, R. E., Minnes, S., Short, E. J., & Bearer, C. (2003). Executive functioning in preschool-age children prenatally exposed to alcohol, cocaine, and marijuana. *Alcoholism: Clinical and Experimental Research, 27,* 647–656.

Noland, J. S., Singer, L. T., Short, E. J., Minnes, S., Arendt, R. E., Kirchner, H. L., & Bearer, C. (2005). Prenatal drug exposure and selective attention in preschoolers. *Neurotoxicology and Teratology, 27,* 429–438. doi:10.1016/j.ntt.2005.02.001

Norbeck, J. S., Lindsay, A. M., & Carrieri, V. L. (1981). The development of an instrument to measure social support. *Nursing Research, 30,* 264–269. doi:10.1097/00006199-198109000-00003

Nordstrom Bailey, B., Sood, B. G., Sokol, R. J., Ager, J., Janisse, J., Hannigan, J. H., Covington, C., & Delaney-Black, V. (2005). Gender and alcohol moderate prenatal cocaine effects on teacher-report of child behavior. *Neurotoxicology and Teratology, 27,* 181–189. doi:10.1016/j.ntt.2004.10.004

Ostrea, E. M., Jr., Brady, M., Gause, S., Raymundo, A. L., & Stevens, M. (1992). Drug screening of newborns by meconium analysis: A large-scale, prospective, epidemiologic study. *Pediatrics, 89,* 107–113.

Phillips, R. B., Sharma, R., Premachandra, B. R., Vaughn, A. J., & Reyes-Lee, M. (1996). Intrauterine exposure to cocaine: Effect on neurobehavior of neonates. *Infant Behavior & Development, 19,* 71–81. doi:10.1016/S0163-6383(96)90045-4

Pine, D. S., Coplan, J. D., Wasserman, G., Miller, L. S., Fried, J. A., Davies, M., . . . Parsons, B. (1997). Neuroendocrine response to fenfluramine challenge in boys: Associations with aggressive behavior and adverse rearing. *Archives of General Psychiatry, 54,* 839–846.

Pratt, H. D., & Greydanus, D. E. (2003). Violence: Concepts of its impact on children and youth. *Pediatric Clinics of North America, 50,* 963–1003. doi:10.1016/S0031-3955(03)00083-X

Reisert, I., Engele, C., & Pilgrim, C. (1989). Early sexual differentiation of diencephalic dopaminergic neurons of the rat in vitro. *Cell and Tissue Research, 255,* 411–417. doi:10.1007/BF00224125

Richardson, G. A., Conroy, M. L., & Day, N. L. (1996). Prenatal cocaine exposure: Effects on the development of school-age children. *Neurotoxicology and Teratology, 18,* 627–634. doi:10.1016/S0892-0362(96)00121-3

Richardson, G. A., & Day, N. L. (1994). Detrimental effects of prenatal cocaine exposure: Illusion or reality? *Journal of the American Academy of Child and Adolescent Psychiatry, 33*(1), 28–34. doi:10.1097/00004583-199401000-00005

Richardson, G. A., Hamel, S. C., Goldschmidt, L., & Day, N. L. (1996). The effects of prenatal cocaine use on neonatal neurobehavioral status. *Neurotoxicology and Teratology, 18,* 519–528. doi:10.1016/0892-0362(96)00062-1

Richters, J. E., & Martinez, P. (1993). The NIMH community violence project: I. Children as victims of and witnesses to violence. *Psychiatry, 56*(1), 7–21.

Roberts, J. (1996). Cocaine blamed for infants' emotional problems. *BMJ (Clinical Research Ed.), 312*(7043), 1379.

Romano, A. G., & Harvey, J. A. (1998). Prenatal cocaine exposure: Long-term deficits in learning and motor performance. *Annals of the New York Academy of Sciences, 846,* 89–108. doi:10.1111/j.1749-6632.1998.tb09729.x

Rose-Jacobs, R., Cabral, H., Posner, M. A., Epstein, J., & Frank, D. A. (2002). Do "we just know"? Masked assessors' ability to accurately identify children with prenatal cocaine exposure. *Journal of Developmental and Behavioral Pediatrics, 23,* 340–346.

Savage, J., Brodsky, N. L., Malmud, E., Giannetta, J. M., & Hurt, H. (2005). Attentional functioning and impulse control in cocaine-exposed and control children at age ten years. *Journal of Developmental and Behavioral Pediatrics, 26,* 42–47.

Scafidi, F. A., Field, T. M., Wheeden, A., Schanberg, S., Kuhn, C., Symanski, R., . . . Bandstra, E. S. (1996). Cocaine-exposed preterm infants show behavioral and hormonal differences. *Pediatrics, 97,* 851–855.

Scher, M. S., Richardson, G. A., & Day, N. L. (2000). Effects of prenatal cocaine/crack and other drug exposure on electroencephalographic sleep studies at birth and one year. *Pediatrics, 105,* 39–48. doi:10.1542/peds.105.1.39

Schlesselman, J. J. (1982). *Case-control studies, design, conduct and analysis.* New York, NY: Oxford University Press.

Schroder, M. D., Snyder, P. J., Sielski, I., & Mayes, L. (2004). Impaired performance of children exposed in utero to cocaine on a novel test of visuospatial working memory. *Brain and Cognition, 55,* 409–412. doi:10.1016/j.bandc.2004.02.062

Schuler, M. E., Nair, P., & Kettinger, L. (2003). Drug-exposed infants and developmental outcome: Effects of a home intervention and ongoing maternal drug use. *Archives of Pediatrics & Adolescent Medicine, 157,* 133–138.

Schulman, M., Morel, M., Karmen, A., & Chazotte, C. (1993). Perinatal screening for drugs of abuse: Reassessment of current practice in a high-risk area. *American Journal of Perinatology, 10,* 374–377. doi:10.1055/s-2007-994765

Selzer, M. L. (1971). The Michigan alcoholism screening test: The quest for a new diagnostic instrument. *The American Journal of Psychiatry, 127,* 1653–1658.

Shields, A., & Cicchetti, D. (1998). Reactive aggression among maltreated children: The contributions of attention and emotion dysregulation. *Journal of Clinical Child Psychology, 27,* 381–395. doi:10.1207/s15374424jccp2704_2

Singer, L. T., Arendt, R., Minnes, S., Farkas, K., & Salvator, A. (2000). Neurobehavioral outcomes of cocaine-exposed infants. *Neurotoxicology and Teratology, 22,* 653–666. doi:10.1016/S0892-0362(00)00092-1

Singer, L. T., Arendt, R., Minnes, S., Farkas, K., Salvator, A., Kirchner, H. L., & Kliegman, R. (2002). Cognitive and motor outcomes of cocaine-exposed infants. *JAMA, 287,* 1952–1960. doi:10.1001/jama.287.15.1952

Singer, L. T., Eisengart, L. J., Minnes, S., Noland, J., Jey, A., Lane, C., & Min, M. O. (2005). Prenatal cocaine exposure and infant cognition. *Infant Behavior & Development, 28,* 431–444. doi:10.1016/j.infbeh.2005.03.002

Singer, L. T., Minnes, S., Short, E., Arendt, R., Farkas, K., Lewis, B., . . . Kirchner, H. L. (2004). Cognitive outcomes of preschool children with prenatal cocaine exposure. *JAMA, 291,* 2448–2456. doi:10.1001/jama.291.20.2448

Smith, A. P., Henson, R. N., Dolan, R. J., & Rugg, M. D. (2004). fMRI correlates of the episodic retrieval of emotional contexts. *NeuroImage, 22,* 868–878. doi:10.1016/j.neuroimage.2004.01.049

Sobrian, S. K., Ali, S. F., Slikker, W., & Holson, R. R. (1995). Interactive effects of prenatal cocaine and nicotine. *Molecular Neurobiology, 11,* 121–143. doi:10.1007/BF02740690

Sokol, R., Martier, S., & Ernhart, C. (1985). Identification of alcohol abuse in the prenatal clinic. In N. C. Chang & H. M. Chao (Eds.), *NIAAA Research Monograph 17: Early identification of alcohol abuse.* Washington, DC: U.S. Department of Health and Human Resources.

Sood, B. G., Nordstrom Bailey, B., Covington, C., Sokol, R. J., Ager, J., Janisse, J., . . . Delaney-Black, V. (2005). Gender and alcohol moderate caregiver reported child behavior after prenatal cocaine. *Neurotoxicology and Teratology, 27,* 191–201. doi:10.1016/j.ntt.2004.10.005

Spear, L. P., Campbell, J., Snyder, K., Silveri, M., & Katovic, N. (1998). Animal behavior models. Increased sensitivity to stressors and other environmental experiences after prenatal cocaine exposure. *Annals of the New York Academy of Sciences, 846,* 76–88. doi:10.1111/j.1749-6632.1998.tb09728.x

Stedman, T. L. (2000). *Stedman's medical dictionary, illustrated* (27th ed.). Philadelphia, PA: Lippincott Williams & Wilkins.

Stein, B. D., Jaycox, L. H., Kataoka, S., Rhodes, H. J., & Vestal, K. D. (2003). Prevalence of child and adolescent exposure to community violence. *Clinical Child and Family Psychology Review, 6,* 247–264. doi:10.1023/B:CCFP.0000006292.61072.d2

Taylor, C. L., Freeman, J. H., Jr., Holt, W., & Gabriel, M. (1999). Impairment of cingulothalamic learning-related neuronal coding in rabbits exposed to cocaine in utero: General and sex-specific effects. *Behavioral Neuroscience, 113,* 62–77. doi:10.1037/0735-7044.113.1.62

Thompson, B. L., Levitt, P., & Stanwood, G. D. (2005). Prenatal cocaine exposure specifically alters spontaneous alternation behavior. *Behavioural Brain Research, 164*(1), 107–116. doi:10.1016/j.bbr.2005.06.010

Torres-Reveron, A., & Dow-Edwards, D. L. (2006). Prenatal cocaine dampened behavioral responses to methylphenidate in male and female adolescent rats. *Neurotoxicology and Teratology, 28,* 165–172. doi:10.1016/j.ntt.2005.12.005

Tronick, E. Z., Frank, D. A., Cabral, H., Mirochnick, M., & Zuckerman, B. (1996). Late dose-response effects of prenatal cocaine exposure on newborn neurobehavioral performance. *Pediatrics, 98,* 76–83.

Vitacco, M. J., & Rogers, R. (2001). Predictors of adolescent psychopathy: The role of impulsivity, hyperactivity, and sensation seeking. *Journal of the American Academy of Psychiatry and the Law, 29,* 374–382.

Waschbusch, D. A., Pelham, W. E., Jennings, R. J., Greiner, A. R., Tarter, R. E., & Moss, H. B. (2002). Reactive aggression in boys with disruptive behavior disorders: Behavior, physiology, and affect. *Journal of Abnormal Child Psychology, 30,* 641–656. doi:10.1023/A:1020867831811

Wechsler, D. (1989). *Wechsler Preschool and Primary Scale of Intelligence-Revised.* San Antonio, TX: The Psychological Corporation.

Whaley, S. E., O'Connor, M. J., & Gunderson, B. (2001). Comparison of the adaptive functioning of children prenatally exposed to alcohol to a nonexposed clinical sample. *Alcoholism: Clinical and Experimental Research, 25,* 1018–1024. doi:10.1111/j.1530-0277.2001.tb02311.x

Wilkins, A. S., Genova, L. M., Posten, W., & Kosofsky, B. E. (1998). Transplacental cocaine exposure. 1: A rodent model. *Neurotoxicology and Teratology, 20,* 215–226. doi:10.1016/S0892-0362(97)00125-6

Williams, S. C., Lochman, J. E., Phillips, N. C., & Barry, T. D. (2003). Aggressive and nonaggressive boys' physiological and cognitive processes in response to peer provocations. *Journal of Clinical Child and Adolescent Psychology, 32,* 568–576. doi:10.1207/S15374424JCCP3204_9

Wood, R. D., Bannoura, M. D., & Johanson, I. B. (1994). Prenatal cocaine exposure: Effects on play behavior in the juvenile rat. *Neurotoxicology and Teratology, 16,* 139–144. doi:10.1016/0892-0362(94)90110-4

Wood, R. D., Molina, V. A., Wagner, J. M., & Spear, L. P. (1995). Play behavior and stress responsivity in periadolescent offspring exposed prenatally to cocaine. *Pharmacology, Biochemistry and Behavior, 52,* 367–374. doi:10.1016/0091-3057(95)00120-L

Woods, N. S., Eyler, F. D., Conlon, M., Behnke, M., & Wobie, K. (1998). Pygmalion in the cradle: Observer bias against cocaine-exposed infants. *Journal of Developmental and Behavioral Pediatrics, 19,* 283–285.

Zuckerman, B., & Frank, D. A. (1994). Prenatal cocaine exposure: nine years later. *The Journal of Pediatrics, 124*(5), 731–733. doi:10.1016/S0022-3476(05)81363-0

3

Sex Differences in the Effects of Cocaine Exposure on Dopaminergic Systems During Brain Development

Diana Dow-Edwards and Annelyn Torres-Reveron

It has been over 25 years since the first descriptions of "crack babies" appeared in the news. Since that time, hundreds of clinical and preclinical studies have reported that while cocaine use during pregnancy can be damaging to the developing brain, the effects can be subtle and are not the same in both males and females. Several clinical studies have found that males are more often adversely affected by prenatal cocaine exposure than females (Asher & Aghajanian, 1974; Creese & Iversen, 1975; Hitzemann, Wu, Hom, & Loh, 1980; Torres-Reveron, Weedon, & Dow-Edwards, 2010). In the preclinical arena, males are clearly affected, but females are not spared. For the past 20 years, our laboratory has studied the effects of cocaine on neurobehavioral development and has amassed a sizable database that includes a wide range of sex differences. These sex differences encompass many cognitive and behavioral domains and vary depending on when the drug is administered more so than on the dose of drug administered; however, only subtoxic doses have been studied. To address the issue of "when" an exposure occurs, we present a brief discussion of what is occurring in the developing brain at the time of exposure and the timing of events in brain development in relation to day of birth in humans and rodents.

Critical Periods of Cocaine Exposure

The most recent information equates the maturational state of the rat's brain on the day of birth to gestation week 22 in humans (Clancy, Finlay, Darlington, & Anand, 2007). Therefore, events that occur during the first half of pregnancy in humans occur during prenatal life in the rat, and events that occur during the last half of pregnancy in humans occur during the early postnatal period in the rat. Cell division and migration occur at genetically programmed times for each brain region during the first half of pregnancy in humans (prenatal in the rat). Neurite (immature axons and dendrites), extension synaptogenesis, synaptic loss, and apoptosis (programmed cell death) occur during the latter half of pregnancy in humans and during the postnatal period in the rat. However, neurite expansion and pruning are dependent on multiple factors, including the level of activity in the neurons and synapses. Alterations in action potentials during this active period of development have profound effects on the synaptology (the pattern of synapses), functional responses, and even the anatomic cytoarchitecture of the developing circuits (Hubel & Wiesel, 1962). Because cocaine acts primarily through altering synaptic activity, we hypothesized that it would have the most profound effects on brain functional development if given during the postnatal period, the period of highly active development of neuronal function and architecture. Therefore, we administered cocaine during three periods of development: prenatally, from gestational day (GD) 8 to 22; early postnatal, from postnatal day (PND) 1–10, a period of neuropil (neurites, axons, and dendrites) expansion and synapse formation; or late postnatal, from day 11–20, a period of neuropil retraction and synaptic pruning. For the prenatal dosing, we administered cocaine at 30 or 60 mg/kg/day between GD 8–22 via gastric intubation. For postnatal dosing, we administered cocaine directly to the pup at 25 or 50 mg/kg/day subcutaneously. These doses resulted in blood levels of approximately 5,000 ng/ml and 1,000 ng/ml at the peak for the higher and lower doses, respectively (Dow-Edwards, 1990). We typically dose during one of these developmental periods and then examine behavior, brain function, and neurochemistry at one of three ages: weaning or PND 21, adolescent (PND 40–45), or adult (PND 60).

We see very different effects on brain metabolic function in adult male and female rats exposed to cocaine during the three developmental periods (Table 3.1). The striking aspect of these results is that prenatal cocaine exposure had very little effect in adult females, whereas postnatal cocaine exposure resulted in a stimulated metabolism in females in specific brain regions, which varied depending on the period of drug administration (PND 1–10 or 11–20). Prenatal cocaine exposure results in decreases in brain metabolism in males when measured in exposed adults (Dow-Edwards, Freed, & Fico, 1990). Even weanling rats that have been exposed prenatally to cocaine show the same sexual dimorphism in metabolic responses (Dow-Edwards, Freed-Malen, & Gerkin,

Table 3.1.   Summary of Functional Studies by Exposure Period

Brain region	Prenatal[a]		Postnatal days 1–10[b]		Postnatal days 11–20[c]	
	♀	♂	♀	♂	♀	♂
Cortex	0/7	2/7↓	1/7↑	1/7↓	5/7↑	1/7↑ 1/7↓
Motor	0/5	1/5↓	3/6↑	0/6	4/5↑	0/5
Sensory	0/7	1/7↓	3/6↑	0/6	1/8↑	1/8↑
Limbic	0/11	5/11↓	9/14↑	0/14	5/14↑	1/14↓
Hypothalamus	0/9	5/9↓	0/9	0/9	2/8↑	0/8

Note.   Brain metabolic activity using the 2-deoxyglucose method at 60 days of age with no drug challenge. Cocaine was administered during one of three developmental periods; results are expressed as the number of statistically significant differences/total number of regions analyzed within each functionally defined grouping (e.g., cortex, motor). The arrow indicates the direction of the change. Males and females exhibited very different responses to cocaine when given during the three phases of brain development. [a]Dow-Edwards et al. (1990). [b]Dow-Edwards et al. (1988). [c]Dow-Edwards et al. (1993).

2001). Examination of pyramidal cell branching in cortex of 21-day-old rats exposed to cocaine prenatally shows that males exhibit a reduction in dendritic branching, a finding that supports the reduction in metabolism we observed; females showed the opposite pattern, an increase in dendritic branching compared with that in control females.[1] This increase in branching in females suggests a greater degree of connectivity in cortex, which may support an otherwise depressed metabolism, to within the normal range. The sex difference in response to cocaine is generally believed to be due to estrogen. Because it is well known that estrogens stimulate spine outgrowth in neurites (Cooke & Woolley, 2005), the increase in neurites and presumably synapses may provide an expansive network for cocaine to stimulate and promote synaptic retention.

Roles of Gonadal Hormones in Cocaine's Effects

It is not possible to provide a detailed description of the differences in development of the gonadal axes in male and female rats in the space provided; suffice it to say that both genomic and nongenomic (activational) effects of gonadal hormones influence development throughout prenatal life, postnatal maturation, and adulthood. The differences begin as early as GD 14 in the rat (Reisert et al., 1989); by GD 18, the first wave of "masculinization" occurs with the production of testosterone by the fetal testes. A second spike in testosterone occurs during the early postnatal period to complete the "defeminization" process (Arnold, 1984; Dörner, 1981; McEwen, 1983). A female is produced if these two spikes of testosterone do not occur.

Estrogens alter multiple phases of neuronal proliferation, apoptosis, and differentiation through their receptors, which are transcription factor members of the steroid hormone/retinoic acid receptor superfamily. Estrogens inhibit apoptosis and increase cortical cell proliferation (Sawada et al., 2000; Wade, Oommen, Conner, Earnest, & Rajesh, 1999). Estrogens promote neuritogenesis and synaptogenesis during development (Miranda, Sohrabji, & Toran-Allerand, 1994) and have multiple interactions with neurotrophins (Miranda, Sohrabji, Singh, & Toran-Allerand, 1996; Singh, Meyer, Millard, & Simpkins, 1994). In addition, the activational effects of estrogens, which can be demonstrated by gonadectomy and steroid replacement studies, are well known to modulate the effects of psychostimulants (Becker, Robinson, & Lorenz, 1982; Camp, Becker, & Robinson, 1986; Camp & Robinson, 1988; Forgie & Stewart, 1993; Glick & Hinds, 1984; Hansen-Trench, Segar, & Barron, 1996; Sell, Scalzitti, Thomas, & Cunningham, 2000). In addition, psychostimulants increase levels of allopregnanolone, a metabolite of progesterone, which along with estrogen has many effects on gamma-aminobutyric acid (GABA) and other neurotransmitter systems (Quinones-Jenab et al., 2008). Virtually every hypothesis about cocaine's effects—both developmental and in adulthood—must be reexamined in females.

---

[1]This work was performed by D. L. Dow-Edwards and M. Miller and has not been published.

Effects of Prenatal Cocaine in Adolescent Animals

We have conducted a series of studies looking at the effects of prenatal cocaine exposure on neurobehavioral, neurochemical, and neurofunctional development in the rat.

Behavioral Effects of Prenatal Cocaine: Attention

Previous studies in rats have repeatedly shown that exposure to cocaine during the prenatal period impairs performance in attentional tasks, as well as arousal (Bayer, Brown, Mactutus, Booze, & Strupp, 2000; Bushnell et al., 2000; de Bartolomeis et al., 1994; Garavan et al., 2000; Spear et al., 2002). Many of these studies assessed the effects of prenatal cocaine exposure in adult animals. We tested animals that were exposed to cocaine prenatally during adolescence because modeling of cortical areas involved in controlling attention occurs during this developmental period (Jernigan, Trauner, Hesselink, & Tallal, 1991; Lewis, 1997). We adapted a procedure previously used by Barb Strupp's (1989) group to assess attention, in which the animal has to remove a lid from a box in order to retrieve a cereal reward. We hypothesized that prenatal exposure to cocaine in rats impairs attention as assessed by this simple discrimination task during the adolescent period.

As usual, rats received cocaine 60 mg/kg or water vehicle by intragastric intubation during GDs 8–22. Between PND 34 and 55, rats were food deprived to 90% free feeding weight and tested. All rats learned the initial task as well as the "shift" task in which they had to shift attention from the previous cue to a new cue. However, during the distraction task, when rats had to continue paying attention to the previous cue, male rats treated with cocaine during the prenatal period (Figure 3.1A) showed a significant reduction in the number of correct trials. No difference was observed in cocaine-treated females (Torres-Reveron & Dow-Edwards, 2004).

Our results suggest that prenatal exposure to cocaine does not affect the learning of a simple discriminatory task during adolescence; when distracters are introduced, however, prenatal cocaine exposure produced a pattern of performance predictive of an attention deficit, but only in males. Female rats seem to have either a protective mechanism that prevents a deficit to the same extent as in males, or they have increased motivation to retrieve the food reward, which can also affect performance in this task. Overall, these data suggest that regions of the brain involved in attentional processing, such as the posterior parietal cortex and the prefrontal cortex, are more affected by cocaine in a long-term manner in males than in females.

Behavioral Responses to a Methylphenidate Challenge

It is well stated in the preclinical literature that prenatal cocaine exposure produces selective alterations in the dopaminergic systems (Glatt, Bolanos, Trksak, & Jackson, 2000; Harvey, 2004). In humans, prenatal cocaine-induced deficits

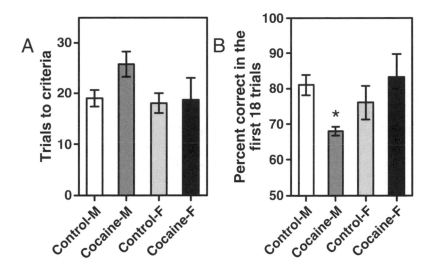

Figure 3.1. Performance during the distraction task on a simple attention task (mean and standard error of the mean). A: Average trials to criteria. B: Percentage of correct trials in the first 3 days or 18 trials of the distraction task. We observed a significantly lower number of correct trials in the cocaine-treated males compared with the other groups. M = males; F = females. *$p < .05$.

include abnormal sustained attention (Bandstra, Morrow, Anthony, Accornero, & Fried, 2001). Children diagnosed with attention-deficit/hyperactivity disorder (ADHD) have been reported to have pronounced deficits in sustained attention as well (Tsal, Shalev, & Mevorach, 2005). Methylphenidate (MPD; e.g., Ritalin, Concerta) is widely prescribed for the treatment of children and adults with ADHD (Swanson et al., 1998; Zito et al., 2000). MPD has a mechanism of action similar to those of cocaine and other psychostimulants by inhibiting the reuptake of dopamine and norepinephrine with fewer effects on serotonin transporters compared with cocaine. Given the emerging evidence of attention problems in children prenatally exposed to cocaine, it is likely that these children might be prescribed MPD at some point during early childhood or adolescence. Because cocaine-exposed children might have permanent alterations in catecholaminergic circuits, the responses to MPD in individuals prenatally exposed to cocaine might be different from those in non-cocaine-exposed individuals. We hypothesized that prenatal cocaine exposure would alter the behavioral responses to MPD. The experiments presented herein used a dose of MPD above the typical doses prescribed to treat individuals with attention problems. However, the dose used in our experiments produces robust behavioral responses in the rat and is in the range of MPD used for recreational purposes by teenagers (Coetzee, Kaminer, & Morales, 2002; Levine, Caplan, & Kauffman, 1986; Morton & Stockton, 2000). Our goal was not to model the clinical scenario in ADHD but to establish the behavioral and neurofunctional responses to MPD in an animal model of prenatal cocaine exposure.

Prenatal cocaine administration was carried out as described previously for the attention task experiments, and behavioral responses to either 10 mg/kg MPD or vehicle were recorded on a single day between PND 41 and PND 44. Locomotion in female MPD-treated rats of the prenatal control group was significantly higher than that in all the other groups that received MPD. Both groups of males that received MPD and females in the prenatal-cocaine group showed a pattern of locomotor activity that was lower than that of the MPD-treated control females (Figure 3.2, A and B). Thus, prenatal cocaine produced a dampening of the locomotor response to MPD but only in females. Because psychostimulants such as MPD can produce stereotyped behavior (repeated seemingly nonsensical behavior) that competes with locomotor activity, we quantified these behaviors using videotaped recordings during the time that the locomotor activity was being recorded. Stereotypy scored from the videotapes was considered *low intensity* if the rat showed repetitive side-to-side movements of the head usually combined with locomotion. *Medium-intensity stereotypy* was scored when the rat showed faster head movements with or without locomotor activity. Male rats that received prenatal cocaine showed a significant decrease in the amount of time spent in low intensity stereotypy compared with the control group. Low-intensity stereotypy in female rats that received MPD was similar between prenatal treatments (Figure 3.2, C and D). Medium-intensity stereotypy, which had a low occurrence overall, was not significantly different across prenatal treatment or sex but showed an average of 92% reduction in the prenatal cocaine groups compared with water controls (Figure 3.2, E and F).

This study showed that prenatal cocaine exposure produced sexually dimorphic responses to MPD during the adolescent period. Our data suggest that the mechanism by which prenatal cocaine decreases the behavioral response to MPD is different in males and females because prenatal cocaine diminishes locomotor responses only in females and stereotyped behavior only in the males. One possible explanation for these differences is that developing dopaminergic neurons of female rats mature before those of males (Beyer, Pilgrim, & Reisert, 1991). Consequently, a similar prenatal cocaine exposure in males and females will result in a longer exposure for dopaminergic striatal cells in females as a result of this earlier maturation. Locomotor activity is associated with mesolimbic dopamine (DA; nucleus accumbens) function, and stereotypy is associated with nigrostriatal (caudate-putamen) function (Asher & Aghajanian, 1974; Creese & Iversen, 1975; Hitzemann et al., 1980). Therefore, we hypothesized that brain imaging studies would show sexually dimorphic changes in function that correlate with the sexually dimorphic behavioral changes.

Brain Metabolic Responses to a Methylphenidate Challenge

We measured brain glucose metabolism in the rats described above as the behavioral responses to MPD or saline were being recorded. Rats were injected with 2-deoxyglucose (2DG, a marker to assess glucose metabolism by autoradiography) through the jugular vein, and the quantified 2DG method (Sokoloff et al.,

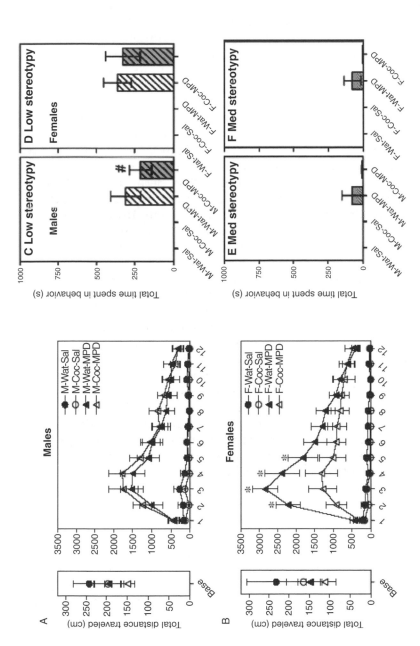

Figure 3.2. Locomotor activity (A and B), low- (C and D), and medium- (E and F) intensity stereotyped behavior after injection of either saline (sal.) or methylphenidate (MPD) in adolescent male rats and female rats that were exposed to prenatal cocaine (COC) or water (WAT; controls). Baseline activity was collected during the initial 20 min and illustrated as an average for that period (base). An asterisk represents significantly lower than same sex control. *Low-intensity stereotypy* refers to repeated side to side head movements with or without locomotion; *medium-intensity stereotypy* refers to more rapid head movements with or without locomotion. E and F: White bars illustrate water pretreated rats and gray bars represent cocaine pretreated rats. There were 10–12 rats per group. Bars represent mean and standard error of the mean. The asterisk denotes significant difference from all other groups; the hash symbol denotes significant difference from prenatal control males that also received MPD. From "Prenatal Cocaine Dampened Behavioral Responses to Methylphenidate in Male and Female Adolescent Rats," by A. Torres-Reveron and D. L. Dow-Edwards. 2006, *Neurotoxicological Teratology. 28*, p. 168. Copyright 2006 by Elsevier. Reprinted with permission.

1977) modified for jugular catheters (Torres-Reveron, Melnick, Stephenson, & Dow-Edwards, 2006) was carried out. Brain structures were grouped by function into motor, mesolimbic, hypothalamic, limbic relay/hippocampal, and sensory regions. For all functional groupings analyzed, MPD increased metabolic rates from 15% to 30% as compared with saline, regardless of prenatal condition. In general, females showed lower rates of brain glucose utilization than males, especially in the limbic structures: medial amygdala, lateral hypothalamus, medial and lateral habenulas, dorsal raphe and CA1 and dentate gyrus regions of the hippocampus. Prenatal treatment did not interact with sex for any of the major functional groupings.

Glucose metabolism reflects both excitatory and inhibitory processes, and so it is difficult to interpret these changes without relating metabolism to behavior. Therefore, we examined the correlations between glucose metabolism and locomotor activity and stereotyped behaviors occurring at the same time that metabolism was determined (Torres-Reveron et al., 2010). Because locomotion is classically thought to be mediated by the nucleus accumbens and stereotypy by the dorsal striatum (caudate-putamen; Asher & Aghajanian, 1974; Creese & Iversen, 1975; Hitzemann et al., 1980), we wanted to see if the prenatal treatments altered the pattern of correlations of metabolism in these regions with each behavior. That is, rates of brain metabolism in structures within the n. accumbens and d. striatum were correlated with locomotor and stereotyped behavior during the 15 min following the 2DG administration, within individual animals using the Pearson product–moment correlation and assessed for significance according to prenatal treatment and sex grouping. For example, locomotor activity was correlated with glucose metabolism in nine regions of the d. striatum of cocaine preexposed males, but not for cocaine preexposed females or for control males and females (see Table 3.2). For stereotyped behavior defined as the time spent in sniffing and low- and medium-intensity stereotypy, the control males and the cocaine-exposed males and females showed tight coupling of metabolism within the d. striatum and stereotypy. This was not seen in the control females. Surprisingly, metabolism in n. accumbens was not tightly coupled with locomotion in any prenatal treatment group. Stereotypy, however, was moderately correlated with metabolism in mesolimbic regions in both male and female prenatal cocaine groups.

Together, the patterns of correlations of metabolism and behavior suggest that prenatal treatment with cocaine produces a tighter coupling of metabolism and behavior than that observed in control rats. A reasonable explanation for this observation is that prenatal cocaine produced a dysregulation of excitation and inhibition secondary to the imbalance in function of dopamine D1 and D2 receptors observed in prenatally cocaine-exposed animals. This imbalance may be due to the uncoupling of the D1 receptor from its second messenger (Friedman & Wang, 1998; Jones et al., 2000; Wang, Runyan, Yadin, & Friedman, 1995; Zhen, Torres, Wang, & Friedman, 2001), an effect that does not appear to be sex specific. In normal males, homeostatic balance of the D1 and D2 receptors results in little coupling between metabolism and behavior. In cocaine-treated males, hypothetically, the loss of homeostasis makes one system (the D2 system in this case) directly related to the behavioral output through coupling of metabolism and behavior. Figure 3.3 represents a possible mechanistic model for the higher

Table 3.2. Prenatal Cocaine Exposure and Glucose Metabolism at 41 to 45 Days of Age

Brain region	Locomotion				Stereotypy[a]			
	Males		Females		Males		Females	
	Control	Cocaine	Control	Cocaine	Control	Cocaine	Control	Cocaine
n. accumbens[c] 7 regions	0[b]	1	0	0	1	5	0	5
d. striatum[d] 12 regions	2	9	0	0	9	12	0	12

Note. The table gives Pearson product–moment correlations of rates of glucose utilization in brain regions with locomotor activity and stereotyped behavior within individual animals grouped by prenatal condition and sex. [a]Repeated sniffing and movements of the head with or without forward locomotion, typically seen following repeated psychostimulant administration. [b]The number of correlations between metabolism and behavior that were significant. [c]Nucleus accumbens, rostral shell @ 2.7, core 2.2, shell 2.2, core 1.6, shell 1.6, core 1.2, shell 1.2. [d]Caudatoputamen @ 2.2, 1.6, 1.2, and 0.2 and dorsolateral, dorsomedial, ventrolateral, ventromedial quadrants @1.6, and 1.2.

From "Methylphenidate Response in Prenatal Cocaine Exposed Rats: A Behavioral and Brain Functional Study," by A. Torres-Reveron, J. Weedon, and D. L. Dow-Edwards, 2010, *Brain Research, 1337,* pp. 74–84. Copyright 2010 by Elsevier. Adapted with permission.

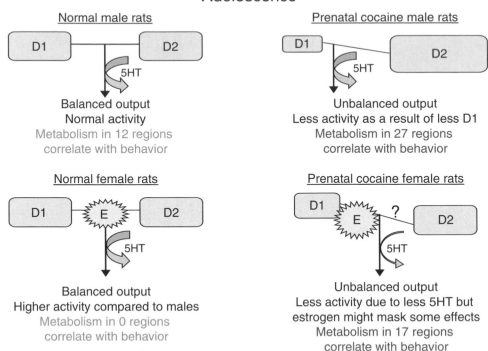

Figure 3.3. Diagram of the proposed model for prenatal cocaine effects on the dorsal caudate-putamen and nucleus accumbens. For simplicity, we illustrate only effects on dopamine and how serotonin (5-HT) can modulate the behavioral output. All significant Pearson product–moment correlations between both locomotor activity and sniffing/stereotypy and metabolism in regions of the accumbens and d. striatum were considered for a possible total of 38 correlations. D1: dopamine D1 receptor, D2: dopamine D2 receptor, E: estrogen.

number of significant correlations of behavior and brain metabolism observed in prenatally cocaine-exposed animals. The important functional relevance is that clinicians evaluating positron emission tomography (PET) scans or functional magnetic resonance imaging (fMRI) data from prenatal cocaine-exposed children may not see abnormal metabolic patterns. However, our data suggest that the underlying regulation of behavioral output is quite abnormal under both baseline and MPD stimulated conditions. That is, the relationship between function (metabolism) and the behavior produced by both the mesolimbic and nigrostriatal systems is abnormal, and this abnormal pattern is different in males and females. In conclusion, prenatal cocaine exposure can produce subtle effects in brain function that are not evident during the adolescent period when measured by conventional brain functional assays alone, but rather become evident when interpreted in the context of behavior, producing sex-specific differences in the coupling of metabolism and behavior. This further suggests that the function of the neuronal circuits underlying behavior is abnormal in prenatal cocaine-exposed adolescents.

Prodynorphin and Proenkephalin Gene Expression in n. Accumbens and d. Striatum

Cocaine alters the responses of medium spiny neurons in the caudate-putamen and nucleus accumbens. These medium spiny neurons differentially contain dynorphin, enkephalin, substance P, and GABA (Gerfen, McGinty, & Young, 1991). The neuropeptides dynorphin and enkephalin are thought to modulate the behavioral output produced by striatal projections (Steiner & Gerfen, 1998). We have previously reported that perinatal cocaine administration (PND 11–20) decreased the expression of prodynorphin messenger ribonucleic acid (mRNA) in the nucleus accumbens when examined during adulthood (Dow-Edwards & Hurd, 1998). However, cocaine administration during adulthood has been reported to increase prodynorphin within the striatum (Adams, Hanson, & Keefe, 2003; Collins et al., 2002; Hurd & Herkenham, 1992). Other researchers have shown that prenatal cocaine does not change prodynorphin expression in juvenile rats at PND 21 (de Bartolomeis et al., 1994) or proenkephalin or mu opioid receptor activation (de Bartolomeis et al., 1994; Meyer, Shani, & Rice, 2000). Therefore, alterations in peptide expression within the striatum apparently depend on the age of the rat during which the cocaine exposure occurred. Our study examined the expression of prodynorphin and proenkephalin mRNA in the adolescent rat striatum after prenatal exposure to cocaine in both sexes. For this, prenatal cocaine exposure was carried out as described in the preceding sections. Proenkephalin and prodynorphin mRNA expression was determined using radioactive in situ hybridization in adolescent animals (PND 41–44).

Cocaine-exposed females showed lower levels of prodynorphin (collapsed for regions) than prenatal control females (Figure 3.4A). No differences among males were observed. Females in the prenatal control group showed higher levels of prodynorphin compared with prenatal control males, a difference not observed between prenatal cocaine treated animals. Unlike prodynorphin, however, there were no effects of prenatal treatment for proenkephalin levels, but we observed that overall males showed higher levels of proenkephalin compared to females regardless of prenatal treatment group (Figure 3.4B).

Our data suggest that striatal projections containing prodynorphin (Steiner & Gerfen, 1998) are more sensitive to cocaine exposure during the prenatal period in females compared with males. Because dopamine D1 receptors have been colocalized in the same neurons as the prodynorphin containing neurons (Hara, Yacovleva, Bakalkin, & Pickel, 2006), the decrease in prodynorphin expression in female rats could be linked to deficient dopaminergic D1 activity. Recall that prenatal cocaine produces uncoupling of D1 receptor from its associated Gs/olf protein (Friedman & Wang, 1998; Wang et al., 1995) in both males and females, according to available information. Therefore, in males the prenatal cocaine exposure must be sufficient to uncouple the D1 receptor but not sufficient to produce downstream effects in prodynorphin expression in these same neurons.

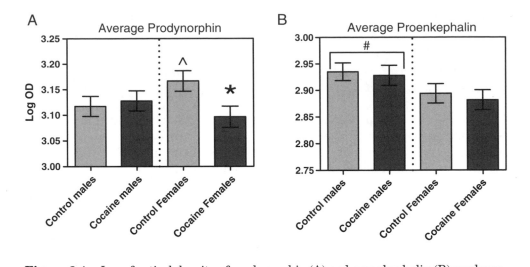

Figure 3.4. Log of optical density of prodynorphin (A) and proenkephalin (B) prodynor-phin messenger ribonucleic acid expression levels collapsed for all regions analyzed (means and standard error of the means). An asterisk represents significantly higher than all other groups; a hash symbol means that both groups of males were significantly different than both groups of females. From "Gender Differences in Prodynorphin but not Proenkephalin mRNA Expression in the Striatum of Adolescent Rats Exposed to Prenatal Cocaine," by A. Torres-Reveron, Y. L. Hurd, and D. L. Dow-Edwards, 2007, *Neuroscience Letters, 421,* p. 214. Copyright 2007 by Elsevier. Reprinted with permission.

Conditioned Place Preference and the Effects of Environmental Enrichment

In a study of the effects of environmental enrichment, rats received cocaine at 30 or 60 mg/kg or water vehicle by intragastric intubation prior to pregnancy and then throughout pregnancy until GD 22. Litters were fostered and weighed twice prior to weaning (PND 21). Then, half of the pups were placed in standard isola-tion cages while the remaining pups were housed in groups of three with toys rotated twice weekly (enriched). These housing conditions continued until PND 42, at which time conditioned place preference training was begun. For this test, rats were placed in open Plexiglas boxes with half of the box having striped walls and a rough floor and the other half having plain white walls and a smooth floor. Rats explored for 30 min while being videotaped. The least preferred side was selected as the side to be paired with cocaine and the preferred side was paired with saline. For the next 3 days, rats received saline injections in the morning on the "saline side," where they remained for 30 min, and 3 hr later received cocaine at 3, 5, 10, 15 or 20 mg/kg intraperitoneally (each rat received one dose only) on the "drug side," where they remained for 30 min. On the 5th day, rats were given free access to both sides of the box and time spent on each side recorded. If the dose of cocaine administered was rewarding to the rat, the rat should spend greater time on the side of the box paired with the drug. We found that in gen-eral, the prenatal 30 mg/kg (C30) group preferred all doses of cocaine tested so far (5, 10 or 15 mg/kg) more so than either the prenatal 60 mg/kg (C60) group or the vehicle group (Figure 3.5). The one exception to this was the females in the enriched condition. Here, both the C30 and the C60 groups showed control-like preferences for cocaine at the doses tested (Dow-Edwards et al., 2010).

These results demonstrate that modification of the environment in which the rat is housed during the juvenile and adolescent period can alter function in the basic reward circuits to dampen the rewarding effects of cocaine and that these effects are in opposite directions in males and females.

Sex Differences in Adult Animals After Postnatal Cocaine Exposure (the Latter Half of Human Pregnancy)

For several years our laboratory has focused on the effects of cocaine during the PND 11–20 period because this is the period when the forebrain and particularly the cortex exhibits maximal plasticity. Synapses are maintained or lost depending on the degree of activation they experience, and cocaine increases glucose metabolism (and presumably synaptic activity), especially in females, following exposure during PND 11–20 (Frick & Dow-Edwards, 1995). That is, the sub-chronic effects of cocaine on glucose metabolism were similar to the effects of the PND 11–20 treatment when studied in adulthood (Table 3.1). Males receiving cocaine during PND 11–20 showed few effects, and females showed wide-ranging increases in metabolism (Dow-Edwards, Freed-Malen, & Hughes, 1993; Frick & Dow-Edwards, 1995). Therefore, in contrast to prenatal exposure, cocaine administration during a period equivalent to the late prenatal period in humans produced acute and lasting increases in metabolism primarily in females.

We have completed many studies in which we examined sex differences in response to cocaine administration during PND 11–20 including adult behavioral responses to challenge with dopamine and serotonin (5-HT) agonists. A large study of over 500 rats receiving either vehicle, cocaine at 25 or 50 mg/kg or GBR 12909, a selective dopamine transporter (DAT) inhibitor, during the same 11–20 day postnatal period demonstrated that cocaine exposure reduced responses to the D1 agonist SKF82958 in adult males but had little effect in females (Figure 3.6; Dow-Edwards & Busidan, 2001). Responses to the D2 agonist, quinpirole, were not altered. Other studies show that PND 11–20 cocaine decreased DAT expression in ventral mesencephalon and preprodynorphin expression in nucleus accumbens shell, suggesting a dampening of function in dopaminergic circuits in exposed adult males. Females were not examined in these studies (Dow-Edwards & Hurd, 1998). Males exposed to cocaine during PND 11–20 showed decreased locomotor and metabolic responses to the D1 agonist SKF82958 (Melnick & Dow-Edwards, 2003). Therefore, although the metabolic alterations in males were fairly subtle in adults following postnatal cocaine treatment, the behavioral responses to a variety of dopaminergic challenges were dampened, and several markers for the dopaminergic systems were reduced. Females, on the other hand, showed increased responses to amphetamine challenge following PND 11–20 cocaine (Figure 3.7). An assessment of the coupling of the D1 receptor to its response element showed that PND 11–20 cocaine had no effect on D1 coupling in striatum but reduced coupling in cortex

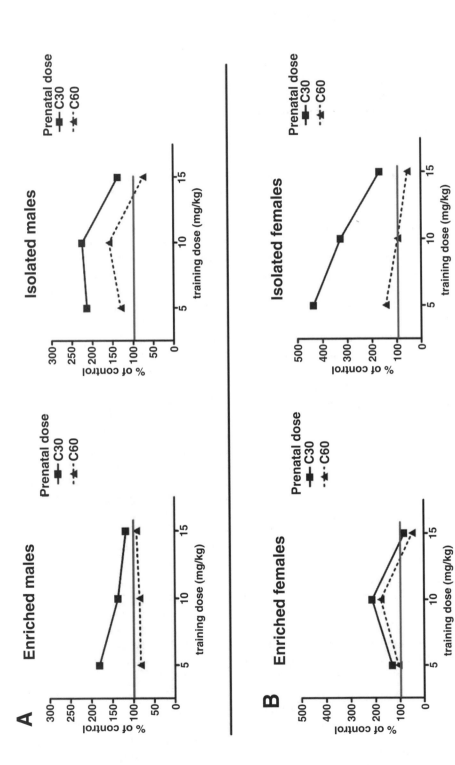

Figure 3.5. Conditioned place preference (CPP) in adolescent rats prenatally exposed to cocaine at 30 or 60 mg/kg/day, raised in an isolated or an enriched environment and conditioned with 5, 10, or 15 mg/kg cocaine. Data is expressed as percentage preference compared to the prenatal control pups (100%) at each training dose. Prenatal 30 mg/kg cocaine increased CPP in all groups except the enriched females, where all prenatal treatment conditions showed similar CPP.

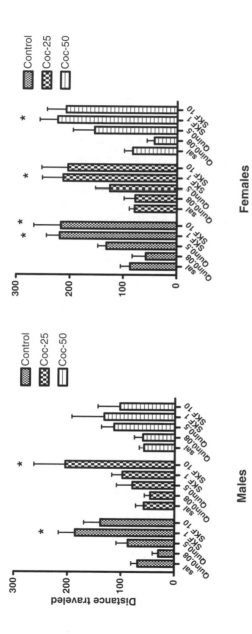

Figure 3.6. Locomotor activity following challenge with dopaminergic drugs: quinpirole (Quin), a selective D2,3, 4 agonist, or SKF82958 (SKF) a selective D 1,5 agonist. Quinpirole was administered at 0.08 or 0.5mg/kg intraperitoneally (ip) and SKF 82958 at 1 or 10 mg/kg ip. Adult males and females had been injected with vehicle, cocaine (COC) at 25 mg/kg/day, or cocaine at 50 mg/kg/day during postnatal days 11–20; means and standard error of the means are presented. An asterisk indicates significantly different from the response to saline within the group. From "Behavioral Responses to Dopamine Agonists in Adult Rats Exposed to Cocaine During the Preweaning Period," by D. L. Dow-Edwards and Y. Busidan, 2001, *Pharmacology, Biochemistry and Behavior, 70,* p. 26. Copyright 2001 by Elsevier. Adapted with permission.

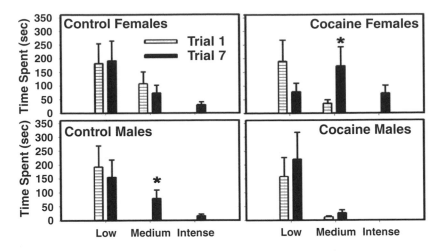

Figure 3.7. Amphetamine sensitization in adult male and female rats exposed to cocaine at 50 mg/kg during postnatal days 11–20 (mean and standard error of the mean). Data for males and females on the first day of treatment are compared to that on day 7 after daily doses of 2 mg/kg amphetamine; the intensities of stereotyped behavior are shown along the X axis. Stereotypies are rated as low (repeated side to side head movement with or without locomotion), medium (more rapid head movements with or without locomotion), or high intensity (rapid, large circular movements without locomotion). An asterisk indicates significant difference from day 1 value within a group. Females treated with cocaine show greatly enhanced stereotyped behavior toward the end of treatment; cocaine produced the opposite effect in males. From "Differential Behavioral Responses to Chronic Amphetamine in Adult Male and Female Rats Exposed to Postnatal Cocaine Treatment," by S. M. Melnick and D. L. Dow-Edwards, 2001, *Pharmacology, Biochemistry and Behavior, 69,* p. 222. Copyright 2001 by Elsevier. Adapted with permission.

(Zhao, Wand, & Dow-Edwards, 2008). Interestingly, there were no sex differences in this measure, and D2 receptor coupling was normal. Male rats exposed to cocaine during PND 11–20 showed dampened responses to D1 drugs consistent with an uncoupling of the D1 receptor from its 2nd messenger, at least in the cortex (Figure 3.8). Females showed more complex responses, with increases in response to amphetamine, which stimulates multiple neurotransmitter systems.

Results of studies with female rats examined for brain metabolic activity as adults suggest that the environment under which measurements of brain metabolism are made predicts the pattern of metabolic changes. PND 11–20 cocaine increased metabolism in the adult females tested on the laboratory bench (as we stated earlier), but similarly treated females habituated to small tents that restrict sensory stimulation and locomotion show a very different pattern of changes in glucose metabolism. When tested in this low-stimulatory environment, females exposed to PND 11–20 cocaine showed decreases in metabolism in almost the same regions that were metabolically increased in females tested in an environment with stimulants such as noise, lights, and odors. On the other hand, male responses were not different under either envi-

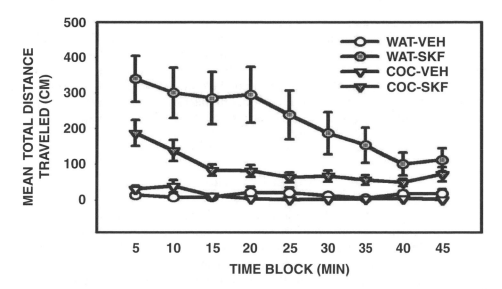

Figure 3.8. Locomotor activity in adult male rats following challenge with SKF 82958 at 5 mg/kg or vehicle intraperitoneally (means and standard error of the means). The rats were initially injected with cocaine (coc) at 50 mg/kg/day or vehicle (water; wat) during postnatal days (PND) 11–20. The PND 11–20 cocaine treatment significantly reduced the locomotor response to SKF but had no effect on the response to saline. From "Blunted Metabolic Response to SKF 82958 in the Mesolimbic System Following Preweaning Cocaine Treatment," by S. M. Melnick and D. L. Dow-Edwards, 2003, *Development Brain Research, 143,* p. 255. Copyright 2003 by Elsevier. Adapted with permission.

ronmental condition (Dow-Edwards & Busidan, 1998).[2] These results parallel those from our laboratory on prenatal cocaine and conditioned place preference for cocaine in that females are more responsive to changes in environment than males (Dow-Edwards et al., 2010).

In studies using 5-HT agonists to assess behavioral effects, PND 11–20 cocaine treatment produced increased responses to 8-OH-DPAT (a 5-HT$_{1A}$ agonist) and quipazine (a 5-HT$_3$ agonist), and increased expression of the 5-HT transporter in dorsal raphe in males (Dow-Edwards, 1996, 1998). On the other hand, females treated with cocaine during the same period of development showed decreased responses to quipazine and no change in 8-OH-DPAT response or in the density of the 5-HT transporter. Because the forebrain dopaminergic regions are densely innervated by 5-HT neurons, which in normal individuals maintain control over behavioral output, one would expect a reduction in dopaminergic function as seen in males to be associated with an increase in 5-HT function. The classical studies administering 6 hydroxydopamine, a neurotoxin used to selectively kill dopaminergic neurons, during the neonatal period provide

---

[2]These findings were also confirmed in unpublished research conducted by G. Frick and D. L. Dow-Edwards.

an extreme example of the re-organization in the brain that occurs with a decrease in DA and an increase in 5-HT innervation (Brown & Gerfen, 2006). This pattern is recapitulated in male rats following PND 11–20 cocaine. The opposite pattern of reorganizing appears to occur in females: an increase in dopaminergic function and a reduction in 5-HT function, which would be consistent with the behavioral and brain metabolic patterns we observe. Therefore, each sex appears to exhibit a unique pattern of DA-5-HT reorganization following PND 11–20 cocaine administration.

General Conclusions

In males, the response patterns following PND 11–20 cocaine administration (equivalent to the late prenatal period in humans) are quite similar to those seen following prenatal exposure (equivalent to the first half of pregnancy in humans). There is a general decrease in DA markers and reactivity perhaps related to the uncoupling of the D1 receptor from its response element. The affected regions shift from the early-developing subcortical regions to the later-developing cortical regions as development progresses. Whereas similar changes in D1 uncoupling are seen in females, behavioral and metabolic responses to drug challenges generally show increases in DA responsivity (except in adolescents) perhaps caused by the effects of estrogen or 5-HT. We have found that a significant factor in the hyperresponsivity of the female is the testing environment, which often obscures underlying neurochemical dysregulation. In addition, underlying sex differences in GABA and glutamate systems, which have been largely unexplored in development, undoubtedly contribute to the sex differences in response to developmental cocaine exposure.

The implications of this work are that cocaine produces many effects on the DA system that are not the same in females and males. Females defy simple relationships between brain function and behavior for several reasons, including the fact that they are more responsive to their environment than are males. Several studies have already described multiple differences across genders in the effects of prenatal cocaine on behavior, and these sex differences should be further examined in humans.

References

Adams, D. H., Hanson, G. R., & Keefe, K. A. (2003). Distinct effects of methamphetamine and cocaine on preprodynorphin messenger RNA in rat striatal patch and matrix. *Journal of Neurochemistry, 84,* 87–93. doi:10.1046/j.1471-4159.2003.01507.x

Arnold, A. P. (1984). Gonadal steroid induction of structural sex differences in the central nervous system. *Annual Review of Neuroscience, 7,* 413–442. doi:10.1146/annurev.ne.07.030184.002213

Asher, I. M., & Aghajanian, G. K. (1974). 6-Hydroxydopamine lesions of olfactory tubercles and caudate nuclei: Effect on amphetamine-induced stereotyped behavior in rats. *Brain Research, 82,* 1–12. doi:10.1016/0006-8993(74)90888-9

Bandstra, E. S., Morrow, C. E., Anthony, J. C., Accornero, V. H., & Fried, P. A. (2001). Longitudinal investigation of task persistence and sustained attention in children with prenatal cocaine exposure. *Neurotoxicology and Teratology, 23,* 545–559. doi:10.1016/S0892-0362(01)00181-7

Bayer, L. E., Brown, A., Mactutus, C. F., Booze, R. M., & Strupp, B. J. (2000). Prenatal cocaine exposure increases sensitivity to the attentional effects of the dopamine D1 agonist SKF81297. *The Journal of Neuroscience, 20,* 8902–8908.

Becker, J. B., Robinson, T. E., & Lorenz, K. A. (1982). Sex differences and estrous cycle variations in amphetamine-elicited rotational behavior. *European Journal of Pharmacology, 80,* 65–72. doi:10.1016/0014-2999(82)90178-9

Beyer, C., Pilgrim, C., & Reisert, I. (1991). Dopamine content and metabolism in mesencephalic and diencephalic cell cultures: Sex differences and effects of sex steroids. *The Journal of Neuroscience, 11,* 1325–1333.

Brown, P., & Gerfen, C. R. (2006). Plasticity within striatal direct pathway neurons after neonatal dopamine depletion is mediated through a novel functional coupling of serotonin 5-HT2 receptors to the ERK 1/2 map kinase pathway. *The Journal of Comparative Neurology, 498,* 415–430. doi:10.1002/cne.21034

Bushnell, P. J., Levin, E. D., Marrocco, R. T., Sarter, M. F., Strupp, B. J., & Warburton, D. M. (2000). Attention as a target of intoxication: Insights and methods from studies of drug abuse. *Neurotoxicology and Teratology, 22,* 487–502. doi:10.1016/S0892-0362(00)00077-5

Camp, D. M., Becker, J. B., & Robinson, T. E. (1986). Sex differences in the effects of gonadectomy on amphetamine-induced rotational behavior in rats. *Behavioral & Neural Biology, 46,* 491–495. doi:10.1016/S0163-1047(86)90527-3

Camp, D. M., & Robinson, T. E. (1988). Susceptibility to sensitization. II. The influence of gonadal hormones on enduring changes in brain monoamines and behavior produced by the repeated administration of D-amphetamine or restraint stress. *Behavioural Brain Research, 30,* 69–88. doi:10.1016/0166-4328(88)90009-5

Clancy, B., Finlay, B. L., Darlington, R. B., & Anand, K. J. (2007). Extrapolating brain development from experimental species to humans. *Neurotoxicology, 28,* 931–937. doi:10.1016/j.neuro.2007.01.014

Coetzee, M., Kaminer, Y., & Morales, A. (2002). Megadose intranasal methylphenidate (Ritalin) abuse in adult attention deficit hyperactivity disorder. *Substance Abuse, 23,* 165–169. doi:10.1080/08897070209511486

Collins, S. L., Kunko, P. M., Ladenheim, B., Cadet, J. L., Carroll, F. I., & Izenwasser, S. (2002). Chronic cocaine increases kappa-opioid receptor density: Lack of effect by selective dopamine uptake inhibitors. *Synapse, 45,* 153–158. doi:10.1002/syn.10091

Cooke, B. M., & Woolley, C. S. (2005). Gonadal hormone modulation of dendrites in the mammalian CNS. *Journal of Neurobiology, 64,* 34–46. doi:10.1002/neu.20143

Creese, I., & Iversen, S. D. (1975). The pharmacological and anatomical substrates of the amphetamine response in the rat. *Brain Research, 83,* 419–436. doi:10.1016/0006-8993(75)90834-3

de Bartolomeis, A., Austin, M. C., Goodwin, G. A., Spear, L. P., Pickar, D., & Crawley, J. N. (1994). Dopaminergic and peptidergic MRNA levels in juvenile rat brain after prenatal cocaine treatment. *Molecular Brain Research, 21,* 321–332. doi:10.1016/0169-328X(94)90263-1

Dörner, G. (1981). Sexual differentiation of the brain. *Vitamins and Hormones, 38,* 325–381. doi:10.1016/S0083-6729(08)60488-4

Dow-Edwards, D., & Busidan, Y. (1998). Ontogenic cocaine effects. *Annals of the New York Academy of Sciences, 846,* 382–385. doi:10.1111/j.1749-6632.1998.tb09761.x

Dow-Edwards, D. L. (1990). Fetal and maternal plasma cocaine levels peak rapidly following intragastric administration in the rat. *Journal of Substance Abuse, 2,* 427–437.

Dow-Edwards, D. L. (1996). Modification of acoustic startle reactivity by cocaine administration during the postnatal period: Comparison with a specific serotonin reuptake inhibitor. *Neurotoxicology and Teratology, 18,* 289–296. doi:10.1016/S0892-0362(96)90029-X

Dow-Edwards, D. L. (1998). Preweaning cocaine administration alters the adult response to quipazine: Comparison with fluoxetine. *Neurotoxicology and Teratology, 20,* 133–142. doi:10.1016/S0892-0362(97)00095-0

Dow-Edwards, D. L., & Busidan, Y. (2001). Behavioral responses to dopamine agonists in adult rats exposed to cocaine during the preweaning period. *Pharmacology, Biochemistry and Behavior, 70,* 23–30. doi:10.1016/S0091-3057(01)00582-2

Dow-Edwards, D. L., Freed, L. A., & Fico, T. A. (1990). Structural and functional effects of prenatal cocaine exposure in adult rat brain. *Developmental Brain Research, 57,* 263–268. doi:10.1016/0165-3806(90)90052-Z

Dow-Edwards, D. L., Freed, L. A., & Milhorat, T. H. (1988). Stimulation of brain metabolism by perinatal cocaine exposure. *Developmental Brain Research, 470,* 137–141. doi:10.1016/0165-3806(88)90209-X

Dow-Edwards, D. L., Freed-Malen, L. A., & Gerkin, L. M. (2001). Sexual dimorphism in the brain metabolic response to prenatal cocaine exposure. *Developmental Brain Research, 129,* 73–79. doi:10.1016/S0165-3806(01)00184-5

Dow-Edwards, D. L., Freed-Malen, L. A., & Hughes, H. E. (1993). Long-term alterations in brain function following cocaine administration during the preweanling period. *Developmental Brain Research, 72,* 309–313. doi:10.1016/0165-3806(93)90198-J

Dow-Edwards, D. L., & Hurd, Y. L. (1998). Perinatal cocaine decreases the expression of prodynorphin mRNA in nucleus accumbens shell in the adult rat. *Molecular Brain Research, 62,* 82–85. doi:10.1016/S0169-328X(98)00218-6

Forgie, M. L., & Stewart, J. (1993). Sex differences in amphetamine-induced locomotor activity in adult rats: Role of testosterone exposure in the neonatal period. *Pharmacology, Biochemistry and Behavior, 46,* 637–645. doi:10.1016/0091-3057(93)90555-8

Frick, G. S., & Dow-Edwards, D. L. (1995). The effects of cocaine on cerebral metabolic function in periweanling rats: The roles of serotonergic and dopaminergic uptake blockade. *Developmental Brain Research, 88,* 158–170. doi:10.1016/0165-3806(95)00094-T

Friedman, E., & Wang, H. Y. (1998). Prenatal cocaine exposure alters signal transduction in the brain D1 dopamine receptor system. *Annals of the New York Academy of Sciences, 846,* 238–247. doi:10.1111/j.1749-6632.1998.tb09741.x

Garavan, H., Morgan, R. E., Mactutus, C. F., Levitsky, D. A., Booze, R. M., & Strupp, B. J. (2000). Prenatal cocaine exposure impairs selective attention: Evidence from serial reversal and extradimensional shift tasks. *Behavioral Neuroscience, 114,* 725–738. doi:10.1037/0735-7044.114.4.725

Gerfen, C. R., McGinty, J. F., & Young, W. S. I. (1991). Dopamine differentially regulates dynorphin, substance P, and enkephalin expression in striatal neurons: In situ hybridization histochemical analysis. *The Journal of Neuroscience, 11,* 1016–1031.

Glatt, S. J., Bolanos, C. A., Trksak, G. H., & Jackson, D. (2000). Effects of prenatal cocaine exposure on dopamine system development: A meta-analysis. *Neurotoxicology and Teratology, 22,* 617–629. doi:10.1016/S0892-0362(00)00088-X

Glick, S. D., & Hinds, P. A. (1984). Sex differences in sensitization to cocaine-induced rotation. *European Journal of Pharmacology, 99,* 119–121. doi:10.1016/0014-2999(84)90442-4

Hansen-Trench, L. S., Segar, T. M., & Barron, S. (1996). Neonatal cocaine and/or ethanol exposure: Effects on a runway task with suckling reward. *Neurotoxicology and Teratology, 18,* 651–657. doi:10.1016/S0892-0362(96)00130-4

Hara, Y., Yakovleva, T., Bakalkin, G., & Pickel, V. M. (2006). Dopamine D1 receptors have subcellular distributions conducive to interactions with prodynorphin in the rat nucleus accumbens shell. *Synapse, 60,* 1–19. doi:10.1002/syn.20273

Harvey, J. A. (2004). Cocaine effects on the developing brain: Current status. *Neuroscience and Biobehavioral Reviews, 27,* 751–764. doi:10.1016/j.neubiorev.2003.11.006

Hitzemann, R., Wu, J., Hom, D., & Loh, H. (1980). Brain locations controlling the behavioral effects of chronic amphetamine intoxication. *Psychopharmacology, 72,* 93–101. doi:10.1007/BF00433812

Hubel, D. H., & Wiesel, T. N. (1962). Receptive fields, binocular interaction and functional architecture in the cat's visual cortex. *Journal of Physiology, 160,* 106–154.

Hurd, Y. L., & Herkenham, M. (1992). Influence of a single injection of cocaine, amphetamine or GBR 12909 on MRNA expression of striatal neuropeptides. *Molecular Brain Research, 16,* 97–104. doi:10.1016/0169-328X(92)90198-K

Jernigan, T. L., Trauner, D. A., Hesselink, J. R., & Tallal, P. A. (1991). Maturation of human cerebrum observed in vivo during adolescence. *Brain: A Journal of Neurology, 114,* 2037–2049. doi:10.1093/brain/114.5.2037

Johns, J. M., Lubin, D. A., Lieberman, J. A., & Lauder, J. M. (2002). Developmental effects of prenatal cocaine exposure on 5-HT$_{1A}$ receptors in male and female rat offspring. *Developmental Neuroscience, 24,* 522–530. doi:10.1159/000069363

Jones, L. B., Stanwood, G. D., Reinoso, B. S., Washington, R. A., Wang, H. Y., Friedman, E., & Levitt, P. (2000). In utero cocaine-induced dysfunction of dopamine D1 receptor signaling and abnormal differentiation of cerebral cortical neurons. *The Journal of Neuroscience, 20,* 4606–4614.

Levine, B., Caplan, Y. H., & Kauffman, G. (1986). Fatality resulting from methylphenidate over-dose. *Journal of Analytical Toxicology, 10,* 209–210.

Lewis, D. A. (1997). Development of the prefrontal cortex during adolescence: Insights into vulner-able neural circuits in schizophrenia. *Neuropsychopharmacology, 16,* 385–398. doi:10.1016/S0893-133X(96)00277-1

McEwen, B. S. (1983). Gonadal steroid influences on brain development and sexual differentiation. *International Review of Physiology, 27,* 99–147.

Melnick, S. M., & Dow-Edwards, D. L. (2001). Differential behavioral responses to chronic amphet-amine in adult male and female rats exposed to postnatal cocaine treatment. *Pharmacology, Biochemistry and Behavior, 69,* 219–224. doi:10.1016/S0091-3057(01)00545-7

Melnick, S. M., & Dow-Edwards, D. L. (2003). Blunted metabolic response to SKF 82958 in the mesolimbic system following preweaning cocaine treatment. *Developmental Brain Research, 143,* 253–259. doi:10.1016/S0165-3806(03)00098-1

Meyer, J. S., Shani, I., & Rice, D. (2000). Effects of neonatal cocaine treatment and gender on opi-oid agonist-stimulated [(35)S]GTP gamma S binding in the striatum and nucleus accumbens. *Brain Research Bulletin, 53,* 147–152. doi:10.1016/S0361-9230(00)00323-3

Miranda, R. C., Sohrabji, F., Singh, M., & Toran-Allerand, C. D. (1996). Nerve growth factor (NGF) regulation of estrogen receptors in explant cultures of the developing forebrain. *Journal of Neurobiology, 31,* 77–87. doi:10.1002/(SICI)1097-4695(199609)31:1<77::AID-NEU7>3.0.CO;2-C

Miranda, R. C., Sohrabji, F., & Toran-Allerand, C. D. (1994). Interactions of estrogen with the neu-rotrophins and their receptors during neural development. *Hormones and Behavior, 28,* 367–375. doi:10.1006/hbeh.1994.1033

Morton, W. A., & Stockton, G. G. (2000). Methylphenidate abuse and psychiatric side effects. *Primary Care Companion to the Journal of Clinical Psychiatry, 2,* 159–164. doi:10.4088/PCC.v02n0502

Paxinos, G., & Watson, C. (1998). *The rat brain in stereotaxic coordinates.* New York, NY: Academic Press.

Quinones-Jenab, V., Minerly, A. C., Niyomchia, T., Akahvan, A., Jenab, S., & Frye, C. (2008). Progesterone and allopregnanolone are induced by cocaine in serum and brain tissues of male and female rats. *Pharmacology, Biochemistry and Behavior, 89,* 292–297.

Reisert, I., Engele, J., & Pilgrim, C. (1989). Early sexual differentiation of diencephalic dopaminer-gic neurons of the rat in vitro. *Cell and Tissue Research, 255,* 411–417. doi:10.1007/BF00224125

Sawada, H., Ibi, M., Urushitani, M., Honda, K., Nakanishi, M., Akaike, A., & Shimohama, S. (2000). Mechanisms of antiapoptotic effects of estrogens in nigral dopaminergic neurons. *The FASEB Journal, 14,* 1202–1214.

Sell, S. L., Scalzitti, J. M., Thomas, M. L., & Cunningham, K. A. (2000). Influence of ovarian hor-mones and estrous cycle on the behavioral response to cocaine in female rats. *The Journal of Pharmacology and Experimental Therapeutics, 293,* 879–886.

Singh, M., Meyer, E., Millard, W., & Simpkins, J. (1994). Ovarian steroid deprivation results in a reversible learning impairment and compromised cholinergic functions in female Sprague-Dawley rats. *Brain Research, 644,* 305–312. doi:10.1016/0006-8993(94)91694-2

Sokoloff, L., Reivich, M., Kennedy, C., Des Rosiers, M. H., Patlak, C. S., Pettigrew, K. D., ... & Shinohara, M. (1977). The [^{14}C]deoxyglucose method for the measurement of local cerebral glucose utilization: Theory, procedure, and normal values in the conscious and anesthetized albino rat. *Journal of Neurochemistry, 28,* 897–916. doi:10.1111/j.1471-4159.1977.tb10649.x

Spear, L. P., Silveri, M. M., Casale, M., Katovic, N. M., Campbell, J. O., & Douglas, L. A. (2002). Cocaine and development: A retrospective perspective. *Neurotoxicology and Teratology, 24,* 321–327. doi:10.1016/S0892-0362(02)00194-0

Steiner, H., & Gerfen, C. R. (1998). Role of dynorphin and enkephalin in the regulation of striatal output pathways and behavior. *Experimental Brain Research, 123,* 60–76. doi:10.1007/s002210050545

Strupp, B. J. (1989). Improvement of memory by a vasopressin fragment: Importance of individual differences in mnemonic function. *Behavioral Neuroscience, 103,* 743–754. doi:10.1037/0735-7044.103.4.743

Swanson, J. M., Swanson, J. M., Sergeant, J. A., Taylor, E., Sonuga-Barke, E. J. S., Jensen, P. S., & Cantwell, D. P. (1998). Attention-deficit hyperactivity disorder and hyperkinetic disorder. *The Lancet, 351,* 429–433. doi:10.1016/S0140-6736(97)11450-7

Torres-Reveron, A., & Dow-Edwards, D. L. (2004). Prenatal cocaine exposure produces attention impairment only in male rats during the adolescent period Society for Neuroscience, Abstract 49.

Torres-Reveron, A., & Dow-Edwards, D. L. (2006). Prenatal cocaine dampened behavioral responses to methylphenidate in male and female adolescent rats. *Neurotoxicology and Teratology, 28,* 165–172.

Torres-Reveron, A., Melnick, S. M., Stephenson, S. I., & Dow-Edwards, D. L. (2006). Standardization of a novel blood-sampling method through the jugular vein for use in the quantified [14C] 2-deoxyglucose method. *Journal of Neuroscience Methods, 150,* 143–149. doi:10.1016/j.jneumeth.2005.05.018

Torres-Reveron, A., Weedon, J., & Dow-Edwards, D. L. (2010). Methylphenidate response in prenatal cocaine exposed rats: A behavioral and brain functional study. *Brain Research, 1337,* 74–84.

Tsal, Y., Shalev, L., & Mevorach, C. (2005). The diversity of attention deficits in ADHD: The prevalence of four cognitive factors in ADHD versus controls. *Journal of Learning Disabilities, 38,* 142–157. doi:10.1177/00222194050380020401

Wade, S. B., Oommen, P., Conner, W. C., Earnest, D. J., & Rajesh, C. (1999). Overlapping and divergent actions of estrogen and the neurotrophins on cell fate and P53-dependent signal transduction in conditionally immortalized cerebral cortical neuroblasts. *The Journal of Neuroscience, 19,* 6994–7006.

Wang, H. Y., Runyan, S., Yadin, E., & Friedman, E. (1995). Prenatal exposure to cocaine selectively reduces D1 dopamine receptor-mediated activation of striatal Gs proteins. *The Journal of Pharmacology and Experimental Therapeutics, 273,* 492–498.

Zhao, N., Wang, H. W., & Dow-Edwards, D. (2008). Cocaine exposure during the early postnatal period diminishes medial frontal cortex Gs coupling to dopamine D1-like receptors in adult rat. *Neuroscience Letters, 438,* 159–162. doi:10.1016/j.neulet.2008.04.014

Zhen, X., Torres, C., Wang, H. Y., & Friedman, E. (2001). Prenatal exposure to cocaine disrupts D1A dopamine receptor function via selective inhibition of protein phosphatase 1 pathway in rabbit frontal cortex. *The Journal of Neuroscience, 21,* 9160–9167.

Zito, J. M., Safer, D. J., dosReis, S., Gardner, J. F., Boles, M., & Lynch, F. (2000). Trends in the prescribing of psychotropic medications to preschoolers. *JAMA, 283,* 1025–1030. doi:10.1001/jama.283.8.1025

4

Gender Influences on the Cognitive and Emotional Effects of Prenatal Cocaine Exposure: Insights From an Animal Model

Stephanie A. Beaudin, Mathew H. Gendle, and Barbara J. Strupp

Beginning in the mid 1980s, a freebase form of cocaine, known as "crack," came to be extensively abused in the United States. Unlike cocaine hydrochloride, crack was extremely cheap and readily available in most urban areas (Hutchings, 1993). This made it extremely attractive, particularly among socially and economically disadvantaged populations, and use of the drug within these groups quickly reached epidemic proportions (Hutchings, 1993). A large percentage of crack users were women of childbearing age, a trend that differed from previous patterns of drug use in the United States (Chavkin, Wise, & Elman, 1998). By the early 1990s, anecdotal and sensational media reports of the effects of prenatal cocaine exposure were common. (Hutchings, 1993). These reports labeled cocaine-exposed children as members of a growing "biologic underclass" (Toufexis, 1991) and fueled a media frenzy surrounding "crack babies," a public health problem that was described as "a devastation that is worse than smallpox" (Krauthammer, July 30, 1989, p. C7).

At the peak of the journalistic and popular fury over "crack babies," no controlled investigations of cocaine-exposed children had been undertaken beyond the neonatal period. With no scientific data to either support or refute these sensational claims, they became the dominant view in both the lay population and scientific circles. However, progress has been made over the past 15 years; many studies have evaluated cognitive and emotional functioning in cocaine-exposed children. These studies have demonstrated that the sequelae of prenatal cocaine exposure are fortunately much less severe than presaged by these early claims. Global measures of cognitive development, such as IQ, have generally not been linked to in utero cocaine exposure (Chasnoff et al., 1998; Espy, Kaufmann, & Glisky, 1999; Granick, 1995; Griffith, Azuma, & Chasnoff, 1994; Hurt et al., 1997; Loebstein & Koren, 1997; Richardson et al., 1996; Rotholz, Snyder, & Peters, 1995; Wasserman et al., 1998). On the other hand, quite a few studies have implicated lasting functional deficits in attention, arousal regulation, and response to stress (Accornero et al., 2007; Alessandri, Imaizumi, & Lewis, 1993; Bandstra, Morrow, Anthony, Accornero, & Fried, 2001; Bendersky, Alessandri, & Lewis, 1996; Bendersky, Alessandri, Sullivan, & Lewis, 1995; Bendersky & Lewis, 1998; Bennett, Bendersky, & Lewis, 2007; Dennis, Bendersky, Ramsay, & Lewis, 2006; Dow-Edwards, Mayes, Spear, & Hurd, 1999; Gaultney, Gingras, Martin, & DeBrule, 2005; Heffelfinger, Craft, & Shyken, 1997; Heffelfinger, Craft, White, & Shyken, 2002; Leech, Richardson, Goldschmidt, & Day, 1999; Mayes, 2002; Mayes, Grillon, Granger, & Schottenfeld, 1998; Molitor, Mays, & Ward, 2003; Noland et al., 2005; Richardson, Conroy, & Day, 1996).

Unfortunately, the conclusions that can be drawn from these reported associations between cocaine use and child functioning are limited by the presence of numerous confounding factors (LaGasse, Seifer, & Lester, 1999). Even in cases where socioeconomic status was controlled by comparing the cocaine-exposed children with controls from the same socioeconomic group, numerous factors other than the exposure itself could account for the deficits observed in the cocaine-exposed children. For example, substance-abusing women often come from families with long histories of chemical dependence, violence, sexual abuse, and various psychopathologies, and a high percentage of them have partners who are also substance abusers (Hans, 1999). Perhaps most important, women who use cocaine during pregnancy almost never use cocaine only: Concomitant use of other licit and illicit drugs is the norm, not the exception (e.g., Bendersky, Alessandri, Gilbert, & Lewis, 1996; Bennett, Bendersky, & Lewis, 2008; Hans, 1999). Because these factors are difficult to accurately quantify and therefore account for statistically, the conclusions that can be drawn regarding the effects of prenatal cocaine exposure alone must be viewed as tentative.

To circumvent the interpretative concerns inherent in these studies of cocaine-exposed children, many researchers have turned to animal models. The early work in this area used subcutaneous (e.g., Dow-Edwards, Freed-Malen, & Hughes, 1993; Heyser, Spear, & Spear, 1995; Snyder, Katovic, & Spear, 1998; Wood, Molina, Wagner, & Spear, 1995) or intragastric (e.g., Dow-Edwards, 1990) methods of administration. These pioneering studies were important in laying the groundwork for subsequent studies in this area, but they suffered from interpretive problems of their own. These routes of administration do not reproduce the acute physiological effects and pharmacokinetic profile seen in humans who self-administer cocaine (Mactutus, Booze, & Dowell, 2000). In addition, the repeated subcutaneous administration of the relatively high cocaine doses used in these studies produces painful necrotic skin lesions at the injection site, as well as signs of maternal toxicity, such as reduced food intake and seizures (Mactutus, Herman, & Booze, 1994). Because some of these effects (e.g., maternal stress, reduced maternal intake, reduced maternal and pup weight) have in themselves been shown to produce lasting cognitive deficits in the offspring, the findings from studies using this type of method of exposure must be viewed as inconclusive.

A significant advance was made in 1994 when Charles Mactutus and Rose Booze developed an intravenous injection protocol for rodent studies of prenatal cocaine exposure (Mactutus et al., 1994; Mactutus et al., 2000). This procedure, which involves the surgical implantation of an intravenous injection catheter in female rats prior to impregnation, eliminates the skin lesions and injection stress of the subcutaneous route. Moreover, this injection regimen accurately mimics the acute physiological effects and pharmacokinetic profile seen in humans self-administering cocaine. Finally, this protocol, which uses much lower doses than the subcutaneous or oral regimens (3.0 mg/kg vs. 40 mg/kg), does not alter the body weight or intake of the dams or pups (Mactutus et al., 1994; Mactutus et al., 2000).

We have been using this intravenous injection protocol for the past decade in a series of studies designed to elucidate the lasting cognitive and affective seque-lae of prenatal cocaine exposure. These studies revealed lasting cognitive and affective dysfunction in the cocaine-exposed animals, but the dysfunction proved to be remarkably selective, affecting only sustained and selective attention as well as arousal regulation. Many other cognitive functions, including basic asso-ciative ability and memory function, proved to be unaffected (see Garavan et al., 2000; Gendle, White, et al., 2004). In broad terms, the pattern of spared and impaired functions was the same in both sexes, but in some instances the magni-tude of the effects and their manifestations varied between the sexes. These areas of similarity as well as differences are outlined in this chapter.

In the studies described in this chapter, testing was conducted in auto-mated testing chambers, which consisted of a large waiting area and a smaller testing alcove containing three response ports. A nose poke into one of three funnel-shaped ports constituted a response; correct responses were reinforced with a 45-mg food pellet. Each daily testing session consisted of 250 trials or 120 min, whichever came first. Additional details of the apparatus or method-ology may be found in previous publications (Alber & Strupp, 1996; Bunsey & Strupp, 1995; Garavan et al., 2000; Hilson & Strupp, 1997).

Selective Attention

Selective attention has proven to be one of the cognitive functions most affected by prenatal cocaine exposure. Our studies indicate that this area of dysfunction is seen in both male and female animals, although, as we describe, there is some evidence that the dysfunction may be more pronounced in the male offspring. Converging evidence for impairment in this domain was provided by the results of four different tasks: extradimensional shift (EDS) tasks, a redundant learn-ing task, a distraction task, and a three-choice olfactory serial reversal learning task series.

The pattern of effects observed in two EDS tasks provided the first clue for impairment in selective attention (Garavan et al., 2000). Prior to the EDS tasks, the animals had mastered a series of simultaneous olfactory discrimina-tions in which they had been reinforced for making a nose poke into the port from which one particular olfactory cue was emanating. Responses to either one of the two other olfactory cues were not rewarded. For the subsequent spa-tial EDS tasks, the same three olfactory cues were presented simultaneously on each trial (as in the prior tasks), but the olfactory cues were no longer predic-tive. Instead, the left port was always correct. Thus, the animals were required to disregard the previously predictive olfactory cues, attend to the spatial cues, and learn which of the three port locations was correct. After the animals had mastered this task, the predictive dimension was again shifted, so that now the olfactory cues were predictive and the spatial information was irrelevant. Finally, a third EDS was performed such that spatial cues were again predictive (the right port was now correct) and the olfactory cues were not predictive. Analyses of learning rate (errors to criterion) demonstrated that the cocaine animals of both sexes were significantly impaired in the two spatial EDS tasks but not in the olfactory EDS task. This pattern of results provides important clues to the specific nature of the observed impairment. First, task difficulty per se can be excluded as the pivotal factor; a comparison of the number of errors committed in each task indicated that the spatial tasks were mastered more easily than the olfactory task. Second, the timing of the impairment in the spatial EDS tasks (i.e. it was specific to the later learning stages; see Figure 4.1), coupled with the absence of any impairment in the olfactory EDS tasks, suggests that attentional shifting per se was not impaired by prenatal cocaine exposure. The observation that the cocaine-related impairment on the spatial EDS tasks was evident only in the later stages of the task (after the animals had made eight consecutive correct responses) suggests that the impairment was not in asso-ciative ability. This conclusion was corroborated by the absence of impairment in a variety of learning tasks, including the more difficult olfactory EDS tasks. Instead, the most parsimonious explanation, when also considering data from other tasks, is that attention in the cocaine animals is "captured" by the most salient environmental cues. When the dominant cues were the predictive stim-uli (as in the olfactory tasks), the cocaine-exposed animals were not impaired. However, when these salient cues were distracters, impairment emerged.

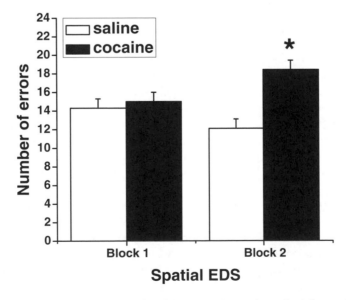

Figure 4.1. Mean (+/− standard error of the mean) number of trials per block for the spatial extradimensional shift (EDS) tasks. *$p < .05$. **$p < .01$, relative to controls. From "Prenatal Cocaine Exposure Impairs Selective Attention: Evidence From Serial Reversal and Extradimensional Shift Tasks," by H. Garavan et al., 2000, *Behavioral Neuroscience, 114,* p. 733. Copyright 2000 by the American Psychological Association.

Under these conditions, apparently the treated animals had trouble consistently attending to the predictive, but less salient, spatial cues, and hence performed less consistently as a result of lapses in attentional control. This dysfunction was comparable in the two sexes for this series of tasks.

The results of a visual attention task with periodic olfactory distracters (Gendle, White, et al., 2004) suggested a similar conclusion. In this distraction task, the animals were required to wait until one of the three light-emitting diodes was briefly illuminated and then to make a nose poke into the port below the light. One of nine olfactory cues (distracters) was presented during the interval prior to light illumination on one third of the trials. The location and onset time of both the visual cue and the distracter varied randomly across trials in a given test session. This task, too, revealed a specific and subtle deficit in the cocaine-exposed animals: They were not impaired on the trials in which no distracter was presented (the nondistraction trials), but they were significantly more disrupted by the presentation of the olfactory distracters than controls (see Figure 4.2). Again, the most parsimonious explanation is that prenatal cocaine exposure impaired selective attention, particularly under conditions of salient irrelevant environmental cues. As in the EDS tasks, this effect was seen in both sexes of exposed animals, to a comparable degree.

Converging evidence for an alteration in selective attention was provided by the results of a redundant learning task (Morgan, Garavan, Mactutus, Booze, & Strupp, 1998; Strupp, Morgan, Garavan, Mactutus, & Booze, 1998), but in this task only the male offspring were impaired. All animals first learned a three-choice simultaneous olfactory discrimination, in which three different odors were presented on each trial (one from each of the three response ports). A nose poke into the port from which the "correct" stimulus was emanating was rewarded with a food pellet. After the animals mastered this olfactory discrimination task, they entered a "redundant" phase, in which the correct port was designated by illumination of a small light-emitting diode above the port, in addition to the olfactory cues; hence, the light cue provided redundant information. During a final phase, only the light cue designated the correct port; the olfactory cues were no longer presented. The cocaine-exposed males performed significantly more poorly than controls on "probe" trials administered during the redundant phase (see Figure 4.3), and they learned the visual discrimination task (the final phase) significantly more slowly. Notably, comparison groups administered only the visual discrimination task (i.e. without the prior redundant phase) did not reveal differences between cocaine-exposed and control animals. Based on the overall pattern of results, it seems likely that during the redundant phase, attention in the cocaine-exposed males was captured by the salient olfactory cues, and as a result, they learned less about the redundant visual cues. In this task, however, contrary to the results of the EDS and distraction tasks, the cocaine-exposed females did not differ from the female controls, suggesting that the impairment in this domain may be more pronounced in cocaine-exposed males than females, perhaps because these different tasks differ in their sensitivity in detecting dysfunction in this domain. Note that this redundant learning task involved the same cohort of animals as the EDS task series; thus, sampling error cannot account for the detection of an effect in the females in the EDS task but not in this redundant learning task.

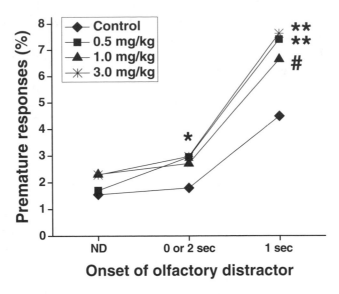

Figure 4.2. Mean percentage premature responses in the distraction task. Three distraction conditions were used: (a) trials on which no distractor was presented (ND), (b) trials on which an olfactory distractor was presented 0 or 2 s following trial onset (moderately distracting), or (c) trials on which a distractor was presented 1 s after trial onset (highly distracting). The unpredictable presentation of an olfactory distractor disrupted the performance of cocaine-exposed rats significantly more than that of controls, with the largest group differences seen under the most distracting conditions. $\# p < .06$; $^*p < .05$; $^{**}p < .01$, relative to controls. From "Enduring Effects of Prenatal Cocaine Exposure on Selective Attention and Reactivity to Errors: Evidence From an Animal Model," by M. H. Gendle et al., 2004, *Behavioral Neuroscience, 118,* p. 293. Copyright 2004 by the American Psychological Association.

Further evidence that prenatal cocaine exposure produces lasting impairment in selective attention but also that this effect is more pronounced in males was provided by the results of an olfactory serial reversal learning task, a task series given to the same cohort of rats that exhibited deficits in the EDS and redundant learning tasks. In this task series, three olfactory cues were presented on each trial, one from each response port, with one of the three odors being "correct." After a high level of performance was achieved, the contingencies were changed such that now a different odor was correct and the previously correct odor was incorrect (a reversal). Four such reversals were administered to each animal. Male rats exposed to cocaine in utero performed more poorly than saline-treated males on the three-choice, but not the two-choice, serial reversal task series. There were no treatment-related effects for females in either the two- or three-choice tasks. The subsequent in-depth analyses provided insight into the nature of the deficit. The fact that the cocaine-treated males did not differ from controls in the three-choice tasks on nontrial and alcove latency measures rules out differences in motivation, frustration, or emotional reactivity on these tasks, corroborated by the absence of a treatment effect on the two-choice task series. Furthermore, the learning phase analyses revealed

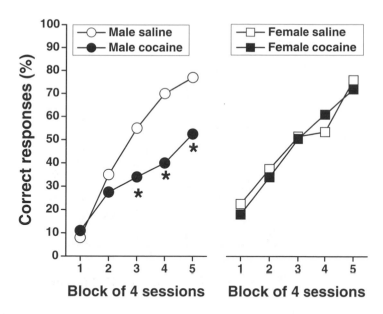

Figure 4.3. Mean percentage of correct responses on probe trials during the redundant phase of a redundant learning task as a function of the five blocks of testing (four sessions per block). In this task, the rats first mastered an olfactory discrimination, with continued testing on a redundant phase in which both olfactory cues and a visual cue (light illumination) indicated which port was correct. During this redundant phase (250 trials/session), the olfactory cues were not presented on 12 randomly presented probe trials. These probe trials provided an index of the rate at which the rats learned about the redundant visual cues. The males exposed to cocaine prenatally (left panel) performed more poorly than control males on these probe trials; no differences were seen in the females (right panel). *$p < .05$. From "Impaired Redundant Learning in Male Rats Exposed to Cocaine Prenatally" by R. E. Morgan, D. A. Levitsky, and B. J. Strupp, 1996 (unpublished data).

that the three-choice task impairment was not due to a prolonged period of perseverative responding to the previously correct cue, the type of response often assumed to underlie impaired reversal learning. Similarly, lapses of inhibitory control, indicated by preferential responding to the previously correct odor in the postperseverative period, did not differentiate the treatment groups. This conclusion was confirmed by the finding that the impairment of the cocaine-exposed males was similar across all five tasks (the initial discrimination and the subsequent four reversals). Finally, the phase analysis indicated that the cocaine-related dysfunction did not stem from an associative deficit. As seen in Figure 4.4, the impairment of the cocaine-exposed males emerged when the rats' performance surpassed 66% correct and was most pronounced in the final phase, a period in which the rats had already mastered the new contingencies. One would expect that an associative deficit would produce its most pronounced effect on performance in the chance and early postchance phases and would not alter the final learning phase—a pattern very different from that seen here. Instead, the most parsimonious explanation, based on the locus of the performance

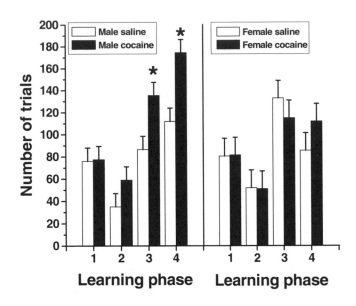

Figure 4.4. Mean number of trials (+/– standard error of the mean) in each of five sequential learning phases for a series of three-choice olfactory serial reversal learning tasks (collapsed across four reversals). Prenatal cocaine exposure significantly increased the duration of phase 3 (the late postchance phase; 66–88% correct) and phase 4 (the criterial phase) for the male offspring (left panel) but not for the females (right panel). Note that the exposed males did not differ from controls during phase 1 (the chance phase; < 46% correct), nor during phase 2 (the early postchance phase; 46–66% correct). * $p < .05$, relative to controls. From "Prenatal Cocaine Exposure Impairs Selective Attention: Evidence From Serial Reversal and Extradimensional Shift Tasks," by H. Garavan et al., 2000, *Behavioral Neuroscience, 114,* p. 731. Copyright 2000 by the American Psychological Association.

impairment and coupled with the other findings from these rats and their littermates, is that the deficit in this serial reversal task also reflects a dysfunction in selective attention, to which the males appeared especially vulnerable.

In summary, these four tasks provide converging evidence for a very specific type of attentional change: The attentional focus of cocaine-exposed animals is heavily influenced by the relative salience of environmental cues. As a result, they are more easily distracted on tasks that depend on learning about less salient environmental cues. In contrast, learning and performance are normal under conditions in which attending to the most salient cues is commensurate with reward contingencies. This area of dysfunction was seen in both sexes but was more pronounced in the males.

Sustained Attention

A dose–response study conducted in our laboratory several years ago (Gendle et al., 2003) revealed impaired sustained attention in cocaine-exposed adult offspring, although in this domain the manifestations of this dysfunction proved to vary as a function of the sex of the offspring. This area of impairment was seen in a variant of the distraction task just described. In this task, designed to tap inhibitory control and sustained attention, one of the three light-emitting diodes (one above each response port), was briefly illuminated following a variable pre-cue delay. To receive a reward, the rats were required to withhold responding prior to presentation of the light cue and then make a nose poke into the port under the illuminated light-emitting diode. The spatial location (left, center, right port), duration of cue illumination (200, 400, or 700 ms), and prestimulus delay (0, 3, 6, or 9 s) varied pseudorandomly across the trials in each test session. Thus, this sustained attention task assesses the animals' ability to detect and respond to brief and unpredictable visual cues over a large number (200–250) of trials per testing session.

The 3.0 mg/kg exposed males, but not those treated with two lower doses (0.5, 1.0 mg/kg), committed significantly more omission errors than control males, but only during the final third of each testing session and only on trials that followed an error (see Figure 4.5). This pattern implicates the combined effects of impaired sustained attention and heightened reactivity to committing an error. The behavior of the exposed females also suggested an impaired ability to sustain attention, but the doses at which this effect was seen and the manifestation

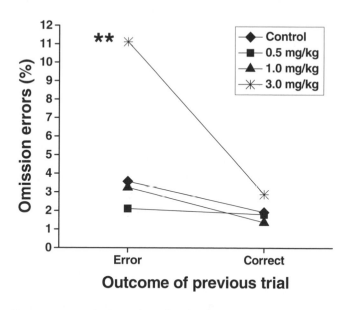

Figure 4.5. Percentage omission errors for the males in the final block of trials (trials 168–250) in each daily testing session for the sustained attention task (collapsed across the five sessions) as a function of the outcome of the previous trial. The increase in omission errors produced by committing an error was significantly greater for the exposed males (3.0 mg/kg) than for control males. Note that during this same block of trials (end of session), the groups did not differ in rate of omission errors on trials that followed a correct response ($p = .3$). ** $p < .01$. From "Impaired Sustained Attention and Altered Reactivity to Errors in an Animal Model of Prenatal Cocaine Exposure," by M. H. Gendle et al., 2003, *Developmental Brain Research, 147*(1–2), p. 90. Copyright 2003 by Elsevier.

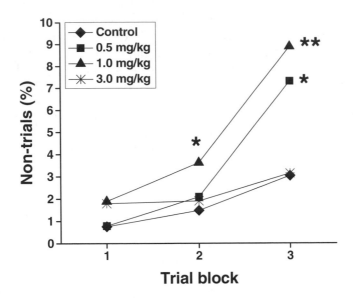

Figure 4.6.   Percentage of nontrials committed by the females in the sustained attention task as a function of three blocks of trials in each 250-trial test session. The increase in nontrials over the course of each session was significantly more pronounced for the females exposed prenatally to the two intermediate cocaine doses than for control females. * $p < .05$. ** $p < .01$. *** $p < .001$, relative to control females. From "Impaired Sustained Attention and Altered Reactivity to Errors in an Animal Model of Prenatal Cocaine Exposure," by M. H. Gendle et al., 2003, *Developmental Brain Research, 147*(1–2), p. 90. Copyright 2003 by Elsevier.

of this impairment differed between the two sexes. During the final third of each testing session, the 0.5 and 1.0 mg/kg exposed females (but not the 3.0 mg/kg group) took significantly longer to enter the testing alcove at trial onset, and they did not enter the alcove at trial onset more frequently than control females (see Figure 4.6). Because these effects were not seen in other tasks of similar duration and reinforcement density, these findings suggest impaired sustained attention. This inference is supported by the finding that the increase in omission errors in the final block of trials in each daily session (relative to earlier in the session) was significantly greater for the 1.0 mg/kg females than for controls, a trend also seen for the 0.5 mg/kg group. Unlike the cocaine-exposed males, who remained engaged in the task when attention began to wane, the cocaine-exposed females appeared to opt for another strategy, namely, refusing to participate when their ability to sustain attention was surpassed.

Reaction to Errors

Numerous studies of prenatal cocaine exposure, involving human and animal subjects, have concluded that stress reactivity is altered by prenatal cocaine exposure (cited below). In our studies, we have evaluated this type of dysfunction by examining how the animals react to committing an error, the type of mildly stressful event that commonly occurs in life. We have studied error reactivity in both rats and mice in numerous tasks over many years. On trials following an error (relative to trials following a correct response), they take significantly longer to enter the testing alcove and make a response, and the likelihood of committing all types of errors (premature responses, omission errors, and inaccurate responses) is also significantly greater. This behavioral pattern of posterror changes in performance parallels some of the disruptions seen in monkeys (Rushworth, Hadland, Gaffan, & Passingham, 2003) and humans (Elliott et al., 1996; Laming, 1979; Rabbitt & Rodgers, 1977; Robertson, Manly, Andrade, Baddeley, & Yiend, 1997) in studies of error monitoring and indicates that rats are sensitive to their own errors. We have intentionally studied error reactivity after task rules have been mastered, such that the errors likely reflect impulsivity or execution errors ("slips") and are distinct from errors of knowledge or mistakes, which typically occur in the context of learning a new task (Reason, 1990). Our studies have revealed that rats exposed to cocaine in utero react differently than controls to committing an error. The nature of this effect varied in different tasks and, in some instances, by sex, as described later.

Evidence from numerous tasks has indicated that the cocaine-exposed males were consistently more disrupted than control males by committing an error on the previous trial. In the distraction task described earlier (Gendle, White, et al., 2004), the 3.0-mg/kg males committed significantly more omission errors than controls on trials following an error, but they did not differ on trials following a correct response (see Figure 4.7). These exposed males exhibited this same type of effect on the sustained attention task (see Figure 4.5; Gendle et al., 2003). In addition, in the distraction task, all three cocaine-exposed groups (0.5, 1.0, 3.0 mg/kg) were significantly more likely than controls to commit a premature response on trials following an error but not on trials following a correct response (see Figure 4.8). Because this was the only task and error type for which the two lower dose groups exhibited this heightened error reactivity, it is likely that this effect reflects the conjoint influence of the increased reactivity produced by committing an error on the prior trial and generalized disruption produced by the unpredictable presentation of the potent distracters, which together impaired inhibitory control on trials following an error. Thus, for males, the heightened reactivity to committing an error produced by prenatal cocaine exposure exhibits a graded dose–effect function across the range of doses tested here: This effect was seen for the high-dose males (3.0 mg/kg) in all tasks examined, whereas for the lower dose groups (0.5 and 1.0 mg/kg), this effect became manifest only when combined with the unpredictable presentation of potent olfactory distracters.

A less consistent pattern was seen for the cocaine-exposed females, although here, too, the evidence suggests altered reactivity to mild stressors. In the distraction task, females in all three cocaine-exposed groups (0.5, 1.0, 3.0 mg/kg) were significantly more likely than controls to commit a premature response on trials following an error, but not on trials following a correct response, as seen in the cocaine-exposed males (Figure 4.8). However, this was the only task in which the exposed females exhibited heightened reactivity to errors or stressors. In fact, in several other tasks administered to this cohort of rats, the cocaine-exposed

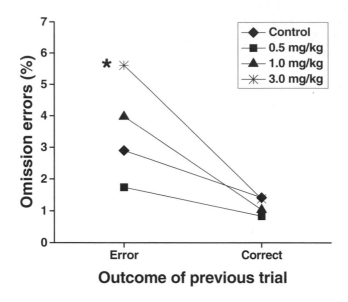

Figure 4.7. Mean percentage of omission errors committed by the male rats in the distraction task as a function of the outcome of the previous trial. Note that the rate of omission errors was significantly higher for the 3.0 mg/kg males than for controls on trials that followed an error but not on trials that followed a correct response ($p = .80$). *$p < .05$, relative to controls. From "Enduring Effects of Prenatal Cocaine Exposure on Selective Attention and Reactivity to Errors: Evidence From an Animal Model," by M. H. Gendle et al., 2004, *Behavioral Neuroscience, 118*(2), p. 294. Copyright 2004 by the American Psychological Association.

females reacted less to mild stressors than did control females (see Gendle et al., 2003; Gendle, White, et al., 2004). One explanation that can accommodate the different results seen for the exposed females in these different tasks is provided by an interesting observation by Linda Mayes and colleagues concerning arousal regulation in cocaine-exposed children. These investigators noted that cocaine-exposed children require more stimulation to reach optimal states of arousal but modulate higher states of arousal less well and therefore often quickly become overaroused (Mayes et al., 1998). Thus, it is possible that prenatal exposure to cocaine alters the regulation of arousal or emotions, with the consequence that both increased and decreased levels of reactivity (relative to controls) may be found, depending on many factors, including the stress of the testing environment. The cocaine-exposed females reacted less to committing an error than controls in the sustained attention task, which did not involve potent olfactory distracters, whereas in the distraction task they were more adversely affected by an error than controls. One interpretation is that in this former task the cocaine-exposed females were less aroused than controls by task demands (e.g., waiting during unpredictable delays), whereas in the distraction task the combined effects of committing an error and the unpredictable presentation of the olfactory distracters overaroused the cocaine-exposed

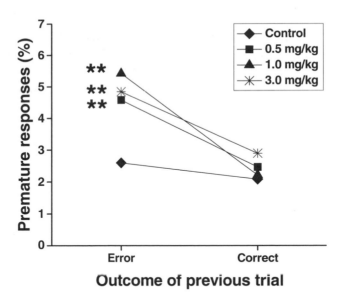

Figure 4.8. Mean percentage of premature responses in the distraction task as a function of the outcome of the previous trial. The increase in premature responses produced by committing an error was significantly greater for all cocaine-exposed animals than for controls. Note that the groups did not differ in rate of premature responses on trials that followed a correct response ($p = .3$). $**p < .01$, relative to controls. From "Enduring Effects of Prenatal Cocaine Exposure on Selective Attention and Reactivity to Errors: Evidence From an Animal Model," by M. H. Gendle et al., 2004, *Behavioral Neuroscience, 118*(2), p. 294. Copyright 2004 by the American Psychological Association.

females, with the result that they performed less well than controls on trials following an error.

Thus, cocaine-exposed animals (like cocaine-exposed children) do not appear to be consistently in a state of overarousal or underarousal. In many tasks, the performance of the cocaine-exposed animals did not differ from controls on trials following a correct response, whereas group differences often emerged specifically on trials following an error. However, the influence of prenatal cocaine exposure on the degree to which an error disrupted performance varied by sex and by type of task. Exposed males exhibited greater disruption following an error than their nonexposed counterparts, regardless of specific task characteristics. In contrast, for exposed females, both overreactivity and underreactivity to errors were observed, depending on task demands.

This demonstration that prenatal cocaine exposure causes lasting changes in reactivity to errors and mild task-related stress represents an important extension of the literature concerning altered reactivity of cocaine-exposed animals to physical stressors such as foot shock and forced swimming (Campbell, Bliven, Silveri, Snyder, & Spear, 2000; Elsworth, Morrow, & Roth, 2001; Huber, Darling, Park, & Soliman, 2001; Overstreet et al., 2000; Spear, Campbell, Snyder, Silveri, & Katovic, 1998). The present findings provide the strongest evidence to date that prenatal cocaine exposure produces lasting changes in the ability to regulate arousal in response to mild stressors. Although many studies of exposed children have suggested this type of effect (Alessandri et al., 1993; Bendersky et al., 1995; Bendersky, Alessandri, & Lewis, 1996; Bendersky & Lewis, 1998; Dennis et al., 2006; Kable, Coles, Lynch, & Platzman, 2008; Li et al., 2009; Mayes, 2002; Mayes et al., 1998), including an increased risk for arousal dysregulation in boys (Bendersky et al., 1995; Kable et al., 2008), interpretation of these findings has been complicated by the fact that the environments of the exposed children differed from controls across several dimensions (e.g., exposure to violence and maternal depression) that are likely to affect this aspect of functioning. As a result, these latter studies have not demonstrated a causal relationship between prenatal cocaine exposure and dysregulation of affect or arousal. In contrast, these studies with animal models do allow this inference, because of the random assignment of treatment condition and absence of confounders.

Summary and Conclusions

Our studies have revealed both similarities and differences in the behavioral effects of in utero cocaine exposure on male and female offspring. The most pervasive area of dysfunction—impaired selective attention—was seen in both sexes, although the dysfunction seemed to be more pronounced in the males. Impaired sustained attention was also seen in both sexes, although here both the doses at which these effects were seen and the manifestation of the impairment differed by sex. Finally, disruption in the regulation of emotion or negative affect, as indexed by error reactivity, was also seen in both sexes, but again some sex differences emerged. Exposed males consistently exhibited greater disruption following an error than controls. In contrast, exposed females exhibited a blunted reaction to errors in tasks that were only mildly arousing, whereas in tasks that were arousing for the animals (e.g., a task involving potent distracters), they too exhibited heightened reactivity relative to controls. Like cocaine-exposed children, they may require more stimulation than nonexposed children to reach optimal levels of arousal, but they are less able to modulate higher states of arousal when they occur (Mayes, 2002; Mayes et al., 1998).

The specific pattern of cognitive and affective impairments observed in cocaine-exposed rats in these studies implicates dysfunction in catecholaminergic modulation of the prefrontal cortex. This conclusion is based, in part, on the similarity in clinical symptoms seen following dysfunction of this part of the brain (Arnsten & Li, 2005; Devinsky, Morrell, & Vogt, 1995) and that seen following prenatal cocaine exposure. Converging evidence is provided by pharmacological, neurochemical, and anatomical studies of animals exposed to cocaine prenatally (e.g., Booze et al., 2006; Ferris et al., 2007; Harvey, 2004; Morrow, Elsworth, & Roth, 2003; Morrow, Hajszan, Leranth, Elsworth, & Roth, 2007; Snow et al., 2004; Wang, Jenkins, Choi, & Murphy, 1996; Wang, Levitt, Grayson, & Murphy, 1995). More recent clinical studies that have begun to evaluate the long-term effects of in utero cocaine exposure on the human brain using event-related potential, imaging, and other methodologies (Li et al., 2009; Mayes, Molfese, Key, & Hunter, 2005; Rao et al., 2007; Smith et al., 2001; Warner et al.,

2006), although less conclusive, are broadly consistent with this view. The neural data emerging from these studies, although beyond the scope of this chapter, implicate developmental alterations in the dopamine (DA) and norepinephrine (NE) neuronal systems and their projections to prefrontal cortex as the putative substrate of the attentional and arousal impairments seen in individuals prenatally exposed to cocaine. (For an excellent review of the preclinical work, see Harvey, 2004.) As with the behavioral studies in this area, sex differences in the response to in utero cocaine on brain neurochemistry and morphology have not been systematically studied in general. Nonetheless, some evidence of sex-mediated differences has been found in cocaine-exposed animals in response to drug challenge with the noradrenergic agonist idazoxan but not for the dopaminergic agonist SKF81297 (Bayer, Brown, Mactutus, Booze, & Strupp, 2000; Bayer, Kakumanu, Mactutus, Booze, & Strupp, 2002). Sexual dimorphism has also been observed in the development of the locus coeruleus (LC; Snow et al., 2004) and in the expression of cortical and subcortical DA and NE receptors following in utero cocaine exposure in adolescent and adult offspring (Booze et al., 2006; Ferris et al., 2007). The influence of gender on stress hyperactivation of DA and NE neurons in medial frontal and related areas (e.g., LC) by in utero cocaine is not known because these studies used only one sex (Elsworth et al., 2001; Morrow, Elsworth, & Roth, 2001, 2002; but see Elsworth et al., 2007).

Unfortunately, research investigating potential pharmacotherapies for ameliorating attentional and arousal deficits that result from prenatal cocaine exposure has been limited. Given the existing evidence for gender differences on the neuronal, behavioral, and cognitive outcomes affected by prenatal cocaine exposure, it stands to reason that novel pharmacotherapeutic approaches must be evaluated within the context of the potential gender differences; compounds that modify cortical DA or NE activity are likely to be different in exposed males and females. Consistent with this prediction, recent work has demonstrated a sex-specific effect of the alpha-2A noradrenergic agonist guanfacine in animals exposed to cocaine prenatally using the intravenous technique described earlier (Beaudin, Mactutus, Booze, & Strupp, 2011). In this work, guanfacine enhanced attentional accuracy under distracting conditions for cocaine-exposed females, but it impaired attentional accuracy in exposed males under the same conditions of distraction. Findings such as these emphasize the importance of considering the role of gender in the assessment of potential pharmacotherapies. A "one size fits all" approach in the clinical management of these functional impairments may not be optimal across individuals, and consideration of not only the sex-specific effects of prenatal cocaine exposure on the developing brain but also its impact on neuropsychological and behavioral functions is critical.

References

Accornero, V. H., Amado, A. J., Morrow, C. E., Xue, L., Anthony, J. C., & Bandstra, E. S. (2007). Impact of prenatal cocaine exposure on attention and response inhibition as assessed by continuous performance tests. *Journal of Developmental and Behavioral Pediatrics, 28,* 195–205. doi:10.1097/01.DBP.0000268560.72580.f9

Alber, S. A., & Strupp, B. J. (1996). An in-depth analysis of lead effects in a delayed spatial alternation task: Assessment of mnemonic effects, side bias, and proactive interference. *Neurotoxicology and Teratology, 18,* 3–15. doi:10.1016/0892-0362(95)02026-8

Alessandri, S. M., Imaizumi, S., & Lewis, M. (1993). Learning and emotional responsivity in cocaine-exposed infants. *Developmental Psychology, 29,* 989–997. doi:10.1037/0012-1649.29.6.989

Arnsten, A. F. T., & Li, B. M. (2005). Neurobiology of executive functions: Catecholamine influences on prefrontal cortical functions. *Biological Psychiatry, 57,* 1377–1384. doi:10.1016/j.biopsych. 2004.08.019

Bandstra, E. S., Morrow, C. E., Anthony, J. C., Accornero, V. H., & Fried, P. A. (2001). Longitudinal investigation of task persistence and sustained attention in children with prenatal cocaine exposure. *Neurotoxicology and Teratology, 23,* 545–559. doi:10.1016/S0892-0362(01)00181-7

Bayer, L. E., Brown, A., Mactutus, C. F., Booze, R. M., & Strupp, B. J. (2000). Prenatal cocaine exposure increases sensitivity to the attentional effects of the dopamine D1 agonist SKF81297. *The Journal of Neuroscience, 20,* 8902–8908.

Bayer, L. E., Kakumanu, S., Mactutus, C. F., Booze, R. M., & Strupp, B. J. (2002). Prenatal cocaine exposure alters sensitivity to the effects of idazoxan in a distraction task. *Behavioural Brain Research, 133,* 185–196. doi:10.1016/S0166-4328(02)00002-5

Beaudin, S. A. Mactutus, C. F., Booze, R. M., & Strupp, B. J. (2011). *Guanfacine treatment of attention and arousal deficits in adult rats exposed* in utero *to low IV cocaine doses.* Manuscript in preparation.

Bendersky, M., Alessandri, S., Gilbert, P., & Lewis, M. (1996). Characteristics of pregnant substance abusers in two cities in the northeast. *The American Journal of Drug and Alcohol Abuse, 22,* 349–362. doi:10.3109/00952999609001664

Bendersky, M., Alessandri, S. M., & Lewis, M. (1996). Emotions in cocaine exposed infants. In M. Lewis & M. W. Sullivan (Eds.), *Emotional development in atypical children* (pp. 89–108). Hillsdale, NJ: Erlbaum.

Bendersky, M., Alessandri, S. M., Sullivan, M. W., & Lewis, M. (1995). Measuring the effects of prenatal cocaine exposure. In M. Lewis & M. Bendersky (Eds.), *Mothers, babies, and cocaine: The role of toxins in development* (pp. 163–178). Hillsdale, NJ: Erlbaum.

Bendersky, M., & Lewis, M. (1998). Arousal modulation in cocaine-exposed infants. *Developmental Psychology, 34,* 555–564. doi:10.1037/0012-1649.34.3.555

Bennett, D. S., Bendersky, M., & Lewis, M. (2007). Preadolescent health risk behavior as a function of prenatal cocaine exposure and gender. *Journal of Developmental and Behavioral Pediatrics, 28,* 467–472. doi:10.1097/DBP.0b013e31811320d8

Bennett, D. S., Bendersky, M., & Lewis, M. (2008). Children's cognitive ability from 4 to 9 years old as a function of prenatal cocaine exposure, environmental risk, and maternal verbal intelligence. *Developmental Psychology, 44,* 919–928. doi:10.1037/0012-1649.44.4.919

Booze, R. M., Wallace, D. R., Silvers, J. M., Strupp, B. J., Snow, D. M., & Mactutus, C. F. (2006). Prenatal cocaine exposure alters alpha2 receptor expression in adolescent rats. *BMC Neuroscience, 7*(33). doi:10.1186/1471-2202-7-33

Bunsey, M. D., & Strupp, B. J. (1995). Specific effects of idazoxan in a distraction task: Evidence that endogenous norepinephrine plays a role in selective attention in rats. *Behavioral Neuroscience, 109,* 903–911. doi:10.1037/0735-7044.109.5.903

Campbell, J. O., Bliven, T. D., Silveri, M. M., Snyder, K. J., & Spear, L. P. (2000). Effects of prenatal cocaine on behavioral adaptation to chronic stress in adult rats. *Neurotoxicology and Teratology, 22,* 845–850. doi:10.1016/S0892-0362(00)00104-5

Chasnoff, I. J., Anson, A., Hatcher, R., Stenson, H., Iaukea, K., & Randolph, L. A. (1998). Prenatal exposure to cocaine and other drugs. Outcome at four to six years. *Annals of the New York Academy of Sciences, 846,* 314–328. doi:10.1111/j.1749-6632.1998.tb09748.x

Chavkin, W., Wise, P. H., & Elman, D. (1998). Policies towards pregnancy and addiction. Sticks without carrots. *Annals of the New York Academy of Sciences, 846,* 335–340. doi:10.1111/j.1749-6632.1998.tb09750.x

Dennis, T., Bendersky, M., Ramsay, D., & Lewis, M. (2006). Reactivity and regulation in children prenatally exposed to cocaine. *Developmental Psychology, 42,* 688–697. doi:10.1037/0012-1649. 42.4.688

Devinsky, O., Morrell, M. J., & Vogt, B. A. (1995). Contributions of anterior cingulate cortex to behaviour. *Brain: A Journal of Neurology, 118,* 279–306. doi:10.1093/brain/118.1.279

Dow-Edwards, D. L. (1990). Fetal and maternal cocaine levels peak rapidly following intragastric administration in the rat. *Journal of Substance Abuse, 2,* 427–437.

Dow-Edwards, D. L., Mayes, L., Spear, L., & Hurd, Y. (1999). Cocaine and development: Clinical, behavioral, and neurobiological perspectives—a symposium report. *Neurotoxicology and Teratology, 21,* 481–490.

Dow-Edwards, D. L., Freed-Malen, L. A., & Hughes, H. E. (1993). Long-term alterations in brain function following cocaine administration during the preweanling period. *Developmental Brain Research, 72,* 309–313. doi:10.1016/0165-3806(93)90198-J

Elliott, R., Sahakian, B. J., McKay, A. P., Herrod, J. J., Robbins, T. W., & Paykel, E. S. (1996). Neuropsychological impairments in unipolar depression: The influence of perceived failure on subsequent performance. *Psychological Medicine: A Journal of Research in Psychiatry and the Allied Sciences, 26,* 975–989. doi:10.1017/S0033291700035303

Elsworth, J. D., Morrow, B. A., Nguyen, V. T., Mitra, J., Picciotto, M. R., & Roth, R. H. (2007). Prenatal cocaine exposure enhances responsivity of locus coeruleus norepinephrine neurons: Role of autoreceptors. *Neuroscience, 147,* 419–427. doi:10.1016/j.neuroscience.2007.04.036

Elsworth, J. D., Morrow, B. A., & Roth, R. H. (2001). Prenatal cocaine exposure increases mesoprefrontal dopamine neuron responsivity to mild stress. *Synapse, 42*(2), 80–83. doi:10.1002/syn.1102

Espy, K. A., Kaufmann, P. M., & Glisky, M. L. (1999). Neuropsychological function in toddlers exposed to cocaine in utero: A preliminary study. *Developmental Neuropsychology, 15,* 447–460. doi:10.1080/87565649909540761

Ferris, M. J., Mactutus, C. F., Silvers, J. M., Hasselrot, U., Beaudin, S. A., Strupp, B. J., & Booze, R. M. (2007). Sex mediates dopamine and adrenergic receptor expression in adult rats exposed prenatally to cocaine. *International Journal of Developmental Neuroscience, 25,* 445–454.

Garavan, H., Morgan, R. E., Mactutus, C. F., Levitsky, D. A., Booze, R. M., & Strupp, B. J. (2000). Prenatal cocaine exposure impairs selective attention: Evidence from serial reversal and extra-dimensional shift tasks. *Behavioral Neuroscience, 114,* 725–738. doi:10.1037/0735-7044.114.4.725

Gaultney, J. F., Gingras, J. L., Martin, M., & DeBrule, D. (2005). Prenatal cocaine exposure and infants' preference for novelty and distractibility. *The Journal of Genetic Psychology: Research and Theory on Human Development, 166,* 385–406. doi:10.3200/GNTP.166.4.385-406

Gendle, M. H., Strawderman, M. S., Mactutus, C. F., Booze, R. M., Levitsky, D. A., & Strupp, B. J. (2003). Impaired sustained attention and altered reactivity to errors in an animal model of prenatal cocaine exposure. *Developmental Brain Research, 147*(1–2), 85–96. doi:10.1016/j.devbrainres.2003.10.002

Gendle, M. H., Strawderman, M. S., Mactutus, C. F., Booze, R. M., Levitsky, D. A., & Strupp, B. J. (2004). Prenatal cocaine exposure does not alter working memory in adult rats. *Neurotoxicology and Teratology, 26,* 319–329. doi:10.1016/j.ntt.2003.12.001

Gendle, M. H., White, T. L., Strawderman, M., Mactutus, C. F., Booze, R. M., Levitsky, D. A., & Strupp, B. J. (2004). Enduring effects of prenatal cocaine exposure on selective attention and reactivity to errors: Evidence from an animal model. *Behavioral Neuroscience, 118,* 290–297. doi:10.1037/0735-7044.118.2.290

Granick, S. (1995). Psychological functioning of children exposed to cocaine prenatally. *Journal of Child & Adolescent Substance Abuse, 4,* 1–16. doi:10.1300/J029v04n03_01

Griffith, D. R., Azuma, S. D., & Chasnoff, I. J. (1994). Three-year outcome of children exposed prenatally to drugs. *Journal of the American Academy of Child & Adolescent Psychiatry, 33*(1), 20–27. doi:10.1097/00004583-199401000-00004

Hans, S. L. (1999). Demographic and psychosocial characteristics of substance-abusing pregnant women. *Clinics in Perinatology, 26*(1), 55–74.

Harvey, J. A. (2004). Cocaine effects on the developing brain: Current status. *Neuroscience and Biobehavioral Reviews, 27,* 751–764. doi:10.1016/j.neubiorev.2003.11.006

Heffelfinger, A. K., Craft, S., & Shyken, J. (1997). Visual attention in children with prenatal cocaine exposure. *Journal of the International Neuropsychological Society, 3,* 237–245.

Heffelfinger, A. K., Craft, S., White, D. A., & Shyken, J. (2002). Visual attention in preschool children prenatally exposed to cocaine: Implications for behavioral regulation. *Journal of the International Neuropsychological Society, 8*(1), 12–21. doi:10.1017/S135561770281102X

Heyser, C. J., Spear, N. E., & Spear, L. P. (1995). Effects of prenatal exposure to cocaine on Morris water maze performance in adult rats. *Behavioral Neuroscience, 109,* 734–743. doi:10.1037/0735-7044.109.4.734

Hilson, J. A., & Strupp, B. J. (1997). Analyses of response patterns clarify lead effects in olfactory reversal and extradimensional shift tasks: Assessment of inhibitory control, associative ability, and memory. *Behavioral Neuroscience, 111* 532–542. doi:10.1037/0735-7044.111.3.532

Huber, J., Darling, S., Park, K., & Soliman, K. F. (2001). Altered responsiveness to stress and NMDA following prenatal exposure to cocaine. *Physiology & Behavior, 72*(1–2), 181–188. doi:10.1016/S0031-9384(00)00410-8

Hurt, H., Malmud, E., Betancourt, L., Braitman, L. E., Brodsky, N. L., & Giannetta, J. (1997). Children with in utero cocaine exposure do not differ from control subjects on intelligence testing. *Archives of Pediatrics & Adolescent Medicine, 151,* 1237–1241.

Hutchings, D. E. (1993). The puzzle of cocaine's effects following maternal use during pregnancy: Are there reconcilable differences? *Neurotoxicology and Teratology, 15,* 281–286. doi:10.1016/0892-0362(93)90021-F

Kable, J. A., Coles, C. D., Lynch, M. E., & Platzman, K. (2008). Physiological responses to social and cognitive challenges in 8-year olds with a history of prenatal cocaine exposure. *Developmental Psychobiology, 50,* 251–265. doi:10.1002/dev.20285

Krauthammer, C. (1989, July 30). Children of cocaine. *The Washington Post,* p. C07.

LaGasse, L. L., Seifer, R., & Lester, B. M. (1999). Interpreting research on prenatal substance exposure in the context of multiple confounding factors. *Clinics in Perinatology, 26*(1), 39–54.

Laming, D. (1979). Choice reaction performance following an error. *Acta Psychologica, 43,* 199–224. doi:10.1016/0001-6918(79)90026-X

Leech, S. L., Richardson, G. A., Goldschmidt, L., & Day, N. L. (1999). Prenatal substance exposure: Effects on attention and impulsivity of 6-year-olds. *Neurotoxicology and Teratology, 21,* 109–118. doi:10.1016/S0892-0362(98)00042-7

Li, Z., Coles, C. D., Lynch, M. E., Hamann, S., Peltier, S., LaConte, S., & Hu, X. P. (2009). Prenatal cocaine exposure alters emotional arousal regulation and its effects on working memory. *Neurotoxicology and Teratology, 31,* 342–348. doi:10.1016/j.ntt.2009.08.005

Loebstein, R., & Koren, G. (1997). Pregnancy outcome and neurodevelopment of children exposed in utero to psychoactive drugs: The Motherisk experience. *Journal of Psychiatry & Neuroscience, 22*(3), 192–196.

Mactutus, C. F., Booze, R. M., & Dowell, R. T. (2000). The influence of route of administration on the acute cardiovascular effects of cocaine in conscious unrestrained pregnant rats. *Neurotoxicology and Teratology, 22,* 357–368. doi:10.1016/S0892-0362(99)00084-7

Mactutus, C. F., Herman, A. S., & Booze, R. M. (1994). Chronic intravenous model for studies of drug (Rabbitt & Rodgers) use in the pregnant and/or group-housed rat: An initial study with cocaine. *Neurotoxicology and Teratology, 16,* 183–191. doi:10.1016/0892-0362(94)90116-3

Mayes, L. C. (2002). A behavioral teratogenic model of the impact of prenatal cocaine exposure on arousal regulatory systems. *Neurotoxicology and Teratology, 24,* 385–395. doi:10.1016/S0892-0362(02)00200-3

Mayes, L. C., Grillon, C., Granger, R., & Schottenfeld, R. (1998). Regulation of arousal and attention in preschool children exposed to cocaine prenatally. *Annals of the New York Academy of Sciences, 846,* 126–143. doi:10.1111/j.1749-6632.1998.tb09731.x

Mayes, L. C., Molfese, D. L., Key, A. P., & Hunter, N. C. (2005). Event-related potentials in cocaine-exposed children during a Stroop task. *Neurotoxicology and Teratology, 27,* 797–813. doi:10.1016/j.ntt.2005.05.011

Molitor, A., Mayes, L. C., & Ward, A. (2003). Emotion regulation behavior during a separation procedure in 18-month-old children of mothers using cocaine and other drugs. *Development and Psychopathology, 15*(1), 39–54. doi:10.1017/S0954579403000038

Morgan, R. E., Garavan, H., Mactutus, C. F., Booze, R. M., & Strupp, B. J. (1998). Increased selectivity of attention in adult males following prenatal cocaine exposure [Abstract]. *Neurotoxicology and Teratology, 20,* 360–361.

Morgan, R. E., Levitsky, D. A., & Strupp, B. J. (1996). *Impaired redundant learning in male rats exposed to cocaine prenatally.* Unpublished data.

Morrow, B. A., Elsworth, D. J., & Roth, R. H. (2001). Prenatal exposure to cocaine reduces the number and enhances reactivity of A10 dopaminergic neurons to environmental stress. *Synapse, 41,* 337–344. doi:10.1002/syn.1090

Morrow, B. A., Elsworth, D. J., & Roth, R. H. (2002). Male rats exposed to cocaine in utero demonstrate elevated expression of Fos in the prefrontal cortex in response to environment. *Neuropsychopharmacology, 26,* 275–285. doi:10.1016/S0893-133X(01)00359-1

Morrow, B. A., Elsworth, D. J., & Roth, R. H. (2003). Axo-axonic structures in the medial prefrontal cortex of the rat: Reduction by prenatal cocaine exposure. *The Journal of Neuroscience, 23,* 5227–5234.

Morrow, B. A., Hajszan, T., Leranth, C., Elsworth, J. D., & Roth, R. H. (2007). Prenatal exposure to cocaine is associated with increased number of spine synapses in rat prelimbic cortex. *Synapse, 61,* 862–865. doi:10.1002/syn.20430

Noland, J. S., Singer, L. T., Short, E. J., Minnes, S., Arendt, R. E., Kirchner, H. L., & Bearer, C. (2005). Prenatal drug exposure and selective attention in preschoolers. *Neurotoxicology and Teratology, 27,* 429–438. doi:10.1016/j.ntt.2005.02.001

Overstreet, D. H., Moy, S. S., Lubin, D. A., Gause, L. R., Lieberman, J. A., & Johns, J. M. (2000). Enduring effects of prenatal cocaine administration on emotional behavior in rats. *Physiology & Behavior, 70*(1-2), 149–156. doi:10.1016/S0031-9384(00)00245-6

Rabbitt, P., & Rodgers, B. (1977). What does a man do after he makes an error? An analysis of response programming. *The Quarterly Journal of Experimental Psychology, 29,* 727–743. doi:10.1080/14640747708400645

Rao, H., Wang, J., Giannetta, J., Korczykowski, M., Shera, D., Avants, B. B., . . . Hurt, H. (2007). Altered resting cerebral blood flow in adolescents with in utero cocaine exposure revealed by perfusion functional MRI. *Pediatrics, 120,* e1245–e1254. doi:10.1542/peds.2006-2596

Reason, J. (1990). *Human error.* New York: Cambridge University Press.

Richardson, G. A., Conroy, M. L., & Day, N. L. (1996). Prenatal cocaine exposure: Effects on the development of school-age children. *Neurotoxicology and Teratology, 18,* 627–634. doi:10.1016/S0892-0362(96)00121-3

Robertson, I. H., Manly, T., Andrade, J., Baddeley, B. T., & Yiend, J. (1997). "Oops!": Performance correlates of everyday attentional failures in traumatic brain injured and normal subjects. *Neuropsychologia, 35,* 747–758. doi:10.1016/S0028-3932(97)00015-8

Rotholz, D. A., Snyder, P., & Peters, G. (1995). A behavioral comparison of preschool children at high and low risk from prenatal cocaine exposure. *Education & Treatment of Children, 18,* 1–18.

Rushworth, M. F., Hadland, K. A., Gaffan, D., & Passingham, R. E. (2003). The effect of cingulate cortex lesions on task switching and working memory. *Journal of Cognitive Neuroscience, 15,* 338–353. doi:10.1162/089892903321593072

Smith, L. M., Chang, L., Yonekura, M. L., Grob, C., Osborn, D., & Ernst, T. (2001). Brain proton magnetic resonance spectroscopy and imaging in children exposed to cocaine in utero. *Pediatrics, 107,* 227–231. doi:10.1542/peds.107.2.227

Snow, D. M., Carman, H. M., Smith, J. D., Booze, R. M., Welch, M. A., & Mactutus, C. F. (2004). Cocaine-induced inhibition of process outgrowth in locus coeruleus neurons: Role of gestational exposure period and offspring sex. *International Journal of Developmental Neuroscience, 22,* 297–308. doi:10.1016/j.ijdevneu.2004.06.004

Snyder, K. J., Katovic, N. M., & Spear, L. P. (1998). Longevity of the expression of behavioral sensitization to cocaine in preweanling rats. *Pharmacology, Biochemistry and Behavior, 60,* 909–914. doi:10.1016/S0091-3057(98)00078-1

Spear, L. P., Campbell, J., Snyder, K., Silveri, M., & Katovic, N. (1998). Animal behavior models. Increased sensitivity to stressors and other environmental experiences after prenatal cocaine exposure. *Annals of the New York Academy of Sciences, 846,* 76–88. doi:10.1111/j.1749-6632.1998.tb09728.x

Strupp, B. J., Morgan, R. E., Garavan, H., Mactutus, C. F., & Booze, R. M. (1998). Prenatal cocaine exposure: An emerging cognitive profile. *Neurotoxicology and Teratology, 20,* 355. doi:10.1016/S0892-0362(98)80587-4

Toufexis, A. (1991, May 13). Innocent victims. *Time, 137,* 56–60.

Wang, X. H., Jenkins, A. O., Choi, L., & Murphy, E. H. (1996). Altered neuronal distribution of parvalbumin in anterior cingulate cortex of rabbits exposed in utero to cocaine. *Experimental Brain Research, 112,* 359–371. doi:10.1007/BF00227942

Wang, X. H., Levitt, P., Grayson, D. R., & Murphy, E. H. (1995). Intrauterine cocaine exposure of rabbits: Persistent elevation of GABA-immunoreactive neurons in anterior cingulate cortex but not visual cortex. *Brain Research, 689,* 32–46. doi:10.1016/0006-8993(95)00528-X

Warner, T. D., Behnke, M., Eyler, F. D., Padgett, K., Leonard, C., Hou, W., . . . Blackband, S. J. (2006). Diffusion tensor imaging of frontal white matter and executive functioning in cocaine-exposed children. *Pediatrics, 118,* 2014–2024. doi:10.1542/peds.2006-0003

Wasserman, G. A., Kline, J. K., Bateman, D. A., Chiriboga, C., Lumey, L. H., Friedlander, H., . . . Heagarty, M. C. (1998). Prenatal cocaine exposure and school-age intelligence. *Drug and Alcohol Dependence, 50,* 203–210. doi:10.1016/S0376-8716(98)00037-4

Wood, R. D., Molina, V. A., Wagner, J. M., & Spear, L. P. (1995). Play behavior and stress responsivity in periadolescent offspring exposed prenatally to cocaine. *Pharmacology, Biochemistry and Behavior, 52,* 367–374. doi:10.1016/0091-3057(95)00120-L

Part II _____

Tobacco and Marijuana

5

Examination of Gender Differences in Effects of Tobacco Exposure

Claire D. Coles, Julie A. Kable, and Mary Ellen Lynch

Although there are several ways in which a child can be exposed to tobacco, most attention has been directed toward maternal use during gestation or prenatal tobacco exposure. This use of cigarettes by pregnant women naturally raises concerns about teratogenic effects on the embryo and fetus. It has been demonstrated that during such tobacco exposure, the contents of the smoke, particularly nicotine, reach the fetus. Nicotine and its by-product, cotinine, are found in fetal serum and amniotic fluid at concentrations 15% higher than those found in maternal blood (Slotkin, 1998) and can persist for 15 to 20 hr. There can be some additional environmental tobacco smoke (ETS) exposure as a result of use by other household members, but the drug levels from this other environmental exposure during pregnancy are very small in comparison with those resulting from maternal use prenatally. Postnatally, nicotine and cotinine can be transferred to infants through nursing by smoking mothers (Polifka, 1998) and through secondhand smoke exposure from other household members and from the environment. The frequency of such exposure is significant. Eiden (2009) reported that 46% of 2,189 women screened either smoked or lived with a smoker. Among nonsmoking women, 19.4% lived with a smoker. Schuster, Franke, and Pham (2002) reported that 35% of children lived in smoking households and even when both parents did not smoke, 16% were exposed in the home. The environmental context for secondhand smoke exposure includes both the home and various public spaces. In addition, vehicles in which the child is traveling are another very significant source (Emerson et al., 1994). A final source of exposure is use by children themselves, a risk that increases with age and becomes significant during adolescence, with 47.1% of 12th graders in the Monitoring the Future study reporting having used tobacco at some time (Johnston, O'Malley, Bachman, & Schulenberg, 2006). Whereas the focus of this chapter is on the effects of prenatal exposure, many recent studies also address these other sources of exposure, and increasing attention is being paid to such environmental exposures.

Epidemiology of Tobacco Use in Pregnancy

In the United States, although smoking has declined in recent years, a significant proportion of women still use cigarettes during pregnancy, reflecting the number of women who continue to smoke overall. Since the late 1990s, reports concerning smoking rates for women of childbearing age have ranged from 20% to 25% (National Center for Health Statistics, 2007), with the rate for 2008 estimated to be 21.1% (National Center for Health Statistics, 2008). Thus, it is not surprising that, despite warnings about the effects of prenatal smoking on infant health and legal restrictions on where individuals can smoke, a large percentage of women (estimated at 12% to 22%) still continue to smoke during pregnancy (Centers for Disease Control and Prevention, 2004). In addition, unlike users of many other addictive substances, pregnant smokers often do not stop or significantly decrease use once pregnant. Of those women participating in the National Health Interview Survey, only 27% were able to quit use immediately when told that they were pregnant; an additional 12% were able to quit by the third trimester (Fingerhut, Kleinman, & Kendrick, 1990). In 2004, Ershoff, Ashford and Goldenberg reported that it was rare for cessation programs for pregnant smokers to achieve quit rates above 20%. Taken together, these rates suggest a basis for concern about the effects on the fetus and the developing child.

Social and Environmental Factors Associated With Maternal Tobacco Use

Smoking in pregnancy is frequently associated with other maternal characteristics that are related to less optimal outcomes for children. These include low socioeconomic status, maternal psychopathology, and life stress (e.g., Fergusson, Woodward, & Horwood, 1998; Kodl & Wakschlag, 2004; Maughan, Taylor, Caspi, & Moffitt, 2004). In human studies, it can be difficult to disentangle the direct teratogenic effects of prenatal tobacco exposure from the effect of these associated factors. An examination of demographic variables suggests that pregnant women who smoke are more likely than nonsmokers to be less well educated, to come from low-income families, and, in some studies, to be unmarried (e.g., Fergusson et al., 1998; Flick et al., 2006; Maughan et al., 2004; Pickett, Wood, Adamson, D'Souza, & Wakschlag, 2008; Weaver, Campbell, Mermelstein, & Wakschlag, 2008). Not surprisingly, such women experience more life stress. Wakschlag et al. (2003) found that persistent smoking in pregnancy was related to both difficulties with adaptive functioning (including experience of stressful life events) and interpersonal problems (e.g., aggressive interactions, difficult partner relationships).

Several studies suggest that women who smoke in pregnancy are more likely than nonsmokers to exhibit signs or symptoms of current or childhood psychopathology, including being more likely to engage in antisocial behavior or to meet criteria for externalizing disorders (e.g., Flick et al., 2006; Kodl & Wakschlag, 2004; Maughan et al., 2004; Wakschlag et al., 2003). On the basis of more than 700 psychiatric interviews with pregnant women who were eligible for Medicaid, Flick et al. (2006) reported that smokers were nearly 3 times more likely than nonsmokers to meet or to have met criteria for behavior or psychiatric disorders. Kodl and Wakschlag (2004) reported that persistent smoking in pregnancy was associated with maternal report of childhood externalizing problems. Other studies suggest that there is a relationship between smoking in pregnancy and internalizing problems, that is to say, depression or anxiety (Maughan et al., 2004; Pickett et al., 2008).

Wakschlag et al. (2003) suggested that persistent smoking in pregnancy may be viewed as one part of a pattern of maternal problem behavior. They emphasized that smoking is frequently not the only problem behavior exhibited by pregnant women "but rather, part of a long-standing pattern of problematic behavior across interpersonal, adaptive, and health domains" (p. 2450). These differences in background and personal characteristics between mothers who do and do not smoke during pregnancy may affect the care provided to the child. Although an impact on child health and nutrition is certainly possible, it seems likely that these factors affect behavioral and developmental characteristics in children and adolescents (e.g., Wakschlag, Leventhal, Pine, Pickett, & Carter, 2006; Wakschlag, Pickett, Cook, Benowitz, & Leventhal, 2002). This perspective seems particularly true in the current social environment in which smoking is viewed as an antisocial act. Understanding outcomes from this perspective may provide an interpretation with more explanatory power for findings that link smoking in pregnancy to negative behavioral outcomes in children, particularly when different responses are observed for males and females.

Developmental Impact of Prenatal Tobacco Exposure and Sex Differences

There are a number of areas of potential effects on development. The research on a number of these areas is examined in this section.

Growth and Development

Growth retardation, specifically birth weight, was the first area to be a focus of concern about the effects of prenatal exposure (Simpson, 1957), and growth differences have been found consistently (Abel, 1984; Werler, Pober, & Holmes, 1985; Willford, Day, & Cornelius, 2006). As early as 1957, Simpson reported that smokers' infants were twice as likely to have low birth weight, a finding that has been replicated frequently (Willford et al., 2006). For those who continue to smoke during pregnancy, the risk for a small-for-gestational-age infant is 2 to 4 times higher, with exposed neonates averaging 200 to 300 grams less than nonsmokers' infants (Kearney, 1999). A clear dose–response relationship between number of cigarettes used per day and birth weight has been observed even when other potentially confounding factors are controlled (i.e. age, parity, maternal weight gain, pre-pregnancy weight:height ratio, gestational age, socioeconomic status, and race; Abel, 1984; Werler et al., 1985; Willford et al., 2006).

There is little in the literature to suggest that this impact on growth differs by gender. Two studies (Conter, Cortinovis, Rogari, & Riva, 1995; Wertelecki, Hoff, & Zansky, 1987) have reported a significantly greater decrement in birth weight in males, whereas a study in Japan (Saito, 1991) found that the deficit was greater in females. Given the extensive literature in this area that reports no effects, these studies are not persuasive.

A second question concerns postnatal growth. Consistent with recent research on the consequence of low birth weight (J. S. Huang, Lee, & Lu, 2007), smokers' infants who showed an initial impact on growth at birth are sometimes more likely to be overweight as older children (Cornelius, Goldschmidt, Day, & Larkby, 2002; Fried, Watkinson, & Gray, 1999; Ong, Preece, Emmett, Ahmed, & Dunger, 2002; Toschke, Koletzko, Slikker, Hermann, & von Kries, 2002; Vik, Jacobsen, Vatten, & Bakketig, 1996) and as adults (Power & Jefferis, 2002). There is also evidence that these children may have an increased risk for diabetes and other obesity-related health conditions (R. C. Huang et al., 2007; Montgomery & Ekbom, 2002). Overall, prenatal tobacco exposure appears to be related to an initial growth retardation that is not maintained and may be associated with excessive weight gain over time (Willford, Day, & Cornelius, 2006). However, this weight gain is not always seen. Cornelius, Leech, and Larkby (2007) reported that the weight differential noted at 6 years (Cornelius et al., 2002) was not present in the same children at 10 years.

There is little evidence for sex differences in postnatal growth. Most investigators have not used sex as a factor in such analyses but instead have controlled for it statistically (Cornelius to Claire Coles, personal communication, December 15, 2009). However, in their longitudinal cohort study, Fried et al. (1999), who found no growth-related gender differences at birth, reported that the weight gain in male versus female toddlers exposed to tobacco was significantly greater.

A few studies have examined the effect on pubertal onset in the children of smokers. Fried, James, and Watkinson (2001) reported that heavy (>16 cigarettes/day) prenatal tobacco exposure was associated with early appearance of pubertal milestones in males but not in females. In contrast, Reynolds et al. (2004) found evidence for early onset of menarche in the California Teachers Study Cohort. This finding was supported initially by Windham, Bottomley, Birner, and Fenster (2004), who found that both prenatal and postnatal environmental exposure were associated with early menarche. However, in a follow-up study using data from the Collaborative Perinatal Project, the same group found the opposite effect, with daughters of heavy smokers showing a significant delay in puberty onset (Windham, Zhang, Longnecker, & Klebanoff, 2008). Thus, there are both limited research and inconsistent results on the effect of tobacco smoke exposure on pubertal onset. Finally, in one study, fecundity in women was examined as a function of prenatal exposure, with children of smokers showing reduced fertility (Weinberg, Wilcox, & Baird, 1989).

Respiratory Problems and Ear Infections

The health of tobacco-exposed infants has been a major concern, and a number of problems have been reported. In interpreting these results, it is important to keep in mind that prenatal and postnatal exposure are clearly confounded in many cases. In general, tobacco exposure is associated with decreased lung function (Moshammer et al., 2006) and increased airway responsivity. A high risk for obstructive sleep apnea has been reported in infants of mothers who smoked during pregnancy (Sawnani, Jackson, Murphy, Beckerman, & Simakajornboon,

2004), and bronchitis and pneumonia are more common in early studies (Colley, Holland, & Corkhill, 1974; Harlap & Davies, 1974). An increased incidence of asthma, although not allergy-based asthma, has been associated with tobacco exposure (Jaakkola & Gissler, 2004; Kershaw, 1987) as well as an aggravation of asthmatic symptoms (Evans et al., 1987). Asthma is generally found to be exacerbated by ETS, but there is inconsistent evidence for asthma induction (Wang & Pinkerton, 2008). With the exception of a few studies, the suggestion of sex difference in this outcome area has not been supported or has yielded contradictory data. For instance, Alati, Mamun, O'Callaghan, Najman, and Williams (2006) reported that girls in an Australian cohort were more susceptible to asthma, whereas Jaakkola and Gissler (2007) specifically examined this question in relation to asthma in a large Finnish cohort and concluded that there were no such differences. Li et al. (2000) examined medical history and tobacco exposure in 5,263 participants in the Children's Health Study and found that both males and females showed effects on lung function when they were exposed to tobacco prenatally. In addition, the relationship between ETS, asthma, and gender were examined. Males were more likely to be affected if they had a history of asthma, whereas females were more affected if they did not have such a history.

There has been a good deal of attention to ear infections in children of smokers. There are multiple reviews of the relationship between tobacco exposure and otitis media (e.g., Cook, Strachean, & Carey, 1998) as well as meta-analyses of the relationship between tobacco exposure, especially ETS, and otitis media, with the majority of these studies concluding that there is an increased risk in this area (e.g., Adair-Bischoff & Sauve, 1998; Ilicali, Keles, Deier, Saiun, & Guldiken, 2001). In addition, there is evidence that prenatal exposure is associated with a greater risk than postnatal exposure (Stathis et al., 1999). There is no indication of gender differences in this area.

Overall, recent reviews (DiFranza, Aligne, & Weitzman, 2004; Wang & Pinkerton, 2008) of the impact of tobacco exposure on infant and child health have emphasized that it is very difficult to discriminate the effects of prenatal and postnatal exposure, although prenatal exposure seems to have a greater effect in some areas (e.g., lung function; Cunningham, Dockery, & Speizer, 1994; Li et al., 2000). In addition, given the wealth of research in this area and the lack of significant effects on sex differences, it is difficult to conclude that there is evidence for gender differences in the impact of tobacco exposure on respiratory health or otitis media.

Cognition and Learning

The evidence for an impact of tobacco exposure on cognition and learning is somewhat mixed. The examination of neurocognitive and behavioral development has produced contradictory results, particularly for general cognitive status and overall academic achievement (e.g., Butler & Goldstein, 1973; Cornelius, Ryan, Day, Goldschmidt, & Willford, 2001; Dunn, McBurney, Ingram, & Hunter, 1977; Fergusson & Lloyd, 1991; Fogelman, 1980; Fried & Watkinson, 1990; Fried, Watkinson, & Gray, 1998, 2003; Hardy & Mellits,

1972; MacArthur, Knox, & Lancashire, 2001; Naeye & Peters, 1984; Streissguth, Barr, Sampson, Darby, & Martin, 1989; Trasti, Vik, Jacobsen, & Bakketeigg, 1999). Olds (1997) suggested that design and methodological issues may account for the lack of clarity in the existing data. There are many factors associated with tobacco (e.g., socioeconomic status) that have a significant effect on cognition and achievement and that, unless controlled, can affect results. Such systematic bias can be a particular problem in this area of research because attitudes about smoking have been changing dramatically over a relatively short time period (historically), and such changes probably affect the extent to which outcomes are influenced by such potentially confounding factors. The relationship between the cognitive outcomes of maternal smoking and potentially confounding factors has been investigated recently by Batty, Der, and Deary (2006) and Breslau, Paneth, Lucia, and Paneth-Pollak (2005). Both groups of investigators used large cohorts to evaluate the effects of maternal smoking on ability level (i.e., IQ) when social and familial factors are controlled. In both studies, the initial significant relationships between smoking and IQ are explained when maternal socioeconomic status, IQ, and education are considered. No differences by gender are reported.

Although these previous results argue against an effect of tobacco exposure on global cognition, there is some evidence that there may be more specific effects. In a study that controlled for other prenatal substance exposure, current tobacco exposure, and multiple socioeconomic status covariates, Cornelius, Ryan, et al. (2001) found a relationship among prenatal tobacco exposure, verbal learning and memory, and hand–eye coordination in a sample of 10-year-olds. Gender was included as a control variable, but no systematic differences were noted.

Problems with academic achievement have been documented (see a review by Eskenazi & Castorina, 1999, on ETS but including prenatal exposure). With a sample from the National Collaborative Perinatal Project, deficits in learning and achievement were noted, particularly problems in reading and spelling (Hardy & Mellits, 1972; Makin, Fried, & Watkinson, 1991; Naeye & Peters, 1984). In a large Finnish sample followed from birth through 12 years, Martin, Dombrowski, Mullis, Wisenbaker, and Huttunen (2006) found both decreased achievement and increased immaturity and distractibility attributable to prenatal smoking. However, other investigators have reported no academic problems (Fergusson & Lloyd, 1991).

Sex Differences

Collins, Wileyto, Murphy, and Munafo (2007) used a British cohort to examine the impact of prenatal tobacco exposure on academic achievement, specifically the likelihood of passing the required "O" level and "A" level examination by male and female adolescents. This study, which followed children born in 1958, yielded contradictory results: Exposed females were less likely to pass the ordinary or O level examinations, and males were less likely to pass the advanced A levels. In contrast, Martin et al. (2006) looked for but did not find gender effects on achievement and behavior in their Finnish cohort.

Auditory Processing and Language

Although it is difficult to come to a conclusion about general effects on cognition and achievement, there is stronger evidence that prenatal tobacco exposure, as well as postnatal exposure, specifically compromises auditory functioning. These effects have been observed across the life span by several investigators who used a variety of methodologies. In the prenatal period, fetal monitoring has indicated that fetuses of women who were smokers were less responsive to maternal speech than were those of the nonsmokers (Cowperthwaite, Hains, & Kisilevsky, 2007). Key et al. (2006) used event-related potential to evaluate the impact of prenatal tobacco exposure on the ability of newborns to process speech (consonant sounds); they foundthat response to consonant sounds is altered (slowed). In early infancy, poorer auditory habituation on the Brazelton Neonatal Behavioral Assessment Scale (Brazelton & Nugent, 1995) has been reported by a number of authors (Fried & Makin, 1987; Jacobson, Fein, Jacobson, Schwartz, & Dowler, 1984; Picone, Allen, Olsen, & Ferris, 1982). In polygraphic studies of sleep, Franco et al. (1999) found that infants of smokers showed decreased arousal to auditory stimuli both as newborns and at 12 weeks. At 6 months of age, infants exposed prenatally to tobacco smoke demonstrated poorer cardiac orienting responses to auditory stimuli while performing comparably to a reference group when exposed to visual stimuli (Kable, 1995). In a different sample of 6-month-olds, we found a dose–response relationship between maternal prenatal tobacco use and reduced latency of auditory brainstem evoked responses. These results suggested that there was an impact on sensory encoding of auditory stimuli that may impact auditory perception (Kable, Coles, Lynch, & Carroll, 2009a), and we hypothesized that this finding was probably a result of effects of prenatal nicotine on the cholinergic receptors along the auditory pathway (Slotkin, 2004). At 12 and 24 months, infants demonstrate tobacco-related differences on an auditory cluster derived from the Infant Behavior Record of the Bayley Scales of Infant Development (BSID; Bayley, 1993; Fried & Watkinson, 1988; Kable, Coles, Lynch, & Carroll, 2009b). Among 4- to 7-year-olds, Fried and colleagues found deficits in performance on auditory, but not visual, vigilance tasks (Kristjansson, Fried, & Watkinson, 1989) and among 6- to 11-year-olds, on a central auditory processing task (McCartney, Fried, & Watkinson, 1994).

Although there are very few studies in this area, deficits in early language development and specific aspects of later language development have been observed among offspring of mothers who smoked in pregnancy. Evidence comes mostly from the middle class Ottawa Prenatal Prospective Study cohort, where maternal smoking was associated with lower scores on several measures of language and verbal intelligence (Fried & Watkinson, 1990). Although not observed in infancy, these effects were noticed by 48 months and persisted into middle childhood, affecting verbal memory tasks (Fried, O'Connell, & Watkinson, 1992; Fried, Watkinson, & Gray, 1992) as well as phonology and articulation (Makin et al., 1991) and later verbal memory skills in adolescents (Fried, Watkinson, & Gray, 2003). These negative outcomes were associated with both maternal active smoking status during pregnancy and postnatal passive environmental exposure (Makin et al., 1991). In different samples that provide converging evidence, prelinguistic skills in 6-month-olds (Coles, Kable, Lynch, & Johnson, 2008; Kable, 1995) and vocalization of vowel–consonant combinations in 8-month-olds (Obel, Henriksen, Hedegaard, Secher, & Ostergaard, 1998) were delayed in smokers' children. In a sample of preschoolers, vocabulary expression (Kukla, Hruba, & Tyrlik, 2006) was impaired among children whose mothers smoked in pregnancy. In a study focusing on cocaine exposure but controlling for tobacco, Lewis et al. (2007) found that tobacco exposure affected receptive but not expressive language during the first 6 years of life. In this study, main effects for sex (with males performing more poorly than females) were found, but no interactions with tobacco exposure were reported.

Specific aspects of reading development that are influenced by auditory and phonetic perception skills also appear to be impacted by prenatal exposure. Fried and his colleagues (Fried et al., 2003; Fried, Watkinson, & Siegel, 1997) found no differences in reading vocabulary or comprehension among school-aged children after adjusting for environmental factors but did find that prenatal exposure was related to poorer performance in reading pseudo words suggesting difficulties with understanding the phonological coding of written language (Fried et al., 1997). Negative relationships between maternal smoking and general reading achievement are reported by some investigators (e.g., Bauman, Flewelling, & LaPrelle, 1991; Butler & Goldstein, 1973; Fogelman, 1980; Naeye & Peters, 1984; Sexton, Fox, & Hebel, 1990) but not others (Fergusson & Lloyd, 1991; Hardy & Mellits, 1972; Lefkowitz, 1981).

As a result of such findings, Fried and his colleagues (Fried, 1998; Fried, Watkinson, & Siegel, 1997) hypothesized that the language and reading difficulties in tobacco-exposed children result from problems in auditory functioning. They suggested that impaired auditory processing and phonemic perception disrupt early language development and subsequent reading skills. These links among tobacco exposure, language development, and reading problems were consistently found in the middle class sample followed by this group and have been reported in other samples with different socioeconomic characteristics.

Given these findings, we can look further to determine whether there are gender differences in teratogenic impact. Animal models suggest that the effects of prenatal tobacco exposure may be the result of the impact of nicotine on the cortical cholinergic systems and that there may be sex differences in response (Slotkin et al., 2007). Such systems are implicated in auditory processing and attention. In a human sample ($N = 181$), Jacobsen, Slotkin, Menci, Frost, and Pugh (2007) evaluated effects of both prenatal tobacco exposure and use during adolescence on auditory and visual attention. Based on the animal studies that found different patterns of response in male and female rats, these investigators looked for gender-specific effects on their outcomes. They reported that, among females, either prenatal exposure or adolescent use by the participants themselves was associated with lower performance accuracy on both auditory and visual attention tasks. If girls were exposed at both time points, the effects were greater. In males, exposure at both time points was associated with significant deficits on auditory attention only, although males in all categories performed least well in the auditory attention condition. The auditory effect in tobacco-exposed males was much greater than either of the effects in females. At the same time, there were no gender differences in plasma cotinine levels, which suggests that the current tobacco exposure levels did not differ meaningfully. Reaction time during the procedure was not affected by gender. The authors also noted that children who were exposed prenatally were also exposed to higher levels of ETS as a result of parental smoking. These authors suggested that exposure to tobacco smoke may reduce the efficiency of central auditory processing by reducing the selectivity of auditory perception. This suggestion is consistent with the findings of Key et al. (2007) in newborns and our own work on phonemic perception and language development (Kable et al., 2009a, 2009b). However, Jacobsen et al. (2007) were the only researchers to report a gender effect on these functions.

Behavior and Behavior Regulation

There is a great deal of evidence that tobacco exposure is associated with arousal dysregulation and behavior problems of various severity, including attention-deficit/hyperactivity disorder (ADHD), antisocial behavior, and criminality. Differences in behavior have been observed over the whole of childhood, beginning in the fetal period (Zeskind & Gingras, 2005) and seen in later infancy (Horne, Franco, Adamson, Groswasser, & Kahn, 2004; Leech, Richardson, Goldschmidt, & Day, 1999; Schuetze & Eiden, 2006) and in older children in the areas of poorer attentional control (Fried, Watkinson, & Gray, 1992; Noland et al., 2005; Streissguth, Martin, Barr, & Sandman, 1984) and behavioral and conduct problems (Brook, Zhang, Rosenberg, & Brook, 2006; Cornelius, Leech, & Larkby, 2001; Day, Richardson, Goldschmidt, & Cornelius, 2000; Fergusson, Woodward, & Horwood, 1998; Linnet et al., 2003; Millberger, Biederman, Faraone, & Jones, 1998; Montreaux, Blacker, Biederman, Fitzmaurice, & Buka, 2006; Naeye & Peters, 1984; Nigg & Breslau, 2007; Orlebeke, Knol, & Verhulst, 1999; Rantakallio, Laara, Isohanni, & Moilanen, 1992; Streissguth et al., 1984; Thapar et al., 2003; Wakschlag, Pickett, Kasza, & Loeber, 2006; Wakschlag et al., 1997; Wasserman, Pine, Workman, & Bruder, 1999; Weissman, Warner, Wickramaratne, & Kandel, 1999; Weitzman, Byrd, Aligne, & Moss, 2002; Williams et al., 1998). Martin et al. (2006) followed children from birth to 12 years and found that teachers rated prenatally exposed children as more distractible and immature and less task oriented in academic situations. Epidemiological studies in adulthood also support these findings (e.g., Brennan, Grekin, & Mednick, 1999; Räsänen et al., 1999). However, a number of authors have argued that these effects are the result of social and genetic factors that, when controlled, eliminate significant effects of prenatal tobacco exposure. For instance, Gilman, Gardener, and Buka (2008) used the large Collaborative Perinatal Project cohort (N = 52,919) collected between 1959 and 1974 to study the characteristics of children from birth through 7 years and concluded that smoking more than a pack a day was associated with effects on birth weight and being overweight at 7 years; however, they found that when multiple confounding factors were controlled, there was no evidence of effects on 12 other outcomes, including intelligence, academic achievement, and behavior.

For the most part, studies of tobacco exposure have not had gender differences as a principal focus. Often sex is included as a covariate, and when behavior problems are the outcome, males usually show a greater effect. However, interactions of tobacco exposure with gender are rarely noted. In many articles, this issue is not discussed or is only alluded to. In some cases, it is specifically removed from the analysis. For example, Button, Thapar, and McGuffin (2005) carried out a study of prenatal tobacco exposure and later behavior problems (ADHD and antisocial behavior) in 2,082 pairs of twins in the Cardiff Twin Study. These children were born between 1980 and 1991 and were 5 to 9 years of age when outcome data were collected. In their data analysis the authors used a gender limitation model to identify sex differences in outcomes and found no tobacco exposure-related differences for ADHD and a small but significant difference for antisocial behavior. They reported this finding (without noting which gender is more "antisocial"), and they noted that because this was not focus of their work, they had covaried out the gender effect for further analyses. As this is a common practice, the body of data available to examine the effects of gender or the interaction of gender with prenatal tobacco exposure is limited.

In the studies described in this section, information was available to compare effects in males and females. As part of a study of effects of prenatal exposure on auditory processing and language development, we examined differences in rates of behavior problems in 24-month-olds using the Child Behavior Checklist (CBCL; Achenbach & Rescorla, 2000). On this maternal report measure, there were significant gender differences on the Attention and Aggressive Behavior subscales, with trends for the Externalizing and Total Problems composite as well as for Somatic Complaints, although none of these groups scored in the clinically significant range. More specifically, these were significant Gender X Tobacco Exposure interactions for the Externalizing and Total Problems composites. This interaction occurred because girls were reported to have significantly fewer behavior problems than boys in the control group, but boys and girls were about equal in the smoking groups (Johnson, Lynch, Kable, & Coles, 2009).

However, other studies using the same measures have different conclusions. In the Netherlands, Orlebeke et al. (1999) also evaluated the effects of smoking on behavior using CBCL in a sample of 3-year-old twins. They found increased externalizing behavior, particularly aggression, as a function of maternal tobacco use in pregnancy; males were found to be more aggressive overall. As a result, these investigators evaluated their data to look for interactions between sex and tobacco exposure and found none. In both males and females, prenatal tobacco exposure increased aggression to the same degree. Williams et al. (1998) examined behavior at age 5 in 4,879 Australian children. They noted that externalizing behavior as measured by the CBCL was specifically affected in children of smokers and followed a dose–response pattern. Behavior problems were associated with smoking early in pregnancy rather than later. In addition, children who were exposed only postnatally also demonstrated an increase in behavior problems. However, no sex differences in behavior response were seen. Cornelius, Leech, and Larkby (2001) also used the CBCL as well as the SNAP (to measure symptoms of ADHD, particularly impulsivity; Swanson et al., 2004) with children of teenaged mothers in the Maternal Health Practices and Child Development Project in Pittsburgh. Maternal smoking was found to predict children's activity level (but not externalizing behavior or aggression) at 6 years even when many potential confounding factors were controlled. One of these factors was child gender, which was independently related to impulsivity although not to aggression or total behavior problems as measured by the CBCL. However, sex was not used as a factor in this study and does not appear to interact with tobacco exposure.

Studies in later childhood confirm the persistence of behavior problems in children of smokers. Wakschlag et al. (1997) used a diagnostic interview to do a 6-year follow-up with boys ages 7 to 12 years and reported an increased level of conduct disorder when mothers smoked 10 or more cigarettes daily during pregnancy. However, girls were not included in this sample, making any conclusions about male/female differences impossible. Millberger et al. (1998) carried out similar studies with boys diagnosed with ADHD and a contrast group and concluded, in a retrospective analysis of this clinical sample, that prenatal smoking was more common among children who demonstrated symptoms of ADHD. Weissman et al. (1999) evaluated both males and females in a relatively small sample whose exposure was retrospectively assessed. They noted a significant increase in behavior disorders in male offspring and a fivefold increase in drug use by adolescent girls. This finding could be taken to demonstrate a gender difference but could also be interpreted as showing similar effects for both males and females. Although these findings are suggestive, the design of these studies (retrospective and based on clinic samples) makes it difficult to interpret outcomes in relation to gender differences. Clinic referrals are almost always much higher for male children, and males almost always have higher scores on ratings of behavior problems, factors that might result in systematic ascertainment biases.

Yolton et al. (2008) examined the impact of ETS exposure on behavior in a sample of children (ages 6 to 12 years) enrolled in an asthma intervention trial. Of these, 66% had been exposed to tobacco prenatally and all were exposed postnatally to an average of 13 to 20 cigarettes daily. The Behavior Assessment System for Children (C. R. Reynolds & Kamphaus, 1992) was used to measure child behavior problems. When cotinine was measured, girls showed significantly higher levels, but behavior problems overall were at clinically significant levels only in males. Thus, there was a relationship between current cotinine (indicating current environmental tobacco exposure) and behavior problems in males only. Girls' behavior was predicted by other maternal and caregiving characteristics. In contrast, Braun, Kahn, Froehlich, Auinger, and Lanphear (2006) examined a large sample of American children and evaluated the effects of lead and prenatal tobacco exposure on ADHD symptoms. Although such symptoms are significantly more likely to be found in those exposed to these toxins, no sex differences were reported.

In young adults, Brennan et al. (1999) and Räsänen et al (1999) studied the association between criminality and prenatal tobacco exposure in large cohorts using publicly available records that included prenatal assessment of maternal smoking. These researchers found that in males only, in Denmark and Finland, tobacco exposure was associated with more violent and persistent offenses.

Wakschlag et al. (2002) reviewed the existing literature on severe anti-social behavior reported in offspring of women smoking in pregnancy and found a strong association. They reported on seven studies that addressed this issue. Four evaluated conduct disorder (Fergusson et al., 1998; Wakschlag et al., 1997; Wakschlag & Keenan, 2001; Weissman et al., 1999) and three criminal behavior (Brennan et al., 1999; Gibson, Piquero, & Tibbets, 2000; Räsänen et al., 1999). Three of the studies of conduct disorder were clinic based and retrospective; only Fergusson et al. (1998) reported on a population based, longitudinally followed cohort. All of the studies of criminal behavior employed prospectively followed cohorts with maternal smoking established at birth. As part of this review, the authors examined gender differences in the incidence of antisocial behavior and concluded that tobacco-exposed males were at higher risk of exhibiting such behavior than were unexposed males. However, females were not included in most (six of seven) of these studies because of the generally lower incidence of antisocial behavior in females; in their epidemiological study that included both genders, Gibson et al. (2000) found no sex differences in the increased incidence of antisocial behavior associated with tobacco exposure. Wakschlag et al. (2002) also noted that several factors that might affect the development of antisocial behavior were uncontrolled in these as well as most other studies of effects of tobacco exposure on behavior. Subsequently, Brennan, Grekin, Mortensen, and Mednick (2002) published a study of adult behavior in a Danish cohort that included both males and females. In this study, a dose–response relationship was found between maternal smoking prenatally and both criminal arrest and psychiatric hospitalization particularly in males. In females, criminal arrest was also related to maternal third trimester smoking, but there was not as clear a dose–response relationship; the authors suggested that female arrests are mediated by hospitalization for substance abuse.

Understanding the etiology of behavior problems and ADHD is difficult because there are many different contributors to such behavior. An association between dopamine genes, including the human dopamine transporter (*DAT1*), and ADHD symptoms has been found (Maher, Marazita, Ferrell, & Vanyukov, 2002). However even in these genetic studies, the results in this area are not consistent, causing Becker, El-Faddach, Schmidt, Esser, and Laucht (2008) to suggest that environmental factors, including prenatal tobacco exposure, may be moderating the association. A small number of studies have examined the interaction of genetic factors (specifically dopamine genes) and tobacco exposure on ADHD symptoms (i.e., Becker et al., 2008; Brookes et al., 2006; Kahn, Khoury, Nichols, & Lanphear, 2003; Neuman et al., 2006; Wiebe et al., 2009). These results were inconsistent; two of these studies (Brookes et al., 2006; Neuman et al., 2006) reported no support for an interaction of prenatal tobacco use and genetics on behavior, whereas Kahn et al. (2003), Becker et al. (2008), and Wiebe et al. (2009) found such effects. Becker et al.'s research was carried out in a cohort of German children in middle adolescence, and it not only identified a relationship between prenatal tobacco exposure and the *DAT1* genotype (human dopamine transporter) but also found a sex effect. Only males in this study were more likely to show ADHD-like symptoms if they were prenatally exposed and had the *DAT1* +/+ genotype. Females did not appear to be affected in this way by either prenatal exposure or their genotype but exhibited ADHD symptoms only if they had higher levels of psychosocial adversity. In a prospective study, Wiebe et al. examined gene–environment interactions with the impact of prenatal tobacco exposure. They evaluated neonates' behavior and executive functioning in preschoolers and found that D_2 dopamine receptor expression (A1+) interacted with tobacco exposure in the neonatal period, producing effects on attention and irritability and in the preschool period affecting executive functioning. The combination of A1+ and prenatal exposure was associated with more negative results. However, in this case, there were no gender differences.

Gender Differences in Effects of Tobacco Exposure on Development

An examination of the rather extensive literature on the effects of prenatal tobacco exposure on development suggests a number of conclusions. It appears that the evidence for effects of tobacco exposure, at this time, is strongest for growth, certainly for lower birth weight and, perhaps, later weight gain. Although there is some debate, there is also convincing evidence that tobacco exposure has negative consequences for respiratory functioning and otitis media. Auditory processing, behavioral regulation, and behavior problems also have bodies of evidence suggesting a relationship with tobacco exposure. Other areas seem less well supported at this time.

Although tobacco exposure and particularly prenatal tobacco exposure seem to be associated with a number of outcomes, it is also evident that the effect sizes in most studies are modest. In addition, it is probably the case that, for most of the outcomes evaluated, tobacco exposure is one of many factors that are usually seen in the same people and that contribute to changes in birth weight, cognition, behavior, and other outcomes. Because the effect sizes are small and there are multiple confounding or mediating factors, significance of effects can vary and even seem to come and go depending on the design of the study.

Another research design question concerns the type of sample used. Clinically identified samples tend to have a high incidence of the characteristic being studied (e.g., asthma, conduct disorder) combined with retrospective assessment of tobacco exposure. In such situations, it is well known that associations are usually found. As noted earlier, specific biases associated with clinical referral can affect results. For instance, children with externalizing problems (often male) are more likely to be referred for treatment than those with internalizing problems (often female). Clinical studies tend to find strong relationships between the outcomes that were used for selection and the retrospectively recalled exposure variables, and there may be sample specific findings that are not present if replicated in a different setting. Epidemiological studies, particularly those using existing data sets for a secondary data analysis, often have a relatively low rate of both (or either) the precursor and the outcome variables and tend to find fewer significant effects in studies of prenatal exposure. Exposure studies, using large samples selected for particular exposures and followed longitudinally, provide a third perspective on these questions. Such studies tend to find effects but often with effect sizes much smaller than those from clinical studies.

In reviewing the literature in this area, which covers about 50 years of work, it is interesting to consider how changes in social attitudes about smoking may have affected not the impact of the teratogen but the characteristics of associated factors that are considered to confound or mediate the relationships between smoking and developmental outcomes. Children born in the 1950s when smoking was socially accepted (including several of the large epidemiological studies cited here) may have mothers who have very different socioeconomic status and other substance use characteristics than children born in the first decade of the 21st century, when smoking has come to be regarded as an antisocial behavior. Meta-analyses that compared outcomes across time might be revealing.

Exploration of gender differences must be undertaken within the context of clear evidence that there are significant outcome that can be attributed to tobacco exposure. That is to say, if it is not clear that there is any overall association of prenatal tobacco exposure with cognition (e.g., when associated social and other factors are controlled), it may not be useful to look for gender difference in this area because they are likely to be either nonexistent or attributable to the same associated factors. Gender differences are noted in some of the studies reviewed here, particularly in relation to behavior. However, these results do not present a consistent pattern and, in many cases, no effects are found. Given the wide variety in the published results, it is important not to place too much weight on the results from any particular study or data set. Some of the findings (e.g., Jacobsen et al., 2007) are interesting and would appear to warrant further study. Other findings (e.g., those related to behavior disorders in males) may be attributable to research design and would need to be validated using different methodologies in order to confirm these conclusions. It is certainly true that gender differences have not been the focus of study in this area and, if this is considered to be an important research question, attention should be paid to this area in the future.

Furthermore, research design is an important consideration in interpreting the meaning of the effects of tobacco exposure, in general, and of any gender specific effects, in particular. To take a simple example, as noted above, in some cases in which behavior problems in boys have been attributed to prenatal tobacco exposure, only males were included in the study. In such studies, gender effects were not the research focus. In the future, if we wish to have information about gender differences, studies must be designed that include both males and females and have sufficient numbers to allow gender to be analyzed as an independent factor. In addition, studies would need to account for different base rates between males and females in the behavior under study.

References

Abel, E. L. (1984). Smoking and pregnancy. *Journal of Psychoactive Drugs, 16,* 327–338.

Achenbach, T. M., & Rescorla, L. A. (2000). *The Child Behavior Checklist, language development survey & caregiver-teacher report form for ages 1.5-5.* Burlington: University of Vermont Department of Psychiatry.

Adair-Bischoff, C. E., & Sauve, R. S. (1998). Environmental tobacco smoke and middle ear disease in preschool-age children. *Archives of Pediatrics & Adolescent Medicine, 152,* 127–133.

Alati, R., Mamun, A. A., O'Callaghan, M., Najman, J. M., & Williams, G. M. (2006). In utero and postnatal maternal smoking and asthma in adolescence. *Epidemiology, 17,* 138–144. doi:10.1097/01.ede.0000198148.02347.33

Batty, G. D., Der, G., & Deary, I. J. (2006). Effect of maternal smoking during pregnancy on offspring's cognitive ability: Empirical evidence for complete confounding in the US national longitudinal survey of youth. *Pediatrics, 118,* 943–950. doi:10.1542/peds.2006-0168

Bauman, K. E., Flewelling, R. L., & LaPrelle, J. (1991). Parental cigarette smoking and cognitive performance of children. *Health Psychology, 10,* 282–288. doi:10.1037/0278-6133.10.4.282

Bayley, N. (1993). *Bayley Scales of Infant Development* (2d ed.). San Antonio, TX: Psychological Corporation.

Becker, K., El-Faddach, M., Schmidt, M. H., Esser, G., & Laucht, M. (2008). Interaction of dopamine transporter genotype with prenatal smoke exposure on ADHD symptoms. *The Journal of Pediatrics, 152,* 263–269.e1. doi:10.1016/j.jpeds.2007.07.004

Braun, J. M., Kahn, S. R., Froehlich, T., Auinger, P., & Lanphear, B. P. (2006). Exposure to environmental toxicants and attention deficit hyperactivity disorder in US children. *Environmental Health Perspectives, 114,* 1904–1909.

Brazelton, T. B., & Nugent, J. K. (1995). *Neonatal behavioral assessment scale* (3rd ed.). Clinics in developmental medicine, No. 137. Cambridge, MA: McKeith Press.

Brennan, P. A., Grekin, E., & Mednick, S. (1999). Maternal smoking during pregnancy and adult male criminal outcomes. *Archives of General Psychiatry, 56,* 215–219. doi:10.1001/archpsyc.56.3.215

Brennan, P. A., Grekin, E., Mortensen, E. L., & Mednick, S. (2002). Relationship of maternal smoking during pregnancy with criminal arrest and hospitalization for substance abuse in male and female adult offspring. *The American Journal of Psychiatry, 159,* 48–54. doi:10.1176/appi.ajp.159.1.48

Breslau, N., Paneth, N., Lucia, V. C., & Paneth-Pollak, R. (2005). Maternal smoking during pregnancy and offspring IQ. *International Journal of Epidemiology, 34,* 1047–1053. doi:10.1093/ije/dyi163

Brook, D. W., Zhang, C., Rosenberg, G., & Brook, J. S. (2006). Maternal cigarette smoking during pregnancy and child aggressive behavior. *The American Journal on Addictions, 15,* 450–456. doi:10.1080/10550490600998559

Brookes, K. J., Mill, J., Guindaline, C., Curran, S., Xu, X., Knight, J., . . . Asherson, P. (2006). A common haplotype of the dopamine transporter gene associated with attention-deficit/hyperactivity disorder and interacting with maternal use of alcohol during pregnancy. *Archives of General Psychiatry, 63,* 74–81. doi:10.1001/archpsyc.63.1.74

Butler, N. R., & Goldstein, H. (1973). Smoking in pregnancy and subsequent child development. *British Medical Journal, 4,* 573–575. doi:10.1136/bmj.4.5892.573

Button, T. M., Thapar, A., & McGuffin, P. (2005). Relationship between antisocial behavior, attention-deficit hyperactivity disorder and maternal prenatal smoking. *The British Journal of Psychiatry, 187,* 155–160. doi:10.1192/bjp.187.2.155

Centers for Disease Control and Prevention. (2004). *2004 Surgeon General's Report—The health consequences of smoking: Smoking among adults in the United States: Reproductive health.* Retrieved from http://www.cdc.gov/tobacco/data_statistics/sgr/sgr_2004/highlights/5.htm

Coles, C. D., Kable, J. A., Lynch, M. A., & Johnson, K. C. (2008). *Language development at 6 and 15 months in children of smokers.* Unpublished manuscript.

Colley, J. R., Holland, W. W., & Corkhill, R. T. (1974). Influence of passive smoking and parental phlegm on pneumonia and bronchitis in early childhood. *The Lancet, 304,* 1031–1034. doi:10.1016/S0140-6736(74)92148-5

Collins, B. N., Wileyto, E. P., Murphy, M. F. G., & Munafo, M. R. (2007). Adolescent environmental tobacco smoke exposure predicts academic achievement test failure. *Journal of Adolescent Health, 41,* 363–370. doi:10.1016/j.jadohealth.2007.04.010

Conter, V., Cortinovis, I., Rogari, P., & Riva, L. (1995). Weight growth in infants born to mothers who smoked during pregnancy. *British Medical Journal, 310,* 768–771.

Cook, D. G., Strachean, D., & Carey, I. (1998). Health effects of passive smoking 9: Parental smoking and spirometric indices in children. *Thorax, 53,* 884–893. doi:10.1136/thx.53.10.884

Cornelius, M. D., Goldschmidt, L., Day, N., & Larkby, C. (2002). Prenatal substance use among pregnant teenagers: A six-year follow-up of effects on offspring growth. *Neurotoxicology and Teratology, 24,* 703–710. doi:10.1016/S0892-0362(02)00271-4

Cornelius, M. D., Leech, S., & Larkby, C. (2007). Prenatal substance exposure: Growth outcomes among 10-year-old offspring of teenage mothers. *Neurotoxicology and Teratology, 29,* 409.

Cornelius, M. D., Ryan, C. M., Day, N. L., Goldschmidt, L., & Willford, J. A. (2001). Prenatal tobacco effects on neuropsychological outcomes among pre-adolescents. *Journal of Developmental and Behavioral Pediatrics, 22,* 217–225.

Cowperthwaite, B., Hains, S., & Kisilevsky, B. (2007). Fetal behavior in smoking compared to non-smoking pregnant women. *Infant Behavior & Development, 30,* 422–430. doi:10.1016/j.infbeh.2006.12.004

Cunningham, J., Dockery, D. W., & Speizer, F. E. (1994). Maternal smoking during pregnancy as a predictor of lung function in children. *American Journal of Epidemiology, 139,* 1139–1152.

Day, N. L., Richardson, G. A., Goldschmidt, L., & Cornelius, M. D. (2000). Effects of prenatal tobacco exposure on preschoolers' behavior. *Journal of Developmental and Behavioral Pediatrics, 21,* 180–188.

DiFranza, J. R., Aligne, C. A., & Weitzman, M. (2004). Prenatal and postnatal environmental tobacco smoke exposure and children's health. *Pediatrics, 113,* 1007–1015.

Dunn, H. G., McBurney, A. K., Ingram, S., & Hunter, C. M. (1977). Maternal cigarette smoking during pregnancy and the child's subsequent development: II. Neurological and intellectual maturation to the age of 6 1/2 years. *Canadian Journal of Public Health, 68,* 43–50.

Eiden, R. D. (2009, January). *Orientation to the issue: What we know (and don't know) about cognitive, behavioral, and neurodevelopmental effects of SHS exposure.* Presentation at National Institute on Drug Abuse–sponsored workshop, "Drug Abuse Vulnerability and Neurodevelopmental Effects of Early Exposure to Secondhand Tobacco Smoke: Methodological Issues and Research Priorities," Rockville, MD.

Emerson, J. A., Wahlgren, D. R., Hovell, M. F., Meltzer, S. B., Zakarian, J. M., & Hofstetter, C. R. (1994). Parent smoking and asthmatic children's exposure patterns: A behavioral epidemiology study. *Addictive Behaviors, 19,* 677–689. doi:10.1016/0306-4603(94)90022-1

Ershoff, D., Ashford, T. H., & Goldenberg, R. (2004). Helping pregnant women quite smoking: An overview. *Nicotine & Tobacco Research, 6*(Suppl. 2), S101–S105. doi:10.1080/14622200410001669204

Eskenazi, B., & Castorina, R. (1999). Association of prenatal maternal or postnatal child environment tobacco smoke exposure and neurodevelopmental and behavioral problems in children. *Environmental Health Perspectives, 107,* 991–1000. doi:10.1289/ehp.99107991

Evans, D., Levison, M., Feldman, C., Clark, N. M., Wasilewski, Y., Levin, B., & Mellins, R. B. (1987). The impact of passive smoking on emergency room visits of urban children with asthma. *The American Review of Respiratory Disease, 135,* 567–572.

Fergusson, D. M., & Lloyd, M. (1991). Smoking during pregnancy and its effects on child cognitive ability from the ages of 8 to 12 years. *Paediatric and Perinatal Epidemiology, 5,* 189–200. doi:10.1111/j.1365-3016.1991.tb00700.x

Fergusson, D. M., Woodward, L. J., & Horwood, L. J. (1998). Maternal smoking during pregnancy and psychiatric adjustment in late adolescence. *Archives of General Psychiatry, 55,* 721–727. doi:10.1001/archpsyc.55.8.721

Fingerhut, L. A., Kleinman, J. C., & Kendrick, J. S. (1990). Smoking before, during, and after pregnancy. *American Journal of Public Health, 80,* 541–544.

Flick, L. H., Cook, C. A., Homan, S. M., McSweeney, M., Campbell, C., & Parnell, L. (2006). Persistent tobacco use during pregnancy and the likelihood of psychiatric disorders. *American Journal of Public Health, 96,* 1799–1807. doi:10.2105/AJPH.2004.057851

Fogelman, K. (1980). Smoking in pregnancy and subsequent development of the child. *Child Care, Health and Development, 6,* 233–251. doi:10.1111/j.1365-2214.1980.tb00154.x

Franco, P., Groswasser, J., Hassid, S., Lanquart, J. P., Scaillet, S., & Kahn, A. (1999). Prenatal exposure to cigarette smoking is associated with a decrease in arousal in infants. *The Journal of Pediatrics, 135,* 34–38. doi:10.1016/S0022-3476(99)70324-0

Fried, P. A. (1998). Cigarette smoke exposure and hearing loss. *JAMA, 280,* 963. doi:10.1001/jama.280.11.963

Fried, P. A., James, D. S., & Watkinson, B. (2001). Growth and pubertal milestones during adolescence in offspring exposed to cigarettes and marihuana. *Neurotoxicology and Teratology, 23,* 431–436. doi:10.1016/S0892-0362(01)00161-1

Fried, P. A., & Makin, J. E. (1987). Neonatal behavioural correlates of prenatal exposure to marihuana, cigarettes and alcohol in a low risk population. *Neurotoxicology and Teratology, 9,* 1–7. doi:10.1016/0892-0362(87)90062-6

Fried, P. A., O'Connell, C. M., & Watkinson, B. (1992). 60- and 72-month follow-up of children prenatally exposed to marijuana, cigarettes, and alcohol: Cognitive and language assessment. *Journal of Developmental and Behavioral Pediatrics, 13,* 383–391. doi:10.1097/00004703-199212000-00001

Fried, P. A., & Watkinson, B. (1988). Twelve- and twenty-four-month neurobehavioral follow-up of children prenatally exposed to marijuana, cigarettes, and alcohol. *Neurotoxicology and Teratology, 10,* 305–313. doi:10.1016/0892-0362(88)90032-3

Fried, P. A., & Watkinson, B. (1990). Thirty-six- and forty-eight-month neurobehavioral follow-up of children prenatally exposed to marijuana, cigarettes, and alcohol. *Journal of Developmental and Behavioral Pediatrics, 11,* 49–58. doi:10.1097/00004703-199004000-00003

Fried, P. A., Watkinson, B., & Gray, R. (1992). A follow-up study of attentional behavior in 6-year-old children exposed prenatally to marijuana, cigarettes, and alcohol. *Neurotoxicology and Teratology, 14,* 299–311. doi:10.1016/0892-0362(92)90036-A

Fried, P. A., Watkinson, B., & Gray, R. (1998). Differential effects on cognitive functioning in 9- to 12-year olds prenatally exposed to cigarettes and marihuana. *Neurotoxicology and Teratology, 20,* 293–306. doi:10.1016/S0892-0362(97)00091-3

Fried, P. A., Watkinson, B., & Gray, R. (1999). Growth from birth to early adolescence in offspring prenatally exposed to cigarettes and marijuana. *Neurotoxicology and Teratology, 21,* 513–525. doi:10.1016/S0892-0362(99)00009-4

Fried, P. A., Watkinson, B., & Gray, R. (2003). Differential effects on cognitive functioning in 13- to 16-year olds prenatally exposed to cigarettes and marihuana. *Neurotoxicology and Teratology, 25,* 427–436. doi:10.1016/S0892-0362(03)00029-1

Fried, P. A., Watkinson, B., & Siegel, L. S. (1997). Reading and language in 9- to 12-year olds prenatally exposed to cigarettes and marijuana. *Neurotoxicology and Teratology, 19,* 171–183. doi:10.1016/S0892-0362(97)00015-9

Gibson, C., Piquero, A., & Tibbets, S. (2000). Assessing the relationship between maternal cigarette smoking during pregnancy and age at first police contact. *Justice Quarterly, 17,* 519–542. doi:10.1080/07418820000094651

Gilman, S. E., Gardener, H., & Buka, S. L. (2008). Maternal smoking during pregnancy and children's cognitive and physical development: A causal risk factor? *American Journal of Epidemiology, 168,* 522–531. doi:10.1093/aje/kwn175

Hardy, J. B., & Mellits, E. D. (1972). Does maternal smoking during pregnancy have a long-term effect on the child? *The Lancet, 300,* 1332–1336. doi:10.1016/S0140-6736(72)92777-8

Harlap, S., & Davies, A. M. (1974). Infant admissions to hospital and maternal smoking. *The Lancet, 303,* 529–532. doi:10.1016/S0140-6736(74)92714-7

Horne, R. S., Franco, P., Adamson, T., Groswasser, J., & Kahn, A. (2004). Influences of maternal cigarette smoking on infant arousability. *Early Human Development, 79,* 49–58. doi:10.1016/j.earlhumdev.2004.04.005

Huang, J. S., Lee, T. A., & Lu, M. C. (2007). Prenatal programming of childhood overweigh and obesity. *Maternal and Child Health Journal, 11,* 461–473. doi:10.1007/s10995-006-0141-8

Huang, R. C., Burke, V., Newnham, J. P., Stanley, F. J., Kendall, G. E., Landau, L. I., . . . Beilin, L. J. (2007). Perinatal and childhood origins of cardiovascular disease. *International Journal of Obesity, 31,* 236–244. doi:10.1038/sj.ijo.0803394

Ilicali, O. C., Keles, N., Deier, K., Saiun, O. F., & Guldiken, Y. (2001). Evaluation of the effect of passive smoking on otitis media in children by an objective method: Urinary cotinine analysis. *The Laryngoscope, 111,* 163–167. doi:10.1097/00005537-200101000-00028

Jaakkola, J. J. K., & Gissler, M. (2004). Maternal smoking in pregnancy, fetal development, and childhood asthma. *American Journal of Public Health, 94,* 136–140. doi:10.2105/AJPH.94.1.136

Jaakkola, J. J. K., & Gissler, M. (2007). Are girls more susceptible to the effects of prenatal exposure to tobacco smoke on asthma? *Epidemiology, 18,* 573–576. doi:10.1097/EDE.0b013e31812001d2

Jacobsen, L. K., Slotkin, T. A., Menci, W. E., Frost, S. J., & Pugh, K. R. (2007). Gender-specific effects of prenatal and adolescent exposure to tobacco smoke on auditory and visual attention. *Neuropsychopharmacology, 32,* 2453–2464. doi:10.1038/sj.npp.1301398

Jacobson, S. W., Fein, G. G., Jacobson, J. L., Schwartz, P. M., & Dowler, J. K. (1984). Neonatal correlates of prenatal exposure to smoking, caffeine, and alcohol. *Infant Behavior & Development, 7,* 253–265.

Johnson, K. C., Lynch, M. L., Kable, J. A., & Coles, C. D. (2009). *Effects of prenatal tobacco expo-sure on behavior at 24 months.* Unpublished manuscript.

Johnston, L. D., O'Malley, P. M., Bachman, J. G., & Schulenberg, J. E. (2006, December 21). *Teen drug use continues down in 2006, particularly among older teens; but use of prescription-type drugs remains high.* Ann Arbor: University of Michigan News and Information Services. Retrieved from http://www.monitoringthefuture.org

Kable, J. A. (1995). *Auditory vs. general information processing deficits in infants of mothers who smokes during their pregnancy* (Unpublished doctoral dissertation). Purdue University, West Lafayette, IN.

Kable, J. A., Coles, C. D., Lynch, M. E., & Carroll, J. (2009a). The impact of maternal smoking on fast auditory brainstem responses. *Neurotoxicology and Teratology, 31,* 216–224.doi:10.1016/j.ntt.2009.02.002

Kable, J. A., Coles, C. D., Lynch, M. E., & Carroll, J. (2009b) *Phonemic perception differences in infants of mothers who smoked during pregnancy.* Manuscript in review.

Kahn, R. S., Khoury, J., Nichols, W. C., & Lanphear, B. P. (2003). Role of dopamine transporter genotype and maternal prenatal smoking in childhood hyperactive-impulsive, inattention, and oppositional behaviors. *The Journal of Pediatrics, 143,* 104–110. doi:10.1016/S0022-3476(03)00208-7

Kearney, M. H. (1999). *Perinatal impact of alcohol, tobacco and other drugs.* White Plains, NY: March of Dimes Publishing.

Kershaw, C. R. (1987). Passive smoking, potential atopy and asthma in the first five years. *Journal of the Royal Society of Medicine, 80,* 683–688.

Key, A. P., Ferguson, M., Molfese, D. L., Peach, K., Lehman, C., & Molfese, V. J. (2006). Smoking during pregnancy affects speech-processing ability. *Environmental Health Perspectives, 115,* 623–629. doi:10.1289/ehp.9521

Kodl, M. M., & Wakschlag, L. S. (2004). Does a childhood history of externalizing problems predict smoking during pregnancy? *Addictive Behaviors, 29,* 273–279. doi:10.1016/j.addbeh.2003.08.003

Kristjansson, E. A., Fried, P. A., & Watkinson, B. (1989). Maternal smoking during pregnancy affects children's vigilance performance. *Drug and Alcohol Dependence, 24,* 11–19. doi:10.1016/0376-8716(89)90003-3

Kukla, L., Hruba, D., & Tyrlik, M. (2006). Smoking of mothers during pregnancy in relation to men-tal and motoric development disorders in 4- and 5-year-old children. The Elspac study results. *Psychológia a Patopsychológia Diet'at'a, 41,* 39–49.

Leech, S. L., Richardson, G. A., Goldschmidt, L., & Day, N. (1999). Prenatal substance exposure: Effects on attention and impulsivity of 6-year-olds. *Neurotoxicology and Teratology, 21,* 109–118. doi:10.1016/S0892-0362(98)00042-7

Lefkowitz, M. M. (1981). Smoking during pregnancy: Long-term effects on offspring. *Developmental Psychology, 17,* 192–194. doi:10.1037/0012-1649.17.2.192

Lewis, B. A., Kirchner, H. L., Short, E. J., Minnes, S., Weishampel, P., Satayathum, S., & Singer, P. T. (2007). Prenatal cocaine and tobacco effects on children's language trajectories. *Pediatrics, 120,* e78–e85. doi:10.1542/peds.2006-2563

Li, Y. F., Gilliland, F. D., Berhane, K., McConnell, R., Gauderman, W. J., Rappaport, E. B., & Peters, J. M. (2000). Effects of in utero and environmental tobacco smoke exposure on lung function in boys and girls with and without asthma. *American Journal of Respiratory and Critical Care Medicine, 162,* 2097–2104.

Linnet, K. M., Dalsgaard, S., Obel, C., Wisborg, K., Henriksen, T. B., Rodriquez, A., . . . Jarvelin, M. (2003). Maternal lifestyle factors in pregnancy risk of attention deficit hyperactivity disorder and associated behaviors: Review of the current evidence. *The American Journal of Psychiatry, 160,* 1028–1040. doi:10.1176/appi.ajp.160.6.1028

MacArthur, C., Knox, E. G., & Lancashire, R. J. (2001). Effects at age nine of maternal smoking in pregnancy: Experimental and observational findings. *BJOG: An international journal of obstetrics and gynaecology, 108,* 67–73.

Maher, B. S., Marazita, M. L., Ferrell, R. E., & Vanyukov, M. M. (2002). Dopamine system genes and attention deficit hyperactivity disorder: A meta-analysis. *Psychiatric Genetics, 12,* 207–215. doi:10.1097/00041444-200212000-00003

Makin, J., Fried, P. A., & Watkinson, B. (1991). A comparison of active and passive smoking dur-ing pregnancy: Long-term effects. *Neurotoxicology and Teratology, 13,* 5–12. doi:10.1016/0892-0362(91)90021-N

Martin, R. P., Dombrowski, S. C., Mullis, C., Wisenbaker, J., & Huttunen, M. O. (2006). Smoking during pregnancy: Association with childhood temperament, behavior, and academic performance. *Journal of Pediatric Psychology, 31,* 490–500.

Maughan, B., Taylor, A., Caspi, A., & Moffitt, T. E. (2004). Prenatal smoking and early childhood conduct problems: Testing genetic and environmental explanations of the association. *Archives of General Psychiatry, 61,* 836–843. doi:10.1001/archpsyc.61.8.836

McCartney, J. S., Fried, P. A., & Watkinson, B. (1994). Central auditory processing in school-age children prenatally exposed to cigarette smoke. *Neurotoxicology and Teratology, 16,* 269–276. doi:10.1016/0892-0362(94)90048-5

Millberger, S., Biederman, J., Faraone, S. V., & Jones, J. (1998). Further evidence of an association between maternal smoking during pregnancy and attention deficit hyperactivity disorder: Findings from a high-risk sample of siblings. *Journal of Clinical Child Psychology, 27,* 352–358. doi:10.1207/s15374424jccp2703_11

Montgomery, S. M., & Ekbom, A. (2002). Smoking during pregnancy and diabetes mellitus in a British longitudinal birth cohort. *British Medical Journal, 324,* 26–27. doi:10.1136/bmj.324.7328.26

Montreaux, M. C., Blacker, D., Biederman, J., Fitzmaurice, G., & Buka, S. L. (2006). Maternal smoking during pregnancy and offspring overt and covert conduct problems: A longitudinal study. *Journal of Child Psychology and Psychiatry, 47,* 883–890. doi:10.1111/j.1469-7610.2005.01566.x

Moshammer, H., Hoek, G., Luttmann-Gibson, H., Neuberger, M. A., Antova, T., Gehring, U., . . . Fletcher, T. (2006). Parental smoking and lung function in children: An international study. *American Journal of Respiratory and Critical Care Medicine, 173,* 1255–1263. doi:10.1164/rccm.200510-1552OC

Naeye, R. L., & Peters, E. C. (1984). Mental development of children whose mothers smoked during pregnancy. *Obstetrics and Gynecology, 64,* 601–607.

National Center for Health Statistics. (2007). *2007—With Chartbook on Trends in the health of Americans.* Hyattsville, MD: Author.

National Center for Health Statistics. (2008). *Early release of selected estimates based on data from the January–June 2008 National Health Interview Survey.* Hyattsville, MD: Author. Retrieved from http://www.cdc.gov/NCHS/about/major/nhis/released200812.htm

Neuman, R. J., Lobos, E., Reich, W., Henerson, C. A., Sun, L. W., & Todd, R. D. (2006). Prenatal smoking exposure and dopaminergic genotypes interact to cause a severe ADHD subtype. *Biological Psychiatry, 61,* 1320–1328.

Nigg, J. T., & Breslau, N. (2007). Prenatal smoking exposure, low birth weight, and disruptive behavior disorders. *Journal of the American Academy of Child and Adolescent Psychiatry, 46*(3), 362–369.

Noland, J. S., Singer, L. T., Short, E. J., Minnes, S., Arendt, R. E., Kirchner, H., & Bearer, C. (2005). Prenatal drug exposure and selective attention in preschoolers. *Neurotoxicology and Teratology, 27,* 429–438. doi:10.1016/j.ntt.2005.02.001

Obel, C., Henriksen, T. B., Hedegaard, M., Secher, N. J., & Ostergaard, J. (1998). Smoking during pregnancy and babbling abilities of the 8-month-old infant. *Paediatric and Perinatal Epidemiology, 12,* 37–48. doi:10.1111/j.1365-3016.1998.00094.x

Olds, D. (1997). Tobacco exposure and impaired development: A review of the evidence. *Mental Retardation and Developmental Disabilities Research Reviews, 3,* 257–269. doi:10.1002/(SICI)1098-2779(1997)3:3<257::AID-MRDD6>3.0.CO;2-M

Ong, K. K., Preece, M. A., Emmett, P. M., Ahmed, M. L., & Dunger, D. B. (2002). Size at birth and early childhood growth in relation to maternal smoking, parity and infant breast feeding: Longitudinal birth cohort study and analysis. *Pediatric Research, 52,* 863–867.

Orlebeke, J. F., Knol, D. L., & Verhulst, F. C. (1999). Child behavior problems increased by maternal smoking during pregnancy. *Archives of Environmental Health, 54,* 15–19. doi:10.1080/00039899909602231

Pickett, K. E., Wood, C., Adamson, J., D'Souza, L., & Wakschlag, L. S. (2008). Meaningful differences in maternal smoking behavior during pregnancy: Implications for infant behavioural vulnerability. *Journal of Epidemiology and Community Health, 62,* 318–324. doi:10.1136/jech.2006.058768

Picone, T. A., Allen, L. H., Olsen, P. N., & Ferris, M. E. (1982). Pregnancy outcome in North American women. II. Effects of diet, cigarette smoking, stress, and weight gain on placentas, and on neonatal physical and behavioral characteristics. *The American Journal of Clinical Nutrition, 36,* 1214–1224.

Polifka, J. E. (1998). Drugs and chemicals in breast milk. In W. Slikker & L. W. Chang (Eds.), *Handbook of developmental neurotoxicology* (pp. 383–400). San Diego, CA: Academic Press. doi:10.1016/B978-012648860-9/50027-3

Power, C., & Jefferis, B. J. (2002). Fetal environment and subsequent obesity: A study of maternal smoking. *International Journal of Epidemiology, 31,* 413–419. doi:10.1093/ije/31.2.413

Rantakallio, P., Laara, E., Isohanni, M., & Moilanen, I. (1992). Maternal smoking during pregnancy and delinquency of the offspring: An association without causation? *International Journal of Epidemiology, 21,* 1106–1113. doi:10.1093/ije/21.6.1106

Räsänen, P., Hakko, H., Isohanni, M., Hodgins, S., Jarvelin, M. R., & Tihonen, J. (1999). Maternal smoking during pregnancy and risk of criminal behavior among adult male offspring in the Northern Finland 1966 Birth Cohort. *The American Journal of Psychiatry, 156,* 857–862.

Reynolds, C. R., & Kamphaus, R. W. (1992). *Behavioral assessment system for children.* Circle Pines, MN: American Guidance Services.

Reynolds, P., Hurley, S. E., Hoggatt, K., Anton-Culver, H., Bernstein, L., Deapen, D., . . . Hornross, P. L. (2004). Correlates of active and passive smoking in the California Teachers Study cohort. *Journal of Women's Health, 13,* 778–790. doi:10.1089/jwh.2004.13.778

Saito, R. (1991). The smoking habits of pregnant women and their husbands and the effects on their infants. *Japanese Journal of Public Health, 38,* 124–131.

Sawnani, H., Jackson, T., Murphy, T., Beckerman, R., & Simakajornboon, N. (2004). The effect of maternal smoking on respiratory and arousal patterns in preterm infants during sleep. *American Journal of Respiratory and Critical Care Medicine, 169,* 733–738. doi:10.1164/rccm.200305-692OC

Schuetze, P., & Eiden, R. D. (2006). The association between maternal smoking and secondhand exposure and autonomic functioning at 2–4 weeks of age. *Infant Behavior & Development, 29,* 32–43. doi:10.1016/j.infbeh.2005.07.001

Schuster, M. A., Franke, T., & Pham, C. M. (2002). Smoking patterns of household members and visitors in homes with children in the United States. *Archives of Pediatrics & Adolescent Medicine, 156,* 1094–1100.

Sexton, M., Fox, N. L., & Hebel, J. R. (1990). Prenatal exposure to tobacco: II. Effects on cognitive functioning at age three. *International Journal of Epidemiology, 19,* 72–77. doi:10.1093/ije/19.1.72

Simpson, K. J. (1957). A preliminary report of cigarettes and the incidence of prematurity. *American Journal of Obstetrics and Gynecology, 73,* 808.

Slotkin, T. A. (1998). Fetal nicotine or cocaine exposure: Which one is worse? *The Journal of Pharmacology and Experimental Therapeutics, 285,* 931–945.

Slotkin, T. A. (2004). Cholinergic systems in brain development and disruption by neurotoxicants: Nicotine, environmental tobacco smoke, organophosphates. *Toxicology and Applied Pharmacology, 198,* 132–151. doi:10.1016/j.taap.2003.06.001

Slotkin, T. A., MacKillop, E. A., Rudder, C. L., Ryde, I. T., Tate, C. A., & Siedler, F. J. (2007). Permanent, sex-selective effects of prenatal or adolescent nicotine exposure, separately or sequentially, in rat brain regions: Indices of cholinergic and sertonergic synaptic function, cell signaling, and neuronal cell number and size at 6 months of age. *Neuropsychopharmacology, 32,* 1082–1097. doi:10.1038/sj.npp.1301231

Stathis, S. L., O'Callaghan, M., Williams, G. M., Najman, J. M., Anderson, M. J., & Bor, W. (1999). Maternal cigarette smoking during pregnancy is an independent predictor for symptoms of middle ear disease at five years' postdelivery. *Pediatrics, 104,* e16. doi:10.1542/peds.104.2.e16

Streissguth, A. P., Barr, H. M., Sampson, P. D., Darby, B. L., & Martin, D. C. (1989). IQ at age 4 in relation to maternal alcohol use and smoking during pregnancy. *Developmental Psychology, 25,* 3–11. doi:10.1037/0012-1649.25.1.3

Streissguth, A. P., Martin, D. C., Barr, H. M., & Sandman, B. M. (1984). Intrauterine alcohol and nicotine exposure: Attention and reaction time in 4-year-old children. *Developmental Psychology, 20,* 533–541. doi:10.1037/0012-1649.20.4.533

Swanson, J., Schuck, S., & Mann, M. Carlson, C., Hartman, K., Sergeant, J., . . . McCleary, R. (2004). *Categorical and dimensional definitions and evaluations of symptoms of ADHD: The SNAP and The SWAN Ratings Scales.* Retrieved from http://www.adhd.net

Thapar, A., Fowler, T., Rice, F., Scourfield, J., van den Bree, M., Thomas, H., .Harold, G., & Hay, D. (2003). Maternal smoking during pregnancy and attention deficit hyperactivity disorder symptoms in offspring. *The American Journal of Psychiatry, 160,* 1985–1989. doi:10.1176/appi.ajp.160.11.1985

Toschke, A. M., Koletzko, B., Slikker, W., Hermann, M., & von Kries, R. (2002). Childhood obesity is associated with maternal smoking in pregnancy. *European Journal of Pediatrics, 161,* 445–448. doi:10.1007/s00431-002-0983-z

Trasti, N., Vik, T., Jacobsen, G., & Bakketeigg, L. S. (1999). Smoking in pregnancy and children's mental and motor development at age 1 and 5 years. *Early Human Development, 55,* 137–147. doi:10.1016/S0378-3782(99)00017-1

Vik, T., Jacobsen, G., Vatten, L., & Bakketig, L. S. (1996). Pre- and post-natal growth in children of women who smoked during pregnancy. *Early Human Development, 45,* 245–255. doi:10.1016/0378-3782(96)01735-5

Wakschlag, L. S., & Keenan, K. (2001). Clinical significance and correlates of disruptive behavior symptoms in environmentally at-risk preschoolers. *Journal of Clinical Child Psychology, 30,* 262–275. doi:10.1207/S15374424JCCP3002_13

Wakschlag, L. S., Lahey, B. B., Loeber, R., Green, S. M., Gordon, R. A., & Leventhal, B. L. (1997). Maternal smoking during pregnancy and the risk of conduct disorders in boys. *Archives of General Psychiatry, 54,* 670–676.

Wakschlag, L. S., Leventhal, B. L., Pine, D. S., Pickett, K. E., & Carter, A. S. (2006). Elucidating early mechanisms of developmental psychopathology: The case of prenatal smoking and disruptive behavior. *Child Development, 77,* 893–906. doi:10.1111/j.1467-8624.2006.00909.x

Wakschlag, L. S., Pickett, K. E., Cook, E., Benowitz, N. L., & Leventhal, B. L. (2002). Maternal smoking during pregnancy and severe antisocial behavior in offspring: A review. *American Journal of Public Health, 92,* 966–974. doi:10.2105/AJPH.92.6.966

Wakschlag, L. S., Pickett, K. E., Kasza, K. E., & Loeber, R. (2006). Is prenatal smoking associated with a developmental pattern of conduct problems in young boys? *Journal of the American Academy of Child and Adolescent Psychiatry, 45,* 461–467.

Wakschlag, L. S., Pickett, K. E., Middlecamp, M. K., Walton, L. L., Tenzer, P., & Leventhal, B. L. (2003). Pregnant smokers who quite, pregnant smokers who don't: Does history of problem behavior make a difference? *Social Science & Medicine, 56,* 2449–2460. doi:10.1016/S0277-9536(02)00248-4

Wang, L., & Pinkerton, K. E. (2008). Detrimental effects of tobacco smoke exposure during development on postnatal lung function and asthma. *Birth Defects Research Part C, 84,* 54–60. doi:10.1002/bdrc.20114

Wasserman, G. A., Pine, D. S., Workman, S. B., & Bruder, G. E. (1999). Dichotic listening deficits and the prediction of substance use in young boys. *Journal of the American Academy of Child & Adolescent Psychiatry, 38,* 1032–1039. doi:10.1097/00004583-199908000-00020

Weaver, K., Campbell, R., Mermelstein, R., & Wakschlag, L. S. (2008). Pregnancy smoking in context: The influence of multiple levels of stress. *Nicotine & Tobacco Research, 10,* 1065–1073. doi:10.1080/14622200802087564

Weinberg, C. R., Wilcox, A. J., & Baird, D. D. (1989). Reduced fecundability in women with prenatal exposure to cigarette smoking. *American Journal of Epidemiology, 129,* 1072–1078.

Weissman, M. M., Warner, V., Wickramaratne, P., & Kandel, D. (1999). Maternal smoking during pregnancy and psychopathology in offspring followed to adulthood. *Journal of the American Academy of Child & Adolescent Psychiatry, 38,* 892–899. doi:10.1097/00004583-199907000-00020

Weitzman, M., Byrd, R. S., Aligne, C., & Moss, M. (2002). The effects of tobacco exposure on children's behavioral and cognitive functioning: Implications for clinical and public health policy and future research. *Neurotoxicology and Teratology, 24,* 397–406. doi:10.1016/S0892-0362(02)00201-5

Werler, M. M., Pober, B. R., & Holmes, L. B. (1985). Smoking and pregnancy. *Teratology, 32,* 473–481. doi:10.1002/tera.1420320316

Wertelecki, W., Hoff, C., & Zansky, S. (1987). Maternal smoking: Greater effect on males, fetal tobacco syndrome? *Teratology, 35,* 317–320. doi:10.1002/tera.1420350305

Wiebe, S. A., Espy, K. A., Jameson, T. R., Gilbert, D. G., Stopp, C., Respass, J., . . . Huggenvik, J. I. (2009). Gene–environment interactions across development: Exploring DRD2 genotype and prenatal smoking effects on self-regulation. *Developmental Psychology, 45,* 31–44. doi:10.1037/a0014550

Willford, J. A., Day, N. L., & Cornelius, M. D. (2006) Tobacco use during pregnancy: Epidemiology and effects on offspring. In M. Miller (Ed.), *Brain development: Normal processes and the effects of alcohol and nicotine* (pp. 315–328). New York, NY: Oxford University Press.

Williams, G. M., O'Callaghan, M., Najman, J. M., Bor, W., Andersen, M. J., Richards, D., & U. C. (1998). Maternal cigarette smoking and child psychiatry morbidity: A longitudinal study. *Pediatrics, 102,* e11.

Windham, G. C., Bottomley, C., Birner, C., & Fenster, L. (2004). Age at menarche in relation to maternal use of tobacco, alcohol, coffee and tea in pregnancy. *American Journal of Epidemiology, 159,* 862–871.

Windham, G. C., Zhang, L., Longnecker, M. P., & Klebanoff, M. (2008). Maternal smoking, demographic and lifestyle factors in relation to daughter's age at menarche. *Paediatric and Perinatal Epidemiology, 22,* 551–561. doi:10.1111/j.1365-3016.2008.00948.x

Yolton, K., Khoury, J., Hounung, R., Kietrich, K., Succop, P., & Lanphear, B. (2008). Environmental tobacco smoke exposure and child behavior. *Journal of Developmental and Behavioral Pediatrics, 29,* 450–457. doi:10.1097/DBP.0b013e31818d0c21

Zeskind, P. S., & Gingras, J. L. (2005). Maternal cigarette-smoking during pregnancy disrupts rhythms in fetal heart rate. *Journal of Pediatric Psychology, 31,* 5–14. doi:10.1093/jpepsy/jsj031

6

Sex-Specific Effects of Prenatal Marijuana Exposure on Neurodevelopment and Behavior

Jennifer A. Willford, Gale A. Richardson, and Nancy L. Day

Cannabis is the most widely used illicit drug among pregnant women in the United States (National Institute on Drug Abuse, 1996; Substance Abuse and Mental Health Services Administration, 2000). Cannabinoids cross the placental barrier during gestation (Hutchings, Martin, Gamagaris, Miller, & Fico, 1989) and can be transferred through maternal milk during lactation (Jakubovic, Hattori, & McGreer, 1973), resulting in prenatal exposure and long-term developmental effects. The majority of studies evaluating sex differences in the effects of prenatal marijuana exposure (PME) have used animal models. Although there have been several human studies of the effects of PME, few have investigated sex differences.

This chapter reviews the development of the endogenous cannabinoid receptor system (ECBR), sex differences in the development of the ECBR, and sex differences in animal and human PME studies. The possible mechanisms for PME-related sex differences in developmental outcomes are also discussed.

In humans, PME has significant effects on central nervous system (CNS) functioning. At birth, the presence of these effects has been revealed by measures of CNS maturity such as neurobehavioral assessment (Fried & Makin, 1987), sleep EEGs (Scher, Richardson, Coble, Day, & Stoffer, 1988), and infant cry analyses (Lester & Dreher, 1989). During childhood, detrimental effects of PME have been found on measures of attention, impulsivity, and activity in both the Maternal Health Practices and Child Development (MHPCD) Project and the Ottawa Prenatal Prospective Study (OPPS; Fried & Watkinson, 2001; Fried, Watkinson, & Gray, 1992; Goldschmidt, Day, & Richardson, 2000; Leech, Richardson, Goldschmidt, & Day, 1999; Smith, Fried, Hogan, & Cameron, 2004). The MHPCD Project and the OPPS have also reported that PME is associated with deficits in aspects of memory, verbal reasoning, and executive functioning (Day et al., 1994; Fried & Watkinson, 1990, 2000; Fried, Watkinson, & Gray, 1998, 2003; Goldschmidt, Richardson, Willford, & Day, 2008; Richardson, Ryan, Willford, Day, & Goldschmidt, 2002). PME has been found to predict higher rates of depressive symptoms (Gray, Day, Leech, & Richardson, 2005), delinquent behaviors (Day, Leech, & Goldschmidt, 2011; Goldschmidt et al.,

2000), and substance use in exposed offspring (Day, Goldschmidt, & Thomas, 2006; Porath & Fried, 2005). These findings have parallels in the animal literature, as discussed next.

Most animal studies of gestational cannabis exposure administer tetrahydrocannabinol (THC) orally to the dam from gestational day (GD) 5 until weaning, which occurs at postnatal day (PND) 24. In humans, the brain undergoes a period of rapid neuronal proliferation and synaptogenesis, the brain growth spurt, during the late second and the third trimesters of pregnancy (Bayer, Altman, Russo, & Zhang, 1993). The parallel for this gestational period in rats occurs during the first two postnatal weeks. Thus, pre- and postnatal exposure to THC in the rat allows researchers to model drug exposure during the rat's equivalent of the human late second and third trimester brain growth spurt.

The long-term effects of PME on brain function are due to changes in the temporal sequence of events that occur during normal CNS development. In animal models, developmental exposure to THC leads to sustained activation of the cannabinoid receptor (CB_1) system. This activation results in the disruption of the position, postsynaptic target selectivity, and differentiation of the developing axons (Berghuis et al., 2007). In addition, animal studies provide neurobiological markers of the effects of prenatal THC, indicated by changes in the function and genetic expression of key components of the hypothalamic–pituitary–adrenal (HPA) axis. Additional effects of gestational exposure to THC include changes in neurotransmitters such as dopamine (Fride, 2008), serotonin (Molina-Holgado, Alvarez, González, Antonio, & Leret, 1997; Molina-Holgado, Amaro, González, Alvarez, & Leret, 1996), and opioids (Jutras-Aswad, DiNieri, Harkany, & Hurd, 2009). In the animal model, there are also associations between perinatal THC exposure and developmental outcomes, including drug sensitivity and self-administration of morphine, changes in locomotor activity, emotional reactivity, sexual behavior, pain responsivity, and disruptions in memory (Mereu et al., 2003; Navarro, Rubio, & de Fonseca, 1995; Vela, Fuentes, Bonnin, Fernández-Ruiz, & Ruiz-Gayo, 1995). Thus, the results of the studies from animal models generally parallel those from the human studies of PME.

Development of the ECBR

Endocannabinoids, or endogenous cannabinoids, are produced in the body and are essential to the development and functioning of the CNS. In the adult, the ECBR plays a modulatory role in physiological functions in the CNS, including tonic inhibition of pain (Guindon & Hohmann, 2009); learning and memory (Lovinger, 2010); sleep regulation (Murillo-Rodríguez, 2008); and feeding, metabolism, and appetite (Viveros, de Fonseca, Bermudez-Silva, & McPartland, 2008). The ECBR and dopamine systems also regulate the role of the prefrontal cortex in cognition, stress responsivity, and the occurrence of psychiatric disorders such as schizophrenia (Galve-Roperh, Palazuelos, Aguado, & Guzmán, 2009; Parolaro, Realini, Vigano, Guidali, & Rubino, 2010; Solowij & Michie, 2007).

Cannabinoid receptors and endocannabinoid ligands can be detected in the brain early in development (Berrendero, Sepe, Ramos, Di, & Fernández-Ruiz, 1999; Romero et al., 1997). CB_1 receptors are first detected during week 14 of gestation (Berrendero et al., 1998; Biegon & Kerman, 2001). The appearance of CB_1 receptors early in gestation coincides with the appearance of most of the neurotransmitter systems (Levitt, Harvey, Friedman, Simansky, & Murphy, 1997). After the initial appearance of CB_1 receptors, a progressive increase in receptor levels is observed in the frontal cortex, hippocampus, basal ganglia, and cerebellum (Mato, Del Omo, & Pazos, 2003; Romero et al., 1997). CB_1 receptors also appear transiently in white matter tracts during development, with the highest densities occurring in the pyramidal tract, brachium conjunctivum, and subventricular germinative zone (Mato et al., 2003; Romero et al., 1997). Cannabinoid receptors are also detected in the corpus callosum, stria terminalis, anterior commissure, midbrain, and cerebral cortex (Fernández-Ruiz, Berrendero, Hernández, & Ramos, 2000; Fernández-Ruiz, Gómez, Hernández, de Miguel, & Ramos, 2004; Romero et al., 1997). These receptors play a functional role during brain development, as evidenced by a peak in binding by WIN55, 212-2, a cannabinoid receptor agonist, which occurs at the same time and in the same brain areas as the receptors (Mato et al., 2003). In adult rats, the CB_1 receptor binding peaks around PND 70, and the highest levels are detected in the striatum, hippocampus, and cerebellum (Fernández-Ruiz et al., 2000).

The ECBR has a significant role in controlling important developmental processes in the CNS. For example, CB_1 receptors are critical for the regulation of activity at ion channels, neurotransmitter transporters, metabolic enzymes, and cytoskeletal integrity (Berghuis et al., 2007; Derkinderen et al., 1996; Derkinderen et al., 2003; He et al., 2005; Rios, Gomes, & Devi, 2006; van der Stelt & DiMarzo, 2005). Differential signaling through CB_1 receptors is important for neuronal specification and is accomplished mainly through cross-talk with other signaling systems (Galve-Roperh, Aguado, Rueda, Velasco, & Guzmán, 2006; Harkany et al., 2007). Furthermore, CB_1 receptors in neurogenic proliferative zones provide the extracellular cues that are necessary for neural progenitor survival, differentiation, migration, and cellular identity (Harkany, Keimpema, Barabás, & Mulder, 2008). The ECBR also plays a role in shaping neuronal connectivity through the CB_1 receptor. This is accomplished by controlling the initial phase of neurochemical specification and by exerting effects on growth cone navigation, axonal elongation, and synaptogenesis of inhibitory interneurons and excitatory cells (Berghuis, Dobszay, Ibanez, Ernfors, & Harkany, 2004; Berghuis et al., 2005; Berghuis et al., 2007; Mulder et al., 2008).

During brain development, the endocannabinoid CB_1 receptor system functions in a neuroprotective role (Fride & Shohami, 2002). Administration of WIN55, 212-2, a cannabinoid agonist, at PND 7 prevents both immediate and delayed neuronal loss (Martínez-Orgado et al., 2003), whereas administration of a CB_1 antagonist, SR141716A, reverses the neuroprotective effects (Martínez-Orgado et al., 2003; van der Stelt et al., 2001). In another study, there were increases in the concentration of anandamide in the developing rat brain following head trauma (Hansen et al., 2001), indicating that the neuroprotective role of endocannabinoids was to rescue neurons from glutamate excitotoxicity. Thus, cannabinoids play a neuroprotective role by preventing or reducing both early and delayed neuron loss (Martínez-Orgado et al., 2003).

Finally, the ECBR system modulates the regulation of specific processes during brain development by influencing the expression of proteins and neural adhesion molecules. Gómez et al. (2003) summarized three processes that have been identified for the modulatory role of cannabinoids during brain development: (a) regulation of gene expression of proteins for specific neurotransmitters such as the enzyme tyrosine hydroxylase (Bonnin et al., 1994; Hernández et al., 2000) and the opioid precursor proenkephalin (Pérez-Rosado, Manzanares, Fernández-Ruiz, & Ramos, 2000); (b) apoptosis via the Bcl-2/bax system of specific groups of neurons with a neurotropic role (Fernández-Ruiz et al., 2000; Fernández-Ruiz, Berrendero, Hernández, Romero, & Ramos, 1999); and (c) modulation of gene expression or function of neural adhesion molecules such as L1 (Fernández-Ruiz et al., 2000; Fernández-Ruiz et al., 1999).

In the mature system, the ECBR consists of endocannabinoids, their receptors, the reuptake mechanism, and a hydrolyzing enzyme. Cannabinoid receptors, CB_1 and CB_2, are widely and densely distributed in neural and nonneural tissues (Mackie, 2008). CB_1 receptors are present in very high levels in several brain regions and in lower amounts in a more widespread fashion. These receptors mediate many of the psychoactive effects of cannabinoids (Herkenham et al., 1991). CB_2 receptors have a more restricted distribution, being found in a number of immune cells and in a few neurons (Galiegue et al., 1995). CB_1 receptors are modulators, and their activation leads to reduced levels of neurotransmitter release. Endogenous ligands for the cannabinoid receptors include anandamide (arachidonyl ethanol amide), 2-arachidonoyl glycerol (2-AG), noladin (arachidonyl glyceryl ether), virodhamine, and N-arachidonoyl-dopamine (NADA; Fride, 2004). In the CNS, endocannabinoids are released from postsynaptic neurons after stimulation and diffuse back to the presynaptic neurons where they act on CB_1 receptors. The endocannabinoids are then eliminated by reuptake into neuronal or glial cells via endocannabinoid transporters, and they are hydrolyzed by fatty acid amide hydroxylase (Christie & Vaughan, 2001).

Sex Differences in the Development of the ECBR

There are sex differences in both the development and distribution of endocannabinoid receptors. In one study, female neonates had a higher receptor density in the striatum at PND 2 and a lower rate at PND 5, compared with males (de Fonseca, Ramos, Bonnin, & Fernández-Ruiz, 1993). From PND 10, the ontogeny of CB_1 receptors in the striatum, limbic forebrain, and ventral mesencephalon showed a progressive increase. Receptor density was higher in males in the striatum at PND 10. However, at PND 20, females had higher receptor density than males. In females, the pattern of maturation of the striatum was more advanced, peaking on PND 30, whereas it reached maximum levels in males on PND 40. Thus, there were subtle differences by sex in the density of cannabinoid receptors at a critical period of brain development in the striatum and ventral mesencephalon. There were no sex differences in endocannabinoid receptor density in the limbic forebrain.

In mature animals, there are important sex differences in the effects of cannabinoids on biological and behavioral responses. Fattore and Fratta (2010) reviewed sex differences in cannabinoid action. In summary, in females, cannabinoid-induced effects included increases in analgesia, motor activity, depression, sexual behavior, catalepsy, and anxiety. Males had increased sensitivity to cannabinoid effects on food intake, energy homeostasis, and decreased sexual behavior. Other behaviors, including measures of stress response, impulsivity, hypothermia, cognition, learning, addiction, reward, and memory, showed no sex differences in studies of animals (Fattore & Fratta, 2010). Thus, there were significant sex differences in the development and specific functions of the ECBR in the brain, including analgesia, motor activity, emotional reactivity, homeostasis, and sexual behavior.

Prenatal Marijuana Exposure and Sex Effects

Given that there are sex differences in the development of the ECBR, it has been hypothesized that there are sex differences in the effects of PME. The majority of the research on sex differences in the effects of PME has been conducted with animal samples. These investigations are reviewed in the next section, followed by a review of the few studies that have been conducted with human samples.

Animal Studies

Prenatal exposure to cannabinoids results in alterations in the developmental profile of both anterior pituitary and steroid hormones. Previous studies have shown that exposure to drugs or stress can modify the role of steroids in the brain during development, resulting in sexually dimorphic differences in behavior (Chen & Smith, 1979; Dalterio & Bartke, 1979; Gruen, Deutch, & Roth, 1990; Hughes & Beveridge, 1990; Kuhn, Ignar, & Windh, 1991; McGivern, Clancy, Hill, & Noble, 1984; Peters & Tanf, 1982; Weisz, Brown, & Ward, 1982). Furthermore, marijuana affects endocrine and reproductive functions, inhibits the secretion of gonadotropin from the pituitary gland, and may act directly on the ovary and testis (Khalsa, 2006). Thus, THC administration during gestation could cause sex-specific effects in the fetus that are directly related to the functioning of CB_1 receptors or that indirectly increase stress on these systems.

CORTICOSTERONE. Corticosterone is a glucocorticoid that is important for the regulation of immune reactions and stress responses. Perinatal exposure to THC has subtle and sex-specific effects on motor activity and locomotion, which in animal studies is an indicator of response to novelty, the ability to habituate to changes in the environment, and emotional reactivity. Females with prenatal THC exposure had increased locomotion and rearing activity (Moreno, Escuredo, Muñoz, de Fonseca, & Navarro, 2005; Navarro, Rubio & de Fonseca, 1994; Rubio et al., 1995), which was attributed to a lack of habituation or a decreased behavioral response after repeated exposure to the novel environment. Navarro et al. (1994) showed that females with prenatal THC exposure had behavioral activation in a familiar environment but decreased activity and increased emotionality in a novel environment compared with control females. The underlying mechanism for these behavioral effects may be related to changes in emotion processing. Deficits in the ability to interpret alerting or threatening stimuli would produce a physiological stress response. Evidence for this is based on studies that show an association between prenatal exposure to THC and higher plasma levels of corticosterone (Moreno et al., 2005; Navarro et al., 1994), increased corticotropin-releasing factor (CRF) in the hypothalamus, and increased plasma concentrations of corticosterone (Rubio et al., 1995) in adult females with gestational THC exposure. Females with prenatal THC exposure displayed higher levels of corticosterone and a blunted adrenal response to the HPA-activating effects in the conditioned place preference test, whereas males with prenatal THC exposure had the opposite pattern (Rubio et al., 1998). Locomotor differences were not observed in males with prenatal THC exposure compared with males without exposure. However, exposed males showed altered endocrine responses, including lower plasma levels of corticosterone and CRF in the hypothalamus (Moreno et al., 2005; Navarro et al., 1994). Thus, the effects of prenatal THC exposure on behavioral measures of emotional reactivity and the response to stress are sexually dimorphic. However, both sexes show underlying physiological changes in the response of corticosterone, an important stress hormone.

DOPAMINE. Dopamine (DA), a catecholamine neurotransmitter, and associated receptors (D^1–D^5) function in the brain to modulate cognition, voluntary movement, motivation and reward, sleep, mood, attention, and working memory. Prenatal exposure to THC is associated with changes in DA function. In one study, acute exposure to D^2 receptor agonists, apomorphine and quinpirole, was associated with changes in locomotor activity as indicated by increased immobility induced by a low dose of apomorphine, and decreased locomotion after administration of quinpirole. This effect was detected in both males and females with perinatal THC exposure compared with controls, but it was more pronounced in the male offspring (Moreno, Trigo, Escuredo, de Fonseca & Navarro, 2003). This type of motor inhibition is typical after administration of dopaminergic agonists and is considered a marker of autoreceptor activation (Yarbrough et al., 1984).

At the beginning of a socio-sexual approach task, males with prenatal THC exposure took longer to visit and spent less time near an incentive male, whereas they took a shorter amount of time to visit and spent more time near an incentive female than did control males (Navarro, de Miguel, de Fonseca, Ramos, & Fernández-Ruiz, 1996). This behavioral difference reflected deficits in the ability of the males to correctly evaluate or respond to novel stimuli. These behavioral alterations were not explained by differences in overall locomotor activity. However, they were correlated with significantly decreased levels of 3,4-dihydroxyphenylacetic acid (DOPAC), a metabolite of DA, in limbic forebrain, suggesting decreased activity of DA neurons in this region among males exposed to THC prenatally.

Studies have also evaluated the effects of prenatal THC exposure on pharmacological measures of DA maturation in males and females. There were differences by sex in messenger RNA (mRNA) levels for the tyrosine hydroxylase (TH) gene that appeared on GD 18 and peaked on GD 21. Males had decreased levels of TH mRNA, whereas females had increased levels (Bonnin, de Miguel,

Castro, Ramos & Fernández-Ruiz, 1996). Males with prenatal THC exposure also showed decreased levels of DA and DOPAC on the day prior to birth compared with males with no THC exposure, although females did not (de Fonseca, Hernández, de Miguel, Fernández-Ruiz, & Ramos, 1992).

Among males, prenatal THC predicted a larger number of D^2 receptors in the striatum, decreased D^2 receptor affinity, and a reduction in TH activity (de Fonseca, Cebeira, Hernández, Ramos, & Fernández-Ruiz, 1990). The former change may be an adaptive response to decreased DA synthesis, whereas the latter differences could result from cannabinoid-induced activation of pre-synaptic D^2 receptors (de Fonseca et al., 1990). In adult animals, those with prenatal THC also had sustained decreases in striatal TH activity following cannabinoid treatment and drug withdrawal (de Fonseca, Cebeira, Fernández-Ruiz, Navarro, & Ramos, 1991). Long-term effects of prenatal THC exposure on TH activity in males were also observed in mesolimbic and hypothalamic brain regions and were correlated with increased numbers of D^1 and D^2 receptors (de Fonseca et al., 1991).

Prenatal THC exposure is also associated with changes in DA function and maturation in females, but the effects are subtle and isolated to the limbic regions of the brain. The maturation of midbrain DA neurons, measured by increased levels of DOPAC production during the first days of birth, was accelerated in females but not males (García, de Miguel, Ramos, & Fernández-Ruiz, 1996). Furthermore, females with perinatal THC exposure had increased levels of DOPAC, a higher DA/DOPAC ratio on PND 20, and decreased DA levels on PND 30 (de Fonseca et al., 1991). García et al. (1996) argued that this increased DOPAC production is a consequence of early maturation of DA re-uptake mechanisms induced by prenatal THC exposure in females.

The physiological effects of prenatal THC exposure on the DA systems indicate that there are subtle and sex-specific effects of prenatal THC exposure on behavioral outcomes associated with DA function, mostly related to loco-motor activity. The effects of perinatal THC exposure on motor function, like those reported for corticosterone, are related to behavioral responses to novelty. Whereas only females show these responses in relation to corticosterone function, both males and females show differences in dopaminergic systems. In the studies of DA, the effects are more pronounced in males. Thus, emotional reactivity and responses to novelty are two targets of further investigation with regard to understanding the sexually dimorphic effects in animals and humans and for characterizing the effects of prenatal THC exposure in these domains in humans. In humans, the effect of THC on the function of the DA system would likely be manifested in behavioral changes that include psychiatric symptoms and behavior problems such as delinquency and aggression.

SEROTONIN. Serotonin is a monoamine neurotransmitter that functions in the regulation of mood and pain and in the control of eating, sleep, and arousal. Prenatal THC exposure has direct, sexually dimorphic, long-term effects on the development of the serotonin system. Administration of THC during gestation decreased levels of 5-hydroxytryptamine (5-HT [serotonin]) in the diencephalon at birth, with males being more susceptible than females (Molina-Holgado et al., 1996). In another study, prenatal THC exposure was associated with increased levels of 5-HT in the neostriatum and decreased levels in the anterior hypothalamus, raphe nuclei, and locus coeruleus (Molina-Holgado et al., 1997). At PND 70, males and females with prenatal THC exposure had decreased levels of 5-HT in ventral hippocampus, septum, and midbrain raphe nuclei. Exposed males additionally had decreased levels of 5-HT in the hypothalamus and rostral neostriatum compared with nonexposed males, a difference that was not observed in the females (Molina-Holgado et al., 1997). There were no differences in levels of 5-HT in the cingulate, dorsal hippocampus, preoptic area, and lateral and medial septum regions. Serotonin directly interacts with and regulates the HPA axis via CRF (Le Feuvre, Aisenthal, & Rothwell, 1991). Thus, the effects of prenatal THC on changes in corticosterone levels may be related to changes in the development of the serotonin system.

These studies show that prenatal THC exposure affects the organization of the serotonin neurotransmitter system. Furthermore, the changes in the development of this system may affect the development of the HPA axis and other endogenous steroid hormones. These interactions may be a neurodevelopmental link to the sexually dimorphic effects observed following prenatal THC exposure. In humans, the behavioral effects of changes in the development of serotonin systems could affect mood regulation. This conclusion is supported by the animal studies that have shown changes in emotional reactivity, especially in novel environments.

Opioids. Prenatal exposure to THC leads to long-term changes in the function of the opioid system, which is related to pain response and drug sensitivity. The opioid receptors appear in embryonic brain in the rat on GD 14 (Kent, Pert, & Herkenham, 1981). During development, prenatal THC exposure affects the opioid receptors or their effector systems, leading to permanent changes in the function of the opioid system (Vela et al., 1995), particularly with respect to pain perception and drug sensitivity. Males with prenatal THC exposure showed an increased sensitivity to pain compared with control males, which was not observed in females. Males with prenatal THC exposure had decreased basal sensitivity to radiant heat during the neonatal period and adolescence compared with control males and, as adults, showed significantly increased sensitivity to pain after morphine challenge (Vela et al., 1995).

Among females with prenatal THC exposure, there was an increased rate of self-administered intravenous morphine compared with control females, an effect that was not found in males (Vela et al., 1998). Prenatal THC exposure in females was also associated with a higher density of μ opioid receptors in the prefrontal cortex, hippocampus (CA3 region), amygdala (posteromedial cortical nucleus), ventral tegmental, and periaqueductal gray matter. These results demonstrate that prenatally THC-exposed females were more susceptible to opiate reinforcing effects and showed changes in the density of μ opioid receptor binding in brain regions that are involved in drug-reinforced behavior (Vela et al., 1998). Prenatal exposure to THC affects a different aspect of drug sensitivity in males. In one study, the rewarding effects of morphine were evaluated using the conditioned place preference paradigm. In this test, one environment is associated with the presence of the drug, whereas a separate environment is associated with the absence of the drug. Males with prenatal THC exposure spent more time in the drug-associated compartment. This effect was significantly correlated with an increased level of plasma corticosterone (Rubio et al., 1995). These differences may be the result of underlying physiological mechanisms. In females, the behavior-related changes in drug sensitivity were associated with changes in the μ opioid receptor binding, whereas in males, the changes were associated with increased reactivity in the HPA axis.

During fetal brain development, proenkephalin mRNA levels were increased in females with prenatal THC exposure, but decreased in males with prenatal TIIC exposure, in the caudate-putamen, hypothalamic paraventricular and ventromedial nuclei, and cerebral cortex (Pérez-Rosado et al., 2000). In adulthood, females with prenatal THC exposure had reduced proenkephalin mRNA in the caudate-putamen compared with control females, which could predict increased vulnerability to opiates. There were no effects of prenatal exposure or sex on levels of proenkephalin mRNA in the nucleus accumbens, central amygdala, and prefrontal cingulate cortex (Corchero et al., 1998).

In summary, animal studies show both direct and indirect associations between perinatal THC exposure and the function of the opioid system. The apparent sexually dimorphic effects of perinatal THC exposure on drug sensitivity warrant further investigation. Whereas both males and females with perinatal THC exposure show increased drug sensitivity, the mechanism for this effect may differ by sex. One human study has reported an association between PME and early onset of marijuana use, which indicates a long-term effect of PME on later drug use (Day et al., 2006). However, no sex effects were reported in this study. Animal studies in the area of drug sensitivity could provide critical information to human studies with regard to pathways and mechanisms that underlie substance use.

Human Studies

Few studies in humans have investigated whether there are sex differences in the effects of PME. Most studies control for sex in statistical analyses but do not specifically test for interactions between PME and sex. To our knowledge, only two reports in the literature tested for Sex × Exposure interactions. Porath and Fried (2005) reported that PME-exposed 16- to 21-year-old males were more likely to initiate cigarette use and to use cigarettes daily than were nonexposed males. There were no differences between PME and non-PME females. In another report, Day et al. (2006) found that whereas PME predicted age of onset and the frequency of marijuana use among 14-year-old offspring, there were no sex differences in the effect of PME on either the age of initiation or the frequency of marijuana use at age 14. In general, however, research shows that males are more likely to be marijuana users than are females (Johnston, O'Malley, Bachman, & Schulenberg, 2010a, 2010b).

Important Links Between Animal and Human Studies

The animal studies of sex differences associated with PME demonstrate that specific domains of function are at risk. These include reactivity to stress and novelty, drug sensitivity, pain responsivity, as well as neurotransmitter function and gene expression. These findings highlight the importance of testing Sex × PME interactions in data analyses in human, as well as animal, studies. The studies of animals are also important in identifying the domains that are likely to be affected in humans. Human studies, on the other hand, provide an opportunity to understand the associations between PME, sex, and factors such as socioeconomic characteristics, family history of substance use, psychological characteristics, and parenting styles, which are more difficult to model in animal samples.

Conclusions and Future Implications

There are significant and important sex differences in the effects of prenatal THC exposure in studies of laboratory animals. These sex-specific effects of gestational THC exposure affect the development and long-term functioning of dopaminergic, serotonergic, and opioid neurotransmitters systems and the HPA axis. As would be expected, based on the systems affected, behavioral outcomes such as the response to novelty, pain, and drug sensitivity are also sexually dimorphic.

The results of animal studies suggest that the primary effects of PME on neurodevelopment and behavior lead to changes in important domains of function, including drug sensitivity, emotional reactivity, and responses to stress and novelty. Studies of the effects of PME in humans show consistency in the domains that are affected. These include emotional regulation (Gray et al., 2005), behavior problems (Day et al., 2011; Goldschmidt et al., 2000), deficits in attention (Fried et al., 1992; Leech et al., 1999; Smith et al., 2004), verbal IQ (Day et al., 1994; Goldschmidt et al., 2008; Willford, Day, Severtson, Richardson, & Day, 2010), and drug use (Day et al., 2006). The potential for sexually dimorphic effects should be explored in each of these domains. In addition, based on the animal research, specific measures of response to stress and emotional processing may be important targets for investigation in human studies of PME.

Further studies with animals would be useful to explicate some of the findings in the human literature, specifically the effects of PME on memory (Day et al., 1994; Fried & Watkinson, 1990; Goldschmidt et al., 2008; Richardson et al., 2002) and attention (Fried et al., 1992; Leech et al., 1999; Smith et al., 2004) and to explore whether these consequences are sexually dimorphic. Laboratory studies using animals would also provide important information on the timing of exposure during gestation and the shape of the association, whether threshold or dose response.

Additional studies are also needed to evaluate the proposed pathways for sex-dependent effects of PME. De Fonseca et al. (1992) proposed three pathways through which sex hormones could be related to sex differences following prenatal drug exposure. First, changes in the development of male offspring may be related to a drug-induced deficit in the fetal programming of testosterone that leads to an incomplete masculinization or a demasculinizing effect. Second, cannabinoids could produce sex differences through interactions between estrogens and THC in the pituitary. For example, cannabinoids might mimic or modify the actions of endogenous steroid hormones that play an important role in brain development, which would lead to sexually dimorphic outcomes (McEwen, 1992). Finally, sexual dimorphism in the distribution of CB_1 receptors may explain some of the sex-dependent sensitivity to the effects of perinatal THC exposure (de Fonseca et al., 1992). Although each of these is a plausible explanation for PME-related sex effects, no study has evaluated these mechanisms. Animal studies will be the most important tool for characterizing the underlying neurobiological mechanisms of PME-related sex effects.

The studies reviewed in this chapter demonstrate that there are important differences by sex in the effects of prenatal exposure to THC. Further laboratory studies are necessary to define these sex-specific consequences of exposure and the underlying neurobiological mechanisms. The potential sex differences in the effects of PME on the human fetus are understudied and should be addressed. This is particularly important given the prevalence of marijuana use among pregnant women and the fact that many of the neurodevelopmental sex-dependent changes associated with PME are maintained into adulthood.

References

Bayer, S. A., Altman, J., Russo, R. J., & Zhang, X. (1993). Timetables of neurogenesis in the human brain based on experimentally determined patterns in the rat. *Neurotoxicology, 14,* 83–144.

Berghuis, P., Dobszay, M. B., Ibanez, R. M., Ernfors, P., & Harkany, T. (2004). Turning the heterogeneous into homogeneous: Studies on selectively isolated GABAergic interneuron subsets. *International Journal of Developmental Neuroscience, 22,* 533–543. doi:10.1016/j.ijdevneu.2004.07.012

Berghuis, P., Dobszay, M. B., Wang, X., Spano, S., Ledda, F., Sousa, K. M., . . . Harkany, T. (2005). Endocannabinoids regulate interneuron migration and morphogenesis by transactivating the TrkB receptor. *Proceedings of the National Academy of Sciences of the United States of America, 102,* 19115–19120. doi:10.1073/pnas.0509494102

Berghuis, P., Rajnicek, A. M., Morozov, Y. M., Ross, R. A., Mulder, J., Urban, G. M., . . . Harkany, T. (2007, May 25). Hardwiring the brain: Endocannabinoids shape neuronal connectivity. *Science, 316,* 1212–1216. doi:10.1126/science.1137406

Berrendero, F., García-Gil, L., Hernández, M. L., Romero, J., Cebeira, M., de Miguel, R., . . . Fernández-Ruiz, J. J. (1998). Localization of mRNA expression and activation of signal transduction mechanisms for cannabinoid receptor in rat brain during fetal development. *Development, 125,* 3179–3188.

Berrendero, F., Sepe, N., Ramos, J. A., Di, M., & Fernández-Ruiz, J. J. (1999). Analysis of cannabinoid receptor binding and mRNA expression and endogenous cannabinoid contents in the developing rat brain during late gestation and early postnatal periods. *Synapse, 33,* 181–191. doi:10.1002/(SICI)1098-2396(19990901)33:3<181::AID-SYN3>3.0.CO;2-R

Biegon, A., & Kerman, I. A. (2001). Autoradiographic study of pre- and postnatal distribution of cannabinoid receptors in human brain. *NeuroImage, 14,* 1463–1468. doi:10.1006/nimg.2001.0939

Bonnin, A., de Miguel, R., Castro, J. G., Ramos, J. A., & Fernández-Ruiz, J. J. (1996). Effects of prenatal exposure to delta 9-tetrahydrocannabinol on the fetal and early postnatal development of tyrosine hydroxylase-containing neurons in rat brain. *Journal of Molecular Neuroscience, 7,* 291–308. doi:10.1007/BF02737066

Bonnin, A., de Miguel, R., Rodríguez-Manzaneque, J. C., Fernández-Ruiz, J. J., Santos, A., & Ramos, J. A. (1994). Changes in tyrosine hydroxylase gene expression in mesencephalic catecholaminergic neurons of immature and adult male rats perinatally exposed to cannabinoids. *Developmental Brain Research, 81,* 147–150. doi:10.1016/0165-3806(94)90079-5

Chen, J. J., & Smith, E. R. (1979). Effects of perinatal alcohol on sexual differentiation and open field behavior in rats. *Hormones and Behavior, 13,* 219–231. doi:10.1016/0018-506X(79)90040-0

Christie, M. J., & Vaughan, C. W. (2001, March 29). Cannabinoids act backwards. *Nature, 410,* 527–530. doi:10.1038/35069167

Corchero, J., García-Gil, L., Manzanares, J., Fernández-Ruiz, J. J., Fuentes, J. A., & Ramos, J. A. (1998). Perinatal delta9-tetrahydrocannabinol exposure reduces proenkephalin gene expression in the caudate-putamen of adult female rats. *Life Sciences, 63,* 843–850. doi:10.1016/S0024-3205(98)00341-5

Dalterio, S., & Bartke, A. (1979, September 28). Perinatal exposure to cannabinoids alters male reproductive function in mice. *Science, 205,* 1420–1422. doi:10.1126/science.472762

Day, N. L., Goldschmidt, L., & Thomas, C. (2006). Prenatal marijuana exposure contributes to the prediction of marijuana use at age 14. *Addiction, 101,* 1313–1322. doi:10.1111/j.1360-0443.2006.01523.x

Day, N. L., Leech, S. L., & Goldschmidt, L. (2011). The effects of prenatal marijuana exposure on delinquent behaviors are mediated by measures of neurocognitive functioning. *Neurotoxicology and Teratology, 33,* 129–136

Day, N. L., Richardson, G. A., Goldschmidt, L., Robles, N., Taylor, P., Stoffer, D., . . . Geva, D. (1994). Effect of prenatal marijuana exposure on the cognitive development of offspring at age three. *Neurotoxicology and Teratology, 16,* 169–175. doi:10.1016/0892-0362(94)90114-7

de Fonseca, F. R., Cebeira, M., Fernández-Ruiz, J. J., Navarro, M., & Ramos, J. A. (1991). Effects of pre- and perinatal exposure to hashish extracts on the ontogeny of brain dopaminergic neurons. *Neuroscience, 43,* 713–723. doi:10.1016/0306-4522(91)90329-M

de Fonseca, F. R., Cebeira, M., Hernández, M. L., Ramos, J. A., & Fernández-Ruiz, J. J. (1990). Changes in brain dopaminergic indices induced by perinatal exposure to cannabinoids in rats. *Developmental Brain Research, 51,* 237–240. doi:10.1016/0165-3806(90)90280-C

de Fonseca, F. R., Hernández, M. L., de Miguel, R., Fernández-Ruiz, J. J., & Ramos, J. A. (1992). Early changes in the development of dopaminergic neurotransmission after maternal exposure to cannabinoids. *Pharmacology, Biochemistry and Behavior, 41,* 469–474. doi:10.1016/0091-3057(92)90359-N

de Fonseca, F. R., Ramos, J. A., Bonnin, A., & Fernández-Ruiz, J. J. (1993). Presence of cannabinoid binding sites in the brain from early postnatal ages. *Neuroreport, 4,* 135–138.

Derkinderen, P., Toutant, M., Burgaya, F., Le Bert, M., Siciliano, J. C., de Franciscis, V., . . . Girault, J. A. (1996, September 20). Regulation of a neuronal form of focal adhesion kinase by anandamide. *Science, 273,* 1719–1722. doi:10.1126/science.273.5282.1719

Derkinderen, P., Valjent, E., Toutant, M., Corvol, J. C., Enslen, H., Ledent, C., . . . Girault, J. A. (2003). Regulation of extracellular signal-related kinase by cannabinoids in hippocampus. *The Journal of Neuroscience, 23,* 2371–2382.

Fattore, L., & Fratta, W. (2010). How important are sex differences in cannabinoid action? *British Journal of Pharmacology, 160,* 544–548. doi:10.1111/j.1476-5381.2010.00776.x

Fernández-Ruiz, J., Berrendero, F., Hernández, M. L., & Ramos, J. A. (2000). The endogenous cannabinoid system and brain development. *Trends in Neurosciences, 23,* 14–20. doi:10.1016/S0166-2236(99)01491-5

Fernández-Ruiz, J., Berrendero, F., Hernández, M. L., Romero, J., & Ramos, J. A. (1999). Role of endocannabinoids in brain development. *Life Sciences, 65,* 725–736. doi:10.1016/S0024-3205(99)00295-7

Fernández-Ruiz, J., Gómez, M., Hernández, M., de Miguel, R., & Ramos, J. A. (2004). Cannabinoids and gene expression during brain development. *Neurotoxicity Research, 6,* 389–401. doi:10.1007/BF03033314

Fride, E. (2004). The endocannabinoid-CB(1) receptor system in pre- and postnatal life. *European Journal of Pharmacology, 500,* 289–297. doi:10.1016/j.ejphar.2004.07.033

Fride, E. (2008). Multiple roles for the endocannabinoid system during the earliest stages of life: Pre- and postnatal development. *Journal of Neuroendocrinology, 20*(Suppl. 1), 75–81. doi:10.1111/j.1365-2826.2008.01670.x

Fride, E., & Shohami, E. (2002). The endocannabinoid system: Function in survival of the embryo, the newborn and the neuron. *Neuroreport, 13,* 1833–1841. doi:10.1097/00001756-200210280-00001

Fried, P. A., & Makin, J. E. (1987). Neonatal behavioral correlates of prenatal exposure to marihuana, cigarettes and alcohol in a low risk population. *Neurotoxicology and Teratology, 9,* 1–7. doi:10.1016/0892-0362(87)90062-6

Fried, P. A., & Watkinson, B. (1990). 36- and 48- month neurobehavioral follow-up of children prenatally exposed to marijuana, cigarettes, and alcohol. *Journal of Developmental and Behavioral Pediatrics, 11,* 49–58. doi:10.1097/00004703-199004000-00003

Fried, P. A., & Watkinson, B. (2000). Visuoperceptual functioning differs in 9- to 12-year olds prenatally exposed to cigarettes and marihuana. *Neurotoxicology and Teratology, 22,* 11–20. doi:10.1016/S0892-0362(99)00046-X

Fried, P. A., & Watkinson, B. (2001). Differential effects on facets of attention in adolescents prenatally exposed to cigarettes and marihuana. *Neurotoxicology and Teratology, 23,* 421–430. doi:10.1016/S0892-0362(01)00160-X

Fried, P. A., Watkinson, B., & Gray, R. (1992). A follow-up study of attentional behavior in 6-year-old children exposed prenatally to marihuana, cigarettes, and alcohol. *Neurotoxicology and Teratology, 14,* 299–311. doi:10.1016/0892-0362(92)90036-A

Fried, P. A., Watkinson, B., & Gray, R. (1998). Differential effects on cognitive functioning in 9- to 12-year-olds prenatally exposed to cigarettes and marihuana. *Neurotoxicology and Teratology, 20,* 293–306. doi:10.1016/S0892-0362(97)00091-3

Fried, P. A., Watkinson, B., & Gray, R. (2003). Differential effects on cognitive functioning in 13- to 16-year-olds prenatally exposed to cigarettes and marihuana. *Neurotoxicology and Teratology, 25,* 427–436. doi:10.1016/S0892-0362(03)00029-1

Galiègue, S., Mary, S., Marchand, J., Dussossoy, D., Carrière, D., Carayon, P., . . . Casellas, P. (1995). Expression of central and peripheral cannabinoid receptors in human immune tissues and leukocyte subpopulations. *European Journal of Biochemistry, 232,* 54–61. doi:10.1111/j.1432-1033.1995.tb20780.x

Galve-Roperh, I., Aguado, T., Rueda, D., Velasco, G., & Guzmán, M. (2006). Endocannabinoids: A new family of lipid mediators involved in the regulation of neural cell development. *Current Pharmaceutical Design, 12,* 2319–2325. doi:10.2174/138161206777585139

Galve-Roperh, I., Palazuelos, J., Aguado, T., & Guzmán, M. (2009). The endocannabinoid system and the regulation of neural development: Potential implications in psychiatric disorders. *European Archives of Psychiatry and Clinical Neuroscience, 259,* 371–382. doi:10.1007/s00406-009-0028-y

García, L., de Miguel, R., Ramos, J. A., & Fernández-Ruiz, J. J. (1996). Perinatal delta 9-tetrahydrocannabinol exposure in rats modifies the responsiveness of midbrain dopaminergic neurons in adulthood to a variety of challenges with dopaminergic drugs. *Drug and Alcohol Dependence, 42,* 155–166. doi:10.1016/S0376-8716(96)01276-8

Goldschmidt, L., Day, N. L., & Richardson, G. A. (2000). Effects of prenatal marijuana exposure on child behavior problems at age 10. *Neurotoxicology and Teratology, 22,* 325–336. doi:10.1016/S0892-0362(00)00066-0

Goldschmidt, L., Richardson, G. A., Willford, J. A., & Day, N. L. (2008). Prenatal marijuana exposure and intelligence test performance at age six. *Journal of the American Academy of Child & Adolescent Psychiatry, 47,* 254–263. doi:10.1097/CHI.0b013e318160b3f0

Gómez, M., Hernández, M., Johansson, B., de Miguel, R., Ramos, J. A., & Fernández-Ruiz, J. (2003). Prenatal cannabinoid exposure and gene expression for neural adhesion molecule L1 in the fetal rat brain. *Developmental Brain Research, 147,* 201–207. doi:10.1016/j.devbrainres.2003.10.016

Gray, K. A., Day, N. L., Leech, S., & Richardson, G. A. (2005). Prenatal marijuana exposure: Effect on child depressive symptoms at ten years of age. *Neurotoxicology and Teratology, 27,* 439–448. doi:10.1016/j.ntt.2005.03.010

Gruen, R. J., Deutch, A. Y., & Roth, R. H. (1990). Perinatal diazepam exposure: Alterations in exploratory behavior and mesolimbic dopamine turnover. *Pharmacology, Biochemistry and Behavior, 36,* 169–175. doi:10.1016/0091-3057(90)90144-7

Guindon, J., & Hohmann, A. G. (2009). The endocannabinoid system and pain. *CNS & Neurological Disorders—Drug Targets, 8,* 403–421.

Hansen, H. H., Schmid, P. C., Bittigau, P., Lastres-Becker, I., Berrendero, F., Manzanares, J., . . . Hansen, H. S. (2001). Anandamide, but not 2-arachidonoylglycerol, accumulates during in vivo neurodegeneration. *Journal of Neurochemistry, 78,* 1415–1427. doi:10.1046/j.1471-4159.2001.00542.x

Harkany, T., Guzmán, M., Galve-Roperh, I., Berghuis, P., Devi, L. A., & Mackie, K. (2007). The emerging functions of endocannabinoid signaling during CNS development. *Trends in Pharmacological Sciences, 28,* 83–92. doi:10.1016/j.tips.2006.12.004

Harkany, T., Keimpema, E., Barabás, K., & Mulder, J. (2008). Endocannabinoid functions controlling neuronal specification during brain development. *Molecular and Cellular Endocrinology, 286*(1–2 Suppl. 1), S84-90.

He, J. C., Gomes, I., Nguyen, T., Jayaram, G., Ram, P. T., Devi, L. A., & Iyengar, R. (2005). The G alpha(o/i)-coupled cannabinoid receptor-mediated neurite outgrowth involves Rap regulation of Src and Stat3. *The Journal of Biological Chemistry, 280,* 33426–33434. doi:10.1074/jbc.M502812200

Herkenham, M., Lynn, A. B., Johnson, M. R., Melvin, L. S., de Costa, B. R., & Rice, K. C. (1991). Characterization and localization of cannabinoid receptors in rat brain: A quantitative in vitro autoradiographic study. *The Journal of Neuroscience, 11,* 563–583.

Hernández, M., Berrendero, F., Suárez, I., García-Gil, L., Cebeira, M., Mackie, K., . . . Fernández-Ruiz, J. (2000). Cannabinoid CB(1) receptors colocalize with tyrosine hydroxylase in cultured fetal mesencephalic neurons and their activation increases the levels of this enzyme. *Brain Research, 857,* 56–65. doi:10.1016/S0006-8993(99)02322-7

Hughes, R. N., & Beveridge, I. J. (1990). Sex- and age-dependent effects of prenatal exposure to caffeine on an open-field behavior, emergency latency and adrenal weights in rats. *Life Sciences, 47,* 2075–2088. doi:10.1016/0024-3205(90)90443-U

Hutchings, D. E., Martin, B. R., Gamagaris, Z., Miller, N., & Fico, T. (1989). Plasma concentrations of delta-9-tetrahydrocannabinol in dams and fetuses following acute or multiple prenatal dosing in rats. *Life Sciences, 44,* 697–701. doi:10.1016/0024-3205(89)90380-9

Jakubovic, A., Hattori, T., & McGreer, P. L. (1973). Radioactivity in suckled rats after giving 14 C- tetrahydrocannabinol to the mother. *European Journal of Pharmacology, 22,* 221–223. doi:10.1016/0014-2999(73)90018-6

Johnston, L. D., O'Malley, P. M., Bachman, J. G., & Schulenberg, J. E. (2010a). *Monitoring the Future National Survey results on drug use, 1975–2009. Vol. 1. Secondary school students* (NIH Publication No. 10-7584). Bethesda, MD: National Institute on Drug Abuse.

Johnston, L. D., O'Malley, P. M., Bachman, J. G., & Schulenberg, J. E. (2010b). *Monitoring the Future National Survey results on drug use, 1975–2009: Vol. 2. College students and adults ages 19–50* (NIH Publication No. 10-7585). Bethesda, MD: National Institute on Drug Abuse.

Jutras-Aswad, D., DiNieri, J. A., Harkany, T., & Hurd, Y. L. (2009). Neurobiological consequences of maternal cannabis on human fetal development and its neuropsychiatric outcome. *European Archives of Psychiatry and Clinical Neuroscience, 259,* 395–412. doi:10.1007/s00406-009-0027-z

Kent, J. L., Pert, C., & Herkenham, M. (1981). Ontogeny of opiate receptors in rat forebrain visualization by in vitro autoradiography. *Developmental Brain Research, 254,* 487–504. doi:10.1016/0165-3806(81)90018-3

Khalsa, J. H. (2006). Medical and health consequences of marijuana. In M. A. ElSohly (Ed.), *Forensic science and medicine: Marijuana and the cannabinoids* (pp. 237–252). Totowa, NJ: Humana Press.

Kuhn, C., Ignar, D., & Windh, R. (1991). Endocrine function as a target of perinatal drug effects: Methodological issues. In M. M. Kilbey & K. Asghar (Eds.), *Methodological issues in controlled studies on effects of prenatal exposure to drug abuse* (pp. 206–232) (NIDA Research Monograph 114). Rockville, MD: National Institute on Drug Abuse.

Leech, S. L., Richardson, G. A., Goldschmidt, L., & Day, N. L. (1999). Prenatal substance exposure: Effects on attention and impulsivity of 6-year-olds. *Neurotoxicology and Teratology, 21,* 109–118. doi:10.1016/S0892-0362(98)00042-7

Le Feuvre, R. A., Aisenthal, E., & Rothwell, N. J. (1991). Involvement of corticotrophin releasing factor (CRF) in the thermogenic and anorexic actions of serotonin (5-HT) and related compounds. *Brain Research, 555,* 245–250. doi:10.1016/0006-8993(91)90348-Y

Lester, B. M., & Dreher, M. (1989). Effects of marijuana use during pregnancy on newborn cry. *Child Development, 60,* 765–771. doi:10.2307/1131016

Levitt, P., Harvey, J. A., Friedman, E., Simansky, K., & Murphy, E. H. (1997). New evidence for neurotransmitter influences on brain development. *Trends in Neurosciences, 20,* 269–274. doi:10.1016/S0166-2236(96)01028-4

Lovinger, D. M. (2010). Neurotransmitter roles in synaptic modulation, plasticity and learning in the dorsal striatum. *Neuropharmacology, 58,* 951–961. doi:10.1016/j.neuropharm.2010.01.008

Mackie, K. (2008). Cannabinoid receptors: Where they are and what they do. *Journal of Neuroendocrinology, 20*(Suppl. 1), 10–14. doi:10.1111/j.1365-2826.2008.01671.x

Martínez-Orgado, J., Fernández-Frutos, B., González, R., Romero, E., Urigüen, L., Romero, J., & Viveros, M. P. (2003). Neuroprotection by the cannabinoid agonist WIN-55212 in an in vivo newborn rat model of acute severe asphyxia. *Molecular Brain Research, 114,* 132–139. doi:10.1016/S0169-328X(03)00163-3

Mato, S., Del Omo, E., & Pazos, A. (2003). Otogenetic development of cannabinoid receptor expression and signal transduction functionality in the human brain. *The European Journal of Neuroscience, 17,* 1747–1754. doi:10.1046/j.1460-9568.2003.02599.x

McEwen, B. S. (1992). Steroid hormones: Effect on brain development and function. *Hormone Research, 37,* 1–10. doi:10.1159/000182393

McGivern, R. F., Clancy, A. N., Hill, M. A., & Noble, E. P. (1984, May 25). Prenatal alcohol exposure alters adult expression of sexually dimorphic behaviors in the rat. *Science, 224,* 896–898. doi:10.1126/science.6719121

Mereu, G., Fà, M., Ferraro, L., Cagiano, R., Antonelli, T., Tattoli, M., . . . Cuomo, V. (2003). Prenatal exposure to cannabinoid agonist produces memory deficits linked to dysfunction in hippocampal long-term potentiation and glutamate release. *Proceedings of the National Academy of Sciences of the United States of America, 100,* 4915–4920. doi:10.1073/pnas.0537849100

Molina-Holgado, F., Alvarez, F. J., González, I., Antonio, M. T., & Leret, M. L. (1997). Maternal exposure to delta 9-tetrahydrocannabinol (delta 9-THC) alters indolamine levels and turnover in adult male and female rat brain regions. *Brain Research Bulletin, 43,* 173–178. doi:10.1016/30361-9230(96)00434-0

Molina-Holgado, F., Amaro, A., González, M. I., Alvarez, F. J., & Leret, M. L. (1996). Effect of maternal delta 9-tetrahydrocannabinol on developing serotonergic system. *European Journal of Pharmacology, 316,* 39–42. doi:10.1016/S0014-2999(96)00753-4

Moreno, M., Escuredo, L., Muñoz, R., de Fonseca, F. R., & Navarro, M. (2005). Long-term behavioural and neuroendocrine effects of perinatal activation or blockage of CB1 cannabinoid receptors. *Behavioural Pharmacology, 16,* 423–430. doi:10.1097/00008877-200509000-00015

Moreno, M., Trigo, J. M., Escuredo, L., de Fonseca, F. R., & Navarro, M. (2003). Perinatal exposure to delta 9-tetrahydrocannabinol increases presynaptic dopamine D2 receptor sensitivity: A behavioral study in rats. *Pharmacology, Biochemistry and Behavior, 75,* 565–575. doi:10.1016/S0091-3057(03)00117-5

Mulder, J., Aguado, T., Keimpema, E., Barabás, K., Ballester Rosado, C. J., & Nguyen, L. . . . Harkany, T. (2008). Endocannabinoid signaling controls pyramidal cell specification and long-range axon patterning. *Proceedings of the National Academy of Sciences, U.S.A., 105,* 8760–8765.

Murillo-Rodríguez, E. (2008). The role of the CB1 receptor in the regulation of sleep. *Progress in Neuro-Psychopharmacology & Biological Psychiatry, 32,* 1420–1427. doi:10.1016/j.pnpbp.2008.04.008

Navarro, M., de Miguel, R., de Fonseca, F. R., Ramos, J. A., & Fernández-Ruiz, J. J. (1996). Perinatal cannabinoid exposure modifies the sociosexual approach behavior and the mesolimbic dopaminergic activity of adult male rats. *Behavioural Brain Research, 75,* 91–98. doi:10.1016/0166-4328(96)00176-3

Navarro, M., Rubio, P., & de Fonseca, F. R. (1994). Sex-dimorphic psychomotor activation after perinatal exposure to (-)-delta 9-tetrahydrocannabinol. An ontogenic study in Wistar rats. *Psychopharmacology, 116,* 414–422. doi:10.1007/BF02247471

Navarro, M., Rubio, P., & de Fonseca, F. R. (1995). Behavioural consequences of maternal exposure to natural cannabinoids in rats. *Psychopharmacology, 122,* 1–14. doi:10.1007/BF02246436

National Institute on Drug Abuse. (1996). *National Pregnancy and Health Survey: Drug use among women delivering live births: 1992* (NIH Publication No. 96-3819). Rockville, MD: Author. doi:10.3886/ICPSR02835

Parolaro, D., Realini, N., Vigano, D., Guidali, C., & Rubino, T. (2010). The endocannabinoid system and psychiatric disorders. *Experimental Neurology, 224,* 3–14. doi:10.1016/j.expneurol.2010.03.018

Pérez-Rosado, A., Manzanares, J., Fernández-Ruiz, J., & Ramos, J. A. (2000). Prenatal delta 9-tetrahydrocannabinol exposure modifies proenkephalin gene expression in the female rat brain: Sex-dependent differences. *Developmental Brain Research, 120,* 77–81. doi:10.1016/S0165-3806(99)00170-4

Peters, D. A. V., & Tanf, S. (1982). Sex-dependent biological changes following prenatal nicotine exposure in the rat. *Pharmacology, Biochemistry and Behavior, 17,* 1077–1082. doi:10.1016/0091-3057(82)90497-X

Porath, A. J., & Fried, P. A. (2005). Effects of prenatal cigarette and marijuana exposure on drug use among offspring. *Neurotoxicology and Teratology, 27,* 267–277. doi:10.1016/j.ntt.2004.12.003

Richardson, G. A., Ryan, C., Willford, J., Day, N. L., & Goldschmidt, L. (2002). Prenatal alcohol and marijuana exposure: Effects on neuropsychological outcomes at 10 years. *Neurotoxicology and Teratology, 24,* 311–320. doi:10.1016/S0892-0362(02)00193-9

Rios, C., Gomes, I., & Devi, L. A. (2006). Mu opioid and CB1 cannabinoid receptor interactions: Reciprocal inhibition of receptor signaling and neuritogenesis. *British Journal of Pharmacology, 148,* 387–395. doi:10.1038/sj.bjp.0706757

Romero, J., García-Palomero, E., Berrendero, F., García-Gil, L., Hernández, M. L., Ramos, J. A., & Fernández-Ruiz, J. J. (1997). Atypical location of cannabinoid receptors in white matter areas during rat brain development. *Synapse, 26,* 317–323. doi:10.1002/(SICI)1098-2396(199707)26:3<317::AID-SYN12>3.0.CO;2-S

Rubio, P., de Fonseca, F. R., Martín-Calderón, J. L., Del Arco, I., Bartolomé, S., Villanúa, M. A., & Navarro, M. (1998). Maternal exposure to low doses of delta 9-tetrahydrocannabinol facilitates morphine-induced place conditioning in adult male offspring. *Pharmacology, Biochemistry and Behavior, 61,* 229–238. doi:10.1016/S0091-3057(98)00099-9

Rubio, P., de Fonseca, F. R., Muñoz, R. M., Ariznavarreta, C., Martín-Calderón, J. L., & Navarro, M. (1995). Long-term behavioral effects of perinatal exposure to delta 9-tetrahydrocannabinol in rats: Possible role of pituitary–adrenal axis. *Life Sciences, 56,* 2169–2176. doi:10.1016/0024-3205(95)00204-J

Scher, M. S., Richardson, G. A., Coble, P. A., Day, N. L., & Stoffer, D. S. (1988). The effects of prenatal alcohol and marijuana exposure: Disturbances in neonatal sleep cycling and arousal. *Pediatric Research, 24,* 101–105.

Smith, A. M., Fried, P., Hogan, M., & Cameron, I. (2004). Effects of prenatal marijuana on response inhibition: An fMRI study of young adults. *Neurotoxicology and Teratology, 26,* 533–542. doi:10.1016/j.ntt.2004.04.004

Solowij, N., & Michie, P. T. (2007). Cannabis and cognitive dysfunction: Parallels with endophenotypes of schizophrenia? *Journal of Psychiatry & Neuroscience, 32,* 30–52.

Substance Abuse and Mental Health Services Administration, Office of Applied Studies. (2000). *Summary of findings from the 1999 National Household Survey on Drug Abuse* (DHHS Publication No. SMA99-3328, NHSDA Series H-12). Rockville, MD: U.S. Department of Health and Human Services.

van der Stelt, M., & Di Marzo, V. (2005). Anandamide as an intracellular messenger regulating ion channel activity. *Prostaglandins & Other Lipid Mediators, 77,* 111–122. doi:10.1016/j.prostaglandins.2004.09.007

van der Stelt, M., Veldhuis, W. B., van Haaften, G. W., Fezza, F., Bisogno, T., Bär, P. R., . . . Nicolay, K. (2001). Exogenous anandamide protects rat brain against acute neuronal injury in vivo. *The Journal of Neuroscience, 21,* 8765–8771.

Vela, G., Fuentes, J. A., Bonnin, A., Fernández-Ruiz, J., & Ruiz-Gayo, M. (1995). Perinatal exposure to delta 9-tetrahydrocannabinol (delta 9-THC) leads to changes in opioid-related behavioral patterns in rats. *Brain Research, 680,* 142–147. doi:10.1016/0006-8993(95)00255-O

Vela, G., Martín, S., García-Gil, L., Crespo, J. A., Ruiz-Gayo, M., Fernández-Ruiz, J. J., . . . Ambrosio, E. (1998). Maternal exposure to delta 9-tetrahydrocannabinol facilitates morphine self-administration behavior and changes regional binding to central μ opioid receptors in adult offspring female rats. *Brain Research, 807,* 101–109. doi:10.1016/S0006-8993(98)00766-5

Viveros, M. P., de Fonseca, F. R., Bermudez-Silva, F. J., & McPartland, J. M. (2008). Critical role of the endocannabinoid system in the regulation of food intake and energy metabolism, with phylogenetic, developmental, and pathophysiological implications. *Endocrine, Metabolic & Immune Disorders Drug Targets, 8,* 220–230. doi:10.2174/187153008785700082

Weisz, J., Brown, B. L., & Ward, I. L. (1982). Maternal stress decreases aromatase activity in brains of male and female rat fetuses. *Neuroendocrinology, 35,* 374–379. doi:10.1159/000123410

Willford, J. A., Day, R. D., Severtson, S. G., Richardson, G. A., & Day, N. L. (2010). *Cognitive status in adolescence as a function of prenatal marijuana exposure, child, maternal, and environmental characteristics.* Manuscript submitted for publication.

Yarbrough, G. G., McGuffin-Clineschmidt, J., Singh, D. K., Haubrich, D. R., Bendesky, R. J., & Martin, G. E. (1984). Electrophysiological, biochemical and behavioral assessment of dopamine autoreceptor activation by a series of dopamine agonists. *European Journal of Pharmacology, 99,* 73–78. doi:10.1016/0014-2999(84)90433-3

Part III

Alcohol

7

Sex Differences in Prenatal Alcohol Abuse in Humans

Ann P. Streissguth

It is now well recognized that alcohol is a teratogen. Alcohol crosses the placenta freely, and within minutes the fetus has the same blood alcohol level as the mother. Prenatal alcohol exposure can cause all four of the main teratogenic end points—death, malformations, growth deficiency, and functional deficits (Riley & Vorhees, 1986; West, 1986). As for all teratogens, the impact on the individual offspring depends on the dose, timing, and conditions of exposure, the latter of which include the individual genetic characteristics of both mother and offspring.

In 1990, the Environmental Protection Agency organized a workshop to compare human and animal studies on a variety of substances thought to be neurotoxicants. A small group of scientists wrote a paper on each topic. The paper on alcohol concluded as follows:

> Prenatal alcohol exposure has been shown to affect a wide variety of neurobehavioral outcomes in humans, with effects of greater magnitude associated with higher levels of exposure. There is a sizable body of data indicating deficits in learning, inhibition, attention, regulatory behaviors, and motor performance. While the comparisons between human and animal data are primarily qualitative in nature, the degree of correspondence is noteworthy. (Driscoll, Streissguth, & Riley, 1990, p. 235; see Table 7.1)

The biological foundations for male/female differences in offspring sexual development and function, and how these are affected by alcohol exposure in utero, have been well described in animal models by Otero and Kelly (see Chapter 8, this volume). There is a large body of research on animal models documenting sex differences in the offspring response to alcohol as a teratogen. However, very few studies have been devoted to male/female differences in humans exposed to alcohol in utero, and sex of the offspring is often overlooked even in clinical descriptions of the children.

This work has been supported by National Institute on Alcohol Abuse and Alcohol Grant R37-AA01455 01-34, by Centers for Disease Control and Prevention Grant RO4/CCR008515, and by an Indian Health Service Contract. The content is solely the responsibility of the author and does not necessarily represent the official views of the National Institute on Alcohol Abuse and Alcoholism or the National Institutes of Health.

Table 7.1.   Behavioral Effects Following Prenatal Alcohol Exposure

Humans	Animals
Hyperactivity, Reactivity	Increased activity, exploration and reactivity
Attention deficits, distractibility	Decreased attention
Lack of inhibition	Inhibition deficits
Mental retardation, learning difficulties	Impaired associative learning
Reduced habituation	Impaired habituation
Perseveration	Perseveration
Feeding difficulties	Feeding difficulties
Gait abnormalities	Altered gait
Poor fine and gross motor skills	Poor coordination
Developmental delay (motor, social, language)	Developmental delay
Hearing abnormalities	Altered auditory evoked potentials
Poor state regulation	Poor state regulation

Note.   From "Prenatal Alcohol Exposure: Comparability of Effects in Humans and Animal Models" by C. D. Driscoll, A. P. Streissguth, and E. P. Riley, 1990, *Neurotoxicology & Teratology, 12,* p. 233. Reprinted with permission.

One particular problem in studying alcohol as a teratogen in humans is that heavy ingestion of alcohol by the mother can affect both the offspring and the mother, thereby affecting both the prenatal and the postnatal environment of the offspring. Some teratogens, for example, the rubella virus, can have a devastating effect on the offspring from a case of measles that has little pronounced effect on the mother. Alcohol is different. It is now well known that women are much more sensitive to the effects of alcohol than are men. Women have a higher blood alcohol level than men after similar ethanol intake; get intoxicated more quickly than men from a similar amount of alcohol; and die younger from less lifetime use of alcohol than do men (Califano, 2007; Schenker, 1997; Wagnerberger, Schafer, Schwartz, Bode, & Parlesak, 2007). Women who abuse alcohol die not only from liver cirrhosis and medical problems but also from accidents, misjudgments, and abuse. The obvious confound in studying the substantial impact of the alcohol-abusing mother on her child is that alcohol can affect not only the developing embryo and fetus but also the postnatal environment of the child, in terms of high rates of maternal death, surrogate parenting, child abuse, and neglect.

Only in animal models is it feasible to isolate the prenatal exposure conditions from the postnatal rearing conditions. In this chapter, I present the data on male/female differences in patients diagnosed with fetal alcohol syndrome (FAS) and exposed to heavy alcohol in utero and occasionally resort to the presentation of illustrative patient histories as applicable.

Because there have been (to my knowledge) no specific investigations of sex differences per se in patients with FAS, this chapter takes a historical, clinical perspective, presenting the available data descriptively. Since 1973, articles on FAS have appeared in the medical literature, with gradually increasing sample sizes in which newly diagnosed patients were added to an accruing cohort. Initially, these early patients were seen at the University of Washington Medical School in Seattle, the home of Dr. David W. Smith, often considered the "father of dysmorphology" because of his early publication *Recognizable Patterns of Human Malformation* (1976). These patients were referred to me for psychological evaluation and help (because I was a colleague of Dr. Smith's), and my students and I published papers on this ever-expanding group, which gradually included those in other settings (e.g., New Mexico and Alaska, where Dr. Smith's fellows also began identifying patients with FAS). The statisticians on our team did not feel it was appropriate to perform significance tests on this kind of descriptive data, and this tradition has been continued with this chapter.

Fetal Alcohol Syndrome, Fetal Alcohol Spectrum Disorders, and the Impact of Alcoholism on Mothers of Children With FASD

Nearly 40 years ago, the identification of a new birth defect, FAS (Jones et al., 1973; Jones & Smith, 1973), brought to light earlier work in France by Lemoine, Harousseau, Borteyru, and Menuet (1968), and together these studies stimulated a wave of animal research that documented the teratogenicity of alcohol (e.g., Riley & Vorhees, 1986; West 1986). Although sex differences have been reported in animal studies of alcohol as a teratogen (e.g., Middaugh, Kelley, Brandy, & McGroarty, 1999; Weinberg, Sliwowska, Lan, & Hellemans, 2008; see also Chapter 8, this volume), they have rarely been a focus in clinical studies, other than in connection with descriptions of genital anomalies.

FAS in humans has three defining characteristics: (a) physical deformities, particularly, but not specifically, of the face (including short palpebral fissures, long or smooth philtrum, and thin upper lip); (b) growth deficiencies; and (c) central nervous system damage or dysfunction, or microcephaly. In 1978, Clarren and Smith reviewed the published literature on 245 diagnosed patients from many countries; the sex of patients was not noted.

Whereas the diagnosis of FAS has remained quite stable across the years, the appropriate nomenclature for the rest of the spectrum of prenatal alcohol-related effects on offspring has been difficult to resolve. In early years, alcohol-exposed patients who had some but not all of the specific characteristics of FAS were described as having *fetal alcohol effects* (FAE), a term coined by David W. Smith (1981), who early on recognized the broader impact of prenatal alcohol exposure beyond the specific FAS diagnosis. Although FAE was eventually replaced by a more detailed nomenclature presented by the Institute of Medicine (Stratton, Howe, & Battaglia, 1996), in this chapter we use the diagnostic terms used by Smith and colleagues when these patients were diagnosed, namely, FAS and FAE.

New terminology was presented by the Institute of Medicine (Stratton et al., 1996) in an attempt to bring more rigor into the non-FAS part of the spectrum of effects related to prenatal alcohol exposure. These diagnostic categories included partial fetal alcohol syndrome, alcohol-related birth defects, and alcohol-related neurodevelopmental disorders. In 2004, the National Organization on Fetal Alcohol Syndrome, in conjunction with the National Institute on Alcohol

Abuse and Alcoholism and the Centers for Disease Control and Prevention (CDC), presented a new umbrella term, *fetal alcohol spectrum disorders* (FASD), to encompass all these clinical and diagnostic terms that were associated with prenatal alcohol exposure. Chudley et al. (2005), Hoyme et al. (2005), and Manning and Hoyme (2007) have presented clinical guidelines for diagnosing the components of FASD, and Jones et al. (2006) have described an effective training protocol for pediatricians. The importance of early diagnoses has been recognized in terms of facilitating appropriate early programs and enrichment, but most patients with this disorder are never diagnosed. The differential developmental aspects of males and females with FASD are rarely addressed in the scientific literature.

The animal research has been invaluable in understanding alcohol as a teratogen, because of the extensive postnatal environmental control that is possible. In the human condition, it is traditionally the mother who protects the children in families of alcoholic fathers. When the mother is alcoholic, or both parents are alcoholic, the children are particularly at risk. For example, in an early study of 30 additional patients with FAS (after the first 11 reported from Seattle; Jones & Smith, 1973; Jones, Smith, Ulleland, & Streissguth, 1973), at least three of the 30 mothers were known to have died of consequences of their alcoholism (cirrhosis, anemia, gastritis, pancreatitis, and delirium tremens; Hanson, Jones, & Smith, 1976). In the first study of 61 adolescents and adults with FASD (Streissguth et al., 1991; mean age 18 years), many of the mothers had died prematurely, often of alcohol-related illnesses but also of accidents and violence. In fact, 69% of the mothers were known to be dead; only 3% of the patients were still with their biologic mothers at the time of the study; and nearly one third had never been raised by their biological mothers.

In another study of 415 patients of all ages (Streissguth, Barr, Kogan, & Bookstein, 1996; Streissguth et al., 2004), 72% of the patients studied had experienced physical or sexual abuse or domestic violence, and 80% were not with their biological mothers at the time of the study. Although many of the children identified as having FAS were born into lower income households with high levels of social problems, I also have had the unique opportunity to observe FASD children born into affluent families with strong social supports, as well as adopted at birth into caring and compassionate families in which the parents have raised other children with successful psychosocial outcomes, only to find that the adopted child with FASD responded differently to their home environment.

A small cohort of children with FAS who were born to and raised by upper and middle class alcoholic mothers were diagnosed and followed by a team at the Child Study Clinic at Yale University (Shaywitz, Cohen, & Shaywitz, 1996). At the time of the study, when the children ranged in age from 6.5 to 18 years, two of the mothers were dead. Of the remaining eight mothers, four were undergoing treatment for alcohol-related disabilities, and five were divorced. All of the children had experienced early school failure (although their mean IQ score was 98, with a range from 82 to 113), and all but one were hyperactive. This was one of the earliest reports of increased mortality among mothers of children with FAS.

Alcohol and Sex Effects on Growth, Morphololgy, and Mortality

Initially as infants and young children, the first 11 patients identified with FAS were growth deficient with respect to height, weight, and head circumference (Jones et al., 1973; Jones & Smith, 1973). When diagnosed, they were strikingly underweight for their height, with "weight-for-height ages" (i.e., the appropriate weight for a person with a particular height age) from less than the 1st to the 15th percentile, and no apparent male/female discrepancy. Most showed some catch-up in weight with increasing age. Jones commented in 1975 that anomalous genitalia were noted in 36% of this original sample of 11 patients. These consisted of hypoplastic labia majora in three patients, and a septated vagina in one patient.

In an early report of 23 alcoholic mothers and well-matched controls drawn from the Collaborative Perinatal Project of the National Institute of Neurologic Diseases and Stroke, four babies had died before 1 week of age (a perinatal mortality of 17% compared with 2% for controls, whose sex was not disclosed; Jones, Smith, Streissguth, & Myrianthopoulus, 1974).

In a 10-year follow-up of the first 11 children diagnosed with FAS (Streissguth, Clarren, & Jones, 1985), two of the seven females were dead, and one child, a male, was lost to follow-up. Four of the eight children examined were severely retarded on follow-up; three of these four were females. At that time, knowledge of eight mothers was available; three of these eight mothers were dead of alcohol-related causes. At the 10-year follow-up, one girl and one boy were not yet teenagers. However, among those examined who were 13 to 14 years old, four of the five girls had weight-for-height ages ranging from the 50th to the 85th percentile, and all had reached menarche (all four adolescent girls were still short but three of these four were now overweight). The two boys examined at this age had not yet entered puberty and had a weight-for-height age ranging from the 17th to 20th percentile; the boys were also short, but unlike the girls they were thin as adolescents. At this follow-up, head circumference ranged from nearly 1 to 6 standard deviations below the mean; IQ scores ranged from 1 to over 5 standard deviations below the mean. Four of the children (three girls and one boy) were severely impaired, with IQ scores between 30 and 60 on their first evaluation in 1973, and they remained severely impaired (IQ between 20 and 57) on their second evaluation in 1983. The other four patients were considered to be mildly to moderately impaired, with IQ scores between 50 and 83 in 1973 and between 80 and 86 in 1983.

Weight-for-height age was thought to be the measurement that best summarized the growth deficiency of children and adolescents with FAS, and male/female differences were most clearly observed in physical characteristics, particularly at puberty and into young adulthood. Thus, the characteristic emaciated appearance of the young child with FAS may not remain a salient feature in the affected adolescent, especially for girls. At their 10-year follow-up (Streissguth et al., 1985), short palpebral fissures, hypoplastic philtrum, thin vermillion border of the upper lip, and flat midface were still prominent craniofacial features. However, with age, prominent growth of the nasal bridge and disharmonic growth of the midface and mandible led to relative prognathism with Class III malocclusion in five children (four of these five were females).

Chronic serous otitis media, probably secondary to eustachian tube dysfunction associated with maxillary hypoplasia, required medical and surgical procedures in four patients (three of whom had permanent conductive hearing loss, all females; Streissguth et al., 1985). The first two adults ever diagnosed with FAS as adults were both males. They were both short and thin into their early 20s, with height and head circumference more than 2 standard deviations below the mean (Streissguth, Herman, & Smith, 1978).

As early as 1978, Majewski in Germany described 95 patients with alcohol embryopathy (his term for FAS), which he divided into three degrees of severity, which corresponded to the severity of offspring damage, which in turn correlated with the mother's alcoholism. Five of his patients died between the ages of 5 months and 4 years (data reported on only two males). He reported genital anomalies (generally slight) in nearly half of his patients, including undescended testes or clitoral hypertrophy. However, some boys also had marked hypospadias and some girls had pseudohermaphroditism. In his later follow-up of 200 children, Majewski (1993) reported that "40% exhibited mostly minor anomalies of external genitalia." In 1996, Majewski provided additional descriptive data on the anomalies observed in these patients, now 230 in number, namely, hypospadias, cryptorchidism, and hypoplasia of the labia minora). He concluded that genital anomalies correlated with the degree of FAS: 61% in children with FAS III (the most severe form), 38% in FAS II, and 27% in FAS I (Majewski, 1996).

Several researchers agreed (Spohr, Willms, and Steinhausen, 1993, in a 10-year follow-up of 60 patients in Berlin [36 males, 24 females] as adolescents and in 2007 as young adults; Majewski, 1981, in a follow-up of 108 children; and Streissguth and colleagues, 1991, in a study of 61 adolescents and adults) that males were more growth impaired than females, whereas girls generally showed a strong postpubertal increase in body weight (Spohr, Willms, & Steinhausen, 2007). D. F. Smith, Sandor, et al. (1981) studied the skeletal x-rays and cardiac exams of 76 patients with FAS from British Columbia (43 males and 33 females). They confirmed many previous findings, including microcephaly (53%) and cervical spine fusion (43%), but they did not discuss male/female differences. Similarly, Swayze et al. (1997) conducted the first magnetic resonance imaging study of 10 patients (six males and four females) and did not discuss male/female differences. In his follow-up study, Spohr (1996) confirmed that "the spontaneous arrest of childhood growth deficiency in adolescent females, noted by Streissguth et al 1991, Majewski, 1993, Löser, 1995, is not clearly understood. Until now, no endocrinological disturbances have been found in the female patients studied" (p. 218). Spohr (personal communication, 2009) reported that two of his three patients who died were females. Streissguth and colleagues (1991) presented data on 61 adolescents and adults (38 males and 23 females). They ranged in age from 12 to 40 years, including 43 adolescents and 18 adults; 70% had an FAS diagnosis and 30% were FAE. We concluded that "FAS is not just a childhood disorder; there is a predictable long-term progression of the disorder into adulthood, in which maladaptive behaviors present the greatest challenge to management" (Streissguth et al., 1991, p. 1967). This conclusion has now been reiterated in other major follow-up studies, including Majewski (1993) and Löser (1995).

My colleagues and I have observed clinically what appeared to be male/female differences in the behavior of patients with FASD as they entered puberty (perhaps not unlike the feminizing effect of prenatal alcohol on males described by Otero and Kelly in Chapter 8, this volume), but these have been largely undocumented in the human literature. Although our team did not study this specifically, we noted that girls with FASD appeared to make more overt sexual advances toward males and dressed in a provocative manner as they entered adolescence. At this age, many boys were not only still short and thin but also timid and quiet. However, in some instances, they responded to peer pressure to engage in inappropriate activities, for example, to take the stolen goods into the pawnshop while the collaborators waited in the car, ready to speed off if necessary, or otherwise engage in risky behaviors (sometimes of a sexual nature) with little apparent awareness of the possible consequences.

A Finnish study reported another possible example of apparent hypersensitivity of females to the intrauterine effects of alcohol. Auttï Rämö and Granström (1996) documented the increasing ratio of males to females in relation to increasing prenatal alcohol exposure in a study of infants born to women undergoing alcohol treatment in a large program in Finland. Offspring with only first trimester alcohol exposure were 49% males. Offspring with two trimesters of alcohol exposure were 51% males. Those with three trimesters of alcohol exposure were 61% males. Although this interesting fact is not discussed in either Autti-Rämö and Granström (1996) or in the original paper (Halmesmäki, 1988), it may be a statistic worthy of note: Are girls more vulnerable in utero to prenatal alcohol exposure than boys?

Bookstein, Sampson, Streissguth, and Connor (2001) carried out a brain imaging study of hypervariability of the corpus callosum in 90 adults who were group-matched for age and ethnicity across three diagnostic groups: FAS, FAE, and no diagnosis. They found that both males and females had more variance among the exposed than among the nonexposed, but the site of the particular hypervariation differed by sex: For females, the site of the hypervariability is in the height of the arch, whereas for males it is under the isthmus. In a further analysis of these same brain scans, Bookstein, Streissguth, Connor, and Sampson (2006) also reported a strong differential effect of prenatal alcohol on the FAS female cerebellum that is not observed for males. In a study of cerebellar surface in 90 males and 90 females, surface size of the cerebellum was a very strong discriminator of the adult FAS females (compared with controls), with FAE falling in between. The largest FAS surface area (centroid size) in an adult FAS female is barely larger than the smallest adult control female. Compared with controls, exposed males did not show these large discrepancies noted for adult females. Similar findings were observed for the cerebellar equator: Centroid size of the FAS females is strikingly deficient with respect to female controls and with respect to FAS males (Bookstein et al., 2006).

Alcohol and Sex Effects on Intelligence, Learning, and Behavior

In 1991, the first psychological and growth data on adolescents and adults with FAS and FAE was published; the data were for 61 patients (38 males and 23 females) who ranged in age from 12 to 40 years (Streissguth et al., 1991). A frequency distribution of IQ scores from the Wechsler tests was presented on a sample including 38 patients diagnosed with FAS and 14 with FAE. Although the two distributions overlap, those with the full FAS had an average IQ of 66; those with FAE had an average IQ of 73. No male/female comparisons were reported or investigated.

LaDue, Streissguth, and Randels (1992) reported on 92 adolescents and adults with FAS or FAE with a mean age of 18 years: 77% were Native American, and 20% were White. Maladaptive behaviors were measured by caretaker report on the Vineland Adaptive Behaviors Scale. Females and males were fairly comparable on scales measuring attention deficits (80%), memory problems (72%), and hyperactivity (72%). This study also noted female and male comparability on temper tantrums, disobedience, and lying, as well as truancy (54–52%) and school suspension (30–32%) for females and males, respectively.

Females and males were clearly not comparable, however, in terms of environmental experiences and interpersonal interactions (LaDue et al., 1992): 91% of females and 83% of males had experienced child neglect, 60% of females and 46% of males had experienced physical abuse, and 57% of females and 19% of males had experienced sexual abuse. On the other hand, 18% of females and 38% of males had been sexually inappropriate with others, and 4% of females and 20% of males had had legal problems involving sexual misconduct, but 19% of females and 3% of males had had a child.

Extensive brain anomalies and small head circumference have been documented in heavily exposed offspring, and the range of intelligence test scores in diagnosed patients is extreme, ranging from severely retarded to above normal. Figure 7.1 shows IQ data on a large group of patients with FAS or FAE who were participating in the University of Washington's Secondary Disabilities

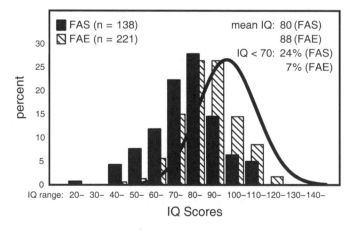

Figure 7.1. IQ scores of patients with fetal alcohol syndrome (FAS) and fetal alcohol effects (FAE) superimposed on the normal curve for IQ. An IQ score of 100 is the mean of the population for IQ. Reprinted from "Risk Factors for Adverse Life Outcomes in Fetal Alcohol Syndrome and Fetal Alcohol Effects," by A. P. Streissguth, F. L. Bookstein, H. M. Barr, P. D. Sampson, K. O'Malley, and J. Kogan Young, 2004, *Journal of Developmental and Behavioral Pediatrics, 25,* p. 232. Copyright 2004 by Wolters Kluwer. Reprinted with permission.

Study. As a group, patients with FAE generally have a higher IQ than those with FAS, but the two distributions have almost complete overlap (Streissguth et al., 2004). The male/female distribution in the Secondary Disabilities Study was 57/43%. The IQ scores of males and females within each of the three age groups (children, adolescents, and adults) were reported to be comparable.

Male/female differences have generally not been discussed in behavioral and psychological studies of patients with FASD (e.g., Aronson 1997; Mattson & Riley 1997; Spohr et al., 2007; Steinhausen, Willms, Metzke, & Spohr, 2003). Mattson, Riley, Gramling, Delis, and Jones (1998) did not discuss sex differences in IQ and neurobehavioral function, but they did report the same ratio of males to females in their study that has been observed in so many other FASD studies: nine males and six females with FAS and seven males and three females with prenatal alcohol exposure. Why is there almost always a paucity of females in these studies, regardless of the country, the year of study, and the age of subjects?

Alcohol and Sex Effects on Secondary Disabilities and Adverse Life Outcomes

In August 1996, the *Final Report to the Centers for Disease Control on the Secondary Disabilities Study* was published, and approximately 30,000 copies were subsequently distributed (Streissguth et al., 1996). Later, a scientific paper (Streissguth et al., 2004) was published with more statistical analyses on the risk factors for adverse life outcomes among patients with FAS or FAE. Data for both publications were derived from a detailed phone interview with a family member as well as the detailed patient records kept over the years, as we tried to respond to the many crises that the patients and their families encountered. The patients studied included the 473 previously diagnosed with FAS or FAE by Smith and his colleagues and referred to the Fetal Alcohol and Drug Unit at the University of Washington Medical School for whom a knowledgeable informant could be reached for a telephone interview. From over 23 years of responding to these families' needs, it was obvious that these patients with FAS or FAE were quite unlike many other mentally handicapped or brain-damaged patients in that they seemed to be more troublesome and difficult for families than patients whose mental handicap was not caused by prenatal alcohol exposure. They were getting expelled from schools that should have been helping them, running away from home, living on the streets, and getting in trouble with the law. After several pilot studies, an intensive interview schedule was developed to systematically measure these life events, which we termed *secondary disabilities*.

Some secondary disabilities show sex effects; others do not. Males with FAS have nearly twice the rate of females with FAS for being expelled, suspended, or dropping out of school; for having trouble with the law; and for being "confined" in jail, prison, mental hospitals, or alcohol/drug treatment centers. Two secondary disabilities, however, show an inverted pattern, with females often having higher rates than males: alcohol and drug problems (ADPs) and inappropriate sexual behavior (ISB; see Figure 7.2).

Surprisingly, females had a 38% rate of ADPs; males had a 32% rate. Both age and diagnosis are also important factors. Adolescent girls with FAS have

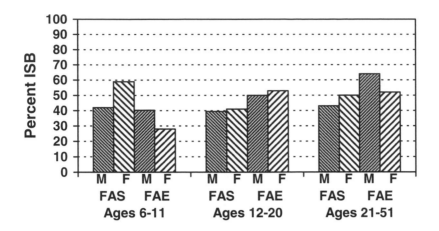

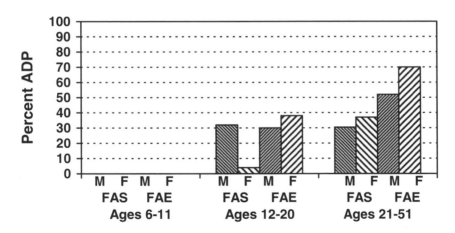

Figure 7.2. Top: history of inappropriate sexual behaviors by sex, diagnosis, and age at interview (*n* = 408). Bottom: history of Alcohol/Drug Problems (ADP) by sex, diagnosis and age at interview (*n* = 243, because no ADP was reported among children). Data were obtained by interviewing the closest available caretaker or informant for each patient who consented to be studied. Data from Streissguth et al., 1996, 2004.

almost no ADPs, possibly because they are likely to be more protected by families (as those with FAS, as a group, have lower IQ scores than those with FAE). Adult women with FAS, on the other hand, have more ADPs than adult men with FAS (around 38% to 30%, respectively). Among patients with FAE, adolescent girls have more ADPs than adolescent boys (around 38% to 30%). However, adult women with FAE have a 70% rate of ADPs compared with about 52% for adult men with FAE.

ISB was coded "yes" if the patient had ever been sentenced to sexual offenders treatment or had ever been reported as "repeatedly" having one or more problems with sexuality and behavior.

ISB is the other secondary disability in which females with FAS have a higher or comparable rate than males with FAS: 60% to 41%, respectively, in the 6- to 11-year range, and 50% and 42%, respectively, among adults with FAS. Promiscuity is twice as frequent for females (22%) as males (11%; Streissguth et al., 2004). Among children with FAE, males have a higher rate of ISB than females. Male and female adolescents with both FAS and FAE are quite comparable for ISB, at around 50% and 52%, respectively.

Speculation about the causes for these data is complicated by the finding that 67% of these patients themselves had experienced physical or sexual abuse or domestic violence (Streissguth et al., 1996). Being a victim of abuse or violence was a strong risk factor for ISB, for example, increasing the odds by fourfold (Streissguth et al., 2004). Furthermore, the Secondary Disabilities Study found that males and females who engaged in ISB were treated very differently by society. The girls were more likely to be sent to therapy, whereas the boys were more likely to be reported to the authorities and thus get into trouble with the law (Streissguth et al., 1996). Thus, one can see the cascade of environmental interactions that confound easy interpretations of male/female differences in humans exposed to alcohol in utero.

Alcohol and Sex Effects on Mental Health, Community Living, and Reproduction

An earlier pilot study using the Structured Clinical Interview for DSM–IV Axis 1 Disorders (SCID-I; *Diagnostic and Statistical Manual of Mental Disorders* (4th ed.; DSM–IV; American Psychiatric Association, 1994) and Structured Clinical Interview for DSM–IV Axis II Personality Disorders (SCID–II) was carried out with 25 diagnosed patients with FAS or FAE who were older than 18 years of age and had an IQ greater than 70 (Famy, Streissguth, & Unis, 1998). Fifteen of 25 patients were diagnosed with alcohol or drug dependence, and 11 of 25 with major depressive disorders. The rate of major depression was surprisingly high, and in contrast to studies of subjects without FASD, the rate of depression was nearly equal among men and women, as was the rate of alcohol or drug dependence (at 60%).

The Secondary Disabilities Study (Streissguth et al., 1996) found no male/female differences in the overall prevalence of mental health problems (over or close to 90% for both sexes). Caregivers reported that around 90% of the entire sample of 415 patients with FAS or FAE had gone to a mental health provider for help. Ninety patients were at least 21 years old at the time of the study. They were evaluated with respect to the prevalence of dependent living and problems with employment. Approximately 80% of the patients with the full FAS were still living dependently after age 21 years, with no male/female differences observed. For those with FAE, 100% of the men but only 70% of the women were still living dependently. Tasks on which these patients required the most supervision were managing money (over 80%), making decisions (nearly 80%), and getting social services (70%). There was a sizable difference between men and women with FAS in terms of employment: 71% of the men and 97% of the women had a history of problems with employment. There was also a male/female discrepancy among patients with FAE, but in the other direction: 75% of the men and only 65% of the women with FAE had had problems with employment. Holding a job was a greater problem for all these patients than getting a job; the biggest problem encountered was becoming easily frustrated on the job.

Of the 253 patients in the Secondary Disabilities Study who were over 12 years old, 44 (17%) had become parents (30 females and 14 males). This represented 28% of the females 12 years and older versus 10% of the males. For females, the average age of the first pregnancy was 18 years. For males, the mean age of fathering a child was 20 years.

The 44 patients with FAS/FAE in this study had produced a total of 76 children, at least half of whom were not in the patient's care. Thirty-six percent of the female patients had had their children removed from their care by child protective services (compared with 9% of the children of male patients). However, 44% of the males gave up raising their children (compared with 30% of the females). An alarming 40% of the female parents were drinking during pregnancy; 17% had a child who had been diagnosed with FAS or FAE, and another 13% had children whom the respondents suspected of being fetal alcohol affected (Grant, Ernst, Streissguth, & Porter, 1997; Streissguth et al., 1996).

In general, patients with FAS/FAE who had become parents had a much higher rate of secondary disabilities than those who had not become parents. Disrupted school experiences (dropping out, being suspended or expelled) characterized 92% of the males with FAS/FAE who had become parents and 80% of the females with FAS/FAE who had become parents; trouble with the law, 91% of the males and 68% of the females; confinement (in jail, mental hospitals, or residential alcohol/drug setting), 19% of the males and 68% of the females; ISB, 70% of the males and 60% of the females; ADPs, 63% of the males and 72% of the females; dependent living, 90% of the males and 68% females; and problems with employment, 60% of the males with FAS/FAE and 89% of the females with FAS/FAE who had become parents, respectively.

Summary

Sex differences among patients with FASD has not been a popular topic, and most articles do not even mention the ratio of males to females in the samples studied, let alone analyze data with respect to gender. This review has focused on patients diagnosed with FAS or FAE, whose mothers consumed substantial quantities of alcohol during pregnancy, usually considered to be abusing alcohol. The major epidemiologic studies evaluating child outcome in relation to varying levels of maternal alcohol use have generally not reported data on male/female differences.

Both prenatal alcohol exposure and sex of offspring appear to be related to physical growth, morphology, and survival. As infants and young children, both males and females with FAS tend to be short and thin, with a smaller than normal head circumference. As adolescents, however, females put on additional body weight and may be short and overweight into adulthood, whereas males tend to remain short and thin into young adulthood.

The early clinical studies of infants and young children born to alcoholic mothers reviewed here often describe more serious physical anomalies and early demise among the female offspring. This would seem to be a topic that could easily be studied if clinical studies more routinely described sex of offspring.

Alcohol is not only an important teratogen in the biological sense, but there is an insidious effect of alcohol on the alcoholic mother herself. The high rate of incapacity and early death among alcoholic mothers compounds the biological impact of maternal alcohol abuse on offspring development.

The frequent physical and sexual abuse of children with FASD, which apparently occurs with greater frequency among female than male children, may well contribute to these children's own sexually inappropriate behaviors, perhaps compounded by their own brain damage sustained in utero, which may compromise their ability to monitor their own behavior or seek help in a troubled environment.

Sex differences were observed for five secondary disabilities: Males had nearly twice the rate of females for disrupted school experiences (expelled, suspended, or dropped out), trouble with the law (any of a long list of possible infractions), and confinement (in jail, prison, or mental health or alcohol/drug inpatient facilities). Females, on the other hand, had a higher rate of ADPs than males, but the data are qualified by age and diagnosis. (As a group, patients with the full FAS have a lower IQ than those with FAE and thus often receive greater supervision during adolescence than during adulthood.) Among adolescents, girls with the full FAS have almost no ADPs, whereas adolescent girls with FAE have higher rates of ADPs than adolescent boys. Among adults, women with the full FAS have more ADPs than men. Adult females with FAE have the highest rates of ADPs of any group.

Female children with FAS had higher rates of ISB than male children with FAS, but females also had experienced more inappropriate sexual behaviors than males as children. No sex differences in ISB were noted among adolescents, but as adults, FAE males are higher than other groups.

Among 90 adults with FAS/FAE who were studied, there were no male/female differences in dependent living among patients with the full FAS (approximately 80% for both sexes), but problems with employment characterized 71% of adult males and 97% of adult females.

For the 473 patients with FAS/FAE on whom IQ data were available, males and females had comparable IQ scores within the categories of children, adolescents, and adults. Secondary disability data reported here have not been controlled for IQ.

Forty-four children were born to the 253 patients over 12 years of age: 28% of the females and 10% of the males were known to have had a child. Child protective services removed 36% of the children born to females with FAS/FAE, but males with FAS/FAE had stopped caring for 44% of their children. Females with FAS/FAE were drinking during 40% of their pregnancies, and 15% had children diagnosed with FAS/FAE.

Finally, careful scrutiny of these data has revealed a possible new finding: Female children with FAS/FAE appear to be more vulnerable for early demise and greater morphological damage than their male counterparts. The first clue to this was the casual reporting of an increased rate of males born to alcoholic mothers who were not able to stop alcohol intake during each trimester of pregnancy (Autti-Rämö & Granström, 1996). The second clue was the curious incidental finding that in almost all studies cited that give the male/female ratio of the participants, there are fewer female than male subjects. The third clue was detected in a careful reading of the earliest case studies on FAS, which often noted incidentally the sex of the offspring being described. As noted earlier, the higher biological vulnerability to alcohol abuse of adult women compared with men is well known and may be another manifestation of this phenomenon.

Further research seems warranted on prenatal alcohol effects on male and female early survival and severity of damage in utero. In addition, the long-term consequences of alcohol and drug abuse among females with FAS/FAE, and the parenting failures of both males and females with FAS/FAE, indicate the need for earlier diagnoses, which in our studies is associated with decreased secondary disabilities, more targeted early interventions for mother and child, and increased familial support.

References

American Psychiatric Association. (1987). *Diagnostic and statistical manual of mental disorders* (3rd ed., rev.). Washington, DC: Author.

American Psychiatric Association. (1994). *Diagnostic and statistical manual of mental disorders* (4th ed.). Washington, DC: Author.

Aronson, M. (1997). Children of alcoholic mothers. In A. P. Streissguth & J. Kanter (Eds.), *The challenge of fetal alcohol syndrome: Overcoming secondary disabilities* (pp. 15–24). Seattle: University of Washington Press.

Autti-Rämö, I., & Granström, M.-L. (1996). Effects of fetal alcohol exposure on early cognitive development. In H.-L. Spohr & H.-C. Steinhausen (Eds.), *Alcohol, pregnancy, and the developing child* (pp. 169–182). Cambridge, England: Cambridge University Press.

Bookstein, F. L., Sampson, P. D., Streissguth, A. P., & Connor, P. D. (2001). Geometric morphometrics of corpus callosum and subcortical structures in the fetal-alcohol-affected brain. *Teratology, 64,* 4–32. doi:10.1002/tera.1044

Bookstein, F. L., Streissguth, A. P, Connor, P. D., & Sampson, P. D. (2006). Damage to the human cerebellum from prenatal alcohol exposure: The anatomy of a simple biometrical explanation. *The Anatomical Record (Part B: New Anat.), 289B,* 195–209.

Califano, J. A. (2007). *High society: How substance abuse ravages America and what to do about it.* New York, NY: Public Affairs.

Chudley, A. E., Conry, J., Cook, J. L., Loock, C., Rosales, T., & LeBlanc, N. (2005). Fetal alcohol spectrum disorder: Canadian guidelines for diagnosis. *CMAJ: Canadian Medical Association Journal, 172,* 1–21.

Clarren, S. K., & Smith, D. W. (1978). The fetal alcohol syndrome. *The New England Journal of Medicine, 298,* 1063–1067. doi:10.1056/NEJM197805112981906

Driscoll, C. D., Streissguth, A. P., & Riley, E. P. (1990). Prenatal alcohol exposure: Comparability of effects in humans and animal models. *Neurotoxicology and Teratology, 12,* 231–237. doi:10.1016/0892-0362(90)90094-S

Famy, C., Streissguth, A. P., & Unis, A. S. (1998). Mental illness in adults with fetal alcohol syndrome or fetal alcohol effects. *The American Journal of Psychiatry, 155,* 552–554.

Grant, T. M., Ernst, C. C., Streissguth, A. P., & Porter, J. (1997). An advocacy program for mothers with FAS/FAE. In A. P. Streissguth & J. Kanter (Eds.), *The challenge of fetal alcohol syndrome: Overcoming secondary disabilities* (pp. 102–112). Seattle: University of Washington Press.

Halmesmäki, E. (1988). Alcohol counseling of 85 pregnant problem drinkers: Effect on drinking and fetal outcome. *British Journal of Obstetrics and Gynaecology, 95,* 243–247. doi:10.1111/j.1471-0528.1988.tb06864.x

Hanson, J. W., Jones, K. L., & Smith, D. W. (1976). Fetal alcohol syndrome: Experience with 41 patients. *JAMA, 235,* 1458–1460. doi:10.1001/jama.235.14.1458

Hoyme, H. E., May, P. A., Kalberg, W. O., Kodituwakku, P., Gossage, J. P., Trujillo, P. M., . . . Robinson, L. K. (2005). A practical clinical approach to diagnosis of fetal alcohol spectrum disorders: Clarification of the 1996 institute of medicine criteria. *Pediatrics, 115,* 39–47. doi:10.1542/peds.2005-0702

Jones, K. L. (1975). The fetal alcohol syndrome. *Addictive Diseases, 2,* 79–88.

Jones, K. L., Robinson, L. K., Bakherieva, L. N., Marintcheva, M., Storojev, V., Strahova, A., . . . Chambers, C. D. (2006). Accuracy of the diagnosis of physical features of fetal alcohol syndrome by pediatricians after specialized training. *Pediatrics, 118,* e1734–1737. doi:10.1542/peds.2006-1037

Jones, K. L., & Smith, D. W. (1973). Recognition of the fetal alcohol syndrome in early infancy. *The Lancet, 302,* 999–1001. doi:10.1016/S0140-6736(73)91092-1

Jones, K. L., Smith, D. W., Streissguth, A. P., & Myrianthopoulos, N. C. (1974). Outcome in offspring of chronic alcoholic women. *The Lancet, 303,* 1076–1078. doi:10.1016/S0140-6736(74)90555-8

Jones, K. L., Smith, D. W., Ulleland, C. N., & Streissguth, A. P. (1973). Pattern of malformation in offspring of chronic alcoholic mothers. *The Lancet, 301,* 1267–1271. doi:10.1016/S0140-6736(73)91291-9

LaDue, R. A., Streissguth, A. P., & Randels, S. P. (1992). Clinical considerations pertaining to adolescents and adults with fetal alcohol syndrome. In T. B. Sonderegger (Ed.), *Perinatal substance abuse: Research findings and clinical implications* (pp. 104–131). Baltimore, MD: The Johns Hopkins University Press.

Lemoine, P., Harousseau, H., Borteyru, J. P., & Menuet, J. C. (1968). *Children of alcoholic parents: Abnormalities observed in 127 cases. Selected Translations of International Alcoholism Research (STIAR).* Rockville, MD: National Institute on Alcohol Abuse and Alcoholism.

Löser, H. (1995). *Alcohol Embryopathie und Alkoholeffekte.* Stuttgart, Germany: Fiscer.

Majewski, F. (1978). *Über schädigene Einflüsse des Alkohols auf die Nachkommen* [The damaging effects of alcohol on offspring]. *Der Nervenarzt, 49,* 410–416.

Majewski, F. (1981). Alcohol embryopathy: Some facts and speculations about pathogenesis. *Neurobehavioral Toxicology and Teratology, 3,* 129–144.

Majewski, F. (1993). Alcohol embryopathy: Experience in 200 patients. *Developmental Brain Dysfunction, 6,* 248–265.

Majewski, F. (1996). Clinical symptoms in patients with fetal alcohol syndrome. In H.-L. Spohr and H.-C. Steinhausen (Eds.), *Alcohol, pregnancy, and the developing child* (pp. 15–39). New York, NY: Cambridge University Press.

Manning, M. A., & Hoyme, E. H. (2007). Fetal alcohol spectrum disorders: A practical clinical approach to diagnosis. *Neuroscience and Biobehavioral Reviews, 31,* 230–238. doi:10.1016/j.neubiorev.2006.06.016

Mattson, S. N., & Riley, E. P. (1997). Neurobehavioral and neuroanatomical effects of heavy prenatal exposure to alcohol. In A. Streissguth & J. Kanter (Eds.), *The challenge of fetal alcohol syndrome: Overcoming secondary disabilities* (pp. 3–14). Seattle: University of Washington Press.

Mattson, S. N., Riley, E. P., Gramling, L., Delis, D. C., & Jones, K. L. (1998). Neuropsychological comparison of alcohol-exposed children with or without physical features of fetal alcohol syndrome. *Neuropsychology, 12,* 146–153. doi:10.1037/0894-4105.12.1.146

Middaugh, L. D., Kelley, B. M., Brandy, A.-L. E., & McGroarty, K. K. (1999). Ethanol consumption by C57BL/6 Mice: Influence of gender and procedural variables. *Alcohol, 17,* 175–183. doi:10.1016/S0741-8329(98)00055-X

Riley, E. P., & Vorhees, C. V. (1986). *Handbook of behavioral teratology.* New York, NY: Plenum Press.

Schenker, S. (1997). Medical consequences of alcohol abuse: Is gender a factor? *Alcoholism: Clinical and Experimental Research, 21,* 179–181. doi:10.1111/j.1530-0277.1997.tb03746.x

Shaywitz, S. E., Cohen, D. J., & Shaywitz, B. A. (1980). Behavior and learning difficulties in children of normal intelligence born to alcoholic mothers. *The Journal of Pediatrics, 96,* 978–982. doi:10.1016/S0022-3476(80)80621-4

Smith, D. F., Sandor, G. G., MacLeod, P. M., Tredwell, S., Wood, B., & Newman, D. E. (1981). Intrinsic defects in the fetal alcohol syndrome: Studies on 76 cases from British Columbia and the Yukon Territory. *Neurobehavioral Toxicology and Teratology, 3,* 145–152.

Smith, D. W. (1976). *Recognizable patterns of human malformation; Genetic, embryologic, and clinical aspects* (2nd ed.). Philadelphia, PA: Saunders.

Smith, D. W. (1981). Fetal alcohol syndrome and fetal alcohol effects. *Neurobehavioral Toxicology and Teratology, 3,* 127.

Spohr, H. L. (1996). Fetal alcohol syndrome in adolescence: Long-term perspective of children diagnosed in infancy. In H.-L. Spohr & H.-C. Steinhausen (Eds.), *Alcohol, pregnancy, and the developing child* (pp. 207–226). Cambridge, England: Cambridge University Press.

Spohr, H. L., Willms, J., & Steinhausen, H. C. (1993). Prenatal alcohol exposure and long-term developmental consequences. *The Lancet, 341,* 907–910. doi:10.1016/0140-6736(93)91207-3

Spohr, H. L., Willms, J., & Steinhausen, H. C. (2007). Fetal alcohol spectrum disorders in young adulthood. *The Journal of Pediatrics, 150,* 175–179.e1. doi:10.1016/j.jpeds.2006.11.044

Steinhausen, H. C., Willms, J., Metzke, C. W., & Spohr, H. L. (2003). Behavioural phenotype in foetal alcohol syndrome and foetal alcohol effects. *Developmental Medicine & Child Neurology, 45,* 179–182. doi:10.1111/j.1469-8749.2003.tb00927.x

Stratton, K., Howe, C., & Battaglia, F. (Eds.). (1996). *Fetal alcohol syndrome: Diagnosis, epidemiology, prevention, and treatment.* Washington, DC: National Academy Press.

Streissguth, A. P., Aase, J. M., Clarren, S. K., Randels, S. P., LaDue, R. A., & Smith, D. F. (1991). Fetal alcohol syndrome in adolescents and adults. *JAMA, 265,* 1961–1967. doi:10.1001/jama.265.15.1961

Streissguth, A. P., Barr, H. M., Kogan, J., & Bookstein, F. L. (1996). *Understanding the occurrence of secondary disabilities in clients with fetal alcohol syndrome and fetal alcohol effects (FAE)* (Final Report to the Centers for Disease Control and Prevention, Grant No. RO4/CCR008515). Seattle, WA: University of Washington School of Medicine, Department of Psychiatry and Behavioral Sciences, Fetal Alcohol and Drug Unit.

Streissguth, A. P., Bookstein, F. L., Barr, H. M., Sampson, P. D., O'Malley, K., & Kogan Young, J. (2004). Risk factors for adverse life outcomes in fetal alcohol syndrome and fetal alcohol effects. *Journal of Developmental and Behavioral Pediatrics, 25,* 228–238. doi:10.1097/00004703-200408000-00002

Streissguth, A. P., Clarren, S. K., & Jones, K. L. (1985). Natural history of the fetal alcohol syndrome: A ten-year follow-up of eleven patients. *The Lancet, 326,* 85–91. doi:10.1016/S0140-6736(85)90189-8

Streissguth, A. P., Herman, C. S., & Smith, D. W. (1978). Intelligence, behavior, and dysmorphogenesis in the fetal alcohol syndrome: A report on 20 patients. *The Journal of Pediatrics, 92,* 363–367. doi:10.1016/S0022-3476(78)80420-X

Swayze, V. W., Johnson, V. P., Hanson, J. W., Piven, J., Sato, Y., Giedd, J. N., . . . Andreasen, N. C. (1997). Magnetic resonance imaging of brain anomalies in fetal alcohol syndrome. *Pediatrics, 99,* 232–240. doi:10.1542/peds.99.2.232

Wagnerberger, S., Schafer, C., Schwarz, E., Bode, C., & Parlesak, A. (2007). Is nutrient intake a gender-specific cause for enhanced susceptibility to alcohol-induced liver disease in women? *Alcohol and Alcoholism, 43,* 9–14. doi:10.1093/alcalc/agm161

Weinberg, J., Sliwowska, J. H., Lan, N., & Hellemans, K. G. (2008). Prenatal alcohol exposure: Foetal programming, the hypothalamic-pituitary-adrenal axis and sex differences in outcome. *Journal of Neuroendocrinology, 20,* 470–488. doi:10.1111/j.1365-2826.2008.01669.x

West, J. (1986). *Alcohol and brain development.* New York, NY: Oxford University Press.

8

Sex Differences in the Teratogenic Effects of Alcohol: Findings From Animal Models

Nicha K. H. Otero and Sandra J. Kelly

Fetal alcohol spectrum disorder (FASD) refers to the range of teratogenic effects on the developing fetus caused by maternal alcohol consumption. A diagnosis of fetal alcohol syndrome (FAS) lies on the most severe end of this spectrum and is characterized by growth deficiency, central nervous system dysfunction, craniofacial dysmorphology, and deficits in cognition and learning (Jones & Smith, 1973; Streissguth & O'Malley, 2000). In the clinical literature on prenatal alcohol effects, the research is often unavoidably confounded by other factors, such as genetic heritability, demographics, maternal use of other drugs of abuse, poor nutrition, and individual variations in alcohol consumption throughout the course of pregnancy. Whereas these factors can be controlled statistically, another approach is to use nonhuman animal models of FASD, which allows confounds to be controlled to some extent and also allows detailed examination of brain deficits specific to alcohol exposure in utero (Samson & Diaz, 1982; West, Goodlett, & Kelly, 1987). Fortunately, there is a significant amount of overlap between the findings from studies using nonhuman animal models and studies with people with FASD (for reviews, see Driscoll, Streissguth, & Riley, 1990; and Kelly, Day, & Streissguth, 2000). Although there are a variety of animal models of FASD, a substantial amount of research has used rodents, including rats and mice, and this review focuses on the findings from rat and mice models of FASD.

A major contribution of rodent models of FASD includes the delineation of the sexually dimorphic effects of alcohol exposure during development. The period of development in rodents that is equivalent to three trimesters in humans, at least with respect to brain growth, includes both the prenatal and early postnatal period (Bayer, Altman, Russo, & Zhang, 1993); thus, studies using either prenatal or postnatal exposure to alcohol are included in the review. Previously published reviews on the sexually dimorphic effects of ethanol exposure during development (see McGivern & Barron, 1991; Weinberg, 1993; Weinberg, Sliwowska, Lan, & Hellemans, 2008; Zhang, Sliwowska, & Weinberg, 2005) have been detailed and are usually focused on a particular aspect of the brain or behavior. It should be noted that much of the literature on animal models of

The research reported in this chapter was supported by National Institute on Alcohol Abuse and Alcoholism Grant RO1 11566.

FASD has either not included sex as a factor in the statistical analyses or has not included enough power in the design to actually detect interactions of sex with alcohol exposure, making conclusions of no sex differences in these studies not justified or conclusions of sex differences unreliable. This review is not intended to be exhaustive but instead focuses on key and replicated findings and suggests future directions for research on sex differences in FASD. We begin with a brief description of typical sexual differentiation of the rat followed by a description of the sexually dimorphic effects of alcohol exposure during development using rodent models of FASD. We conclude with some discussion of future directions of research in this field.

Typical Sexual Differentiation in Rats

Sexual differentiation in rodents begins during the prenatal period and continues into the postnatal period. The presence or absence of the Y chromosome determines the differentiation of the gonads into testes or ovaries, and this in turn determines the relative concentrations of gonadal hormones. In females, the ovaries secrete very low levels of hormones during the gestation period. However, the male gonads produce both the anti-Müllerian hormone and testosterone, which ultimately lead to the suppression of female internal organs and the development of male internal and external physical characteristics respectively (Becker, Breedlove, & Crews, 1993).

The testosterone surge in male rats occurs both in the late prenatal period and the early postnatal period (McEwen, 1992). Testosterone, either directly or via its metabolite, estradiol, has myriad effects during development and results in permanent alterations in behavior and brain (Schwarz & McCarthy, 2008). Both the absence of this steroid and the presence of high levels of alpha-fetoprotein in females result in the representation of more feminine-type behaviors. This protein protects the female from the masculinizing effects of the estradiol by binding to estradiol, stopping any interaction between the hormone and its receptor (Schwarz & McCarthy, 2008). In the rat, the sexual differentiation of the brain gives rise to sexually dimorphic reproductive behavior and also nonsexual behavior such as learning and memory (for reviews, see Beatty, 1979; and Kelly, Ostrowski, & Wilson, 1999). Examples of differences in nonreproductive behavior include aggression, learning, pain, and spatial skills observed in rodent models (Beatty, 1979). However, these differences in behaviors between the genders are not influenced solely by genetics and hormones. The long-standing "nature versus nurture" debate has underlined the added influences of environmental factors on behavior. For instance, in rats, the amount of anogenital stimulation to pups by their mother has influences on excretion, the development of sexual function and behavior in the males, prevention of cell death, and hyporesponsiveness to stress (Moore, Dou, & Juraska, 1996; Moore & Morelli, 1979). Clearly another environmental factor is exposure to drugs, alcohol in particular, during early development. Because the period in the rat that is equivalent to all three trimesters in the human with respect to brain growth includes both the prenatal and early postnatal periods (Bayer et al., 1993), rat models of FASD include exposure during the prenatal period, postnatal period, or both (perinatal) periods. Alcohol crosses the placental barrier easily, and exposure to the dam results in equivalent blood alcohol concentrations in both dam and fetuses (Brien, Clarke, & Richardson, 1985).

Sex Differences in Morphology After Alcohol Exposure During Development

Body weight in rats generally is reduced by alcohol exposure during development, particularly during the second half of gestation (Abel, 1985; Tran, Cronise, Marino, Jenkins, & Kelly, 2000). Although consistent sex differences in body weight have not been observed, there may be sex differences in how the reduced body weight is manifested. Examination of the anogenital distance has consistently revealed a feminizing or demasculinizing effect of alcohol exposure during development on male rats. In newborn rat pups, a small anogenital distance is indicative of a female; a larger distance indicates a male. In male rats exposed prenatally to alcohol, this distance is significantly smaller when compared with controls (Blanchard & Hannigan, 1994; Parker, Udani, Gavaler, & Van Thiel, 1984; Udani, Parker, Gavaler, & Van Thiel, 1985). Other studies have also reported lower weights in male reproductive organs, such as the testes and prostate, after exposure to alcohol in utero (Blanchard, Hannigan, & Riley, 1987; Kelce, Rudeen, & Ganjam, 1989; McGivern et al., 1988). Delayed vaginal opening in female rats after exposure to alcohol during the prenatal period has also been consistently demonstrated (Boggan, Randall, & Dodds, 1979; Esquifino, Sanchis, & Guerri, 1986).

The anatomy of several brain regions that are sexually differentiated in typical subjects is also affected by maternal alcohol consumption. The sexually dimorphic nucleus of the preoptic area is significantly larger in male compared with female rats and has been shown to be considerably decreased in volume and size in male rats following prenatal, postnatal, or perinatal alcohol exposure (Barron, Tieman, & Riley, 1988; Rudeen, 1986; Rudeen, Kappel, & Lear, 1986). Similarly, prenatal alcohol exposure has been shown to alter the corpus callosum and cerebral asymmetry in the male rat, reducing it to a size comparable with that of a female rat and thus eliminating the sex differences in these brain areas that are usually observed in control animals (Zimmerberg & Mickus, 1990; Zimmerberg & Reuter, 1989; Zimmerberg & Scalzi, 1989).

Most of the findings on sexually dimorphic effects of alcohol on brain morphology have found them in structures that are sexually dimorphic in control animals. This suggests that there is a disruption of sexual differentiation in rats exposed to alcohol during development.

Sex Differences in Hormonal and Neurotransmitter Systems After Fetal Alcohol Exposure

Specific hormonal and neurotransmitter systems have been shown to be altered by perinatal alcohol exposure in a sexually dimorphic manner. However, again, these sex differences in alcohol effects are almost always in systems that are different in the two sexes in control animals. Much of the research has focused on the hypothalamic–gonadal and hypothalamic–pituitary–adrenal axes.

Because of its possible role in the mechanism underlying alcohol's sexually dimorphic effects, many investigations have focused on testosterone levels (for a review, see McGivern & Barron, 1991). Testosterone levels in the male rat increased during the late gestational and early postnatal period as part of the process of typical sexual differentiation. Perinatal alcohol exposure in the male rat has been shown to blunt this testosterone surge (McGivern et al., 1988; McGivern, Handa, & Raum, 1998; McGivern, Handa, & Redei, 1993), a deficit believed to be due to an alcohol-related decrease in enzymatic activity that produces these steroids in the testes (Kelce et al., 1989; McGivern et al., 1988; Udani et al., 1985; O. B. Ward, Ward, Denning, French, & Hendricks, 2002; O. B. Ward, Ward, Denning, Hendricks, & French, 2002). Moreover, testosterone levels continue to be reduced in adult male rats after alcohol exposure during development (Dalterio, Bartke, Blum, & Sweeney, 1981; Lugo, Marino, Gass, Wilson, & Kelly, 2006; Udani et al., 1985).

In addition to reliable effects on testosterone levels, alcohol exposure during development lowers estradiol levels and responsiveness in female rats (Handa, McGivern, Noble, & Gorski, 1985; Minetti & Fulginiti, 1991; Wilson, Kelly, & Wilson, 1996). There are also effects on luteinizing hormone in males and females exposed to alcohol during development (Creighton-Taylor & Rudeen, 1991; Handa et al., 1985).

There is an extensive literature showing that alcohol exposure during development generally affects responsiveness to stress and that frequently the alcohol effect is sexually dimorphic (for a recent review, see Weinberg et al., 2008). The stress response in rats is sexually dimorphic in many parameters (for a review, see Luine, Beck, Fownman, Frankfurt, & Maclusky, 2007). The effect of alcohol on the stress response is complicated because of the use of different stressors, different alcohol exposure parameters, and different ages for testing. In addition, because the administration of alcohol during development is always a stressor, this literature is also rife with effects of the administration procedures itself (e.g., pair-feeding of liquid diet, artificial rearing, postnatal intubation) on the response to stress in later life, making the interpretation of any alcohol effects difficult. Nevertheless, alcohol-exposed newborn pups show increased corticosterone levels right after birth (Weinberg, 1989; Weinberg & Gallo, 1982) and blunted responses to stressors during the first 2 weeks of life (Osborn, Kim, Yu, Herbert, & Weinberg, 1996; Weinberg, 1989), whereas alcohol-exposed rats during the pubertal stage and adulthood show hyperresponsiveness to stress, all compared with nontreated controls (Glavas, Ellis, Yu, & Weinberg, 2007; Kelly, Mahoney, Randich, & West, 1991; Weinberg, 1988; Weinberg, Taylor, & Gianoulakis, 1996). Females exposed to alcohol not only show a heightened responsiveness to stress but also take a longer time to show decreases in corticosterone levels after the termination of stress exposure (Newman Taylor, Branch, Liu, & Kokka, 1982; Weinberg, 1988). Alcohol-exposed males, on the other hand, seem to show this same increased reaction only when the stressor is chronic and more prolonged (Kim, Giberson, Yu, Zoeller, & Weinberg, 1999; Weinberg, 1992).

Sex differences in neurotransmitter systems after ethanol exposure during development have not been examined in a systematic manner. There are hints in the literature that sexually dimorphic effects of ethanol exposure during development occur when the neurotransmitter response to stress is measured (Kelly, 1996a, 1996b; Kelly & Dillingham, 1994). Given the discussion above, sexually dimorphic effects of alcohol on the responsiveness to stress are likely involved, and these neurotransmitter changes may be secondary to changes in stress responsiveness. The few other studies showing sex differences in basal levels of receptors, neurotransmitters (Rudeen & Weinberg, 1993), and metabolites (Kelly & Dillingham, 1994) need replication. Clearly, more research is needed in this area.

Sex Differences in Behavior After Alcohol Exposure During Development

Generally, there are few sex differences in the effects of alcohol exposure during development on simple behaviors such as reflexes or basic sensory processing (Kelly, Hulsether, & West, 1987), although these have not been examined extensively. However, in complex behaviors, perinatal alcohol exposure can frequently cause sexually dimorphic alterations. In most cases, the behavior that is altered in a sexually dimorphic manner is sexually dimorphic in the control rats. The explanation of the ethanol effects is complicated by the number of factors, including stress responsivity, motivation, and learning, that affect complex behaviors.

Saccharin preference has been shown by some researchers to be a sexually dimorphic behavior, with females consuming more than males (McGivern et al., 1984). Both prenatal (McGivern et al., 1984) and early postnatal (Barron, Razani, Gallegos, & Riley, 1995) exposure to alcohol results in an increase in saccharin preference in males and a decrease in saccharin preference in females. There have been failures to replicate this effect, but in these studies there were no sex differences in the saccharin preference in control rats (Abel & Dintcheff, 1986). A similar pattern is seen in play behavior and active social interactions. In studies where there is a sex difference in the control rats, alcohol exposure during development decreased play behavior and active social interaction in male rats and increased both behaviors in female rats (Kelly & Dillingham, 1994; Meyer & Riley, 1986). In another study where no sex difference is observed in the play behavior in control rats, there was an effect of alcohol exposure during development on play, but the effect was not sexually dimorphic (Lawrence, Bonner, Newsom, & Kelly, 2008).

Studies of sex differences in the performance in spatial tasks and other hippocampal-dependent tasks in rodents have shown very mixed results; findings have depended on species, strain, testing parameters, stress levels, and rearing conditions (for a review, see McCarthy & Konkle, 2005). Whereas many of the studies have shown a male superiority in performance on spatial tasks such as the Morris water maze and radial arm maze, some studies have shown clear female superiority (McCarthy & Konkle, 2005). Given these contradictory findings about baseline behavior, it is not surprising that the literature on how alcohol exposure during development affects spatial learning in the two sexes is also contradictory. Prenatal alcohol exposure has been shown to cause greater deficits in males than in females in some studies (Blanchard, Riley, & Hannigan, 1987;

Zimmerberg, Mattson, & Riley, 1989), opposite effects in the two sexes in other studies (McGivern, Clancy, Hill, & Noble, 1984), and equal deficits in both sexes in other studies (Gianoulakis, 1990) in measures of performance in spatial tasks. Similarly, early postnatal exposure to alcohol has been shown to cause greater deficits in adult females (Kelly, Goodlett, Hulsether, & West, 1988), greater deficits in adult males (Johnson & Goodlett, 2002), equal deficits in juvenile rats of both sexes, and no effects in adult rats (Cronise, Tran, Marino, & Kelly, 2001). These studies vary according to alcohol administration procedures, timing of alcohol exposure and exact parameters, and type of spatial test. In the review by Weinberg, Zimmerberg, and Sonderegger (1992), a couple of suggestions were made as to the possible reasons for so much discrepancy in sex differences within this type of research. These include possible sex differences in the level of motivation to escape one type of aversive situation versus another (e.g., hunger from food deprivation, escape from submersion in cold water), differences in the amount or level of motor activity required to perform a task, or differences in the stress response, which would in turn affect performance.

Given the discussion on effects of alcohol exposure during development on sex steroids, it is not surprising that there are effects on both male and female sexual behavior and also on maternal behavior in rats. These behaviors are clearly sexually dimorphic and also heavily dependent upon hormonal events. In adult male rats, exposure to alcohol in utero has led to decreased copulation in the presence of a receptive female, lower initial penile reflexes, lower frequencies of intromission, longer latency to reach ejaculation, and manifestation of a more feminine-type sexual behavior known as *lordosis* (Blanchard & Hannigan, 1994; Hård et al., 1984; Parker et al., 1984; Udani et al., 1985). In an interesting series of studies, researchers have examined the changes in male sexual behavior after alcohol exposure, stress, and the combination of the two procedures during the prenatal period (I. L. Ward et al., 2003; O. B. Ward, Ward, Denning, Hendricks, & French, 2002; O. B. Ward, Ward, Denning, French, & Hendricks, 2002). Most of their findings suggest that whereas prenatal alcohol exposure alters male sexual behavior, much more severe effects are observed when prenatal alcohol exposure is combined with prenatal stress. As mentioned previously, stress is inherent in all of the alcohol administration paradigms used in this field, and the research literature suggests that this synergy may play a role in the findings on male sexual behavior.

In addition to male sexual behavior, alcohol exposure during development has been shown to impact aggression in rats, which has been shown to be influenced by testosterone levels (Edwards, 1969). The direction of the effects vary across studies, with some studies showing enhanced aggression (Brain, Ajarem, & Petkov, 1987; Elis & Kršiak, 1975; Kršiak, Elis, Pöschlová, & Masek, 1977; Royalty, 1990; Yanai & Ginsburg, 1977) and others showing reduced aggression (Lugo et al., 2006; Yanai & Ginsburg, 1977) in rodents exposed to alcohol during development. These studies vary according to timing and method of alcohol exposure, type of rodent, and assessment of aggression. The reduction in aggression after alcohol exposure during development is a finding that is consistent with the literature on effects of testosterone, but it should be noted that aggression even in rodents is a complex response with multiple determinants.

The impact of alcohol exposure during development on female sexual behavior has not been studied as much as that on male sexual behavior. Whereas alcohol exposure during development does not interfere with the estrus cycle, there are delays in the age of vaginal opening and puberty (Boggan et al., 1979; Hård et al., 1984; Minetti & Fulginiti, 1991) as well as lower levels and less sensitivity to estradiol (Minetti & Fulginiti, 1991; Wilson et al., 1996). In one study, the pacing behavior of female rats exposed to alcohol during the perinatal period suggested changes in sexual motivation or processing of sensory cues during sexual behavior (Gass, Jenkins, Marino, Lugo, & Kelly, 2007). Clearly, this study needs to be replicated, but these behavioral findings are consistent with the hormonal changes. Similarly consistent with the hormonal changes, the pup-directed behavior of adult females and juveniles of both sexes exposed to alcohol during the perinatal period is disrupted (Barron & Riley, 1985; Fernandez, Caul, Haenlein, & Vorhees, 1983; Wilson et al., 1996).

Clearly, there are sex differences seen in behavior after exposure to alcohol during development. However, there also are some contradictory findings in the literature, particularly with more complex behaviors. The contradictory findings are likely due to the multiple factors involved in complex behaviors, which can vary in animal models and across testing situations (and laboratories) in unpredictable ways.

Possible Mechanisms Underlying Sexual Dimorphic Effects of Alcohol Exposure During Development

There are clear sex differences in the effects of alcohol exposure during development, and the most consistent findings are in sex steroids and behaviors that are tightly linked to the organizational and activational effects of sex steroids. The blunting of the testosterone surge during the prenatal and early postnatal periods in male rats by alcohol exposure during development (McGivern, Raum, Salido, & Redei, 1988; I. L. Ward et al., 2003) should affect the organization of the brain and thus is a likely mechanism. However, there have been few direct tests of this possibility. Some studies have tried to ameliorate alcohol-induced effects with testosterone supplements during the prenatal period without success (McGivern, 1989; McGivern, Holcomb, & Poland, 1987). However, a dose response analysis of the impact of testosterone supplements is necessary prior to making any conclusions, and it is important to examine the impact of testosterone supplements during the early postnatal period.

The mechanism underlying changes in female rats after alcohol exposure during development remains unknown. It is clear that there are reliable effects of alcohol exposure during development on gonadal hormones in female rats. These effects may be mediated by direct impact of alcohol on the ovaries or by some changes in brain regulation of hormonal cycles. These possible mechanisms require more investigation to determine relative contributions and more specificity.

In our opinion, the most intriguing avenue for investigation of the mechanisms underlying sex differences in the impact of alcohol exposure during development is to explore the impact on the stress response, as described by

Weinberg and colleagues (2008; Zhang et al., 2005). Alcohol exposure during the prenatal period clearly elicits physiological responses resembling stress in the pregnant animal and this, in turn, can affect the fetus (Weinberg et al., 2008; Weinberg & Bezio, 1987; Weinberg & Gallo, 1982; Zhang et al., 2005). Impact on the fetus can include the underlying neurohormonal bases of the stress response and sex hormones (as discussed in Weinberg et al., 2008; and Zhang et al., 2005), which in turn affects a large number of behaviors, including complex behaviors such as learning, in a sexually dimorphic manner. Given the resemblance of the response to alcohol to the response to stress (Weinberg & Gallo, 1982) and the prevalence of sex-specific effects of prenatal stress (Weinstock, 2007), this whole area of research deserves further study.

Postnatal handling has been shown to dampen the stress response in rats, and there have been attempts to use this procedure to reverse the findings on alcohol-induced changes in the hypothalamic–pituitary axis without success (Gabriel, Yu, Ellis, & Weinberg, 2000). However, it may be that the impact of postnatal handling was not intensive enough. Environment enrichment can alleviate some of the effects of alcohol exposure during development (Hannigan, O'Leary-Moore, & Berman, 2007), and it is plausible (but not known) that this effect may be mediated through an impact on the stress response.

Another way to tackle the problem of mechanism is to vary the suspect variable systematically and examine the outcome. This is an additive factors approach, which is used routinely in cognitive psychology (Sternberg, 1969) and is similar to a dose–response approach in pharmacology. It can be used quite effectively in behavioral neuroscience (for examples, see Lawrence et al., 2008; Lugo, Marino, Cronise, & Kelly, 2003) for further refining the underlying mechanism or mechanisms of a behavioral change in a complex behavior. For example, in tests of learning, it is possible to increase the stress level and examine the performance of the subjects. If alcohol-induced sex differences in performance in a spatial task occur because of sex differences in the stress response, then different patterns of sex differences would emerge with different levels of stress. If the deficit is affected by sex differences in the stress response, it would be predicted that alcohol-induced deficits would be similar in both sexes under low stress levels, with sex differences emerging as stress levels are increased. The same type of approach could be used with pharmacological manipulations. For example, sex differences in deficits of animals exposed to alcohol during development may emerge strongly with increasing doses of dexamethasone or increasing blockade of sex steroids in certain brain regions.

Conclusion

Broadly speaking, research on sex differences in the effect of alcohol during development in rodent models has two overarching goals. The first goal for this type of basic research is that it should contribute to our understanding of the sexual differentiation of the brain and the underlying neural bases of behavioral differences. The research findings that have been reviewed suggest that sex differences in the stress response and gonadal hormones may be critical in a variety of behaviors (as has been known for a long time) and that it may be important to examine components of a complex behavior when trying to determine the reason for sex differences in behavior (McCarthy & Konkle, 2005).

The second goal is translation of the research findings in rodents into studies on people with FASD, which will eventually give rise to more effective treatments. Effective treatment may well be gender specific. The prevalence and type of sex differences in alcohol-exposed rodents suggest that sex differences in deficits of affected people are likely to be present in behaviors that are sexually dimorphic in nonexposed people and in behaviors that are tightly linked to hormonal responses. The known literature on sex differences in FASD is reviewed in Chapter 7 of this volume. To translate the findings in rodent models to the clinical realm, it is important to select behavioral outcomes that are known to show sex differences and then include enough power in the design to actually detect an interaction between gender and alcohol exposure. Such noted outcome variables include performance in spatial tasks, hormonal responses to either drugs or social cues (or both), and sexual behavior. The latter point about power in the design is frequently a flaw in many studies, which do not detect gender differences. In human-based research, it is important to control for the use of birth control pills and also hormonal status. To move the field forward, it is essential to continue to facilitate the communication between basic and clinical researchers and take ideas or findings from one domain and test them in the other.

References

Abel, E. L. (1985). Prenatal effects of alcohol on growth: A brief overview. *Federation Proceedings, 44,* 2318–2322.

Abel, E. L., & Dintcheff, B. A. (1986). Saccharin preference in animals prenatally exposed to alcohol: No evidence of altered sexual dimorphism. *Neurobehavioral Toxicology & Teratology, 8,* 521–523.

Barron, S., Razani, L. J., Gallegos, R. A., & Riley, E. P. (1995). Effects of neonatal ethanol exposure on saccharin consumption. *Alcoholism: Clinical and Experimental Research, 19,* 257–261. doi:10.1111/j.1530-0277.1995.tb01500.x

Barron, S., & Riley, E. P. (1985). Pup-induced maternal behavior in adult and juvenile rats exposed to alcohol prenatally. *Alcoholism: Clinical and Experimental Research, 9,* 360–365. doi:10.1111/j.1530-0277.1985.tb05560.x

Barron, S., Tieman, S. B., & Riley, E. P. (1988). Effects of prenatal alcohol exposure on the sexually dimorphic nucleus of the preoptic area of the hypothalamus in male and female rats. *Alcoholism: Clinical and Experimental Research, 12,* 59–64. doi:10.1111/j.1530-0277.1988.tb00133.x

Bayer, S. A., Altman, J., Russo, R. J., & Zhang, X. (1993). Timetables of neurogenesis in the human brain based on experimentally determined patterns in the rat. *Neurotoxicology, 14,* 83–144.

Beatty, W. W. (1979). Gonadal hormones and sex differences in non-reproductive behaviors in rodents: Organization and activational effects. *Hormones and Behavior, 12,* 112–163. doi:10.1016/0018-506X(79)90017-5

Becker, J. B., Breedlove, S. M., & Crews, D. (1993). *Behavioral endocrinology.* Cambridge, MA: MIT Press.

Blanchard, B. A., & Hannigan, J. H. (1994). Prenatal ethanol exposure: Effects on androgen and nonandrogen dependent behaviors and on gonadal development in male rats. *Neurotoxicology and Teratology, 16,* 31–39. doi:10.1016/0892-0362(94)90006-X

Blanchard, B. A., Hannigan, J. H., & Riley, E. P. (1987). Amphetamine-induced activity after fetal alcohol exposure and undernutrition in rats. *Neurotoxicology and Teratology, 9,* 113–119. doi:10.1016/0892-0362(87)90087-0

Blanchard, B. A., Riley, E. P., & Hannigan, J. H. (1987). Deficits on a spatial navigation task following prenatal exposure to ethanol. *Neurotoxicology and Teratology, 9,* 253–258. doi:10.1016/0892-0362(87)90010-9

Boggan, W. O., Randall, C. L., & Dodds, H. M. (1979). Delayed sexual maturation in female C57Bl/6J mice prenatally exposed to alcohol. *Research Communications in Chemical Pathology and Pharmacology, 23,* 117–125.

Brain, P. F., Ajarem, J. S., & Petkov, V. V. (1987). The utility of ethological assessments of murin agonistic interactions in behavioural teratology: The fetal alcohol syndrome. In B. Olivier, J. Mos, & P. F. Brain (Eds.), *Ethnopharmacology of agonistic behaviour in animals and humans* (pp. 110–121). Boston, MA: Martinus Nijhoff.

Brien, J. F., Clarke, D. W., & Richardson, B. P. J. (1985). Disposition of ethanol in maternal blood, fetal blood and amniotic fluid of third-trimester pregnant ewes. *American Journal of Obstetrics and Gynecology, 152,* 583–590.

Creighton-Taylor, J. A., & Rudeen, P. K. (1991). Fetal alcohol exposure and effects of LHRH and PMA on LH beta-mRNA expression in the female rat. *Alcoholism: Clinical and Experimental Research, 15,* 1031–1035. doi:10.1111/j.1530-0277.1991.tb05206.x

Cronise, K., Tran, T. D., Marino, M., & Kelly, S. J. (2001). Hippocampal-based learning in rats exposed to alcohol during different periods of development. *Behavioral Neuroscience, 115,* 138–145. doi:10.1037/0735-7044.115.1.138

Dalterio, S., Bartke, A., Blum, K., & Sweeney, C. (1981). Marihuana and alcohol: Perinatal effects on development of male reproductive functions in mice. *Progress in Biochemical Pharmacology, 18,* 143–154.

Driscoll, C. D., Streissguth, A. P., & Riley, E. P. (1990). Prenatal alcohol exposure: Comparability of effects in humans and animal models. *Neurotoxicology and Teratology, 12,* 231–237. doi:10.1016/0892-0362(90)90094-S

Edwards, D. A. (1969). Early androgen stimulation and aggressive behavior in male and female mice. *Physiology & Behavior, 4,* 333–338. doi:10.1016/0031-9384(69)90185-1

Elis, J., & Kršiak, M. (1975). Effect of alcohol administration during pregnancy on social behaviour of offspring of mice. *Activitas Nervosa Superior, 17,* 281–282.

Esquifino, A. I., Sanchis, R., & Guerri, C. (1986). Effect of prenatal alcohol exposure on sexual maturation of female rat offspring. *Neuroendocrinology, 44,* 483–487. doi:10.1159/000124690

Fernandez, K., Caul, W. F., Haenlein, M., & Vorhees, C. V. (1983). Effects of prenatal alcohol on homing behavior, maternal responding, and open-field activity in rats. *Neurobehavioral Toxicology & Teratology, 5,* 351–356.

Gabriel, K. I., Yu, W., Ellis, L., & Weinberg, J. (2000). Postnatal handling does not attenuate hypothalamic–pituitary–adrenal hyperresponsiveness after prenatal ethanol exposure. *Alcoholism: Clinical and Experimental Research, 24,* 1566–1574. doi:10.1111/j.1530-0277.2000.tb04576.x

Gass, J. T., Jenkins, W. J., Marino, M. D., Lugo, J. N., Jr., & Kelly, S. J. (2007). Alcohol exposure during development: Analysis of effects on female sexual behavior. *Alcoholism: Clinical and Experimental Research, 31,* 2065–2072. doi:10.1111/j.1530-0277.2007.00525.x

Gianoulakis, C. (1990). Rats exposed prenatally to alcohol exhibit impairment in spatial navigation test. *Behavioural Brain Research, 36,* 217–228. doi:10.1016/0166-4328(90)90060-R

Glavas, M. M., Ellis, L., Yu, W. K., & Weinberg, J. (2007). Effects of prenatal ethanol exposure on basal limbic–hypothalamic–pituitary–adrenal regulation: Role of corticosterone. *Alcoholism: Clinical and Experimental Research, 31,* 1598–1610. doi:10.1111/j.1530-0277.2007.00460.x

Handa, R. J., McGivern, R. F., Noble, E. P., & Gorski, R. A. (1985). Exposure to alcohol in utero alters the adult pattern of luteinizing hormone secretion in male and female rats. *Life Sciences, 37,* 1683–1690. doi:10.1016/0024-3205(85)90295-4

Hannigan, J. H., O'Leary-Moore, S. K., & Berman, R. F. (2007). Postnatal environmental or experiential amelioration of neurobehavioral effects of perinatal alcohol exposure in rats. *Neuroscience and Biobehavioral Reviews, 31,* 202–211. doi:10.1016/j.neubiorev.2006.06.019

Hård, E., Dahlgren, I. L., Engel, J., Larsson, K., Liljequist, S., Lindh, A.-S., .Musi, B. (1984). Development of sexual behavior in prenatally ethanol-exposed rats. *Drug and Alcohol Dependence, 14,* 51–61. doi:10.1016/0376-8716(84)90019-X

Johnson, T. B., & Goodlett, C. R. (2002). Selective and enduring deficits in spatial learning after limited neonatal binge alcohol exposure in male rats. *Alcoholism: Clinical and Experimental Research, 26,* 83–93.

Jones, K. L., & Smith, D. W. (1973). Recognition of fetal alcohol syndrome in early infancy. *The Lancet, 302,* 999–1001. doi:10.1016/S0140-6736(73)91092-1

Kelce, W. R., Rudeen, P. K., & Ganjam, V. K. (1989). Prenatal ethanol exposure alters steroidogenic enzyme activity in newborn rat testes. *Alcoholism: Clinical and Experimental Research, 13,* 617–621. doi:10.1111/j.1530-0277.1989.tb00392.x

Kelly, S. J. (1996a). Alcohol exposure during development alters hypothalamic neurotransmitter concentrations. *Journal of Neural Transmission, 103,* 55–67. doi:10.1007/BF01292616

Kelly, S. J. (1996b). Effects of alcohol exposure and artificial rearing during development on septal and hippocampal neurotransmitters in adult rats. *Alcoholism: Clinical and Experimental Research, 20,* 670–676. doi:10.1111/j.1530-0277.1996.tb01670.x

Kelly, S. J., Day, N., & Streissguth, A. P. (2000). Effects of prenatal alcohol exposure on social behavior in humans and other species. *Neurotoxicology and Teratology, 22,* 143–149. doi:10.1016/S0892-0362(99)00073-2

Kelly, S. J., & Dillingham, R. R. (1994). Sexually dimorphic effects of perinatal alcohol exposure on social interactions and amygdala DNA and DOPAC concentrations. *Neurotoxicology and Teratology, 16,* 377–384. doi:10.1016/0892-0362(94)90026-4

Kelly, S. J., Goodlett, C. R., Hulsether, S. A., & West, J. R. (1988). Impaired spatial navigation in adult female but not adult male rats exposed to alcohol during the brain growth spurt. *Behavioural Brain Research, 27,* 247–257. doi:10.1016/0166-4328(88)90121-0

Kelly, S. J., Hulsether, S. A., & West, J. R. (1987). Alterations in sensorimotor development: Relationship to postnatal alcohol exposure. *Neurotoxicology and Teratology, 9,* 243–251. doi:10.1016/0892-0362(87)90009-2

Kelly, S. J., Mahoney, J. C., Randich, A., & West, J. R. (1991). Indices of stress in rats: Effects of sex, perinatal alcohol and artificial rearing. *Physiology & Behavior, 49,* 751–756. doi:10.1016/0031-9384(91)90314-E

Kelly, S. J., Ostrowski, N. L., & Wilson, M. A. (1999). Gender differences in brain and behavior: Hormonal and neural bases. *Pharmacology, Biochemistry and Behavior, 64,* 655–664. doi:10.1016/S0091-3057(99)00167-7

Kim, C. K., Giberson, P. K., Yu, W., Zoeller, R. T., & Weinberg, J. (1999). Effects of prenatal ethanol exposure on hypothalamic–pituitary–adrenal responses to chronic cold stress in rats. *Alcoholism: Clinical and Experimental Research, 23,* 301–310.

Kršiak, M., Elis, J., Pöschlová, N., & Mašek, K. (1977). Increased aggressiveness and lower brain serotonin levels in offspring of mice given alcohol during gestation. *Journal of Studies on Alcohol, 38,* 1696–1704.

Lawrence, R. C., Bonner, H. C., Newsom, R. J., & Kelly, S. J. (2008). Effects of alcohol exposure during development on play behavior and c-Fos expression in response to play. *Behavioural Brain Research, 188,* 209–218.

Lugo, J. N., Jr., Marino, M. D., Cronise, K., & Kelly, S. J. (2003). Effects of alcohol exposure during development on social behavior in rats. *Physiology & Behavior, 78,* 185–194. doi:10.1016/S0031-9384(02)00971-X

Lugo, J. N., Jr., Marino, M. D., Gass, J. T., Wilson, M. A., & Kelly, S. J. (2006). Ethanol exposure during development reduces resident aggression and testosterone in rats. *Physiology & Behavior, 87,* 330–337. doi:10.1016/j.physbeh.2005.10.005

Luine, V. N., Beck, K. D., Fownman, R. E., Frankfurt, M., & Maclusky, N. J. (2007). Chronic stress and neural function: Accounting for sex and age. *Journal of Neuroendocrinology, 19,* 743–751. doi:10.1111/j.1365-2826.2007.01594.x

McCarthy, M. M., & Konkle, A. T. M. (2005). When is a sex difference not a sex difference? *Frontiers in Neuroendocrinology, 26,* 85–102. doi:10.1016/j.yfrne.2005.06.001

McEwen, B. S. (1992). Steroid hormones: Effect on brain development and function. *Hormone Research in Paediatrics, 37*(Supplement 3), 1–10.

McGivern, R. F. (1989). Low birthweight in rats induced by prenatal exposure to testosterone combined with alcohol, pair-feeding, or stress. *Teratology, 40,* 335–338. doi:10.1002/tera.1420400405

McGivern, R. F., & Barron, S. (1991). Influence of prenatal alcohol exposure on the process of neurobehavioral sexual differentiation. *Alcohol Health & Research World, 15,* 115–125.

McGivern, R. F., Clancy, A. N., Hill, M. A., & Noble, E. P. (1984, May 25). Prenatal alcohol exposure alters adult expression of sexually dimorphic behavior in the rat. *Science, 224,* 896–898. doi:10.1126/science.6719121

McGivern, R. F., Handa, R. J., & Raum, W. J. (1998). Ethanol exposure during the last week of gestation in the rat: Inhibition of the prenatal testosterone surge in males without long-term alterations in sex behavior. *Neurotoxicology and Teratology, 20,* 483–490. doi:10.1016/S0892-0362(98)00009-9

McGivern, R. F., Handa, R. J., & Redei, E. (1993). Decreased postnatal testosterone surge in male rats exposed to ethanol during the last week of gestation. *Alcoholism: Clinical and Experimental Research, 17,* 1215–1222. doi:10.1111/j.1530-0277.1993.tb05232.x

McGivern, R. F., Holcomb, C., & Poland, R. E. (1987). Effects of prenatal testosterone propionate treatment on saccharin preference of adult rats exposed to ethanol in utero. *Physiology & Behavior, 39,* 241–246. doi:10.1016/0031-9384(87)90016-3

McGivern, R. F., Raum, W. J., Salido, E., & Redei, E. (1988). Lack of prenatal testosterone surge in fetal rats exposed to alcohol: Alterations in testicular morphology and physiology. *Alcoholism: Clinical and Experimental Research, 12,* 243–247. doi:10.1111/j.1530-0277.1988.tb00188.x

Meyer, L. S., & Riley, E. P. (1986). Social play in juvenile rats prenatally exposed to alcohol. *Teratology, 34,* 1–7. doi:10.1002/tera.1420340102

Minetti, S. A., & Fulginiti, S. (1991). Sexual receptivity of adult female rats prenatally intoxicated with alcohol on gestational day 8. *Neurotoxicology and Teratology, 13,* 531–534. doi:10.1016/0892-0362(91)90061-Z

Moore, C. L., Dou, H., & Juraska, J. M. (1996). Number, size, and regional distribution of motor neurons in the dorsolateral and retrodorsolateral nuclei as a function of sex and neonatal stimulation. *Developmental Psychobiology, 29,* 303–313. doi:10.1002/(SICI)1098-2302(199605)29:4<303::AID-DEV1>3.0.CO;2-U

Moore, C. L., & Morelli, G. A. (1979). Mother rats interact differently with male and female offspring. *Journal of Comparative and Physiological Psychology, 93,* 677–684. doi:10.1037/h0077599

Newman Taylor, A., Branch, B. J., Liu, S. H., & Kokka, N. (1982). Long-term effects of fetal ethanol exposure on pituitary–adrenal response to stress. *Pharmacology, Biochemistry and Behavior, 16,* 585–589. doi:10.1016/0091-3057(82)90420-8

Osborn, J. A., Kim, C. K., Yu, W., Herbert, L., & Weinberg, J. (1996). Fetal ethanol exposure alters pituitary–adrenal sensitivity to dexamethasone suppression. *Psychoneuroendocrinology, 21,* 127–143. doi:10.1016/0306-4530(95)00037-2

Parker, S., Udani, M., Gavaler, J., & Van Thiel, D. H. (1984). Adverse effects of ethanol upon adult sexual behavior of male rats exposed in utero. *Neurobehavioral Toxicology & Teratology, 6,* 289–293.

Royalty, J. (1990). Effects of prenatal ethanol exposure on juvenile play-fighting and postpubertal aggression in rats. *Psychological Reports, 66,* 551–560. doi:10.2466/PR0.66.2.551-560

Rudeen, P. K. (1986). Reduction of the volume of the sexually dimorphic nucleus of the preoptic area by in utero ethanol exposure in male rats. *Neuroscience Letters, 72,* 363–368. doi:10.1016/0304-3940(86)90542-2

Rudeen, P. K., Kappel, C. A., & Lear, K. (1986). Postnatal or in utero ethanol exposure reduction of the volume of the sexually dimorphic nucleus of the preoptic area in male rats. *Drug and Alcohol Dependence, 18,* 247–252. doi:10.1016/0376-8716(86)90056-6

Rudeen, P. K., & Weinberg, J. (1993). Prenatal ethanol exposure: Changes in regional brain catecholamine content following stress. *Journal of Neurochemistry, 61,* 1907–1915. doi:10.1111/j.1471-4159.1993.tb09833.x

Samson, H. H., & Diaz, J. (1982). Effects of neonatal ethanol exposure on brain development in rodents. In E. L. Abel (Ed.), *Fetal alcohol syndrome* (3rd ed., pp. 131–150). Boca Raton, FL: CRC Press.

Schwarz, J. M., & McCarthy, M. M. (2008). Steroid-induced sexual differentiation of the developing brain: Multiple pathways, one goal. *Journal of Neurochemistry, 105,* 1561–1572. doi:10.1111/j.1471-4159.2008.05384.x

Sternberg, S. (1969). The discovery of processing stages: Extensions of Donders' method. *Acta Psychologica, 30,* 276–315. doi:10.1016/0001-6918(69)90055-9

Streissguth, A. P., & O'Malley, K. (2000). Neuropsychiatric implications and long-term consequences of fetal alcohol spectrum disorders. *Seminars in Clinical Neuropsychiatry, 5,* 177–190. doi:10.1053/scnp.2000.6729

Tran, T. D., Cronise, K., Marino, M. D., Jenkins, W. J., & Kelly, S. J. (2000). Critical periods for the effects of alcohol exposure on brain weight, body weight, activity, and investigation. *Behavioural Brain Research, 116,* 99–110. doi:10.1016/S0166-4328(00)00263-1

Udani, M., Parker, S., Gavaler, J., & Van Thiel, D. H. (1985). Effects of in utero exposure to alcohol upon male rats. *Alcoholism: Clinical and Experimental Research, 9,* 355–359. doi:10.1111/j.1530-0277.1985.tb05559.x

Ward, I. L., Ward, O. B., Affuso, J. D., Long, W. D., III, French, J. A., & Hendricks, S. E. (2003). Fetal testosterone surge: Specific modulations induced in male rats by maternal stress and/or alcohol consumption. *Hormones and Behavior, 43,* 531–539. doi:10.1016/S0018-506X(03)00061-8

Ward, O. B., Ward, I. L., Denning, J. H., French, J. A., & Hendricks, S. E. (2002). Postparturitional testosterone surge in male offspring of rats stressed and/or fed ethanol during late pregnancy. *Hormones and Behavior, 41,* 229–235. doi:10.1006/hbeh.2001.1746

Ward, O. B., Ward, I. L., Denning, J. H., Hendricks, S. E., & French, J. A. (2002). Hormonal mechanisms underlying aberrant sexual differentiation in male rats prenatally exposed to alcohol, stress, or both. *Archives of Sexual Behavior, 31,* 9–16. doi:10.1023/A:1014018931977

Weinberg, J. (1988). Hyperresponsiveness to stress: Differential effects of prenatal ethanol on males and females. *Alcoholism: Clinical and Experimental Research, 12,* 647–652. doi:10.1111/j.1530-0277.1988.tb00258.x

Weinberg, J. (1989). Prenatal ethanol exposure alters adrenocortical development of offspring. *Alcoholism: Clinical and Experimental Research, 13,* 73–83. doi:10.1111/j.1530-0277.1989.tb00287.x

Weinberg, J. (1992). Prenatal ethanol effects: Sex differences in offspring stress responsiveness. *Alcohol, 9,* 219–223. doi:10.1016/0741-8329(92)90057-H

Weinberg, J. (1993). Neuroendocrine effects of prenatal alcohol exposure. *Annals of the New York Academy of Sciences, 697,* 86–96. doi:10.1111/j.1749-6632.1993.tb49925.x

Weinberg, J., & Bezio, S. (1987). Alcohol-induced changes in pituitary adrenal activity during pregnancy. *Alcoholism: Clinical and Experimental Research, 11,* 274–280. doi:10.1111/j.1530-0277.1987.tb01307.x

Weinberg, J., & Gallo, P. V. (1982). Prenatal ethanol exposure: Pituitary–adrenal activity in pregnant dams and offspring. *Neurobehavioral Toxicology & Teratology, 4,* 515–520.

Weinberg, J., Sliwowska, J. H., Lan, N., & Hellemans, K. G. (2008). Prenatal alcohol exposure: Foetal programming, the hypothalamic–pituitary–adrenal axis and sex differences in outcome. *Journal of Neuroendocrinology, 20,* 470–488. doi:10.1111/j.1365-2826.2008.01669.x

Weinberg, J., Taylor, A. N., & Gianoulakis, C. (1996). Fetal ethanol exposure: Hypothalamic–pituitary–adrenal and beta-endorphin responses to repeated stress. *Alcoholism: Clinical and Experimental Research, 20,* 122–131. doi:10.1111/j.1530-0277.1996.tb01054.x

Weinberg, J., Zimmerberg, B., & Sonderegger, T. B. (1992). Gender-specific effects of perinatal exposure to alcohol and other drugs. In T. B. Sonderegger (Ed.), *Perinatal substance abuse: Research findings and clinical implications* (pp. 51–89). Baltimore, MD: Johns Hopkins Press.

Weinstock, M. (2007). Gender differences in the effects of prenatal stress on brain development and behaviour. *Neurochemical Research, 32,* 1730–1740. doi:10.1007/s11064-007-9339-4

West, J. R., Goodlett, C. R., & Kelly, S. J. (1987). Alcohol and brain development [Review]. *NIDA Research Monograph, 78,* 45–60.

Wilson, J. H., Kelly, S. J., & Wilson, M. A. (1996). Early postnatal alcohol exposure in rats: Maternal behavior and estradiol levels. *Physiology & Behavior, 59,* 287–293. doi:10.1016/0031-9384(95)02094-2

Yanai, J., & Ginsburg, B. E. (1977). A developmental study of ethanol effects on behavioural and physical development in mice. *Alcoholism: Clinical and Experimental Research, 1,* 325–333. doi:10.1111/j.1530-0277.1977.tb05789.x

Zhang, X., Sliwowska, J. H., & Weinberg, J. (2005). Prenatal alcohol exposure and fetal programming: Effects on neuroendocrine and immune function. *Experimental Biology and Medicine, 230,* 376–388.

Zimmerberg, B., Mattson, S., & Riley, E. P. (1989). Impaired alternation test performance in adult rats following prenatal alcohol exposure. *Pharmacology, Biochemistry and Behavior, 32,* 293–299. doi:10.1016/0091-3057(89)90246-3

Zimmerberg, B., & Mickus, L. A. (1990). Sex differences in corpus callosum: Influence of prenatal alcohol exposure and maternal undernutrition. *Developmental Brain Research, 537,* 115–122. doi:10.1016/0006-8993(90)90347-E

Zimmerberg, B., & Reuter, J. M. (1989). Sexually dimorphic behavioral and brain asymmetries in neonatal rats: Effects of prenatal alcohol exposure. *Developmental Brain Research, 46,* 281–290. doi:10.1016/0165-3806(89)90291-5

Zimmerberg, B., & Scalzi, L. V. (1989). Commissural size in neonatal rats: Effects of sex and prenatal alcohol exposure. *International Journal of Developmental Neuroscience, 7,* 81–86. doi:10.1016/0736-5748(89)90046-4

Part IV

Environmental Toxins

9

Gender (Sex) Differences in Response to Prenatal Lead Exposure

Nancy L. Fiedler

Although lead has been used for more than 8,000 years and recognized as a neurotoxicant for more than 2,000 years, the exposure concentrations at which health effects occur remain controversial. Lead has many industrial uses but no known biological function; moreover, it has adverse effects on every organ system. But while the scientific community's sophistication in detecting the deleterious effects of lead has improved, no clear lead threshold for nervous system effects has emerged. Since 1991, blood lead concentration of more than 10 µg/dl in children has defined lead poisoning (Centers for Disease Control [CDC], 1991). However, data from animal and human studies challenge this standard, showing deleterious effects on learning and behavior at or below 10 µg/dl blood lead (Lanphear, Dietrich, Auinger, & Cox, 2000; U.S. Environmental Protection Agency, 2006). The current blood lead standard for children was based on observations of significant developmental delay among 2-year-olds with prenatal lead exposures greater than 10 µg/dl relative to those with blood lead less than 10µg/dl as documented from umbilical cord blood (Bellinger, Levitron, Waternaux, Needleman, & Rabinowitz, 1987). Although several subsequent studies have found that the adverse effects of prenatal exposures were attenuated in later childhood (e.g., Bellinger, Stiles, & Needleman, 1992; Wasserman et al., 1997), evidence from animal studies has provided cause for reconsideration (White et al., 2007), with some investigators calling for further reduction of the blood lead standard (S. G. Gilbert & Weiss, 2006; Lidsky & Schneider, 2003).

The scientific and regulatory communities probably understand more about the cognitive and behavioral effects of lead than any other neurotoxicant, and yet we are just beginning to appreciate the breadth of lead's effects on the developing organism. Moreover, we know little about the interaction of prenatal lead exposure with other concomitant risk factors (e.g., poverty, nutrition) or how males and females may be differentially affected. The purpose of this chapter is to review animal and human studies of prenatal lead exposure, with special focus on sex as an effect modifier for cognitive, motor, and social development.

Measurement Issues and Prenatal Lead Exposure

The effects of postnatal lead exposure on cognitive function and behavior are well documented (U.S. Environmental Protection Agency, 2006). The majority of studies dating back to the 1970s rely on current blood lead as an indicator of exposure. However, a growing body of evidence indicates that the developmental period in which exposure occurs determines the significance and permanence of lead's effects on function. Without question, the neonate is uniquely susceptible to neurotoxicant exposures, but this vulnerability varies widely over the course of pregnancy (Mendola, Selevan, Gutter, & Rice, 2002). Although exogenous sources of lead exposure have declined significantly with the removal of lead from gasoline (see Table 9.1), the mother is an endogenous source of lead exposure because of the mobilization of maternal skeletal lead during pregnancy (Gomaa et al., 2002; Hu & Hernandez-Avila, 2002; Tellez-Rojo et al., 2004). Thus, lead exposure to unborn children has persisted long after the environmental sources of exposure have declined (Hu & Hernandez-Avila, 2002). For example, even after controlling for cord blood lead and other covariates, the mother's patellar (kneecap) bone lead was a significant and independent predictor of reduced Bayley Mental Development Index (MDI) scores in 24-month-old infants (Gomaa et al., 2002). The composition of patella bone is primarily trabecular and more porous or spongy than tibia or shin bone, which is more compact (cortical bone). Thus, patella bone is expected to release more lead to the fetus because of greater bone resorption during pregnancy (R. Smith & Phillips, 1998). Furthermore, Gomaa et al. (2002) did not find an association between 12- and 24-month postnatal blood lead values and MDI scores, underscoring the relative importance of prenatal versus postnatal exposure on mental development. Gomaa et al. recruited mother–infant pairs and covaried sex as an important determinant of infant neurodevelopment, but the interaction of sex and lead exposure was not a focus of the analysis.

Table 9.1.   U.S. Blood Lead Levels (µg/dl)

Gender	NHANES II (1976–1980)		NHANES III (1988–1991)		NHANES III (1991–1994)	
	M[a]	CI	M[b]	CI	M[b]	CI
Overall	16.3	15.2–17.4	4.1	3.7–4.5	3.1	2.8–3.5
White						
Males	15.6	14.3–16.9	3.5	3.1–4.1	2.8	2.5–3.2
Females	14.5	13.3–15.7	3.6	3.0–4.3	2.6	2.0–3.2
Black						
Males	20.2	18.0–22.4	6.3	5.6–7.2	5.4	4.6–6.3
Females	21.7	19.6–23.8	5.8	5.1–6.5	4.2	3.4–5.0

Note.   Data for the second National Health and Nutrition Examination Survey (NHANES II) are for children ages 6 months to 2 years. The findings are reported in Amnest and Mahaffey, 1984. Data for the third NHANES, 1988–1991, are taken from Brody et al., 1994; the 1991–1994 data are taken from Pirkle et al., 1994. CI = confidence interval.
[a]Arithmetic mean. [b]Geometric mean.

Although maternal and fetal blood lead levels are similar and highly correlated (Gardella, 2001), the measurement of fetal dose throughout pregnancy is not well characterized. Thus, differences in study results depend on accurate characterization of the timing and dose of prenatal lead exposure. For example, some studies have measured maternal whole blood lead at different trimesters, whereas others have used umbilical cord blood lead as an indicator of dose during pregnancy. Maternal whole blood lead may not be the most accurate marker of lead in the fetal brain, because 99% of lead is bound to red cells and cannot cross the placenta (Hu et al., 2006). Instead, Hu et al. (2006) used plasma lead because it more closely represents lead in circulation that can be readily exchanged with peripheral target tissues (e.g., brain) and therefore is regarded as a more accurate indicator of fetal dose (D. Smith, Hernandez-Avila, Tellez-Rojo, Mercado, & Hu, 2002). Animal studies support that the uptake of lead is more efficient in the fetus as opposed to the postnatal period (Rossouw, Offermeier, & Van Rooyen, 1987).

Behavioral Effects of Prenatal Lead Exposure

Mental or cognitive development and overall indices of intelligence are the outcomes most often measured to determine the effects of lead on behavioral function. However, fewer studies have also evaluated social and emotional behavior to include early sociability, hyperactivity, aggressiveness, and antisocial or delinquent behavior (e.g., Carpenter & Nevin, 2010; Dietrich, Ris, Succop, Berger, & Bornschein, 2001; Mendolsohn et al., 1998; Needleman, Riess, Tobin, Biesecker, & Greenhouse, 1996; Nevin, 2007). The Bayley Scales of Infant Development are the scales most often used to evaluate mental and motor development during early childhood (Bayley, 1969). The mental scales of the Bayley (MDI) evaluate sensory–perceptual abilities, acquisition of object constancy and memory, learning and problem solving, verbal communication, and the ability to form classifications (abstract thinking). Follow-up studies have used standardized tests of intelligence to include the Wechsler Intelligence Scales for Children (Wechsler, 1991), the McCarthy Scale of Children's Ability (McCarthy, Baghurst, Robertson, Vimpani, & Wigg, 1985), and the Kaufman Assessment Battery for Children (Kaufman & Kaufman, 2004). Teacher checklists, the Child Behavior Checklist (Achenbach, 1991) for parents and teachers, and the Bayley Behavior Rating Scale (Bayley, 1969) are measures used to assess emotional and social behavior.

Studies of early development have found that low-level fetal lead exposure was associated with lower birth weight (Dietrich et al., 1986), shorter gestation (McMichael, Vimpani, Robertson, Baghurst, & Clark, 1986), and increased risk for minor anomalies (Needleman, Rabinowitz, Leviton, Linn, & Schoenbaum, 1984). These studies recruited newborns and either did not address the effect of sex or reported that sex was unrelated to lead exposure (Needleman et al., 1984). Subsequent studies from these and other groups have shown modest relationships between low-level prenatal lead exposure and poorer motor control and attention in neonates with no evaluation of the interaction with sex (Emory, Patillo, Archibold, Bayorh, & Sung, 1999). Tang et al. (1999) reported less sociability and lower 5-hydroxyindoleacetic acid levels, an indicator of serotonergic function, among 9-month-old children with prenatal lead expo-sure, but they did not evaluate the effect of sex.

In the late 1970s and early 1980s, birth cohorts in Cincinnati, Ohio (Dietrich et al., 1987); Port Pirie, Australia (McMichael et al., 1986); and Boston, Massachusetts (Bellinger et al., 1984) were developed to prospectively evaluate the effects of prenatal lead exposure on child development. Studies from these cohorts documented that after control for covariates, increases in umbilical cord blood lead were associated with significant reductions in the Bayley MDI (see Table 9.2). Furthermore, these deficits persisted up to 2 years of age in some cases (Bellinger et al., 1987; Dietrich et al., 1987; Wigg et al., 1988). However, the effects were not universal among other samples recruited in a similar time frame (Cooney et al., 1989; Ernhart, Morrow-Tlucak, Marler, & Wolf, 1987), although later birth cohorts from Yugoslavia (Wasserman et al., 1992) and Shanghai, China (Shen et al., 1998), reported similar results for the MDI at 2 years of age.

Among the positive studies, children from the Cincinnati and Boston cohorts evaluated and reported sex differences in response to prenatal lead exposure. A prenatal Blood Lead × Sex interaction indicative of stronger dose-related MDI deficit among male infants was observed in the Cincinnati cohort (Dietrich et al., 1987). On the basis of questionnaires completed by teachers, however, girls from the Boston cohort were more vulnerable to the effects of postnatal lead exposure, showing reading and spelling problems, whereas boys were relatively more vul-nerable to the effects of prenatal lead exposure (i.e., cord blood lead $\geq$ 10 µg/dl) as indicated by difficulty following directions (Leviton et al., 1993). As for the stud-ies of lead's effect on newborns, analyses of the data evaluating mental develop-ment did not focus on the effect of sex. Some investigators did not perform any evaluation of the Sex × Lead interaction on development (e.g., Cooney et al., 1989; Ernhart et al., 1987), whereas others used sex as a covariate (Wasserman et al., 1992). For example, in the Port Pirie cohort, Wigg et al. (1988) reported that sex had no effect on blood lead values and then did not evaluate the effect of sex on developmental outcomes.

Follow-up studies of these cohorts have revealed continuing decrements in cognitive performance as measured with the Kaufman Assessment Battery for Children and the McCarthy Scales of Children's Ability (Bellinger et al., 1992; McMichael et al., 1988; Wasserman et al., 1994), but continuing decrements were not universally observed (Dietrich, Succop, Berger, Hammond, & Bornschein, 1991). In both the Boston and Port Pirie cohorts, postnatal blood lead was the strongest predictor of cognitive performance after adjustment for confounders. Some investigators (Bellinger et al., 1992; Wasserman et al., 1994) have con-trolled for sex (a known correlate of cognitive development) in the analysis to improve the precision of estimates for lead's effect on cognitive function, but others (Dietrich et al., 1991; McMichael et al., 1988) have investigated sex as a factor that could interact and alter the effects of lead on cognitive function. For the sample of children living near a smelter in Yugoslavia, both prenatal (maternal and cord blood lead levels) and postnatal blood lead levels significantly predicted decrements in intelligence up to age 7 even after controlling for confounders. However, it should be noted that certain subgroups experienced more persistent effects of prenatal or early natal lead exposure. For example, neonatal blood lead

Table 9.2. Studies of Prenatal Lead Exposure and Mental Development

Birth cohorts	Cord blood lead values	Age at testing	Behavioral effects	Gender effects	References
Cincinnati, Ohio (1979–1984) ($N = 305$)	$M = 6.3$ µg/dl ($SD = 4.5$)	3 months	6 MDI point reduction per 10 µg/dl increase in lead	6 month old males: 8 MDI point reduction per 10µg/dl increase in maternal prenatal blood lead	Dietrich et al., 1987
Port Pirie, Australia (1979–1982) ($N = 723$)	Geometric mean = 8.3 (CI = 8.0–8.6)	2 years	MDI reduction	None reported	Wigg et al., 1988
Boston, Massachusetts (1979–1981) ($N = 249$)	low = < 3 µg/dl; medium = 6.5 µg/dl; high = > 10 µg/dl	6 months	6 point MDI reduction per 10 µg/dl for low vs. high blood lead	None reported	Bellinger et al., 1984
Cleveland, Ohio ($N = 359$)	$M = 5.99$ µg/dl ($SD = 2.11$)	6 months	No consistent effect on MDI	None reported	Ernhart et al., 1987

Note. The Birth cohorts column gives the location of the study, the years of the birth cohort, and the number of pregnant women recruited in the original sample. The Behavioral effects column refers to the Bayley Scales of Infant Development: Mental (MDI) and motor development; effects are reported after control for significant covariates. CI = confidence interval.

(10 days postnatal) predicted cognitive performance at age 4 among the poorest families in the Cincinnati cohort (Dietrich et al., 1991); in the Boston cohort, children with higher cord blood lead were more adversely affected by higher postnatal lead exposure than were those with lower cord blood lead (Bellinger et al., 1992). The more deleterious effects on males observed at 6 months of age in the Cincinnati cohort were not reported at 4 years of age, but females in the Boston cohort with the highest prenatal exposures showed the greatest recovery of function on the general cognitive index of the McCarthy Scales (Bellinger, Leviton, & Sloman, 1990). Finally, in a follow-up study evaluating the neuropsychological effects of prenatal and postnatal lead exposure among adolescents from the Cincinnati cohort, males showed significant reductions on measures of attention and visuoconstruction (Ris, Dietrich, Succop, Berger, & Bernschein, 2004).

Although earlier studies addressed the effect of prenatal lead exposure on development, the relative contribution of prenatal versus postnatal lead exposure remains unclear. Recent studies, such as the Mexico City Prospective Lead Study, documented that third trimester lead exposure was a significant log linear predictor of IQ at 6 to 10 years of age after controlling for other prenatal and postnatal lead measures (Schnaas et al., 2006). Sex was not a significant factor along with other covariates in the model predicting IQ. Moreover, the largest IQ changes occurred at the lower maternal lead value of 1 to 6 μg/dl. In a carefully controlled study, Hu and colleagues (2006) sought to determine the effects of lead exposure measured during each trimester of pregnancy, from cord blood, and postnatally at 12 and 24 months. Only maternal plasma and whole blood lead during the first trimester were significant predictors of reduced MDI scores. As noted by the authors, previous studies did not consistently measure maternal blood lead during each trimester of pregnancy and therefore could not clearly address whether the trimester in which lead exposure occurred made a difference in outcomes. Although sex was included in the multivariate model, it was treated as a covariate (p = .13), and the interaction effect of sex and plasma lead on MDI scores was not reported.

The focus of the literature has been on cognitive and psychomotor function among infants and children exposed to lead in utero and during childhood. However, some studies evaluated other indicators to include brainstem auditory evoked responses, electroretinographic (ERG) a and b wave amplitudes, and behavior including observational ratings of attention and sociability. In the Mexico City cohort, maternal blood lead at midpregnancy (20 weeks) was associated with brainstem auditory evoked responses in newborns and at 3 months and 67 months of age (Rothenberg, Poblano, & Garza-Morales, 1994; Rothenberg, Poblano, & Schnaas, 2000). These effects on auditory function appear to be permanent because auditory response latencies reach adult values by approximately age 4. Moreover, the investigators suggest that alterations in the auditory brainstem could result in problems detecting sound transitions and distinguishing speech sound or the spatial location of sounds. These deficits could underlie some of the cognitive decrements observed in lead-exposed children. Compromised visual function, measured by ERG, has also been related to cord blood lead concentrations (Rothenberg et al., 2002).

Low-level prenatal lead exposure has been associated with less sociability in 9-month-old children and poorer attention as assessed by direct observation of infant attention (Emory et al., 1999; Plusquellec et al., 2007). Again, sex was treated as a covariate in the analysis of these outcomes. Even minor decrements in the basic visual, auditory, and attentional capacities may explain the pathways through which higher order cognitive function later in development is compromised with prenatal lead exposure.

Based on innovative animal studies suggesting that prenatal lead exposure is associated with permanent alterations in the hypothalamic–pituitary–adrenal (HPA) axis function, Gump and colleagues evaluated cortisol in response to an acute stressor, the cold pressor task, among 9-year-old children enrolled in the longitudinal Oswego Children's Study (Gump, Stewart, et al., 2007). Prenatal blood lead values, adjusted for covariates and postnatal blood lead, were significantly associated with increasing salivary cortisol responses at 21, 40, and 60 min after the stressor. Unlike many previous studies, these investigators explicitly evaluated the Sex × Lead interaction largely because of the sex differences noted in animal studies, but they found no significant interaction. The levels of prenatal cord blood lead values ranged from < 1 μg/dl to 4.4 μg/dl, clearly below the CDC value of 10 μg/dl. In the same cohort, Gump et al. (2005) documented a significant association between cord blood lead values and higher baseline systolic blood pressure after adjustment for confounders and childhood blood lead values. However, childhood lead values but not cord blood leads were associated with total peripheral resistance (TPR) in response to mirror tracing and reaction time tasks (Gump et al., 2005). Furthermore, childhood lead values mediated the relationship between socioeconomic status and TPR response to acute stressors (Gump, Reihman, et al., 2007). That is, lower family socioeconomic status was associated with higher childhood blood lead levels, and the latter was a mediator for the TPR response to acute stressors. No significant sex effects were observed. These are unique studies that build on animal work documenting the significant impact of lead on the HPA axis (see the discussion that follows) and a potential mechanism for the association of lead with the development of hypertension in adulthood.

Evidence is accumulating to suggest that even low prenatal exposure levels, as documented by maternal and cord blood values, have significant effects on sensory, intellectual, adrenocortical, and emotional function that could persist throughout life. For example, a follow-up study of the Cincinnati cohort revealed that higher prenatal lead exposure was significantly associated with increased parental reports of delinquent and antisocial behaviors for males and females (Dietrich et al., 2001) and with lower attention and visuoconstruction performance for male but not female adolescents (Ris et al., 2004). Furthermore, childhood blood lead concentrations for the 19- to 24-year-old subjects from this cohort were associated with loss of frontal gray matter; this loss was much greater for men than women even though the average childhood lead values were comparable (i.e., ~ 13 μg/dl +/- 6; Cecil et al., 2008). In an ecological assessment of the relationship between prenatal or early childhood lead exposure (or both) at the population level and crime statistics, Carpenter and Nevin (2010) associated a significant decline in violent crime rates with the decline in blood leads that began in the 1970s with removal of lead from gasoline. They further suggested that this trend is seen internationally (Nevin, 2007) with approximately a 20-year lag in crime reduction based on changes in lead exposure in early development. Males are more likely to commit violent crime, which has been attributed to rising levels of testosterone combined with impoverished environment. However, this ecologic assessment also proposes that the behavioral alterations of reduced attention and increased impulsivity, seen disproportionately among lead-exposed males, may contribute to increased risk of antisocial behavior. Moreover, the disproportionate loss of gray matter in brain regions associated with executive function, mood regulation, and decision making among lead-exposed males further supports their increased vulnerability to the effects of lead on behavior (Cecil et al., 2008).

In summary, studies of prenatal and postnatal lead exposure in children have suggested that lead has a differential effect on males and females but that this effect probably depends on a multitude of other factors that have yet to be adequately characterized, such as the developmental period of exposure, social and nutritional status, and genetic factors influencing metabolism of lead (Bellinger, Leviton, & Sloman, 2000; Lidsky & Schneider, 2003). There are no clear sex differences in blood lead levels among young children (e.g., Baghurst et al., 1992). Therefore, any differences in function are more likely due to biological differences between the sexes. Although a number of studies have documented sex differences in lead burden related to pregnancy, lactation, and menopause, sex differences in lead metabolism have been inadequately studied even among adults (Vahter, Akesson, Liden, Ceccatelli, & Berglund, 2007).

Overall, testing the interaction of sex and lead on the outcome variables measured was not planned in the studies cited, and therefore power may not have been sufficient to adequately test this interaction and certainly not sufficient to evaluate relevant three-way interactions (e.g., Sex × Lead × Social Class; Bellinger, 2000; Tong, McMichael, & Baghurst, 2000). Thus, some researchers have observed greater effects of lead in boys (Bellinger et al., 1990; Dietrich et al., 1987; Pocock, Smith, & Baghurst, 1994), whereas others have found girls to be more affected (McMichael et al., 1992; Rabinowitz, Wang, & Soong, 1993; Tong et al., 2000). Moreover, resilience and recovery from lead exposure may be differentially affected by both sex and social class. For example, environmental enrichment concomitant with higher social class contributed to recovery from exposure related cognitive effects, but only for females (Bellinger, 2000).

Prenatal Lead Exposure in Animal Models

Rat models of prenatal lead exposure have revealed that effects are altered by the developmental period during which exposure occurs, the combination of stress in the mother and offspring, the sex of the offspring, and the neurotransmitter and behavioral outcomes measured (White et al., 2007). In a series of studies from Cory-Slechta and colleagues, the offspring of dams, exposed 2 months before breeding and continuously through lactation to 0 and 150 parts per million (ppm) lead acetate in drinking water (blood lead = 39 µg/dl) with and without stress, exhibited significantly increased basal corticosterone at age 9 months, but at age 14 months basal corticosterone was reduced to approximately 50% of control levels (Cory-Slechta, Virgolini, Thiruchelvam, Weston, & Bauter, 2004). Male animals were relatively more susceptible than females to the effects of prenatal lead exposure, but the effects observed in both sexes were mediated by prenatal lead exposure, not stress. Although basal corticosterone levels at 9 months were approximately 50% higher than controls among females, males approximately doubled their basal corticosterone relative to their controls. Because lead exposure ended at 21 days of age when weaning occurred, Cory-Slechta et al. (2004) concluded that the changes in basal corticosterone signified permanent alteration in the HPA axis function that was dynamic over time and different for males and females. Further studies of these female offspring also revealed that their stress responsivity was altered in response to the combined maternal lead and stress exposure (Virgolini, Chen, Weston, Bauter, & Cory-Slechta, 2005). Relative to controls, female offspring whose mothers were exposed to lead and stress exhibited reduced rates of responding to a fixed interval task and reduced corticosterone levels following a cold stressor, potentially modeling effects on both the HPA axis and on neurobehavioral function in children (Virgolini et al., 2005).

Male and female rats exposed through their mothers during gestation and lactation also differed in dopamine levels and dopamine turnover in frontal cortex, nucleus accumbens, and striatum at 10 months of age. For example, female offspring were more vulnerable, showing significant increases in frontal dopamine levels relative to controls among those whose mothers were exposed to lead and stress (Cory-Slechta et al., 2004). The same effect was not observed for dopamine levels in the frontal cortex of male offspring. Differential effects of sex and exposure were also observed in dopamine levels in other brain regions. These studies are informative because they created animal models that included exposure to lead and stress as a model for lower socioeconomic status human exposure. Furthermore, they highlight the differential effect of sex that varies depending on the outcome measured.

Lead exposure in utero but terminating at weaning produced permanent impairment of long-term potentiation, the cellular mechanisms supporting learning in the hippocampus (M. E. Gilbert, Mack, & Lasley, 1996, 1999) and altered the glutamate transmitter release function (Lasley & Gilbert 1996; Lasley, Green, & Gilbert, 1999). As for the HPA axis function, these studies illustrate that early exposure terminating at weaning is sufficient to produce permanent impairment in neurochemical release function (White et al., 2007). Studies with monkeys also show neurobehavioral deficits following steady state in utero exposure of about 11 µg/dl (U.S. Environmental Protection Agency, 2006). Moreover, the role of early lead exposure on the later development of neurodegenerative diseases is a subject of current exploration with rodent models of disease (e.g., Basha et al., 2005).

Sex differences in immunotoxicity have also been documented after low levels of lead exposure (single exposure of 5 or 10 µg) during embryonic development of chickens and rats (Bunn, Marsh, & Dietert, 2000; Bunn, Parsons, Kao, & Dietert, 2001). For example, lead caused a persistent alteration in the immune response of male chickens, but adult female rats had more severe immunotoxicity than males with maternal exposure to 250 ppm lead throughout gestation. As for neurobehavioral and HPA axis function, timing during development, dose, and sex all contributed differentially to immune function changes that persisted into adulthood.

Conclusions and Future Directions

Among neurotoxicants, lead has received more research attention than any other poison. In response to increasing scientific information, public health standards for lead exposure have declined steadily in the developed world. Despite this progress, children from the developing world and those living in lower socio-economic neighborhoods in the United States continue to be exposed to lead, resulting in blood lead levels exceeding the CDC's accepted standard of 10 µg/dl blood lead. Furthermore, the current CDC action level of 10 µg/dl has more recently been challenged in light of growing evidence of behavioral and cognitive effects of blood lead exposures below the recommended standard. Moreover, none of the existing standards adequately protect the developing fetus with its unique susceptibility during critical stages of development. As is evident from the literature cited in this chapter, maternal blood levels reflected in maternal whole blood and cord blood values less than 10 µg/dl have consistently been associated with developmental delay. Whether these effects persist into adulthood remains controversial, but evidence from animal studies is accumulating to suggest that prenatal exposure may permanently alter biological mechanisms (e.g., HPA axis) and thus form the basis of later dysfunction and disease.

Despite all that is known about lead, this chapter is evidence of how little is known about whether sex modifies the effect of lead on developmental outcomes. Although some studies suggest that males may be more vulnerable to the effects of lead, this finding is by no means universal and seems to depend on the outcome measured and the stage of development when exposure occurred. Thus, males and females may have differential vulnerability, but we know little about the mechanisms that drive that differential vulnerability. For example, Gochfeld (2007) reviewed how toxicokinetics (e.g., absorption, distribution, metabolism) and toxicodynamics (dose to target organs) may differ between males and females and called for stratification to evaluate these potential differences. None of the studies reviewed intentionally designed their protocols to evaluate the effects of sex on the outcomes measured. Some investigators justified this decision based on data suggesting no difference in blood lead levels between boys and girls (e.g., Wigg et al., 1988), whereas others cited the same association between lead and the outcome of interest (e.g., blood pressure) for men and women as justification for hypothesizing no differences in the responses of boys and girls to lead (e.g., Gump et al., 2005). As pointed out by Bellinger (2000) and Gochfeld (2007), when studies are not designed to systematically evaluate how sex modifies the effects of exposure, then power to determine these effects is often inadequate. Moreover, this could result in over or underestimation of the effect of lead on the outcome of interest if sex has a differential effect and thus miss important information to identify vulnerability (Bellinger, 2000).

Because sex has been included in the data analysis rather than the study design of lead exposure's effect on child development, we may be missing important information about the differential susceptibility of males and females to lead exposure. Even if blood lead levels do not differ between boys and girls, this does not necessarily mean that they are not differentially susceptible to the effects of lead on either mental or social development. In fact, some intriguing differences in male and female responses to lead exposure suggest that later antisocial behavior may be more closely related to early lead exposure among boys rather than girls. Future studies could use the developmental exposure literature in animals to develop hypotheses about the interaction of sex and lead in children exposed in utero and during early development. Because lead levels have declined significantly, such interaction effects are difficult to detect without careful study design that includes adequate sample size to systematically evaluate effect modification by sex. Although environmental lead levels have declined, disadvantaged women of child-bearing age may continue to confer increased risk of lead exposure during pregnancy as a result of the mobilization of bone lead stores. The extent of this risk is not well characterized, but we need to understand its impact in order to prevent the ongoing legacy of lead exposure for vulnerable populations. Unfortunately, lead exposure continues at higher levels in the developing world, and future work that includes these populations will further our understanding of the mechanisms involved in lead's effect on cognitive and social development.

References

Achenbach, T. M. (1991). *Manual for the Child Behavior Checklist / 4-16 and 1991 Scoring Profile.* Burlington: University of Vermont Department of Psychiatry.

Annest, J. L., & Mahaffey, K. (1984). *Blood lead levels for persons ages 6 months - 74 years, United States, 1976-80, vol. 84* [DHHS Pub. No. (PHS) 84-1683]. Hyattsville, MD: National Center for Health Statistics.

Baghurst, P. A., Tong, S.-L., McMichael, A. J., Robertson, E. F., Wigg, N. R., Vimpani, G. V., . . . Tong, S.-L. (1992). Determinants of blood lead concentrations to age 5 years in a birth cohort study of children living in the lead smelting city of Port Pirie and surrounding areas. *Archives of Environmental Health, 47,* 203–210. doi:10.1080/00039896.1992.9938350

Basha, M. R., Wei, W., Bakheet, S. A., Benitez, N., Siddiqi, H. K., Ge, Y.- . . . Zawia, N. H. (2005). The fetal-basis of amyloidogenesis: Exposure to lead and latent over-expression of amyloid precursor protein and B-amyloid in the aging brain. *The Journal of Neuroscience, 25,* 823–829. doi:10.1523/JNEUROSCI.4335-04.2005

Bayley, N. (1969). *The Bayley Scales of Infant Development.* New York, NY: The Psychological Corporation.

Bellinger, D. C. (2000). Effect modification in epidemiologic studies of low-level neurotoxicant exposures and health outcomes. *Neurotoxicology and Teratology, 22,* 133–140. doi:10.1016/S0892-0362(99)00053-7

Bellinger, D. C., Leviton, A., & Sloman, J. (1990). Antecedents and correlates of improved cognitive performance in children exposed in utero to low levels of lead. *Environmental Health Perspectives, 89,* 5–11. doi:10.2307/3430890

Bellinger, D. C., Leviton, A., Waternaux, C., Needleman, H., & Rabinowitz, M. (1987). Longitudinal analyses of prenatal and postnatal lead exposure and early cognitive development. *The New England Journal of Medicine, 316,* 1037–1043. doi:10.1056/NEJM198704233161701

Bellinger, D. C., Needleman, H. L., Leviton, A., Waternaux, C., Rabinowitz, M. B., & Nichols, M. L. (1984). Early sensory-motor development and prenatal exposure to lead. *Neurobehavioral Toxicology & Teratology, 6,* 387–402.

Bellinger, D. C., Stiles, K. M., & Needleman, H. L. (1992). Low-level lead exposure, intelligence and academic achievement: A long-term follow-up study. *Pediatrics, 90,* 855–861.

Brody, D. J., Pirkle, J. L., Kramer, R. A., Flegal, K. M., Matte, T. E., Gunter, E. W., & Paschal, D. C. (1994). Blood lead levels in the US population. Phase I of the Third National Health and Nutrition Examination Study (NHANES III, 1988 to 1991). *JAMA, 272,* 277–283. doi:10.1001/jama.272.4.277

Bunn, T. L., Marsh, J. A., & Dietert, R. R. (2000). Gender differences in developmental immunotoxicity to lead in the chicken: Analysis following a single early low-level exposure in ovo. *Journal of Toxicology and Environmental Health, 61,* 677–693. doi:10.1080/00984100050195152

Bunn, T. L., Parsons, P. J., Kao, E., & Dietert, R. R. (2001). Gender-based profiles of developmental immunotoxicity to lead in the rat: Assessment in juveniles and adults. *Journal of Toxicology and Environmental Health, 64,* 223–240. doi:10.1080/15287390152543708

Carpenter, D. O., & Nevin, R. (2010). Environmental causes of violence. *Physiology & Behavior, 99,* 260–268. doi:10.1016/j.physbeh.2009.09.001

Cecil, K. M., Brubaker, C. J., Adler, C. M., Dietrich, K. N., Altaye, M., Eglehoff, J. C., . . . Lanphear, B. P. (2008). Decreased brain volume in adults with childhood lead exposure. *PLoS Medicine, 5*(5), e112. doi:10.1371/journal.pmed.0050112

Centers for Disease Control. (1991). *Preventing lead poisoning in young children.* Atlanta, GA: U.S. Department of Health and Human Services, Public Health Service.

Cooney, G. H., Bell, A., McBride, W., & Carter, C. (1989). Neurobehavioural consequences of prenatal low level exposures to lead. *Neurotoxicology and Teratology, 11,* 95–104. doi:10.1016/0892-0362(89)90047-0

Cory-Slechta, D. A., Virgolini, M. B., Thiruchelvam, M., Weston, D. D., & Bauter, M. R. (2004). Maternal stress modulates the effects of developmental lead exposure. *Environmental Health Perspectives, 112,* 717–730. doi:10.1289/ehp.6481

Dietrich, K. N., Krafft, K. M., Bier, M., Succop, P. A., Berger, O., & Bornschein, R. L. (1986). Early effects of fetal lead exposure: Neurobehavioral findings at 6 months. *International Journal of Biosocial Research, 8,* 151–168.

Dietrich, K. N., Krafft, K. M., Bornschein, R. L., Hammond, P. B., Berger, O., Succop, P. A., & Bier, M. (1987). Low-level fetal lead exposure effect on neurobehavioral development in early infancy. *Pediatrics, 80,* 721–730.

Dietrich, K. N., Ris, M. D., Succop, P. A., Berger, O. G., & Bornschein, R. L. (2001). Early exposure to lead and juvenile delinquency. *Neurotoxicology and Teratology, 23,* 511–518. doi:10.1016/S0892-0362(01)00184-2

Dietrich, K. N., Succop, P. A., Berger, O. G., Hammond, P. B., & Bornschein, R. L. (1991). Lead exposure and the cognitive development of urban preschool children: The Cincinnati lead study cohort at age 4 years. *Neurotoxicology and Teratology, 13,* 203–211. doi:10.1016/0892-0362(91)90012-L

Emory, E., Pattillo, R., Archibold, E., Bayorh, M., & Sung, F. (1999). Neurobehavioral effects of low-level lead exposure in human neonates. *American Journal of Obstetrics and Gynecology, 181*(1), S2–S11. doi:10.1016/S0002-9378(99)70465-5

Ernhart, C. B., Morrow-Tlucak, M., Marler, M. R., & Wolf, A. W. (1987). Low level lead exposure in the prenatal and early preschool periods: Early preschool development. *Neurotoxicology and Teratology, 9,* 259–270. doi:10.1016/0892-0362(87)90011-0

Gardella, C. (2001). Lead exposure in pregnancy: A review of the literature and argument for routine prenatal screening. *Obstetrical & Gynecological Survey, 56,* 231–238. doi:10.1097/00006254-200104000-00024

Gilbert, M. E., Mack, C. M., & Lasley, S. M. (1996). Chronic developmental lead (Pb^{2+}) exposure increases threshold for long-term potentiation in the rat dentate gyrus in vivo. *Brain Research, 736,* 118–124. doi:10.1016/0006-8993(96)00665-8

Gilbert, M. E., Mack, C. M., & Lasley, S. M. (1999). Developmental lead exposure reduces the magnitude of long-term potentiation: A dose-response analysis. *Neurotoxicology, 20,* 71–82.

Gilbert, S. G., & Weiss, B. (2006). A rationale for lowering the blood lead action level from 10 to 2 ug/dL. *Neurotoxicology, 27,* 693–701. doi:10.1016/j.neuro.2006.06.008

Gochfeld, M. (2007). Framework for gender differences in human and animal toxicology. *Environmental Research, 104,* 4–21. doi:10.1016/j.envres.2005.12.005

Gomaa, A., Hu, H., Bellinger, D., Schwartz, J., Tsaih, S.-W., Gonzalez-Cossio, T., . . . Hernandez-Avila, M. (2002). Maternal bone lead as an independent risk factor for fetal neurotoxicity: A prospective study. *Pediatrics, 110,* 110–118. doi:10.1542/peds.110.1.110

Gump, B. B., Reihman, J., Stewart, P., Lonky, E., Darvill, T., & Matthews, K. A. (2007). Blood lead (Pb) levels: A potential environmental mechanism explaining the relation between socio-economic status and cardiovascular reactivity in children. *Health Psychology, 26,* 296–304. doi:10.1037/0278-6133.26.3.296

Gump, B. B., Stewart, P., Reihman, J., Lonky, E., Darvill, T., Matthews, K. A., & Parsons, P. J. (2005). Prenatal and early childhood blood lead levels and cardiovascular functioning in 9 ½ year old children. *Neurotoxicology and Teratology, 27,* 655–665. doi:10.1016/j.ntt.2005.04.002

Gump, B. B., Stewart, P., Reihman, J., Lonky, E., Darvill, T., Parsons, P. J., & Granger, D. A. (2007). Low-level prenatal and postnatal blood lead exposure and adrenocortical responses to acute stress in children. *Environmental Health Perspectives, 116,* 249–255. doi:10.1289/ehp.10391

Hu, H., & Hernandez-Avila, M. (2002). Invited commentary: Lead, bones, women, and pregnancy—the poison within? *American Journal of Epidemiology, 156,* 1088–1091. doi:10.1093/aje/kwf164

Hu, H., Tellez-Rojo, M., Bellinger, D., Smith, D., Ettinger, A. S., Lamadrid-Figueroa, H., . . . Hernández-Avila, M. (2006). Fetal lead exposure at each stage of pregnancy as a predictor of infant mental development. *Environmental Health Perspectives, 114,* 1730–1735.

Kaufman, A. S., & Kaufman, N. L. (2004). *KABC-II: Kaufman Assessment Battery for Children* (2nd ed.). Minneapolis, MN: Pearson.

Lanphear, B. P., Dietrich, K., Auinger, P., & Cox, C. (2000). Cognitive deficits associated with blood lead concentrations <10 ug/dL. *Public Health Reports, 115,* 521–529. doi:10.1093/phr/115.6.521

Lasley, S. M., & Gilbert, M. E. (1996). Presynaptic glutamatergic function in a hippo-campal dentate gyrus is diminished by chronic exposure to inorganic lead. *Brain Research, 736,* 125–134. doi:10.1016/0006-8993(96)00666-X

Lasley, S. M., Green, M. C., & Gilbert, M. E. (1999). Influence of exposure period on in vivo hippocampal glutamate and GABA release in rats chronically exposed to lead. *Neurotoxicology, 20,* 619–629.

Leviton, A., Bellinger, D., Allred, E. N., Rabinowitz, M., Needleman, H., & Schoenbaum, S. (1993). Pre- and postnatal low-level lead exposure and children's dysfunction in school. *Environmental Research, 60,* 30–43. doi:10.1006/enrs.1993.1003

Lidsky, T. I., & Schneider, J. S. (2003). Lead neurotoxicity in children: Basic mechanisms and clinical correlates. *Brain: A Journal of Neurology, 126,* 5–19. doi:10.1093/brain/awg014

McCarthy, A. J., Baghurst, P. A., Robertson, E. F., Vimpani, G. V., & Wigg, N. R. (1985). Manual for the McCarthy Scales of Children's Abilities. *The Medical Journal of Australia, 143,* 499–503.

McMichael, A. J., Baghurst, P. A., Vimpani, G. V., Robertson, E. F., Wigg, N. R., & Tong, S. L. (1992). Sociodemographic factors modifying the effect of environmental lead on neuropsychological development in early childhood. *Neurotoxicology and Teratology, 14,* 321–327. doi:10.1016/0892-0362(92)90038-C

McMichael, A. J., Baghurst, P. A., Wigg, N. R., Vimpani, G. V., Robertson, E. F., & Roberts, R. J. (1988). Port Pirie Cohort study: Environmental exposure to lead and children's abilities at the age of four years. *The New England Journal of Medicine, 319,* 468–475. doi:10.1056/NEJM198808253190803

McMichael, A. J., Vimpani, G. V., Robertson, E. F., Baghurst, P. A., & Clark, P. D. (1986). The Port Pirie cohort study: Maternal blood lead and pregnancy outcome. *Journal of Epidemiology and Community Health, 40*(1), 18–25. doi:10.1136/jech.40.1.18

Mendola, P., Selevan, S. G., Gutter, S., & Rice, D. (2002). Environmental factors associated with a spectrum of neurodevelopmental deficits. *Mental Retardation and Disabilities Research Reviews, 8,* 188–197. doi:10.1002/mrdd.10033

Mendelsohn, A. L., Dreyer, B. P., Fierman, A. H., Rosen, C. M., Legano, L. A., Kruger, H. A., . . . Courtlandt, C. D. (1998). Low-level lead exposure and behavior in early childhood. *Pediatrics, 101,* e10. doi:10.1542/peds.101.3.e10

Needleman, H. L., Rabinowitz, M., Leviton, A., Linn, S., & Schoenbaum, E. (1984). The relationship between prenatal exposure to lead and congenital anomalies. *JAMA, 251,* 2956–2959. doi:10.1001/jama.251.22.2956

Needleman, H. L., Riess, J. A., Tobin, M. J., Biesecker, G. E., & Greenhouse, J. B. (1996). Bone lead levels and delinquent behavior. *JAMA, 275,* 363–369. doi:10.1001/jama.275.5.363

Nevin, R. (2007). Understanding international crime trends: The legacy of preschool lead exposure. *Environmental Research, 104,* 315–336. doi:10.1016/j.envres.2007.02.008

Pirkle, J. L., Kaufmann, R. B., Brody, D. J., Hickman, T., Gunter, E. W., & Paschal, D. C. (1994). The decline in blood lead levels in the United States. The National Health and Nutrition Examination Surveys (NHANES). *JAMA, 272,* 284–291. doi:10.1001/jama.272.4.284

Plusquellec, P., Muckle, G., Dewailly, E., Ayotte, P., Jacobson, S. W., & Jacobson, K. L. (2007). The relation of low-level prenatal lead exposure to behavioral indicators of attention in Inuit infants in Arctic Quebec. *Neurotoxicology and Teratology, 29,* 527–537. doi:10.1016/j.ntt.2007.07.002

Pocock, S. J., Smith, M., & Baghurst, P. (1994). Environmental lead and children's intelligence: A systematic review of the epidemiological evidence. *British Medical Journal, 309,* 1189–1197.

Rabinowitz, M., Wang, J. D., & Soong, W. T. (1993). Lead and classroom performance at seven primary schools in Taiwan. *Research in Human Capital and Development, 7,* 253–272.

Ris, M. D., Dietrich, K. N., Succop, P. A., Berger, O. G., & Bornschein, R. (2004). Early exposure to lead and neuropsychological outcome in adolescence. *Journal of the International Neuropsychological Society, 10,* 261–270. doi:10.1017/S1355617704102154

Rossouw, J., Offermeier, J., & Van Rooyen, J. M. (1987). Apparent central neurotransmitter receptor changes induced by low-level lead exposure during different developmental phases in the rat. *Toxicology and Applied Pharmacology, 91,* 132–139. doi:10.1016/0041-008X(87)90200-6

Rothenberg, S. J., Poblano, A., & Garza-Morales, S. (1994). Prenatal and perinatal low level lead exposure alters brainstem auditory evoked responses in infants. *Neurotoxicology, 15,* 695–699.

Rothenberg, S. J., Poblano, A., & Schnaas, L. (2000). Brainstem auditory evoked response at five years and prenatal and postnatal blood lead. *Neurotoxicology and Teratology, 22,* 503–510. doi:10.1016/S0892-0362(00)00079-9

Rothenberg, S. J., Schnaas, L., Salgado-Valladares, M., Casanueva, E., Geller, A. M., Hudnell, H. K., & Fox, D. A. (2002). Increased ERG a- and b-wave amplitudes in 7- to 10-year-old children resulting from prenatal lead exposure. *Investigative Ophthalmology & Visual Science, 43,* 2036–2044.

Schnaas, L., Rothenberg, R. J., Flores, M.-F., Martinez, S., Hernandez, C., Osorio, E., Velasco, S. R., & Perroni, E. (2006). Reduced intellectual development in children with prenatal lead exposure. *Environmental Health Perspectives, 114,* 791–797.

Shen, X.-M., Yan, C.-H., Guo, D., Wu, S.-M., Li, R.-Q., Huang, H., . . . Tang, J. M. (1998). Low-level prenatal lead exposure and neurobehavioral development of children in the first year of life: A prospective study in Shanghai. *Environmental Research, 79,* 1–8. doi:10.1006/enrs.1998.3851

Smith, D., Hernandez-Avila, M., Tellez-Rojo, M. M., Mercado, A., & Hu, H. (2002). The relationship between lead in plasma and whole blood in women. *Environmental Health Perspectives, 110,* 263–268. doi:10.1289/ehp.02110263

Smith, R., & Phillips, A. J. (1998). Osteoporosis during pregnancy and its management. *Scandinavian Journal of Rheumatology Supplement, 107,* 66–67.

Tang, H.-W., Huel, G., Campagna, D., Hellier, G., Boissinot, C., & Blot, P. (1999). Neurodevelopmental evaluation of 9-month-old infants exposed to low levels of lead in utero: Involvement of monoamine neurotransmitters. *Journal of Applied Toxicology, 19,* 167–172. doi:10.1002/(SICI)1099-1263(199905/06)19:3<167::AID-JAT560>3.0.CO;2-8

Téllez-Rojo, M. M., Hernandez-Avila, M., Lamadrid-Figueroa, H., Smith, D., Hernandez-Cadena, L., Mercado, A., Aro, A., Schwartz, J., & Hu, H. (2004). Impact of bone lead and bone resorption on plasma and whole blood lead levels during pregnancy. *American Journal of Epidemiology, 160,* 668–678. doi:10.1093/aje/kwh271

Tong, S., McMichael, A. J., & Baghurst, P. A. (2000). Interactions between environmental lead exposure and sociodemographic factors on cognitive development. *Archives of Environmental Health, 55,* 330–335. doi:10.1080/00039890009604025

U.S. Environmental Protection Agency. (2006). *Air quality criteria for lead* (Vol. I and II). Research Triangle Park, NC: National Center for Environmental Assessment. Retrieved from http://cfpub.epa.gov/ncea/cfm/recordisplay.cfm?deid=15882

Vahter, M., Akesson, A., Liden, C., Ceccatelli, S., & Berglund, M. (2007). Gender differences in the disposition and toxicity of metals. *Environmental Research, 104,* 85–95. doi:10.1016/j.envres.2006.08.003

Virgolini, M. B., Chen, K., Weston, D. D., Bauter, M. R., & Cory-Slechta, D. A. (2005). Interactions of chronic lead exposure and intermittent stress: Consequences for brain catecholamine systems and associated behaviors and HPA axis function. *Toxicological Sciences, 87,* 469–482. doi:10.1093/toxsci/kfi269

Wasserman, G., Graziano, J. H., Factor-Litvak, P., Popovac, D., Morina, N., Musabegovic, A., . . . Stein, Z. (1992). Independent effects of lead exposure and iron deficiency anemia on developmental outcome at age 2 years. *The Journal of Pediatrics, 121,* 695–703. doi:10.1016/S0022-3476(05)81895-5

Wasserman, G. A., Graziano, J. H., Factor-Litvak, P., Popovac, D., Morina, N., Musabegovic, A., . . . Stein, Z. (1994). Consequences of lead exposure and iron supplementation on childhood development at age 4 years. *Neurotoxicology and Teratology, 16,* 233–240. doi:10.1016/0892-0362(94)90044-2

Wasserman, G. A., Liu, X., Lolacono, N. J., Factor-Litvak, P., Kline, J. K., Popovac, D., . . . Graziano, J. H. (1997). Lead exposure and intelligence in 7-year-old children: The Yugoslavia prospective study. *Environmental Health Perspectives, 105,* 956–962. doi:10.1289/ehp.97105956

Wechsler, D. (1991). *Wechsler Intelligence Scale for Children* (3rd ed.). San Antonio, TX: The Psychological Corporation.

White, L. D., Cory-Slechta, D. A., Gilbert, M. E., Tiffany-Castiglioni, E., Zawia, N. H., Virgolini, M., . . . Basha, R. (2007). New and evolving concepts in the neurotoxicology of lead. *Toxicology and Applied Pharmacology, 225,* 1–27. doi:10.1016/j.taap.2007.08.001

Wigg, N. R., Vimpani, G. V., McMichael, A. J., Baghurst, P. A., Robertson, E. F., & Roberts, R. J. (1988). Port Pirie cohort study: Childhood blood lead and neuropsychological development at age two years. *Journal of Epidemiology and Community Health, 42,* 213–219. doi:10.1136/jech.42.3.213

10

The Sexually Dimorphic Nature of the Effects of Polychlorinated Biphenyls on the Central Nervous System in the Developing Animal

Elizabeth M. Sajdel-Sulkowska and Noriyuki Koibuchi

Perinatal exposure to polychlorinated biphenyls (PCBs) elicits sexually dimorphic effects in developing animals, with males being more vulnerable than females. This review focuses on the neurotoxic effects of PCBs in the developing animal brain, discusses sex differences in the developing brain structure and function, and provides examples of sexually dimorphic effects of PCBs on organ and endocrine systems, behavior, and neurotransmitters, leading to the discussion of possible molecular mechanisms underlying the sexually dimorphic nature of the response. Although the developmental neurotoxicity of PCBs could be mediated by alterations in thyroid hormone (TH), the sex-specific effects are more on par with the disruption of the estrogen signaling pathway by PCBs. However, it is becoming clear that although hormones are major players in the sexual dimorphic response to PCBs, they do not fully account for all aspects of this response because PCBs are not unique in that respect, and a number of other environmental toxins and pharmacological substances elicit different responses in males and in females. It is possible that genetic sex determines developmental gene expression and that PCBs activate several signaling pathways. It is tempting to suggest that PCB-induced oxidative stress, and specifically higher oxidative capacity in females than in males, contributes to the dimorphic nature of their effects. Understanding the molecular mechanism or mechanisms that cause these sex differences may help in understanding the mechanisms involved in the pathology of neurodevelopmental disorders, such as autism, dyslexia, or attention-deficit/hyperactivity disorder, that affect disproportionately more males than females.

This chapter discusses the evidence of the sexually dimorphic effects of PCBs in animals and is intended to complement Chapter 11 in this volume, which discusses PCB effects in humans. The sex-dependent effects of PCBs in animals

We thank Mrs. Patricia McCann for her input and excellent editorial work on this manuscript and the Autism Research Institute for its continuing support. The lead author dedicates this chapter to the memory of her son, Zachary L. Sulkowski, a budding neuroscientist.

are discussed from the viewpoint of a developmental neuroscientist. Perinatal exposure to PCBs appears to interact with genetics and impacts the course of central nervous system (CNS) development in both humans and animals. However, whereas many of the PCB effects are observed in both humans and animals, some aspects of the response to PCBs, such as the critical time of exposure, differ. The emphasis is placed on the sex-dependent effects of PCBs on the CNS in sexually immature laboratory animals, particularly rodents, but the evidence for sex differences in the effect of PCBs on organ and endocrine systems, behavior, and neurotransmitters is also reviewed. The review of different PCB effects leads to a discussion of the possible molecular mechanisms underlying that response. Although it is likely that the dimorphic response to PCBs is in part determined by their structure, alternative explanations must also be considered because the sex-dependent nature of the response is not unique to PCBs but extends to a number of environmental toxins. Understanding the underlying molecular mechanisms may unravel the causes behind a greater preponderance of environmentally linked neuropsychological disorders in males.

Effects of Perinatal PCB Exposure on Organ Systems and Behavior in Animals

This section focuses on the neurotoxic effects of PCBs in the developing animal, and specifically the developing CNS.

PCB Structure and Sex-Dependent Absorption and Accumulation

At the core of PCBs is a diphenyl ring structure; different PCBs display different number of chlorines bonded to different carbons. Chlorines in positions 2 or 6 are orthosubstituted, those in positions 3 or 6 are metasubstituted, and those in positions 4 are parasubstituted. The specific combination of chlorine substitutions transforms the structure PCB either into a coplanar or noncoplanar configuration. Thus, the PCB congeners are divided into two main classes, "dioxin-like" coplanar PCBs and non-coplanar PCBs. Figure 10.1 shows the classification of different PCB congeners discussed in this chapter.

Based on laboratory animal data, it appears that the effects of PCBs, in terms of both their toxicity and neurotoxicity, depend on a structure of particular PCB congeners. In general, coplanar, non-ortho or mono-orthosubstituted dioxinlike congeners are more toxic, and their effects are thought to be mediated via binding to aryl hydrocarbon receptor (AhR), a transcription factor. Non-coplanar, orthosubstituted, non-dioxinlike congeners are more active neurotoxins, which interfere with intracellular calcium-dependent signal transduction and TH and are able to modify cognitive processes. Aroclor 1254 contains a mixture of these two classes of congeners (Veith, Kuel, Puglisi, Glass, & Eaton, 1977); consequently, the effects of Aroclor may be more complex than those of pure congeners. Both classes of PCBs are absorbed and deposited initially in muscle fat before reaching the liver, lungs, and brain (Bachour, Failing, Georgii, Elmadfa, & Brunn, 1998). However, PCBs in humans accumulate in the mus-

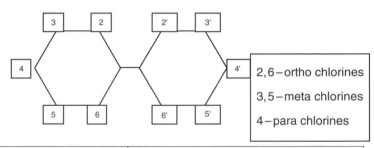

COPLANAR, DIOXINLIKE PCB CONGENERS	NONCOPLANAR ORTHOSUBSTITUTED PCB CONGENERS
no or one chlorine in positions 2 or 6	
two chlorines in positions 3 and 5	two or more chlorines in positions 2 and 6
at least one chlorine in position 4	
77 (3,3',4,4'-tetrachlorobiphenyl)	47 (2,2',4,4'-tetrachlorobiphenyl)
106 (2,3,3',4,5-Pentachlorobiphenyl)	95 (2,2',3,5',6-pentachlorobiphenyl)
107 (2,3,3',4',5-pentachlorobiphenyl)	101 (2,2',4,5,5'-pentachlorobiphenyl)
118 (2,3',4,4',5-pentachlorobiphenyl)	128 (2,2',3,3',4,4'-hexachlorobiphenyl)
126 (3,3',4,4',5-pentachlorobiphenyl)	153 (2,2',4,4',5,5v-hexachlorobiphenyl)
156 (2,3,3',4,4',5-hexachlorobiphenyl)	
169 (3,3',4,4',5,5'-hexachlorobiphenyl)	

Figure 10.1. Classification of different PCB congeners discussed in this chapter. Aroclor 1254 is a mixture of coplanar and noncoplanar PCBs.

cle tissue; PCBs in animals accumulate in the liver (Bachour et al., 1998). In rats, PCBs affect liver morphology; in the case of coplanar PCBs, the effect is more pronounced in females (Singh, Chu, & Villeneuve, 1996), whereas no sex differences were found with respect to non-coplanar PCBs (Gilroy, Singh, Chu, & Villeneuve, 1996; Peng, Singh, Ireland, & Chu, 1997; Singh, Connell, & Chu, 2000). Both coplanar and non-coplanar PCBs pass through the placenta and breast milk (Roth-Härer et al., 2001; Tilson, Jacobson, & Rogan, 1990). Although the brain appears to be relatively protected by the blood–brain barrier (Bachour et al., 1998), some congeners cross the blood–brain barrier and accumulate in the brain (Darnerud, Morse, Klasso-Wehler, & Brouwer, 1996; J. D. McKinney,

1989). For example, coplanar PCBs (PCB 169) do not accumulate appreciably in the brain but are retained at threefold higher level in the liver than non-coplanar PCBs; non-coplanar PCBs preferentially accumulate in brain tissue. Accumulation of non-coplanar PCB 153 in brains is four- to ninefold higher than that of PCB 169 and appears to be brain region–specific, with high accumulation in the cerebellum (Saghir, Hansen, Holmes, & Kodavanti, 2000). With respect to PCB absorption and accumulation, sex differences have not been explored.

Effects of PCBs on Growth

Perinatal exposure to PCBs results in a lower birth weight (Fein, Jacobson, Jacobson, Schwartz, & Dowler, 1984) and growth retardation in humans (Jacobson, Jacobson, & Humphrey, 1990a), monkeys (Allen, Barsotti, & Carstens, 1980), rats (Overmann, Kostas, Wilson, Shain, & Bush, 1987), and mice (Chou, Miike, Payne, & Davis, 1979); sex differences in the response to PCBs were not considered in these studies. Our own observations indicated that whereas the body mass of perinatally PCB-exposed male and female pups was not affected at birth, it was significantly lower in female pups on postnatal day (PND) 21 (Nguon, Baxter, & Sajdel-Sulkowska, 2005).

Effect of PCBs on Brain Structure

Histological, neuroimaging, and behavioral evidence indicates that there is sexual dimorphism in CNS structure and function in both humans and animals. One such affected structure is the cerebellum, the focus of our discussion.

The cerebellum develops relatively late during the last trimester in humans and during the early postnatal period in rats. Cell proliferation and migration patterns and progression of regional development are parallel, although the time scale is in days for rodents and weeks to months in humans. For example, exposure to environmental insult during week 4 of gestation in humans or on gestational day (GD) 11 in rats is expected to interfere with neurogenesis in hindbrain structure; the same insult at the end of gestation in humans and in the first postnatal week in rats might affect neurogenesis in the cerebellum and hippocampus. The rat cerebellum is an especially appropriate model to study the effect of maternal PCB exposure on both brain structure and functions because it demonstrates many of the same developmental processes observed in other brain regions and its protracted developmental stages are similar to those of the human cerebellum (Porterfield & Hendrich, 1993). In the rat cerebellum, these developmental stages continue after birth, making that period one of enhanced vulnerability to environmental impacts. Based on the timeline of the developmental landmarks, cerebellar development from midpregnancy to birth corresponds to the second trimester of human CNS development. Changes in the cerebellum from birth to PND 10 can be related to changes in the human CNS during the last trimester of pregnancy. Furthermore, accumulating behavioral evidence indicates that the human cerebellum is involved in learning, motor planning, cognitive flexibility, sensory processing, exploratory activity (Pierce & Courchesne, 2001), and other higher cognitive processes (Schmahmann, 1991).

More directly, studies of genetically and nongenetically lesioned rats suggest that the cerebellum plays a role in spatial learning (Lalonde & Strazielle, 2003).

Human data suggest that prenatal PCB exposure results in a decreased head circumference (Fein et al., 1984); the sex differences were not noted in this study. In the general population, cerebellar volume appears to be larger in males (Raz, Gunning-Dixon, Head, Williamson, & Acker, 2001; Rhyu et al., 1999), but females have a higher rate of cerebellar metabolism (Volkow et al., 1997). Animal studies show greater dendritic segmentation in the female rat cerebellum (Juraska, 1990).

Our own studies showed that PCB exposure of rats during the perinatal period results in decreased cerebellar weight that is more pronounced in males than in females (Nguon, Baxter, & Sajdel-Sulkowska, 2005). Neither human (Mayhew, MacLaren, & Henery, 1990) nor animal studies (Mwamengele, Mayhew, & Dantzer, 1993) suggest sex-related differences in the number of Purkinje cell number, although a lower number of Purkinje cells was observed in heterozygous male than in female Reeler mice (Hadj-Sahraoui, Frederic, Delhaye-Bouchaud, & Mariani, 1996). PCB exposure has been shown to increase Purkinje cell height only in rat male offspring gestationally exposed to PCBs (Roegge et al., 2006).

We have also observed a sex-dependent increase in cerebellar glial fibrillary acidic protein (GFAP) expression suggesting increased gliosis (Nguon, Baxter, & Sajdel-Sulkowska, 2005), but decreased synaptophysin expression in male offspring. These changes in protein expression appear to be brain region–specific: GFAP was increased in the cerebellum and olfactory tract but decreased in the brain stem (Morse, Seegal, Borsch, & Brouwer, 1996).

Sex-Dependent Effect of PCBs on Behavior

In humans, prenatal PCB exposure affects cognitive functioning, such as memory (Jacobson, Jacobson, & Humphrey, 1990b) and attention (Jacobson & Jacobson, 2003), and results in lower IQ scores (Jacobson & Jacobson, 1996). In nonhuman primates, postnatal exposure to Aroclor mixtures results in long-lasting learning deficits (Faroon, Jones, & Rosa, 2000).

Several behavioral abnormalities in perinatally PCB-exposed rats or mice parallel those found in humans, for example, impaired spatial learning (Gilbert, Mundy, & Crofton, 2000) and spatial working and reference learning memory (Roegge, Seo, Crofton, & Schantz, 2000), with males being more affected than females but with females being more affected by gestational exposure (Schantz, Moshtaghian, & Ness, 1995). PCB exposure results in impaired spatial discrimination–reversal learning (Widholm, Villareal, Seegal, & Schantz, 2004), with male rats showing different patterns of mistakes than female offspring (Widholm et al., 2001), impaired active avoidance learning (Lilienthal & Winneke, 1991), altered performance on the T-maze (Schantz, Seo, Moshtaghian, Peterson, & Moore, 1996) and Morris maze (Zahalka, Ellis, Goldey, Stanton, & Lau, 2001), and impaired habituation in male offspring on open-field tests (Meerts et al., 2004). Behavioral abnormalities also included altered social interaction (Fanini, Palumbo, Giorgi, & Panteleoni, 1990), diminished exploration

(Fanini et al., 1990), hyperactivity (Berger et al., 2001; Carpenter, Hussain, Berger, Lombardo, & Park, 2002; Holene, Nafstad, Skaare, & Sagvolden 1998), and auditory impairment (Goldey, Kehn, & Crofton, 1993; Goldey, Kehn, Lau, Rehnberg, & Crofton, 1995; Overmann et al., 1987; Powers, Widholm, Lasky, & Schantz, 2006), with postnatal exposure associated with more pronounced effects (Crofton, Ding, Padich, Taylor, & Henderson, 2000).

In PCB-exposed rats, behavioral abnormalities frequently reflect impairment of cerebellar structure and function and include altered motor development as suggested by increased righting time (Bowers et al., 2004; Overmann et al., 1987) and impaired motor behavior measured by rotarod performance, with males more affected than females (McFadyen, Kusek, Bolivar, & Flaherty, 2003). Our own studies of the effects of PCB exposure during the gestation through lactation period showed an impaired rotarod performance between PND 12 and PND 21, with PCB-exposed male pups being more affected than female pups (Nguon, Baxter, & Sajdel-Sulkowska, 2005). PND 12 male pups also show greater improvement on repeated rotarod trials relative to female pups, a difference that is eliminated by PCB treatment. Furthermore, PND 21 male pups perform better in afternoon testing than morning testing, whereas no such difference was observed in female rats. PCBs also contribute to motor stereotypy (Chou et al., 1979) suggesting abnormalities in nigro-striatum system. Thus, it is of interest that the gestational exposure to PCB 106 has been shown to affect striatal gene expression (Takahashi et al., 2009).

PCBs as Hormonal Disruptors

PCBs are classified as endocrine disruptors (Nguon, Baxter, & Sajdel-Sulkowska, 2005; Nguon, Ladd, Baxter, & Sajdel-Sulkowska, 2005; Sajdel-Sulkowska & Koibuchi, 2002) interfering specifically with the TH and estrogen status.

PCBs may act directly on the hypothalamic–pituitary–thyroid (HPT) axis and result in lower plasma TH levels (see the discussion below) or interfere with peripheral metabolism of TH (Gaitan, 1998). Severe deficiencies in TH, which is crucial for brain development, lead to cytoarchitectual abnormalities and mental retardation known as cretinism (Barres, Lazar, & Raff, 1994; Nicholson & Altman, 1972a, 1972b), whereas milder hypothyroidism results in attention deficits (Alvarez et al., 1999). It has been proposed that hypothyroidism induced by PCB exposure contributes to growth deficits, motor dysfunction, and hearing disorders, because similar defects are observed in developing hypothyroid animals (Goldey, Kehn, Lau, Rehnberg, & Crofton, 1995; Goldey, Kehn, Rehnberg, & Crofton, 1995) and can be attenuated with thyroxine (Goldey & Crofton, 1998).

Depending on the structure, and specifically the position and number of chlorine substitutions, different PCBs elicit pleiotropic biologic responses involving the estrogenic signaling pathway (Garritano et al., 2006; Safe, 1994) that includes the metabolism of estradiol or the induction of estrogen-regulated enzymes (Bonefeld-Jørgensen, Andersen, Rasmussen, & Vinggard, 2001). Brain estrogen levels are derived from testosterone by aromatase, and maternal exposure to PCBs results in decreased aromatase activity in newborn male rats (Hany et al., 1999; Kaya et al., 2002). PCB-exposed female weanlings exhibit elevated uterine wet weight suggesting increased estrogenic activity (Hany et al., 1999).

Exposure to Aroclor 1254 during pregnancy results in decreased blood estrogen and testosterone levels in adult offspring and the elevation of sweet preference in male offspring, indicating feminization of this sexually dimorphic behavior (Kaya et al., 2002). The estrogenic activity of PCBs may play a critical role in the sexually dimorphic nature of the response.

Sex-Dependent Disruption of the HPT Axis by PCBs

The HPT axis consists of the hypothalamus producing thyrotropin-releasing hormone (TRH), the pituitary that releases thyrotropin (TSH) in response to TRH, and the thyroid gland that in response to TSH releases thyroxine (T4) and a small amount the active form of TH, triiodothyronine (T3). Most of the active T3 is produced in the peripheral organs by specific deiodinases and then released to the circulation. PCBs disrupt the HPT axis in animals (Khan & Hansen, 2003) and in humans (Osius, Karmaus, Krause, & Witten, 1999) at several critical points. There is evidence that maternal exposure to a pharmacological dose of PCB 77 alters T4 secretion and results in decreased fetal and neonatal plasma T4 levels (Roth-Härer et al., 2001). Similarly, exposure to Aroclor 1254 in rats results in decreased neonatal plasma T4 levels (Crofton et al., 2000; Goldey, Kehn, Lau, et al., 1995; Goldey, Kehn, Rehnberg, & Crofton, 1995; Morse et al., 1996) and brain T4 levels (Morse et al., 1996). Generally, exposure to PCBs during lactation appears to have a more dramatic effect than exposure during gestation (Crofton et al., 2000). PCB may also interfere with TH transport. It has been proposed that PCBs, which are similar in structure to TH, can bind to the TH serum binding protein, transhyretin (Chauhan, Kodavanti, & McKinney, 2000; Hallgren & Darnerud, 2002). In humans, exposure to PCB 118 has been shown to increase TSH levels (Osius et al., 1999). The prenatal administration of Aroclor results in a differential accumulation of PCBs and increased AhR expression only in the male hypothalamus (Pravettoni, Colciago, Negro-Cesi, Villa, & Celotti, 2005), suggesting greater sensitivity of the male hypothalamus to the disruptive effects of PCBs.

Sex-Dependent Effect on Brain Neurotransmitters

PCB exposure affects several neurotransmitter systems including the dopaminergic, cholinergic, and serotonergic systems.

Perinatal exposure to the coplanar PCB 77 results in a significant elevation of dopamine concentration in the frontal cortex and substantia nigra, but the exposure to orthosubstituted non-coplanar PCB 47 exposure causes a decrease in dopamine levels (Seegal, Brosch, & Okoniewski, 1997). Furthermore, developmental exposure to coplanar PCB 107 results in a significant decrease in 3,4-dihydroxyphenylacetic acid, a major dopamine metabolite, levels in nucleus accumbens only in males (Meerts et al., 2004).

Perinatal exposure to Aroclor 1254 affects the cholinergic system with a significant elevation in activity of choline acetyltransferase (an index of cholinergic functions regulated by steroid hormones) in the basal forebrain (Provost, Juarez de Ku, Zender, & Meserve, 1999). On the other hand, a mixture of orthosubstituted and nonsubstituted PCB congeners results in a depression of choline acetyltransferase activity in the hippocampus (Donahue, Dougherty, & Meserve, 2004).

Changes in serotonin (5-HT) levels (Roth-Härer et al., 2001) and brain region–specific long-term alterations in serotonin metabolism (Morse et al., 1996) following perinatal PCB exposure have also been observed with embryonic exposure, resulting in a decrease in serotonergic cell growth (Kreiling, Stephens, Kuzirian, Jessen-Eller, & Reinisch, 2000). Because 5-HT plays a trophic role during development (Whitaker-Azmitia, 2001) facilitating neurite extension, dendrite stabilization, and the formation and maintenance of synapses (N. Okado, Narita, & Narita, 2001), a deficit in serotonin during critical periods of development results in retardation of Bergman glial cell maturation, granule cell migration, and dendritic arborization of Purkinje cells (Del Angel-Meza, Ramirez-Cortes, Olvera-Cortes, Perez-Vega, & Gonzalez-Burgos, 2001), decreased synaptic density, and a deficit in spatial learning (Mazer et al., 1997). In rats, hypothalamic 5-HT concentrations are transiently sexually differentiated in the second week postpartum, with higher levels in the female. Furthermore, the presynaptic 5-HT turnover shows a sexually dimorphic pattern (Ferrari et al., 1999). It is of interest that the level of 5-hydroxyindole-3-acetic acid (5-HIAA), a major serotonin metabolite, was significantly increased in frontal cortex of PCB 107-treated male offspring (Meerts et al., 2004). It is possible that the PCB altering 5-HT levels may work within the context of this dimorphic developmental regulation of the serotonergic system. Both nondioxin (PCB 153)- and dioxin (PCB 126)-like congeners decrease the number of muscarinic receptors in the developing cerebellum, with the effect being greater in males (Coccini et al., 2007).

Evidence for the dimorphic effect of PCBs on organ and endocrine systems is summarized in Figure 10.2.

Possible Molecular Mechanisms Involved in Sex-Dependent Effects of PCBs

This section discusses the possible molecular mechanisms underlying the sexually dimorphic effects of developmental PCB exposure.

Sex-Dependent Effects of PCBs on Oxidative Stress: Apoptosis and Neurotrophins

PCBs are environmental toxins that induce oxidative stress. PCBs have been shown to generate reactive oxygen species in rat synaptosomes (Voie & Fonnum, 2000), cerebellar granule cells (Mariussen, Myhre, Reistad, & Fonnum, 2002), and dopamine cell cultures (D. W. Lee & Opanashuk, 2004). Thus, it is of interest that the steps of the oxidative stress cascade appear to be sex dependent, with female rats showing a higher oxidative capacity than males (Valle, Guevara, Garcia-Palmer, Roca, & Oliver, 2007). Environmentally triggered oxidative stress results in increased protein carboxylation and a reduced ratio of reduced/oxidized forms of glutathione in the hippocampus of the newborn male but not female rat pups (Lanté et al., 2007).

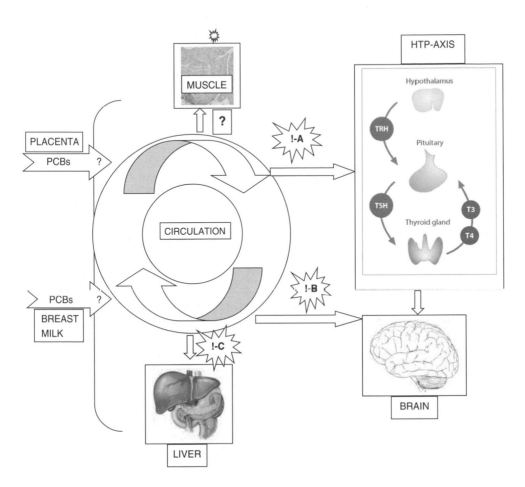

Figure 10.2.   Possible sites of sexually dimorphic effects of PCBs on organ and endocrine systems based on animal studies. The sunburst indicates the sites with documented dimorphic effect in males and in females; the question mark indicates lack of direct evidence for that effect. HPT = hypothalamic–pituitary–thyroid; TRH = thyrotropin-releasing hormone; TSH = thyrotropin; T3 = triiodothyronine; T4 = thyroxine; PCB = polychlorinated biphenyls. !-A: Pravettoni et al. (2005); !-B: Hany et al. (1999); Kaya et al. (2002); Nguon et al. (2005); !-C: Singh et al. (1996).

PCB-induced oxidative stress may contribute to the cell apoptosis observed in dopamine neurons (D. W. Lee & Opanashuk, 2004), SK-N-MC cells (J. Y. Lee et al., 2004), and AtT20 pituitary cells in culture (Johansson et al., 2006). It has been suggested that oxidative stress contributes to cell apoptosis (Numakawa et al., 2007) by increasing cellular Ca^{2+} (Oyama, Okazaki, Chikahisa, Nagano, & Sdakata, 1996).

We recently demonstrated that oxidative stress affects brain neurotrophin expression (Sajdel-Sulkowska, Xu, & Koibuchi, 2009). Brain neurotrophins exhibit a sexually dimorphic profile of expression (Gilmore, Jarskog, & Vadlamudi, 2003). Whereas the in vivo effect of PCBs on neurotrophin expression has not been studied, the in vitro exposure of glial cells to Aroclor 1254 increases nerve growth factor secretion, suggesting a disruption of neutrophin signaling (Gurley, Jelaso, Ide, & Spitsergen, 2007). This effect appears to involve the protein kinase C (PKC) pathway.

Intracellular Ca^{2+} Dependent PKC Pathway: Sexually Dimorphic PKC Isoforms

Exposure to PCBs affects the PKC signaling pathway (Kodavanti, Ward, McKinney, & Tilson, 1995; Kodavanti et al., 1998; Sharma, Derr-Yellin, House, & Kodavanti, 2000) essential for normal brain development and is further implicated in the modulation of motor behavior, learning, and memory. It appears that PCBs disrupt cellular calcium homeostasis (Kodavanti, Shin, Tilson, & Harry, 1993) by stimulating rapid elevation in intracellular calcium (Ca^{2+}; J. Okada, Shimokawa, & Koibuchi, 2005). In unrelated studies of the role of calcium in vascular functions, males were more sensitive to intracellular Ca^{2+} influx, whereas females were more sensitive to the actual intracellular Ca^{2+} levels (Eatman, Stallone, Rutecki, & Whittier, 1998). It is thus possible that the PCB-induced effect on Ca^{2+} trafficking may exert different effects in males and in females. PCBs contribute to PKC translocation, and the action appears to be limited to ortho-substituted non-coplanar congeners (Yang, Derr-Yellin, & Kodavanti, 2003; Yang & Kodavanti, 2001). It has been suggested that this action of PCBs may be relevant to altered expression of Ca^{2+} regulated genes, such as c-Jun, following PCB exposure (Shimokawa, Miyazaki, Iwasaki, & Koibuchi, 2006). PCBs affect the activity of individual developmentally regulated PKC isoforms (Yang et al., 2003) that are specifically involved in motor behavior, learning, and memory. PCBs also alter brain region–specific binding of Ca^{2+} to its ryanodine receptors (Schantz, Seo, Wong, & Pessah, 1997).

PCB Binding to Hormone Receptors: Sexually Dimorphic Regulation of Transcription

The sexually dimorphic effect of PCBs is associated with binding to specific receptors and disruption of transcription. The coplanar, dioxinlike PCB congeners bind to and activate AhRs and disrupt transcription (Safe et al., 1985). Exposure to Aroclor results in a significant increase in DNA binding of several transcription factors (Basha, Raddy, Zawia, & Kodavanti, 2006).

It has been proposed that non-coplanar PCBs that are similar in structure to TH can bind to TH receptors (TRs; J. McKinney et al., 1987; Porterfield, 2000) and interfere with the biological action of the hormone at the transcriptional level (Iwasaki, Miyazaki, Takeshita, Kuroda, & Koibuchi, 2002; Miyazaki, Iwasaki, Takeshita, Kuroda, & Koibuchi, 2004). Because TRs are intimately associated with estrogen receptors (ERs), a key to understanding the sex-dependent actions of these compounds may involve the TR–ER interaction. Indeed, the effect of PCBs on TR-mediated transcription can be correlated with the dissociation of TR from the TRH complexes (Miyazaki, Iwasaki, Takeshita, Tohyama, & Koibuchi, 2008). PCBs also bind to ERs, exert an antiestrogenic effect (Connor et al., 1997), and inhibit ERs in neuronal cells (Salama, Chakraborty, Ng, & Gore,

2003). In addition, PCBs decrease the expression of androgen receptors (AR) in the female hypothalamus (Colciago et al., 2006) and interfere with transcriptional activation of the AR by a direct binding to AR ligand-binding domain (Portigal et al., 2002).

In male pups, testosterone is converted to estrogen by the developmentally regulated aromatase, which may play an important role in sexual brain differentiation (Kanagawa, 1982). Aromatase activity has been detected in GD 14 rats, decreasing slightly until birth and increasing drastically during the postnatal period (Kanagawa 1982), overlapping with a critical brain development period. Because maternal exposure to PCBs results in decreased aromatase activity in the brain of newborn male rats (Hany et al., 1999; Kaya et al., 2002), the resulting deficit in brain estrogen levels during critical periods of brain development may in part explain the sexual dimorphism of developmental effects of some PCB congeners.

Sexually Dimorphic Gene Expression and the Effect of PCBs in Males and Females

It is tempting to suggest that the sexually dimorphic effect of PCBs on the developing brain is in part determined by the PCBs interfering with differentiation events that are themselves regulated by sex hormones. Thus, a reduction in brain aromatase following PCB exposure in the male brain (Hany et al., 1999) may result in a relative deficiency of estradiol and consequently affect the expression of genes and those processes dependent on estradiol. On the other hand, in PCB-exposed females showing increased estrogen levels, the same pathways may be differentially affected contributing to the dimorphic effect of PCB exposure.

Furthermore, during the neonatal period Purkinje cells use cholesterol to synthesize progesterone (Sakamoto, Mezaki, Shikimi, Ukena, & Tsutsui, 2003). Progesterone receptors in the brain are differentially expressed (Quadros, Lopez, De Vries, Chung, & Wagner, 2002) and regulated (Guerra-Araiza, Coyoy-Salgado, & Camacho-Arroyo, 2002) by estradiol in male and female neonates. Purkinje cells also express aromatase, the key enzyme for the formation of estradiol from testosterone (Sakamoto et al., 2003) that is down-regulated by PCBs (Hany et al., 1999; Kaya et al., 2002). Thus, PCB inhibition of etradiol formation affects the sex-specific expression of estrogen-regulated progesterone receptors in the developing rat cerebellum (Quadros et al., 2002) and could further contribute to the sexual dimorphic effect of PCBs in the developing brain.

Another important issue is the neuroprotective role of brain estrogen (Lang & McCullough, 2008; Numakawa et al., 2007). Thus, in the developing male brain the relative deficit of estrogen brought about by PCBs could exacerbate their neurotoxicity.

Although it is likely that the dimorphic response to PCBs is in great part related to their endocrine-disruptive properties, alternative explanations must also be considered because the sex-dependent nature of the responses is not unique to PCBs. Sex-dependent responses to a number of environmental and pharmacological manipulations, such as chlorpyrifos, organophosphate pesticides (Dam, Seidler, & Slotkin, 2000), methylazoxymethanol acetate (Ferguson,

Paule, & Holson, 1996), glucocorticoids (Vicedomini, Nonneman, DeKosky, & Scheff, 1986), naltrexone (De Cabo de la Vega & Paz Viveros, 1997), ethanol (Rintala et al., 2001), and daily handling (Rhees, Lephart, & Eliason, 2001), have been observed. Rats exposed prenatally to cocaine show impaired motor coordination, with males being more affected than females (Markowski, Cox, & Weiss, 1998). It is tempting to suggest that oxidative stress induced by these environmental perturbations, including exposure to PCBs, plays a key role in their effects and that a higher oxidative capacity in females than in males (Valle et al., 2007) contributes to the dimorphic nature of their effects.

Possible molecular mechanisms involved in the sexually dimorphic effects of PCBs are summarized in Figure 10.3.

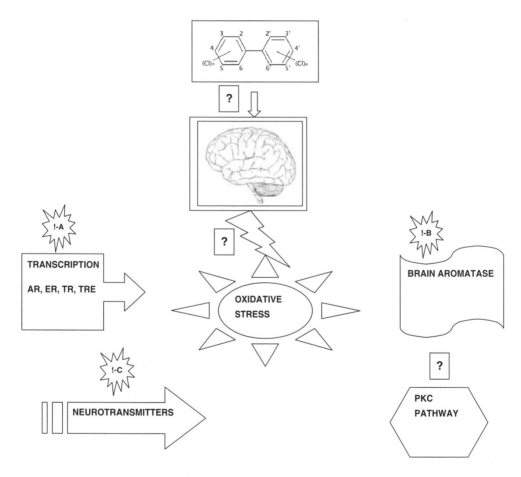

Figure 10.3. Possible molecular mechanisms involved in sex-dependent effects of PCBs in the developing animal brain. The sunburst indicates the processes with documented dimorphic effect in males and in females; the question mark indicates lack of direct evidence for that effect. AR = androgen receptors; ER = estrogen receptors; TR = thyroid hormone receptors; TRE = thyroid hormone response element; PKC = protein kinase C. !-A: Colciago et al. (2006); !-B: Hany et al. (1999); Kaya et al. (2002); !-C: Meerts et al. (2004); Coccini et al. (2007).

Summary

Although the sex-dependent effects of PCBs have been observed in animals, they have not been explored in depth by comparing the response between males and females. The mechanism underlying the sexually dimorphic nature of PCB effects remains obscure. Although developmental neurotoxicity of PCBs could be mediated by alterations in the thyroid signaling pathway, the sex-specific effect is more on par with the disruption of the estrogen signaling pathway by PCBs. However, it is becoming clear that although hormones are major players in the sexual dimorphic responses to PCBs, they do not fully account for all aspects of this response. It is possible that genetic sex determines developmental gene expression and that several signaling pathways are activated by PCBs. It is tempting to suggest that PCB-induced oxidative stress, and specifically higher oxidative capacity in females than in males, contributes to the dimorphic nature of their effects. Understanding the molecular mechanism or mechanisms that cause these sex differences may help in understanding the mechanisms involved in the pathology of neurodevelopmental disorders, such as autism, dyslexia, or attention-deficit/hyperactivity disorder, that affect disproportionately more males than females.

References

Allen, J. R., Barsotti, D. A., & Carstens, L. A. (1980). Residual effects of polychlorinated biphenyls on adult nonhuman primates and their offspring. *Journal of Toxicology and Environmental Health, 6,* 55–66. doi:10.1080/15287398009529830

Alvarez, M., Guell, R., Daniel, L., Berazain, A. R., Machdo, C., & Pascual, A. (1999). Neuro-cognitive condition of 8-year-old children with congenital hypothyroidism treated early. *Revista de Neurologia, 28,* 701–706.

Bachour, G., Failing, K., Georgii, S., Elmadfa, I., & Brunn, H. (1998). Species and organ specific dependence of PCB contamination in fish, foxes, roe deer and humans. *Archives of Environmental Contamination and Toxicology, 35,* 666–673. doi:10.1007/s002449900429

Barres, B. A., Lazar, M. A., & Raff, M. C. (1994). A novel role for thyroid hormone, glucocorticoids and retinoic acid in timing oligodendrocyte development. *Development, 120,* 1097–1108.

Basha, M. R., Raddy, N. S., Zawia, N. H., & Kodavanti, P. R. (2006). Ontogenic alterations in prototypical transcription factors in the rat cerebellum and hippocampus following perinatal exposure to a commercial PC mixture. *Neurotoxicology, 27,* 118–124. doi:10.1016/j.neuro.2005.07.006

Berger, D. F., Lombardo, J. P., Jeffers, P. M., Hunt, A. E., Bush, B., Casey, A., & Quimby, F. (2001). Hyperactivity and impulsiveness in rats fed diets supplemented with either Aroclor 1248 or PCB-contaminated St. Lawrence river fish. *Behavioural Brain Research, 126,* 1–11. doi:10.1016/S0166-4328(01)00244-3

Bonefeld-Jørgensen, E. C., Andersen, H. R., Rasmussen, T. H., & Vinggard, A. M. (2001). Effect of highly bioaccumulated polychlorinated biphenyl congeners on estrogen and androgen receptor activity. *Toxicology, 158,* 141–153. doi:10.1016/S0300-483X(00)00368-1

Bowers, W. J., Nakai, J., Chu, I., Wade, M. G., Moir, D., Yagminas, A., . . . Meuller, R. (2004). Early developmental neurotoxicity of a PCB/organochlorine mixture in rodents after gestational and lactational exposure. *Toxicological Sciences, 77,* 51–62. doi:10.1093/toxsci/kfg248

Carpenter, D. O., Hussain, R. J., Berger, D. F., Lombardo, J. P., & Park, H. Y. (2002). Electrophysiologic and behavioral effects of perinatal and acute exposure of rats to lead and polychlorinated diphenyls. *Environmental Health Perspectives, 3,* 377–386.

Chauhan, K. R., Kodavanti, P. R., & McKinney, J. D. (2000). Assessing the role of ortho-substitution on polychlorinated biphenyl binding to transthyretin, a thyroxine transport protein. *Toxicology and Applied Pharmacology, 162,* 10–21. doi:10.1006/taap.1999.8826

Chou, S. M., Miike, T., Payne, W. M., & Davis, G. J. (1979). Neuropathology of "spinning syndrome" induced by prenatal intoxication with PCB in mice. *Annals of the New York Academy of Sciences, 320,* 373–395.

Coccini, T., Roda, E., Castoldi, A. F., Goldoni, M., Poli, D., Bernocchi, G., & Manzo, L. (2007). Perinatal co-exposure to methylmercury and PCB126 or PCB126 in rats alters the cerebral cholinergic Muscarinic receptors at weaning and puberty. *Toxicology, 238,* 34–48. doi:10.1016/j.tox.2007.05.018

Colciago, A., Negri-Cesi, P., Pravettoni, A., Mornati, O., Casati, L., & Celotti, F. (2006). Prenatal Aroclor 1254 exposure and brain sexual differentiation: Effect on the expression of testosterone metabolizing enzymes and androgen receptors in the hypothalamus of male and female rats. *Reproductive Toxicology, 22,* 738–745. doi:10.1016/j.reprotox.2006.07.002

Connor, K., Raamoorthy, K., Moore, M., Mustain, M., Chen, I., Safe, S., . . . Balaguer, P. (1997). Hydroxylated polychlorinated biphenyls (PCBs) as estrogens and antiestrogens: Structure–activity relationships. *Toxicology and Applied Pharmacology, 145,* 111–123. doi:10.1006/taap.1997.8169

Crofton, K. M., Ding, D., Padich, R., Taylor, M., & Henderson, D. (2000). Hearing loss following exposure during development to polychlorinated biphenyls: A cochlear site of action. *Hearing Research, 144,* 196–204.

Crofton, K. M., Kodavanti, P. R., Derr-Yellin, E. C., Casey, A. C., & Kehn, L. S. (2000). PCBs, thyroid hormone, and ototoxicity in rats: Cross-fostering experiments demonstrate the impact of postnatal lactation exposure. *Toxicological Sciences, 57,* 131–140. doi:10.1093/toxsci/57.1.131

Dam, K., Seidler, F. J., & Slotkin, T. A. (2000). Chlorpyrifos exposure during a critical neonatal period elicits gender-selective deficits in the development of coordination skill and locomotor activity. *Developmental Brain Research, 121,* 179–187. doi:10.1016/S0165-3806(00)00044-4

Darnerud, P. O., Morse, D., Klasso-Wehler, E., & Brouwer, A. (1996). Binding of a 3,3',4,4'-tetra-chlorobiphenyl (CB 77) metabolite to fetal transhyretin and effects on fetal thyroid hormone levels in mice. *Toxicology, 106,* 105–114. doi:10.1016/0300-483X(95)03169-G

De Cabo de la Vega, C., & Paz Viveros, M. (1997). Effects of neonatal naltrexone on neurological and somatic development in rats of both genders. *Neurotoxicology and Teratology, 19,* 499–509. doi:10.1016/S0892-0362(97)00043-3

Del Angel-Meza, A. R., Ramirez-Cortes, L., Olvera-Cortes, E., Perez-Vega, M. I., & Gonzales-Burgos, I. (2001). A tryptophan deficient corn-based diet induces plastic responses in cerebellar cortex of rat offspring. *International Journal of Developmental Neuroscience, 19,* 447–453. doi:10.1016/S0736-5748(01)00004-1

Donahue, D. A., Dougherty, E. J., & Meserve, L. A. (2004). Influence of the combination of tetra-chloroiphenyl congeners (PCB47; PCB 77) on thyroid status, choline acetyltransferase (ChAT) activity, short- and long-term memory in 30-day-old Sprague-Dawley rats. *Toxicology, 203,* 99–107. doi:10.1016/j.tox.2004.06.011

Eatman, D., Stallone, J. N., Rutecki, G. W., & Whittier, F. C. (1998). Sex differences in extracellular and intracellular calcium-mediated vascular reactivity to vasopressin in rat aorta. *European Journal of Pharmacology, 361,* 207–216. doi:10.1016/S0014-2999(98)00700-6

Fanini, D., Palumbo, G., Giorgi, R., & Panteleoni, G. (1990). Behavioral effects of PCBs in mice. *Behavioural Pharmacology, 1,* 505–510. doi:10.1097/00008877-199000160-00004

Faroon, O., Jones, D., & Rosa, C. (2000). Effects of polychlorinated biphenyls on the nervous system. *Toxicology and Industrial Health, 16,* 305–333. doi:10.1177/074823370001600708

Fein, G. G., Jacobson, J. L., Jacobson, S. W., Schwartz, P. M., & Dowler, J. K. (1984). Prenatal exposure to poly-chlorinated biphenyls: Effects on birth size and gestational age. *The Journal of Pediatrics, 105,* 315–320. doi:10.1016/S0022-3476(84)80139-0

Ferguson, S. A., Paule, M. G., & Holson, R. R. (1996). Functional effects of methylazoxymethanol-induced cerebellar hypoplasia in rats. *Neurotoxicology and Teratology, 18,* 529–537. doi:10.1016/0892-0362(96)00083-9

Ferrari, P. F., Lowther, S., Tidbury, H., Greengrass, P., Wilson, C. A., & Horton, R. W. (1999). The influence of gender and age on neonatal rat hypothalamic 5-HT1A and 5-HT2A receptors. *Cellular and Molecular Neurobiology, 19,* 775–784.

Gaitan, E. (1988). Goitrogens. *Bailliere's Clinical Endocrinology and Metabolism, 2,* 683–702. doi:10.1016/S0950-351X(88)80060-0

Gilbert, M. E., Mundy, W. R., & Crofton, K. M. (2000). Spatial learning and long-term potentiation in the dentate gyrus of the hippocampus in animals developmentally exposed to Aroclor 1254. *Toxicological Sciences, 57,* 102–111. doi:10.1093/toxsci/57.1.102

Gilmore, J. H., Jarskog, L. F., & Vadlamudi, S. (2003). Maternal infection regulates BDNF and NGF expression in fetal and neonatal brain and maternal–fetal unit of rat. *Journal of Neuroimmunology, 138,* 49–55. doi:10.1016/S0165-5728(03)00095-X

Gilroy, C., Singh, A., Chu, I., & Villeneuve, D. C. (1996). Toxicity of PCB 156 in the rat liver: An ultrastructural and biochemical study. *Journal of Submicroscopic Cytology and Pathology, 28,* 27–32.

Goldey, E. S., & Crofton, K. M. (1998). Thyroxine replacement attenuates hypothyroxinemia, hearing loss, and motor deficits following developmental exposure to Aroclor 1254 in rats. *Toxicological Sciences, 45,* 94–105.

Goldey, E. S., Kehn, L. S., & Crofton, K. M. (1993). The sensitivity to 3'3'-iminodipropionitrile differs for high-and mid-frequency hearing loss in the developing rat. *Hearing Research, 69,* 221–228. doi:10.1016/0378-5955(93)90111-D

Goldey, E. S., Kehn, L. S., Lau, C., Rehnberg, G. L., & Crofton, K. M. (1995). Developmental exposure to poly-chlorinated biphenyls (Aroclor 1254) reduces circulating thyroid hormone concentrations and causes hearing deficits in rats. *Toxicology and Applied Pharmacology, 135,* 77–88. doi:10.1006/taap.1995.1210

Goldey, E. S., Kehn, L. S., Rehnberg, G. L., & Crofton, K. M. (1995). Effects of developmental hypothyroidism on auditory and motor function in the rat. *Toxicology and Applied Pharmacology, 135,* 67–76. doi:10.1006/taap.1995.1209

Guerra-Araiza, C., Coyoy-Salgado, A., & Camacho-Arroyo, I. (2002). Sex differences in the regulation of progesterone receptor isoforms expression in the rat brain. *Brain Research Bulletin, 59,* 105–109.

Gurley, G. H., Jelaso, A. M., Ide, C. F., & Spitsergen, J. M. (2007). Effects of polychlorinated biphenyls (PCBs) on expression of neurotrophic factors in C6 glial cells in culture. *Neurotoxicology, 28,* 1264–1271. doi:10.1016/j.neuro.2007.08.005

Hadj-Sahraoui, N., Frederic, F., Delhaye-Bouchaud, N., & Mariani, J. (1996). Gender effect on Purkinje cell loss in the cerebellum of the heterozygous reeler mouse. *Journal of Neurogenetics, 11,* 45–58. doi:10.3109/01677069609107062

Hallgren, S., & Darnerud, P. O. (2002). Polybrominated diphenyl ether (PBDEs), polychlorinated biphenyls (PCBs) and chlorinated paraffins (CPs) in rats—testing interactions and mechanisms for thyroid hormone effects. *Toxicology, 177,* 227–243. doi:10.1016/S0300-483X(02)00222-6

Hany, J., Lileienthal, H., Roth-Härer, A., Ostendorp, G., Heizow, B., & Winneke, G. (1999). Behavioral effects following single and combined maternal exposure to PCB 77 (3,4,3',4'-tetrachlorobiphenyl) and PCB 47 (2,4,2',4'-tetrachlorobiphenyl) in rats. *Neurotoxicology and Teratology, 21,* 147–156. doi:10.1016/S0892-0362(98)00038-5

Holene, E., Nafstad, I., Skaarc, J. U., & Sagvolden, T. (1998). Behavioural hyperactivity in rats following postnatal exposure to subtoxic doses of polychlorinated biphenyl congeners 153 and 126. *Behavioural Brain Research, 94,* 213–224. doi:10.1016/S0166-4328(97)00181-2

Iwasaki, T., Miyazaki, W., Takeshita, A., Kuroda, Y., & Koibuchi, N. (2002). Polychlorinated biphenyls suppress thyroid hormone-induced transactivation. *Biochemical and Biophysical Research Communications, 299,* 384–388. doi:10.1016/S0006-291X(02)02659-1

Jacobson, J. L., & Jacobson, S. W. (1996). Intellectual impairment in children exposed to polychlorinated biphenyls in utero. *The New England Journal of Medicine, 335,* 783–789. doi:10.1056/NEJM199609123351104

Jacobson, J. L., & Jacobson, S. W. (2003). Prenatal exposure to polychlorinated biphenyls and attention at school age. *The Journal of Pediatrics, 143,* 780–788. doi:10.1067/S0022-3476(03)00577-8

Jacobson, J. L., Jacobson, S. W., & Humphrey, H. B. (1990a). Effects of exposure to PCBs and related compounds on growth and activity in children. *Neurotoxicology and Teratology, 12,* 319–326. doi:10.1016/0892-0362(90)90050-M

Jacobson, J. L., Jacobson, S. W., & Humphrey, H. B. (1990b). Effects of in utero exposure to polychlorinated biphenyls and related contaminants on cognitive functioning in young children. *The Journal of Pediatrics, 116,* 38–45. doi:10.1016/S0022-3476(05)81642-7

Johansson, C., Tofighi, R., Tamm, C., Goldoni, M., Mutti, A., & Ceccatelli, S. (2006). Cell death mechanisms in AtT20 pituitary cells exposed to polychlorinated biphenyls (PCB 126 and PCB 153) and methylmercury. *Toxicology Letters, 167,* 183–190. doi:10.1016/j.toxlet.2006.09.006

Juraska, J. M. (1990). Gender differences in the dendritic tree of granule neurons in the hippocampal dentate gyrus of weaning age rats. *Developmental Brain Research, 53,* 291–294. doi:10.1016/0165-3806(90)90021-P

Kanagawa, Y. (1982). Aromatase activity by the diencephalon of fetal and neonatal rats. [Hokkaido igaku zasshi] *The Hokkaido Journal of Medical Science, 57,* 572–576.

Kaya, H., Hany, J., Fastbend, A., Roth-Härer, A., Winneke, G., & Lilienthal, H. (2002). Effects of maternal exposure to a reconstituted mixture of polychlorinated biphenyls on sex-dependent behaviors and steroid hormone concentrations in rats: Dose–response relationship. *Toxicology and Applied Pharmacology, 178,* 71–81. doi:10.1006/taap.2001.9318

Khan, M. A., & Hansen, L. G. (2003). Ortho-substituted polychlorinated biphenyl (PCB) congeners (95 or 101) decrease pituitary response to thyrotropin releasing hormone. *Toxicology Letters, 144,* 173–182. doi:10.1016/S0378-4274(03)00203-0

Khan, M. A., Lichtensteiger, C. A., Faroon, O., Mumtaz, M., Schaeffer, D. J., & Hansen, L. G. (2002). The hypothalamo–pituitary–thyroid (HPT) axis: A target of nonpersistent ortho-substituted PCB congeners. *Toxicological Sciences, 65*(1), 52–61.

Kodavanti, P. R., Shin, D., Tilson, H. A., & Harry, G. J. (1993). Comparative effects of two polychlorinated biphenyl congeners on calcium homeostasis in rat cerebellar granule cells. *Toxicology and Applied Pharmacology, 123,* 97–106. doi:10.1006/taap.1993.1226

Kodavanti, P. R., Ward, T. R., Derr-Yellin, E. C., Mundy, W. R., Casey, A. C., Bush, B., & Tilson, H. A. (1998). Congener-specific distribution of polychlorinated biphenyls in brain regions, blood, liver, and fat of adult rats following repeated exposure to Aroclor 1254. *Toxicology and Applied Pharmacology, 153,* 199–210. doi:10.1006/taap.1998.8534

Kodavanti, P. R., Ward, T. R., McKinney, J. D., & Tilson, H. A. (1995). Increased [3H]phorbol ester binding in rat cerebellar granule cells by polychlorinated biphenyl mixtures and congeners: Structure–activity relationship. *Toxicology and Applied Pharmacology, 130,* 140–148. doi:10.1006/taap.1995.1018

Kreiling, J. A., Stephens, R. E., Kuzirian, A. M., Jessen-Eller, K., & Reinisch, C. L. (2000). Polychlorinated biphenyls are selectively neurotoxic in the developing *Spisula solidissima* embryo. *Journal of Toxicology and Environmental Health, 61,* 657–675. doi:10.1080/00984100050195143

Lalonde, R., & Strazielle, C. (2003). The effects of cerebellar damage on maze learning in animals. *The Cerebellum, 2,* 300–309. doi:10.1080/14734220310017456

Lang, J. T., & McCullough, L. D. (2008). Pathways to ischemic neuronal cell death: Are sex differences relevant? *Journal of Translational Medicine, 6,* 33. doi:10.1186/1479-5876-6-33

Lanté, F., Meunier, J., Guiramand, J., Maurice, T., Cavalier, M., de Jesus Ferriera, M. C., . . . Barbanel, G. (2007). Neurodevelopmental damage after prenatal infection: Role of oxidative stress in the fetal brain. *Free Radical Biology & Medicine, 42,* 1231–1245. doi:10.1016/j.freeradbiomed.2007.01.027

Lee, D. W., & Opanashuk, L. A. (2004). Polychlorinated biphenyl mixture Aroclor 1254-induced oxidative stress plays a role in dopaminergic cell injury. *Neurotoxicology, 25,* 925–939. doi:10.1016/j.neuro.2004.05.005

Lee, J. Y., Kim, J. W., Cho, S. D., Kim, Y. H., Choi, K. J., Joo, W. H., . . . Moon, J. Y. (2004). Protective effect of ginseng extract against apoptotic cell death induced by 2,2',5,5'-tetrachlorobiphenyl in neuronal SK-N-MC cells. *Life Sciences, 75,* 1621–1634. doi:10.1016/j.lfs.2004.03.016

Lilienthal, H., & Winneke, G. (1991). Sensitive periods for behavioral toxicity of polychlorinated biphenyls: Determination by cross-fostering in rats. *Fundamental and Applied Toxicology, 17,* 368–375. doi:10.1016/0272-0590(91)90226-T

Mariussen, E., Myhre, O., Reistad, T., & Fonnum, F. (2002). The polychlorinated biphenyl mixture Aroclor 1254 induces death of rat cerebellar granule cells: The involvement of the N-methyl-D-aspartate receptor and reactive oxygen species. *Toxicology and Applied Pharmacology, 179,* 137–144. doi:10.1006/taap.2002.9353

Markowski, V. P., Cox, C., & Weiss, B. (1998). Prenatal cocaine exposure produces gender-specific motor effects in aged rats. *Neurotoxicology and Teratology, 20,* 43–53. doi:10.1016/S0892-0362(97)00076-7

Mayhew, T. M., MacLaren, R., & Henery, C. C. (1990). Fractionator studies on Purkinje cells in human cerebellum: Numbers in right and left halves of male and female brains. *Journal of Anatomy, 169,* 63–70.

Mazer, C., Muneyirci, J., Taheny, K., Raio, N., Borell, A., & Whitaker-Azmitia, P. (1997). Serotonin depletion during synaptogenesis leads to decreased synaptic density and learning deficits in the adult rat: A possible model of neurodevelopmental disorders with cognitive deficits. *Brain Research, 760,* 68–73. doi:10.1016/S0006-8993(97)00297-7

McFadyen, M. P., Kusek, G., Bolivar, V. J., & Flaherty, L. (2003). Differences among eight inbred strains of mice in motor ability and motor learning on a rotarod. *Genes, Brain & Behavior, 2,* 214–219. doi:10.1034/j.1601-183X.2003.00028.x

McKinney, J., Fannin, R., Jordan, S., Chae, K., Rickenbachewr, U., & Pedersen, L. (1987). Polychlorinated biphenyls and related compound interactions with specific binding sites for thyroxine in rat liver nuclear extracts. *Journal of Medicinal Chemistry, 30,* 79–86.

McKinney, J. D. (1989). Multifunctional receptor model for dioxin and related compound toxic action: Possible thyroid hormone-responsive effector-linked site. *Environmental Health Perspectives, 82,* 323–336. doi:10.2307/3430790

Meerts, I. A., Liliennthal, H., Hoving, S., van den Berg, J. H., Weijers, B. M., Bergman, A., . . . Brouwer, A. (2004). Developmental exposure to 4-hydroxy-2,3,3',4',5-pentachlororbiphenyl (4-OHCB107): Long-term effects on brain behavior, and brain stem auditory potentials in rats. *Toxicological Sciences, 82,* 207–218. doi:10.1093/toxsci/kfh252

Miyazaki, W., Iwasaki, T., Takeshita, A., Kuroda, Y., & Koibuchi, N. (2004). Polychlorinated biphenyls suppress thyroid hormone receptor-mediated transcription through a novel mechanism. *The Journal of Biological Chemistry, 279,* 18195–18202. doi.10.1074/jbc.M310531200

Miyazaki, W., Iwasaki, T., Takeshita, A., Tohyama, C., & Koibuchi, N. (2008). Identification of the functional domain of thyroid hormone receptor responsible for polychlorinataed biphenyl-mediated suppression of its action in vitro. *Environmental Health Perspectives, 116,* 1231–1236. doi:10.1289/ehp.11176

Morse, D. C., Seegal, R. F., Borsch, K. O., & Brouwer, A. (1996). Long-term alterations in regional brain serotonin metabolism following maternal polychlorinated biphenyl exposure in the rat. *Neurotoxicology, 17,* 631–638.

Mwamengele, G. L., Mayhew, T. M., & Dantzer, V. (1993). Purkinje cell complements in mammalian cerebella and the biases incurred by counting nucleoli. *Journal of Anatomy, 183,* 155–160.

Nguon, K., Baxter, M. G., & Sajdel-Sulkowska, E. M. (2005). Perinatal exposure to polychlorinated biphenyl (PCBs) differentially affects cerebellar and neurocognitive functions in male and female rat neonates. *The Cerebellum, 4,* 1–11.

Nguon, K., Ladd, B., Baxter, M. G., & Sajdel-Sulkowska, E. M. (2005). Sexual dimorphism in cerebellar structure, function, and response to environmental perturbations. *Progress in Brain Research, 148,* 341–351. doi:10.1016/S0079-6123(04)48027-3

Nicholson, J. L., & Altman, J. (1972a). The effect of early hypo- and hypothyroidism on the development of rat cerebellar cortex I. Cell proliferation and differentiation. *Brain Research, 44,* 13–23. doi:10.1016/0006-8993(72)90362-9

Nicholson, J. L., & Altman, J. (1972b). The effect of early hypo- and hyperthyroidism on the development of rat cerebellar cortex II. Synaptogenesis in the molecular layer. *Brain Research, 44,* 25–36. doi:10.1016/0006-8993(72)90363-0

Numakawa, Y., Matsumoto, T., Yokomaku, D., Taguchi, T., Niki, E., Hatanaka, H., . . . Numakawa, T. (2007). 17 bet-estradiol protects cortical neurons against oxidative stress-induced cell death through reduction in the activity of mitogen-activated protein kinase and in the accumulation of intracellular calcium. *Endocrinology, 148,* 627–637. doi:10.1210/en.2006-1210

Okada, J., Shimokawa, N., & Koibuchi, N. (2005). Polychlorinated biphenyl (PCB) alters acid-sensitivity of cultured neurons derived from the medulla oblongata. *The International Journal of Biochemistry & Cell Biology, 37,* 1368–1374. doi:10.1016/j.biocel.2005.02.003

Okado, N., Narita, M., & Narita, N. (2001). A biogenic amine-synapse mechanism for mental retardation and developmental disabilities. *Brain and Development, 23*(Suppl. 1), S1–S15.

Osius, N., Karmaus, W., Krause, H., & Witten, J. (1999). Exposure to polychlorinated biphenyls and levels of thyroid hormones in children. *Environmental Health Perspectives, 107,* 843–849. doi:10.1289/ehp.99107843

Overmann, S. R., Kostas, J., Wilson, L. R., Shain, W., & Bush, B. (1987). Neuroehavioral and somatic effects of perinatal PCB exposure in rats. *Environmental Research, 44,* 56–70. doi:10.1016/S0013-9351(87)80086-5

Oyama, Y., Okazaki, E., Chikahisa, L., Nagano, T., & Sdakata, C. (1996). Oxidative stress-induced increase in intracellular Ca2+ and Ca(2+)-induced increase in oxidative stress: An experimental model using dissociated rat brain neurons. *Japanese Journal of Pharmacology, 72,* 381–385. doi:10.1254/jjp.72.381

Peng, J., Singh, A., Ireland, W. P., & Chu, I. (1997). Polychlorinated biphenyl congener 153-induced ultrastructural alterations in rat liver: A quantitative study. *Toxicology, 120,* 171–183. doi:10.1016/S0300-483X(97)03663-9

Pierce, K., & Courchesne, E. (2001). Evidence for a cerebellar role in reduced exploration and stereotyped behavior. *Biological Psychiatry, 49,* 655–664. doi:10.1016/S0006-3223(00)01008-8

Porterfield, S. P. (2000). Thyroidal dysfunction and environmental chemicals—Potential impact on brain development. *Environmental Health Perspectives, 108,* 433–438. doi:10.2307/3454533

Porterfield, S. P., & Hendrich, C. E. (1993). The role of thyroid hormones in prenatal and neonatal neurological development —Current perspectives. *Endocrine Reviews, 14,* 94–106.

Portigal, C. L., Cowell, S. P., Fedoruk, M. N., Butler, C. M., Rennie, P. S., & Nelson, C. C. (2002). Polychlorinated biphenyls interfere with androgen-induced transcriptional activation and hormone binding. *Toxicology and Applied Pharmacology, 179,* 185–194. doi:10.1006/taap.2002.9371

Powers, B. E., Widholm, J. J., Lasky, R. E., & Schantz, S. L. (2006). Auditory deficits in rats exposed to an environmental PCB mixture during development. *Toxicological Sciences, 89,* 415–422. doi:10.1093/toxsci/kfj051

Pravettoni, A., Colciago, A., Negro-Cesi, P., Villa, S., & Celotti, F. (2005). Ontogenic development, sexual differentiation, and effects of Aroclor 1254 exposure on expression of arylhydrocarbon receptor and on the arylhydrocarbon receptor nuclear translocator in the rat hypothalamus. *Reproductive Toxicology, 20,* 521–530. doi:10.1016/j.reprotox.2005.03.008

Provost, T. L., Juarez de Ku, L. M., Zender, C., & Meserve, L. A. (1999). Dose-and age-dependent alterations in choline acetyltransferase (ChAT) activity, learning and memory, and thyroid hormones in 15- and 30-day old rats exposed to 1.25 or 12.5 PPM polychlorinated biphenyl (PCB) beginning at conception. *Progress in Neuro-Psychopharmacology & Biological Psychiatry, 23,* 915–928. doi:10.1016/S0278-5846(99)00035-4

Quadros, P. S., Lopez, V., De Vries, G. J., Chung, W. C., & Wagner, C. K. (2002). Progesterone receptors and the sexual differentiation of medial preoptic nucleus. *Journal of Neurobiology, 51,* 24–32. doi:10.1002/neu.10040

Raz, N., Gunning-Dixon, F., Head, D., Williamson, A., & Acker, J. D. (2001). Age and sex differences in the cerebellum and the ventral pons: Prospective MR study of healthy adults. *American Journal of Neuroradiology, 22,* 1161–1167.

Rhees, R. W., Lephart, E. D., & Eliason, D. (2001). Effects of maternal separation during early postnatal development on male sexual behavior and female reproductive function. *Behavioural Brain Research, 123,* 1–10. doi:10.1016/S0166-4328(00)00381-8

Rhyu, I. J., Cho, T. H., Lee, N. J., Uhm, C. S., Kim, H., & Suh, Y. S. (1999). Magnetic resonance image-based cerebellar volumetry in health Korean adults. *Neuroscience Letters, 270,* 149–152. doi:10.1016/S0304-3940(99)00487-5

Rintala, J., Jaatinen, P., Kiianmaa, K., Iikonen, J., Kemppainen, O., Sarviharju, M., & Hervonen, A. (2001). Dose-dependent decrease in glial fibrillary acidic protein-immunoreactivity in rat cerebellum after lifelong ethanol consumption. *Alcohol, 23,* 1–8. doi:10.1016/S0741-8329(00)00116-6

Roegge, C. S., Morris, J. R., Villareal, S., Wang, V. C., Powers, B. E., Klintsova, A. Y., . . . Schantz, S. L. (2006). Purkinje cell and cerebellar effects following developmental exposure to PCBs and/or MeHg. *Neurotoxicology and Teratology, 28,* 74–85. doi:10.1016/j.ntt.2005.10.001

Roegge, C. S., Seo, B. W., Crofton, K. M., & Schantz, S. L. (2000). Gestational-lactational exposure to Aroclor 1254 impairs radial-arm maze performance in male rats. *Toxicological Sciences, 57,* 121–130. doi:10.1093/toxsci/57.1.121

Roth-Härer, A., Lilienthal, H., Bubser, M., Kronthaler, U. R., Mundy, W., Ward, T., . . . Winneke, G. (2001). Neurotransmitter concentrations and binding at dopamine receptors in rats after maternal exposure to 3,4,3',4'-tetrachlorobiphenyl: The role of reduced thyroid hormone concentrations. *Environmental Toxicology and Pharmacology, 9,* 103–115. doi:10.1016/S1382-6689(00)00069-7

Safe, S. H. (1994). Polychlorinated biphenyls (PCBs): Environmental impact, biochemical and toxic responses, and implications for risk assessment. *Critical Reviews in Toxicology, 4,* 87–149.

Safe, S. H., Bandiera, S., Sawyer, T., Robertson, L., Safe, L., Parkinson, A., . . . Levin, W. (1985). PCBs: Structure–function relationships and mechanism of action. *Environmental Health Perspectives, 60,* 47–56. doi:10.2307/3429944

Saghir, S. A., Hansen, L. G., Holmes, K. R., & Kodavanti, P. R. (2000). Differential and non-uniform tissue and brain distribution of two distinct 14C-hexachlorobiphenyls in weanling rats. *Toxicological Sciences, 54,* 60–70. doi:10.1093/toxsci/54.1.60

Sajdel-Sulkowska, E. M., & Koibuchi, N. (2002). Impact of thyroid status-disrupting environmental factors on brain development. *Recent Research Developments in Endocrinology, 3,* 101–117.

Sajdel-Sulkowska, E. M., Xu, M., & Koibuchi, N. (2009). Increase in cerebellar neurotrophin-3 and oxidative stress markers in autism. *The Cerebellum, 8,* 366–372. doi:10.1007/s12311-009-0105-9

Sakamoto, H., Mezaki, Y., Shikimi, H., Ukena, K., & Tsutsui, K. (2003). Dendritic growth and spine formation in response to estrogen in the developing Purkinje cell. *Endocrinology, 144,* 4466–4477. doi:10.1210/en.2003-0307

Salama, J., Chakraborty, T. R., Ng, L., & Gore, A. C. (2003). Effects of polychlorinated biphenyls on estrogen receptor-beta expression in the anteroventral perventricular nucleus. *Environmental Health Perspectives, 111,* 1278–1282. doi:10.1289/ehp.6126

Schantz, S. L., Moshtaghian, J., & Ness, D. K. (1995). Spatial learning deficits in adult rats exposed to ortho-substituted PCB congeners during gestation and lactation. *Toxicological Sciences, 26,* 117–126. doi:10.1006/faat.1995.1081

Schantz, S. L., Seo, B. W., Moshtaghian, J., Peterson, R. E., & Moore, R. W. (1996). Effects of gestational and lactational exposure to TCDD or coplanar PCBs on spatial learning. *Neurotoxicology and Teratology, 18,* 305–313. doi:10.1016/S0892-0362(96)90033-1

Schantz, S. L., Seo, B. W., Wong, P. W., & Pessah, I. N. (1997). Long-term effects of developmental exposure to 2,2',3,5',6-pentachlorobiphenyl (PCB 95) on locomotor activity, spatial learning and memory and rain ryanodine binding. *Neurotoxicology, 18,* 457–467.

Schmahmann, J. D. (1991). An emerging concept. The cerebellar contribution to higher function. *Archives of Neurology, 48,* 1178–1187.

Seegal, R. F., Brosch, K. O., & Okoniewski, R. J. (1997). Effects of in utero and lactational exposure of the laboratory rat to 2,4,2',4'- and 3,4,3',4'-tetrachlorobiphenyl on dopamine function. *Toxicology and Applied Pharmacology, 146,* 95–103. doi:10.1006/taap.1997.8226

Sharma, R., Derr-Yellin, E. C., House, D. E., & Kodavanti, P. R. (2000). Age-dependent effects of Aroclor 1254R on calcium uptake by subcellular organelles in selected brain regions of rats. *Toxicology, 156,* 13–25. doi:10.1016/S0300-483X(00)00328-0

Shimokawa, N., Miyazaki, W., Iwasaki, T., & Koibuchi, N. (2006). Low dose hydroxylated PCB induces c-Jun expression in PC12 cells. *Neurotoxicology, 27,* 176–183. doi:10.1016/j.neuro.2005.09.005

Singh, A., Chu, I., & Villeneuve, D. C. (1996). Subchronic toxicity of 2,4,4'-trichlorobiphenyl in the liver: An ultrastructural and biochemical study. *Ultrastructural Pathology, 20,* 275–284. doi:10.3109/01913129609016325

Singh, A., Connell, B. J., & Chu, I. (2000). PCB 128-induced ultrastructural lesions in the rat liver. *Journal of Submicroscopic Cytology and Pathology, 32,* 145–152.

Takahashi, M., Negishi, T., Imamura, M., Sewano, E., Kuroda, Y., & Tashiro, T. (2009). Alterations in gene expression of glutamate receptors and exocytosis-related factors by a hydroxylated-polychlorinated biphenyl in the developing brain. *Toxicology, 257,* 17–24. doi:10.1016/j.tox.2008.12.003

Tilson, H. A., Jacobson, J. L., & Rogan, W. J. (1990). Polychlorinated biphenyls and the developing nervous system: Cross-species comparison. *Neurotoxicology and Teratology, 12,* 239–248. doi:10.1016/0892-0362(90)90095-T

Valle, A., Guevara, R., García-Palmer, F. J., Roca, P., & Oliver, J. (2007). Sexual dimorphism in liver mitochondrial oxidative capacity is conserved under caloric restriction conditions. *American Journal of Physiology. Cell Physiology, 293,* C1302–C1308. doi:10.1152/ajpcell.00203.2007

Veith, G. D., Kuel, D. W., Puglisis, F. A., Glass, G. E., & Eaton, J. G. (1977). Residues of PCBs and DTT in the western Lake Superior ecosystem. *Archives of Environmental Contamination and Toxicology, 5,* 487–499. doi:10.1007/BF02220927

Vicedomini, J. P., Nonneman, A. J., DeKosky, S. T., & Scheff, S. W. (1986). Perinatal glucocorticoids disrupt learning: A sexually dimorphic response. *Physiology & Behavior, 36,* 145–149. doi:10.1016/0031-9384(86)90088-0

Voie, O. A., & Fonnum, F. (2000). Effect of polychlorinated biphenyls on production of reactive oxygen species (ROS) in rat synaptosomes. *Archives of Toxicology, 73,* 588–593. doi:10.1007/s002040050012

Volkow, N. D., Wang, G. J., Fowler, J. S., Hitzemann, R., Pappas, N., Pascani, K., & Wong, C. (1997). Gender differences in cerebellar metabolism: Test–retest reproducibility. *The American Journal of Psychiatry, 154,* 119–121.

Whitaker-Azmitia, P. M. (2001). Serotonin and brain development: Role in human developmental diseases. *Brain Research Bulletin, 56,* 479–485. doi:10.1016/S0361-9230(01)00615-3

Widholm, J. J., Clarkson, G. B., Strupp, B. J., Crofton, K. M., Seegal, R. F., & Schantz, S. L. (2001). Spatial reversal learning in Aroclor 1254-exposed rats: Sex-specific deficits in associative ability and inhibitory control. *Toxicology and Applied Pharmacology, 174,* 188–198. doi:10.1006/taap.2001.9199

Widholm, J. J., Villareal, S., Seegal, R. F., & Schantz, S. L. (2004). Spatial alteration deficits following developmental exposure to Aroclor 1254 or methylmercury in rats. *Toxicological Sciences, 82,* 577–589. doi:10.1093/toxsci/kfh290

Yang, J. H., Derr-Yellin, E. C., & Kodavanti, P. R. (2003). Alterations in brain protein kinase C isoforms following developmental exposure to a polychlorinated biphenyl mixture. *Molecular Brain Research, 111,* 123–135. doi:10.1016/S0169-328X(02)00697-6

Yang, J. H., & Kodavanti, P. R. (2001). Possible molecular targets of halogenated aromatic hydrocarbons in neuronal cells. *Biochemical and Biophysical Research Communications, 280,* 1372–1377. doi:10.1006/bbrc.2001.4283

Zahalka, E. A., Ellis, D. H., Goldey, E. S., Stanton, M. E., & Lau, C. (2001). Perinatal exposure to polychlorinated biphenyls Aroclor 1016 or 1254 did not alter brain catecholamines nor delayed alterations performance in Long-Evans rats. *Brain Research Bulletin, 55,* 487–500. doi:10.1016/S0361-9230(01)00548-2

11

Sexual Differentiation of the Human Brain: Hormonal Control and Effects of Endocrine Disruptors

Erica L.T. van den Akker and Nynke Weisglas-Kuperus

Endocrine disruptors are exogenous substances that act like hormones in the endocrine system and disrupt the physiologic function of endogenous hormones. Some of them, such as polychlorinated biphenyls (PCBs) and dioxins, are persistent environmental pollutants and have been found in virtually all regions of the world. Other active agents, such as diethylstilbestrol (DES), are not environmental pollutants; DES was used as medication to prevent miscarriages until the 1970s. Prenatal hormone exposure influences the development of the reproductive system as well as the development of the brain.

This chapter outlines the current knowledge of hormonal control, endocrine disruptors, and sexual differentiation of the human brain. It is meant to further advance our understanding of the link between gender identity, sexual behavior, neuropsychological function, and endocrine disruptor effects.

Hormonal Control

Development of the Reproductive System

Early in fetal development, gonadal structures are undifferentiated, with precursors for both the female (Müllerian) and male (Wolffian) reproductive tracts; thus, the developing embryo has the potential to be either male or female (for a review, see C. A. Wilson & Davies, 2007). Sexual differentiation in fetal development is influenced by sex hormones such as testosterone, estrogens, and progesterone. Genital development takes place between weeks 6 and 12 of pregnancy. Under the influence of anti-Müllerian hormone produced in the testis, the Müllerian ducts regress, and with testosterone the male phenotype develops further. In the absence of testes, the Wolfian ducts regress, and a female phenotype develops.

Gender Identity and Sexual Behavior

Hormones also direct sex differentiation in the brain. The process of sexual brain differentiation takes place in the second half of pregnancy. The gender-specific morphological and functional phenotype of the body and brain leads to gender identity, sexual orientation, sexual behavior, and sex-specific neurocognitive functions. Primate studies suggest that there may be multiple prenatal sensitive periods when different brain regions and thus behaviors are susceptible to hormonal modulation (Cohen-Bendahan, van de Beek, & Berenbaum, 2005). In humans, prenatal exposure to sex steroids are important in the regulation of sexual orientation and gender identity (Cohen-Bendahan et al., 2005; Swaab, 2004). Masculinization of the brain in most mammals occurs primarily through estradiol, a metabolite of testosterone, acting on estrogen receptors (C. A. Wilson & Davies, 2007).

In humans (and unlike most mammals), testosterone and dihydrotestosterone are the masculinizing agents for the brain. The exact role of estrogen in sexual differentiation of the human brain is unknown. Individuals with 46XY, deficient in androgen receptors (androgen insensitivity syndrome), develop external female phenotype and feminized sexually dimorphic behavior and female gender identity (J. D. Wilson, 1999). Males lacking estradiol synthesis or activity as a result of aromatase insufficiency or mutant estrogen receptors exhibit male psychosexual behavior and gender identity (Swaab, 2004). In congenital adrenal hyperplasia (CAH), an enzymatic defect in the adrenal gland leads to overproduction of androgens. The CAH fetus is exposed to high levels of testosterone from very early gestation. After birth, androgens normalize under treatment. Female CAH children display typical male activities and interests throughout life. Whereas most adult women with CAH are heterosexual, a greater proportion are homosexual compared with the general population (30% vs. 10%; C. A. Wilson & Davies, 2007). Their sexual orientation is masculinized, resulting in a preference for females (Cohen-Bendahan et al., 2005).

Cerebral Lateralization and Neurocognitive Functioning

There are differences between the male and female brain. The right cerebral hemisphere has been found to be larger than the left in male brains (Good et al., 2001). This has been suggested to be the basis of a dominant right hemisphere in males with consequent superiority in spatial perception compared with females and higher frequency of left-handedness. Females have been found to exhibit better speech and language skills, controlled by the left hemisphere. Based on human studies, cerebral lateralization seems to be influenced by prenatal testosterone exposure. For example, abnormal prenatal androgen exposure caused by CAH appears to affect cognition in females. They have higher spatial ability than controls and are more likely to be left-handed (Cohen-Bendahan et al., 2005), although the differences are small and not always found (Berenbaum, Korman, & Everoni, 1995; Wisniewski, Prendeville, & Dobs, 2005). In contrast, individuals with the syndrome of androgen insensitivity have been shown to have relatively higher verbal than performance abilities (Imperato-McGlnley, Pichardo, Gautier, Voyer, & Bryden, 1991; Masica, Money, Ehrhardt, & Lewis, 1969). Control males and females were superior to patients with androgen insensitivity on visuospatial abilities (Imperato-McGlnley et al., 1991). Results from these studies have been interpreted to suggest that the absence of effective androgen contributes to female-typical cognitive patterns.

In animals it has been shown that exposure to sex hormones is influenced by intrauterine position. Whether testosterone levels differ in human opposite-sex twins compared with same-sex twins is presently unknown. In human twins, opposite-sex twin girls (n = 67) had a more lateralized pattern of cerebral lateralization than same-sex dizygotic twin pairs (n = 53), measured by auditory–verbal dichotic listening task. It was hypothesized that this was a result of prenatal exposure of higher testosterone levels in the opposite-sex twin girls (Cohen-Bendahan, Buitelaar, van Goozen, & Cohen-Kettenis, 2004).

Endocrine Disruptor Effects

In the prenatal hormonal regulation of sexual differentiation, brain structures and circuits are fixed for life, a process called *programming*. Endocrine disruptors may interfere with this programming, leading to permanent changes. Endocrine disruptors can mimic the actions of sex steroids and therefore have the potency of causing abnormal sexual differentiation of the reproductive tract and brain. The evidence for an association between endocrine disruptors and impaired sexual differentiation is stronger for wildlife than it is for humans, where only two groups of chemicals, DES and polyhalogenated aromatic hydrocarbons, have been studied; however, reports are inconsistent.

DES

NONREPRODUCTIVE SEX-SPECIFIC BEHAVIOR. Some studies suggest that prenatal exposure to DES, a nonsteroidal synthetic estrogen, may masculinize the gender-role behavior of girls and women. A previous study in prenatally DES-exposed women showed they had increased frequencies of bisexuality and homosexuality and decreased interest in parenting compared with controls (Ehrhardt et al., 1985). However, other studies could not replicate these findings (Lish et al., 1991; Newbold, 1993).

GENDER-RELATED BEHAVIOR. In humans, reports of the effects of prenatal exposure to DES are conflicting. Some authors have reported no effects on gender-related behavior. One study compared 10 males exposed to DES during gestation with their matched, unexposed brothers on measures of brain hemispheric specialization for processing nonlinguistic spatial information and cognitive abilities. DES exposure was associated with reduced hemispheric laterality and lowered spatial ability (Reinisch & Sanders, 1992). In women, masculinized aspects of sexual and nonsexual behaviors have been reported, depending on the time of exposure. In DES-exposed women, exposure early in gestation correlated with masculinized hand preference (increased left-handedness), whereas exposure late in gestation correlated with maculinized improved visuospatial abilities (Smith & Hines, 2000).

PCBs and Dioxins

MECHANISMS OF ACTION. PCBs and dioxins are polyhalogenated aromatic hydrocarbons. PCBs were commercially produced as complex mixtures for a variety of industrial applications and as additives in plastics and many com-mercial products. Their commercial utility was based largely on their chemical and physical stability, including low flammability and their miscibility with organic compounds. The total amount of PCBs produced worldwide from 1929 to the 1980s, when most countries reduced or stopped their production, has been estimated at approximately 1.5 million metric tons (World Health Organization, 1989). Dioxins are generally formed as unwanted and often unavoidable by-products during the synthesis of a wide array of commercial chemical products, especially those based on chlorinated aromatics, precursors, and intermediates. Moreover, they are formed during various combustion processes, such as burn-ing of solid waste from municipal incinerators.

Neurochemical studies have shown that many elements of the central ner-vous system, and especially of the developing central nervous system, are sus-ceptible to exposure to PCBs and dioxins, including cellular and synaptic processes, and endocrine systems (Grandjean, 2007). Estrogenic (Bitman, Cecil, Harris, & Feil, 1978), antiestrogenic (Jansen, Cooke, Porcelli, Liu, & Hansen, 1993; Mortensen & Arukwe, 2008; Nesaretnam, Corcoran, Dils, & Darbre, 1996), and antiandrogenic (Endo, Monsees, Akaza, Schill, & Pflieger-Bruss, 2003; Kaya et al., 2002) effects have been described in vivo and in vitro, possibly depending on congener type or metabolite. Human exposure to PCBs and dioxins occurs for 90% through the diet, with fish being the predominant source (Laden et al., 1999). Because PCBs and dioxins are lipid-soluble and are only slowly degraded, with half-lifetimes in humans ranging from 1.8 years to 9.9 years (Steele, Stehr-Green, & Welty, 1986), these compounds accumulate in adipose tissue. During pregnancy, PCBs and dioxins are transferred through the placenta and are able to cross the blood–brain barrier, exposing the fetus during a vulnerable time of central nervous system development (Masuda et al., 1978). PCBs have been detected in brain tissue of stillborn babies, exposed to environmental levels of PCBs, from 17 weeks of gestational age onward (Lanting et al., 1998).

Effects of perinatal exposure on more specific neurodevelopmental aspects are described. PCBs and dioxins are known to have sex steroid hormone-modulating properties. Steroid hormones play a mediating role in brain devel-opment and may influence not only reproductive but also nonreproductive behaviors that show sex differences, such as childhood play behavior.

NONREPRODUCTIVE SEX-SPECIFIC BEHAVIOR

Yu Cheng Cohort. In human studies, effects of perinatal exposure to PCBs and dioxins on nonreproductive sex-specific behavior have hardly been addressed. The only study that provided some evidence for steroid hormone–mediated behav-ioral effects of prenatal exposure to PCBs and dioxins is the study in the highly exposed children of the Yu Cheng cohort (Guo, Lai, Chen, & Hsu, 1995). In 1979, a large population in Taiwan was accidentally exposed to rice oil that was contam-inated during the manufacturing process with heat transfer fluids containing PCBs, polychlorinated dibenzofurans, and polychlorinated quarterphenyls for relatively short periods. Cognitive functions in this cohort ($n = 118$) showed con-sistent cognitive delays of 5 points from 4 to 7 years of age compared with a matched control group. In the Yu Cheng cohort at 6, 7, 8, and 9 years of age, more spatially related cognitive abilities were differently affected in boys and girls. Only the exposed boys scored lower than their nonexposed matched controls. These results, therefore, provided the first evidence of sex steroid hormone–modulating effects of PCBs and dioxins on cognitive development in humans.

Dutch PCB/Dioxin Study. Four hundred and eighteen children were studied in a Dutch PCB/dioxin cohort. PCB and dioxin levels were measured in maternal blood in the last trimester of pregnancy. In the children of these mothers, follow-up assessments at 6 and 7 years of age were performed, and half of the Rotterdam cohort were invited at 9 years of age as well (Vreugdenhil, Lanting, Mulder, Boersma, & Weisglas-Kuperus, 2002; Vreugdenhil, Mulder, Emmen, & Weisglas-Kuperus, 2004; Vreugdenhil, Slijper, Mulder, & Weisglas-Kuperus, 2002). The assessment included (general) cognitive and motor abilities, gender role-play behavior, neuropsychological functions, and a neurophysiological assessment. At school age, the Dutch version of the McCarthy Scales of Children's Abilities (van der Meulen & Smirkovsky, 1998) was used to assess the general cognitive abilities (General Cognitive Index) and memory and motor skills in children ($n = 376$). Mean age at follow-up was 6.7 years $\pm$ 0.3. Prenatal exposure to PCBs and dioxins was not significantly related to cognitive and motor development at school age. However, it appeared that effects of prenatal exposure to PCBs and dioxins on cognitive and motor abilities were modified by parental and home environmental conditions (i.e., maternal age, parental education level and verbal IQ, and Home Observation for Measurement of the Environment score; Caldwell & Bradley, 1984), such that optimal parental and environmental factors could compensate for the negative effects of PCB and dioxins exposure (Vreugdenhil, Lanting et al., 2002).

As part of the Dutch PCB/dioxin study, sex differences in play behavior were assessed by means of the Pre-School Activity Inventory (PSAI; $n = 160$) at mean age 7.5 years (Vreugdenhil, Slijper, et al., 2002). The PSAI assesses masculine and feminine play behavior scored on three subscales: Masculine, Feminine, and Composite. Higher prenatal PCB levels were related to less masculinized play behavior in boys and more masculinized play behavior in girls. Higher prenatal dioxin levels were associated with more feminized play in boys as well as in girls, assessed by the Feminine subscale. There was no evidence that lactational exposure to PCBs and dioxins was related to play behavior in the total breastfed group and neither in boys and girls separately. The results are suggestive of steroid hormone involvement in the neurotoxic mechanism of action of prenatal exposure to environmental levels of PCBs and dioxins.

GENDER-RELATED BEHAVIOR. Prenatal exposure to PCBs and dioxins can be regarded as chronic exposure of the developing central nervous system, and many processes of the central nervous system are likely to be sensitive to exposure to PCBs and dioxins, including neuronal and glial cells, neurotransmitters, and endocrine systems (Grandjean, 2007). Consequently, effects of prenatal exposure to PCBs and dioxins are likely to be of multifocal or diffuse nature. Human PCB studies suggest effects of prenatal exposure to PCBs on several neurodevelopmental outcome variables, including general cognitive and motor development, processing speed, attention and concentration, memory skills, planning or executive functions, and on a neurophysiological endpoint that assesses processing and evaluation of auditory stimuli (Gladen et al., 1988; Grandjean et al., 2001; Jacobson, Jacobson, & Humphrey, 1990; Koopman-Esseboom et al., 1996; Patandin et al., 1999; Rogan & Gladen, 1991; Stewart, Reihman, Lonky, Darvill, & Pagano, 2003; Vreugdenhil, Lanting et al., 2002; Walkowiak et al., 2001; Winneke, Walkowiak, & Lilienthal, 2002).

Half of the Dutch PCB/dioxin cohort, the lowest prenatally exposed (p25; $n = 26$) and the highest prenatally exposed children (p75; $n = 26$), were invited to participate in neuropsychological and neurophysiological assessments at 9 years of age (Vreugdenhil, Mulder, et al., 2004). The assessment of neuropsychological functions included the Rey Complex Figure Test (Osterrieth, 1944), the Auditory–Verbal Test, the Simple Reaction Time task, and the Tower of London (Kalverboer & Deelman, 1964; Letz, 1994; Lezak, 1995; Shallice, 1982). Prenatally high-exposed children had, after adjusting for confounding variables, longer reaction times and more variation in their reaction times, and lower scores on the Tower of London than prenatally low-exposed children. The results of this study are suggestive of multifocal or diffuse neurotoxic effects of prenatal exposure to PCBs and related compounds. The P300 latency is considered to be a cognitive component of event-related brain potentials and occurs with a latency of about 300 ms when a person is actively processing ("attending to") incoming stimuli. Prenatally high-exposed children had significantly longer P300 latencies than prenatally low-exposed children, adjusted for confounding variables (Vreugdenhil, Van Zanten, Brocaar, Mulder, & Weisglas-Kuperus, 2004). These results suggest that prenatal exposure to PCBs and dioxins delays central nervous system mechanisms that evaluate and process relevant stimuli at school age. For these assessments of neuropsychological functioning, no sex-specific effects were found.

Conclusion

In fetuses and embryos, growth and development are highly controlled by the endocrine system. They are therefore more vulnerable to exposure to endocrine disruptors. Endocrine-disrupting effects have been noted in environmentally exposed animals. Therefore, although endocrine disruption in humans by pollutant chemicals remains largely undemonstrated, the potential for such effects is real (Rogan & Ragan, 2003). Although several studies indicate a possible effect, it is hard to definitively link a particular chemical with a specific effect in humans, taking into account that the exact role of estrogen in sexual differentiation of the human brain is unknown. The low number of studies on gender-specific endocrine disruptor chemical effects in children is striking. Future research studying the possible sex-specific effects of endocrine disruptor chemicals in larger groups is needed. Moreover, long-term follow-up of the observed effects into adulthood is needed.

References

Berenbaum, S. A., Korman, K., & Everoni, C. L. (1995). Early hormones and sex differences in cognitive abilities. *Learning and Individual Differences, 7,* 303–321. doi:10.1016/1041-6080 (95)90004-7

Bitman, J., Cecil, H. C., Harris, S. J., & Feil, V. J. (1978). Estrogenic activity of o,p'-DDT metabolites and related compounds. *Journal of Agricultural and Food Chemistry, 26*(1), 149–151. doi:10.1021/jf60215a002

Caldwell, B., & Bradley, R. (1984). *Home observation of the environment* (Administrative manual). Little Rock, AR.

Cohen-Bendahan, C. C. C., Buitelaar, J. K., van Goozen, S. H., & Cohen-Kettenis, P. T. (2004). Prenatal exposure to testosterone and functional cerebral lateralization: A study in same-sex and opposite-sex twin girls. *Psychoneuroendocrinology, 29,* 911–916. doi:10.1016/j.psyneuen.2003.07.001

Cohen-Bendahan, C. C. C., van de Beek, C., & Berenbaum, S. A. (2005). Prenatal sex hormone effects on child and adult sex-typed behavior: Methods and findings. *Neuroscience and Biobehavioral Reviews, 29,* 353–384. doi:10.1016/j.neubiorev.2004.11.004

Ehrhardt, A. A., Meyer-Bahlburg, H. F., Rosen, L. R., Feldman, J. F., Veridiano, N. P., Zimmerman, I., & McEwen, B. S. (1985). Sexual orientation after prenatal exposure to exogenous estrogen. *Archives of Sexual Behavior, 14*(1), 57–77. doi:10.1007/BF01541353

Endo, F., Monsees, T. K., Akaza, H., Schill, W. B., & Pflieger-Bruss, S. (2003). Effects of single non-ortho, mono-ortho, and di-ortho chlorinated biphenyls on cell functions and proliferation of the human prostatic carcinoma cell line, LNCaP. *Reproductive Toxicology, 17,* 229–236. doi:10.1016/S0890-6238(02)00126-0

Gladen, B. C., Rogan, W. J., Hardy, P., Thullen, J., Tingelstad, J., & Tully, M. (1988). Development after exposure to polychlorinated biphenyls and dichlorodiphenyl dichloroethene transplacentally and through human milk. *The Journal of Pediatrics, 113,* 991–995. doi:10.1016/S0022-3476(88)80569-9

Good, C. D., Johnsrude, I., Ashburner, J., Henson, R. N., Friston, K. J., & Frackowiak, R. S. (2001). Cerebral asymmetry and the effects of sex and handedness on brain structure: A voxel-based morphometric analysis of 465 normal adult human brains. *NeuroImage, 14,* 685–700. doi:10.1006/nimg.2001.0857

Grandjean, P. (2007). [Effect of industrial chemicals on development of the nerve system—secondary publication]. *Ugeskrift for Laeger, 169*(34), 2782–2784. (Republished from *The Lancet,* 368(9553), pp. 2167–2178, by P. Grandjean, 2006)

Grandjean, P., Weihe, P., Burse, V. W., Needham, L. L., Storr-Hansen, E., Heinzow, B., . . . White, R. F. (2001). Neurobehavioral deficits associated with PCB in 7-year-old children prenatally exposed to seafood neurotoxicants. *Neurotoxicology and Teratology, 23,* 305–317. doi:10.1016/S0892-0362(01)00155-6

Guo, Y. L., Lai, T. J., Chen, S. J., & Hsu, C. C. (1995). Gender-related decrease in Raven's progressive matrices scores in children prenatally exposed to polychlorinated biphenyls and related contaminants. *Bulletin of Environmental Contamination and Toxicology, 55*(1), 8–13. doi:10.1007/BF00212382

Imperato-McGinley, J., Pichardo, M., Gautier, T., Voyer, D., & Bryden, M. P. (1991). Cognitive abilities in androgen-insensitive subjects: Comparison with control males and females from the same kindred. *Clinical Endocrinology, 34,* 341–347. doi:10.1111/j.1365-2265.1991.tb00303.x

Jacobson, J. L., Jacobson, S. W., & Humphrey, H. E. (1990). Effects of in utero exposure to polychlorinated biphenyls and related contaminants on cognitive functioning in young children. *The Journal of Pediatrics, 116,* 38–45. doi:10.1016/S0022-3476(05)81642-7

Jansen, H. T., Cooke, P. S., Porcelli, J., Liu, T. C., & Hansen, L. G. (1993). Estrogenic and antiestrogenic actions of PCBs in the female rat: In vitro and in vivo studies. *Reproductive Toxicology, 7,* 237–248. doi:10.1016/0890-6238(93)90230-5

Kalverboer, A. F., Deelman, B. G. (1964). *Voorlopige selectie van enkele tests voor het onderzoeken van geheugenstoornissen van verschillende aard* [Selection of tests in memory deficits]. Groningen, The Netherlands: Groningen University, Department of Neuropsychology.

Kaya, H., Hany, J., Fastabend, A., Roth-Harer, A., Winneke, G., & Lilienthal, H. (2002). Effects of maternal exposure to a reconstituted mixture of polychlorinated biphenyls on sex-dependent behaviors and steroid hormone concentrations in rats: Dose–response relationship. *Toxicology and Applied Pharmacology, 178*(2), 71–81. doi:10.1006/taap.2001.9318

Koopman-Esseboom, C., Weisglas-Kuperus, N., de Ridder, M. A., Van der Paauw, C. G., Tuinstra, L. G., & Sauer, P. J. (1996). Effects of polychlorinated biphenyl/dioxin exposure and feeding type on infants' mental and psychomotor development. *Pediatrics, 97,* 700–706.

Laden, F., Neas, L. M., Spiegelman, D., Hankinson, S. E., Willett, W. C., Ireland, K., . . . Hunter, D. J. (1999). Predictors of plasma concentrations of DDE and PCBs in a group of U.S. women. *Environmental Health Perspectives, 107*(1), 75–81. doi:10.1289/ehp.9910775

Lanting, C. I., Patandin, S., Fidler, V., Weisglas-Kuperus, N., Sauer, P. J., Boersma, E. R., & Touwen, B. C. L. (1998). Neurological condition in 42-month-old children in relation to pre- and postnatal exposure to polychlorinated biphenyls and dioxins. *Early Human Development, 50,* 283–292. doi:10.1016/S0378-3782(97)00066-2

Letz, R. (1994). *NES2 Test users manual* (version 6.6). Winchester, MA: Neurobehavioral Systems.

Lezak, M. D. (1995). *Neuropsychological assessment.* New York, NY: Oxford University Press.

Lish, J. D., Ehrhardt, A. A., Meyer-Bahlburg, H. F., Rosen, L. R., Gruen, R. S., & Veridiano, N. P. (1991). Gender-related behavior development in females exposed to diethylstilbestrol (DES) in utero: An attempted replication. *Journal of the American Academy of Child & Adolescent Psychiatry, 30*(1), 29–37. doi:10.1097/00004583-199101000-00005

Masica, D. N., Money, J., Ehrhardt, A. A., & Lewis, V. G. (1969). IQ, fetal sex hormones and cognitive patterns: Studies in the testicular feminizing syndrome of androgen insensitivity. *The Johns Hopkins Medical Journal, 124*(1), 34–43.

Masuda, Y., Kagawa, R., Kuroki, H., Kuratsune, M., Yoshimura, T., Taki, I., . . . Hayashi, M. (1978). Transfer of polychlorinated biphenyls from mothers to foetuses and infants. *Food and Cosmetics Toxicology, 16,* 543–546. doi:10.1016/S0015-6264(78)80221-1

Mortensen, A. S., & Arukwe, A. (2008). Activation of estrogen receptor signaling by the dioxin-like aryl hydrocarbon receptor agonist, 3,3',4,4',5-pentachlorobiphenyl (PCB126) in salmon in vitro system. *Toxicology and Applied Pharmacology, 227,* 313–324. doi:10.1016/j.taap.2007.11.003

Nesaretnam, K., Corcoran, D., Dils, R. R., & Darbre, P. (1996). 3,4,3',4'-Tetrachlorobiphenyl acts as an estrogen in vitro and in vivo. *Molecular Endocrinology, 10,* 923–936. doi:10.1210/me.10.8.923

Newbold, R. R. (1993). Gender-related behavior in women exposed prenatally to diethylstilbestrol. *Environmental Health Perspectives, 101,* 208–213. doi:10.2307/3431541

Osterrieth, P. A. (1944). Le test de copie d'une figure complex [Rey complex figure test]. *Archives de Psychologie, 30,* 206–356.

Patandin, S., Lanting, C. I., Mulder, P. G., Boersma, E. R., Sauer, P. J., & Weisglas-Kuperus, N. (1999). Effects of environmental exposure to polychlorinated biphenyls and dioxins on cognitive abilities in Dutch children at 42 months of age. *The Journal of Pediatrics, 134,* 33–41. doi:10.1016/S0022-3476(99)70369-0

Reinisch, J. M., & Sanders, S. A. (1992). Effects of prenatal exposure to diethylstilbestrol (DES) on hemispheric laterality and spatial ability in human males. *Hormones and Behavior, 26*(1), 62–75. doi:10.1016/0018-506X(92)90032-Q

Rogan, W. J., & Gladen, B. C. (1991). PCBs, DDE, and child development at 18 and 24 months. *Annals of Epidemiology, 1,* 407–413. doi:10.1016/1047-2797(91)90010-A

Rogan, W. J., & Ragan, N. B. (2003). Evidence of effects of environmental chemicals on the endocrine system in children. *Pediatrics, 112*(1 Pt 2), 247–252.

Shallice, T. (1982). Specific impairments of planning. *Philosophical Transactions of the Royal Society B Biological Sciences, 298,* 199–209.

Smith, L. L., & Hines, M. (2000). Language lateralization and handedness in women prenatally exposed to diethylstilbestrol (DES). *Psychoneuroendocrinology, 25,* 497–512. doi:10.1016/S0306-4530(00)00005-6

Steele, G., Stehr-Green, P., & Welty, E. (1986). Estimates of the biologic half-life of polychlorinated biphenyls in human serum. *The New England Journal of Medicine, 314,* 926–927. doi:10.1056/NEJM198604033141418

Stewart, P. W., Reihman, J., Lonky, E. I., Darvill, T. J., & Pagano, J. (2003). Cognitive development in preschool children prenatally exposed to PCBs and MeHg. *Neurotoxicology and Teratology, 25,* 11–22. doi:10.1016/S0892-0362(02)00320-3

Swaab, D. F. (2004). Sexual differentiation of the human brain: Relevance for gender identity, transsexualism and sexual orientation. *Gynecological Endocrinology, 19,* 301–312. doi:10.1080/09513590400018231

van der Meulen, B. F., & Smirkovsky, M. (1998). *The McCarthy Scales of Children's Abilities* (Dutch version). Lisse, The Netherlands: Swets and Zeitlinger B.V.

Vreugdenhil, H. J., Lanting, C. I., Mulder, P. G., Boersma, E. R., & Weisglas-Kuperus, N. (2002). Effects of prenatal PCB and dioxin background exposure on cognitive and motor abilities in Dutch children at school age. *The Journal of Pediatrics, 140,* 48–56. doi:10.1067/mpd.2002.119625

Vreugdenhil, H. J., Mulder, P. G., Emmen, H. H., & Weisglas-Kuperus, N. (2004). Effects of perinatal exposure to PCBs on neuropsychological functions in the Rotterdam cohort at 9 years of age. *Neuropsychology, 18,* 185–193. doi:10.1037/0894-4105.18.1.185

Vreugdenhil, H. J., Slijper, F. M., Mulder, P. G., & Weisglas-Kuperus, N. (2002). Effects of perinatal exposure to PCBs and dioxins on play behavior in Dutch children at school age. *Environmental Health Perspectives, 110,* a593–a598. doi:10.1289/ehp.021100593

Vreugdenhil, H. J., Van Zanten, G. A., Brocaar, M. P., Mulder, P. G., & Weisglas-Kuperus, N. (2004). Prenatal exposure to polychlorinated biphenyls and breastfeeding: Opposing effects on auditory P300 latencies in 9-year-old Dutch children. *Developmental Medicine & Child Neurology, 46,* 398–405. doi:10.1017/S0012162204000647

Walkowiak, J., Wiener, J. A., Fastabend, A., Heinzow, B., Kramer, U., Schmidt, E., . . . Winneke, G. (2001). Environmental exposure to polychlorinated biphenyls and quality of the home environment: Effects on psychodevelopment in early childhood. *The Lancet, 358,* 1602–1607. doi:10.1016/S0140-6736(01)06654-5

Wilson, C. A., & Davies, D. C. (2007). The control of sexual differentiation of the reproductive system and brain. *Reproduction, 133,* 331–359.

Wilson, J. D. (1999). The role of androgens in male gender role behavior. *Endocrine Reviews, 20,* 726–737.

Winneke, G., Walkowiak, J., & Lilienthal, H. (2002). PCB-induced neurodevelopmental toxicity in human infants and its potential mediation by endocrine dysfunction. *Toxicology, 181–182,* 161–165.

Wisniewski, A. B., Prendeville, M. T., & Dobs, A. S. (2005). Handedness, functional cerebral hemispheric lateralization, and cognition in male-to-female transsexuals receiving cross-sex hormone treatment. *Archives of Sexual Behavior, 34,* 167–172.

World Health Organization. (1989). Levels of PCBs, PCDDs and PCDFs in breast milk: Results of the WHO-coordinated interlaboratory quality control studies and analytical field studies. *Environmental Health Series, 34.*

Index

About the Editors

Michael Lewis, PhD, has published more than 300 articles in scientific journals, and he has written or edited more than 35 books, including *Social Cognition and the Acquisition of Self* (1979); *Children's Emotions and Moods: Developmental Theory and Measurement* (1983); *Shame, The Exposed Self* (1992); and *Altering Fate: Why the Past Does Not Predict the Future* (1997). He edited the *Handbook of Developmental Psychopathology* (2nd ed., 2001), and the *Handbook of Emotions* (3rd ed., 2009). He recently won the Urie Bronfenbrenner Award from the American Psychological Association for Lifetime Contribution to Developmental Psychology in the Service of Science and Society.

Lisa Kestler, PhD, is a senior clinician at MedAvante, Inc., a psychiatric research company in Hamilton, New Jersey. At the Institute for the Study of Child Development, Dr. Kestler served as an investigator on the National Institute on Drug Abuse-funded study on the Developmental Effects of Prenatal Cocaine Exposure, a prospective study spanning the lives of children born to drug-abusing mothers from infancy through adolescence. Drawing on her training in developmental psychopathology at Emory University, Dr. Kestler has been interested in understanding the cognitive, emotional, and behavioral development of children following exposure to intrauterine pathogens as well as postnatal stressors, environmental risk, and parental psychopathology.